ACCOUNTANTS GUIDE TO THE EUROPEAN COMMUNITIES

Accountants Guide to the European Communities

Dennis Evans
MBE, F.S.C.A., F.B.I.M.

MACDONALD AND EVANS

Macdonald & Evans Ltd.
Estover, Plymouth PL6 7PZ

First published 1981

ISBN 0 7121 0156 X

Printed in Great Britain by
Butler & Tanner Ltd, Frome

This anthology is dedicated to my wife Gladys and my two children – Europeans Keith and Gwen who have patiently spent their life with Europe.

FOREWORD

I welcome the publication of this guide. Although it is primarily designed for the Society of Company and Commercial Accountants' Diploma in European Studies (the first of its kind), its comprehensive nature will I believe make it a most valuable guide for a wider range of students of accountancy in business schools generally. Because of its broad coverage of the financial side of the Community's operations, the guide will interest business executives as well.

I welcome the guide for a second reason: simply that it is not merely an accountancy guide. The author clearly knows and shows the human side of the Community – that it is not simply a common market, but is for and about people. As president of the European Commission, I have tried to maintain as one of the criteria of judgment of our work: how will our proposals and our action affect the European citizen? The very first clauses of the preamble of the Treaty of Rome refer to the concern of the founding fathers for the peoples of our continent. Mr. Evans has done both his readers and our Community a service in reminding them and us of this dimension.

Roy Jenkins

25 June 1980

PREFACE AND ACKNOWLEDGMENTS

The European Economic Community is a vast mosaic that is forming the walls of time:

> And we who live in time compose its parts,
> The patterns range from money to people, reflecting
> all that moves in human life,
> When complete will more of light than shadow show
> And will our parts have helped to make it so.

It was these thoughts which prompted me to bring together under one cover some of the many economic and human aspects of the European Community. For obvious reasons no one book can or ever will be written that can bring together in a lifetime this vast mosaic. With my involvement in Europe I have for far too long been concerned at the lack of knowledge and appreciation by the business and academic community of the financial, economic and human problems both large and small of the Community. This book or anthology, however the reader wishes to assess it, sets out to demonstrate the many parts that are forming the walls of time, and is intended as a much needed guide to the political, economic, social and financial facets of the Community and its member states. It covers the organisation and function of the accounting professions in the different countries; company legislation and the establishment of a business; and the statutory and other requirements including EEC directives. At the same time, it presents an economic appraisal of the twelve countries, the functions of the Central Banks, Stock Exchanges, and the Institutions. The controversial Community Budget, a selection of some of the Community Policies and some small and large industries have been chosen to illustrate the problems the Community faces, but being a nation of 260 million people, the Community is involved in trading arrangements with nearly every country in the world. Some human subjects (if Euronet-Diane is a woman), such as going on holiday and retirement, lead to some of the important institutes of learning and business.

I am honoured that the Society of Company and Commerical Accountants have commissioned this book for those persons preparing for the Society's post-graduate Diploma in European Studies: it is the first professional body to realise the need for a European Diploma, and to provide a medium through which may be demonstrated an understanding of the European Community. The Diploma is obtained by examination, entrants to which must have a university degree or professional examination (not necessarily in accounting); it will provide a knowledge of the economic systems of the member states and their forms of business enterprise.

Mr. Roy Jenkins, then President of the Commission of the European Communities, sent a message to the Society in 1979 on its 50th Anniversary, congratulating it on its foresight in launching a Diploma in European Studies:

> In my view it is very important that members of the accounting and other professions should be informed of the economic, legal, financial and social environment which inevitably affects our society; among these factors the European Community introduces a new dimension in your concern.

It is hoped that the book will also be most useful to all university and professional students of accounting and business studies as well as for practising executives.

I wish to take this opportunity of thanking those who helped me make this book a reality. The Information departments of the European Parliament in Luxembourg (Mr. David Millar), the European Commission in Brussels (Mr. Peter Doyle, Editor-in-Chief of *Euroforum*) and the United Kingdom Commission Office in London (Mr. G. Scott and his staff). I am also grateful to the Commission in Brussels for introducing me for certain technical research to the EEC Bulletins of Price Waterhouse and Co., Brussels.

My thanks are especially due to the International Bureau of Fiscal Documentation, Amersterdam, Netherlands, for making research documentation available and I recommend them to all Europeans with a thirst for knowledge of community finance operations.

The Central Banks, Stock Exchanges and Joint Stock Banks throughout the Community have been most helpful, together with the Savings Bank Group, Brussels. I make special mention of the Abecor Association of European Banks especially Barclays Bank Ltd., as well as the National Westminster Bank Ltd., a non-member. Grateful acknowledgment is hereby made of the guidance and opinions of the late Mr. R.H.S. Beacham, B.Com, B.Sc.(Econ.), Executive Director of the Society of Company and Commercial Accountants, whose comments, suggestions, encouragement and expert professional advice I shall always value. My sincere thanks go to Mrs. J. G. Slade, Education Secretary of the Society, for so expertly organising the production of the manuscript. I would particularly like to thank Mr. Brian Davis for his great many invaluable suggestions and his skilled assistance in turning my manuscript into a book.

I am certain to have failed to mention everyone who directly or indirectly made a contribution to my work, and in order to retain friends and business associates add this disclaimer that I do not assume and hereby disclaim any liability to any party for any loss or damage caused by errors or omissions in the *Accountants Guide to the European Communities,* whether such errors result from negligence, accident or any other cause.

December 1980 Dennis Evans

CONTENTS

CHAPTER 1

INTRODUCTION

1. The Establishment of the Community

The background

The Treaty of Paris created the European Coal and Steel Community. Signed on 18 April 1951 the Treaty provided for the establishment of various institutions to run the Community, including a High Authority, an Assembly and a Court of Justice. In 1957 followed the Treaty of Rome (or more properly Treaties of Rome, since *two* Communities were created under separate agreements) which was signed on 25 March 1957. Established under the Treaties were the European Economic Community (EEC) and the European Atomic Energy Committee (EAEC or Euratom). The Institutional framework of the EEC was established at that time as a Commission, a Council of Ministers, a European Assembly (Parliament) and a Court of Justice.

Six countries signed the Treaties at the outset: Belgium, France, the Federal Republic of Germany, Italy, Luxembourg and the Netherlands. The Treaty of Accession (or Treaty of Brussels) was signed by these original six members of the Community and Denmark, Norway, the Republic of Ireland and the United Kingdom on 22 January 1972. Under the Treaty the acceding countries agreed to be bound by the Treaties of Paris (1951) and Rome (1957) subject to amendments and adjustments to these Treaties agreed to in Brussels. On the 1 January 1973 Denmark, the Republic of Ireland and the United Kingdom became members of the Community, Norway having withdrawn following a referendum rejecting membership.

Greece became the tenth member of the Community on 1 January 1981.

The original aims of the Community can be summarised as follows:

(1) to lay down in the aftermath of the Second World War the foundations of a European union which could rule out conflicts between its members and provide the countries with a voice in a world dominated by major Continental powers;

(2) to provide economic recovery and then expansion through the creation of a common market, starting with the coal and steel section – the two basic materials which were the sinews of war – and then extend the experience gained to the whole economy of each member state.

In the early stages, the results exceeded expectations.

(1) During the first five years of the ECSC, trade in coal and steel amongst the six increased by 129 per cent. Between the creation of the European Economic Community in 1958 and its expansion in 1973, trade amongst the six rose from 7 to 54 billion European units of account (see Chapter 4) for all products. Amongst the nine trade reached 168 billion EUA in 1977.

(2) Supplementing the increase in trade with the rest of the world, this development enabled consumers to be supplied with a more extensive range of goods. By stimulating competition – for which the Community is the watchdog – it also helped keep down price rises.

(3) European industry – with a domestic common market of 192 million people at its disposal in 1972 and 260 million at the present moment – has been able to rationalise production and raise productivity. The same has been the case for agriculture.

(4) Europe has consequently seen economic expansion without precedent. Between 1958 and 1972 – the year which signalled the beginning of the international economic crisis – the Community's gross national product had increased by 90 per cent compared with 42 per cent in the United Kingdom and 61 per cent in the United States of America. To take as an example two of the standard of living indications, the number of telephones per thousand inhabitants has risen from 80 in 1958 to 216 in 1962 and 400 in 1980. The indicator for cars has risen from 76 in 1958 to 325 in 1980.

(5) Above all peace was maintained. Human contacts have multiplied between men, women, leaders, politicians, civil servants, trade unionists, employers, farmers and so on, and have helped build up greater trust between peoples who have been divided for too long. Jean Monnet said: "We are not only bringing together countries, we are uniting people." As a sign of the Community's attraction, Greece requested to join in 1975 and Portugal and Spain followed suit in 1977. Greece is now a member, and Portugal and Spain will soon follow.

Common market and interdependence

Throughout the last three decades, the work of the common market has helped develop interdependence between Community countries.

(1) The free movement of men and services has enabled workers, traders and industrialists to move to and work in the countries of their choice. Migrants benefit from equal treatment over wages, social security and trade union rights. The Community is currently working to extend these rights to the liberal professions by harmonising national criteria and qualifications and to encourage language teaching and the mobility of university students.
(2) The free movement of goods has by and large been accomplished. Customs duties were totally abolished for the six founding countries in 1968 and in 1977 for the others. In consequence trade amongst the nine has considerably increased and today represents a little more than half of their total trade. This vast domestic European market enables large scale production costs to be reduced. Countries which decide to turn in on themselves will lose this advantage and will be condemned to decline.
(3) European competition rules have been implemented. The objective is to ensure that companies do not reach agreements or form cartels or abuse dominant positions either to the detriment of other firms or at the expense of the consumer.
(4) In the agricultural sector where state aid is an established tradition, a European policy has been introduced based on common prices and on Community price support. New efforts are necessary to eliminate the distortions created by exchange rate fluctuations, to prevent the creation of surplus stocks, to assure the future of farming in Mediterranean areas and to introduce a common system for fisheries.
(5) Another consequence of the free movement of goods within the Community has been the common customs tariff applicable to the rest of the world. International trade agreements and the introduction of measures to guard against uncontrolled competition from third countries are now within Community powers.

The Community has emerged on the international scene as a single body – the most powerful grouping in the world, since it accounts for over 20 per cent of world trading (excluding intra-Community trade).

The Community has used its power to liberalise international trade and to encourage the development of the Third World which is the principal supplier of raw materials to the leading export markets.

Along with the growth of the Community, contacts have multiplied owing to the need for interdependence in other sectors:

(1) taxation – despite the abolition of customs duties border controls cannot be abolished until VAT rates applied to different goods are harmonised;
(2) environment and consumer protection;
(3) regional policy;
(4) social policy;
(5) scientific policy, and
(6) industrial policy.

Summary

Throughout the world there are a large number of international organisations to bring together the states that wish to co-operate with each other. The European Community goes much further than this:

(1) in its aim – to build a veritable European Union;
(2) in its methods – the operation of the Community is not purely inter-governmental, since Community institutions have their own powers and the organisation of their relationship aims to promote the general interest of Europeans, and
(3) in its results – the Council of Ministers and the Commission, wherever it has autonomous decision-making powers, takes action with the force of law which in many cases is applied directly to European citizens.

Such action may take the form of –

(a) *regulations,* which are applied directly as Community laws;
(b) *decisions,* which are binding only on the member states, companies or individuals to whom they are addressed;
(c) *directives,* which set down compulsory objectives but leave it to the discretion of member states to translate them into their national legislation, or
(d) *recommendations* and *opinions* which are not binding (except for recommendations in the ECSC section, where they are equivalent to directives)

The application of European law is watched over by the Court of Justice which is open to complaints from citizens.

With the direct election by universal suffrage of the members of the European Parliament, the full democratic participation of citizens in the operation of Community institutions will be recognised and institutionalised. In the continuous dialogue which takes place between Community institutions, an elected Parliament will have by that fact alone prestige, authority and increased moral weight. For the rest, the extension of the European Parliament's powers presupposes a revision of the European Treaties and therefore the unanimous agreement of member states in conformity with their own constitutional rules. This will imply other institutional reforms to improve the operation of the Community which will be particularly important with the entry of other countries.

The problems

Factory closures, unemployment, spending cutbacks, declining standard of living, inflation – these words have freely abounded in conversation and newspaper and TV reports throughout Europe in recent years and are a sign of the hardship that Europe has suffered. Recent economic indications show only a slight but not necessarily permanent improvement. More and more citizens have felt the impact of the economic crisis in their everyday lives, a crisis triggered in 1973 by the rise in oil prices which has hit all industrialised countries to greater or lesser degrees.

(1) Unemployment has increased dramatically – 10 per cent in three provinces of Belgium and several other regions of Europe: in Southern Italy 20 per cent in the Campanie and Basilicate. The total unemployed in Community countries is over six million: the average between 1960 and 1970 was two million.
(2) Economic growth rates in Community countries have fallen from 4.6 per cent in the 1960s to 2.6 per cent.
(3) Inflation is now averaging 12 per cent in the Community, compared with an average of 3 per cent between 1958 and 1967. In 1974 and 1975 it was averaging 13 per cent.
(4) Industries in third world countries are competing more and more with community countries in goods such as textiles, shipbuilding and steel: matters given more detailed consideration later in the book. The fourfold oil price increases in 1973 and price rises in other imported raw materials were the first signs of a significant readjustment in the balance of the world economy.
(5) The international monetary crisis has not helped either – especially the constant fall in the value of the US dollar, which still remains the principal means of payment in world trade. Variations in European exchange rates are a measure of divergences in economic efficiency. They discourage trade and therefore industrial investment.
(6) The improvement in standards of living and social welfare characteristic of the years of prosperity have been interrupted. Social and regional inequalities have deepened. The limits on funds available have made it more difficult to find answers to new demands for a better quality of life.

The economic crisis was preceded by a moral crisis, and the limits of badly distributed and purely quantitative economic growth have been evident to a number of social commentators and particularly to the young.

(1) Large pockets of poverty persist in the least developed or declining regions, often in close proximity to opulence. Things are worse in third world countries. One-third of the world's population is hungry.
(2) In addition to the problems experienced by workers are those suffered by consumers. The workers in our programmed society often have boring and repetitive jobs which demand little skill and which they must perform within a rigid hierarchical structure. Consumer needs are accentuated rather than fulfilled by advertising, waste and the multiplication of personal goods.
(3) Economic growth pushes us nearer to human and natural limits. New progress seems to amount to further attacks on the person – noise, fatigue, insecurity – or on the environment. Pollution is increasing and the dwindling reserves of certain raw materials lead to disturbing forecasts.

Economic crises always impose new objectives and so they do with the Community. The scope of the future challenge facing the Community and the interdependence of Community countries calls for joint responses.

In a troubled world only the economic and monetary union of Europe can enable the EEC countries to create a zone of relative stability, and this will depend upon certain objectives being achieved.

Currency and finance

(1) The development of the European Monetary System to provide exchange stability between European currencies, hopefully to include the Pound Sterling. The European Currency Unit (ECU) system is made up of a basket of Community currencies.
(2) More effective coordination of national economic policies – it is difficult to maintain stable relationships between currencies when inflation rates differ by as much as 10 per cent.
(3) Joint action to resolve structural imbalances. In the framework of the new monetary system a sum of six million EUA will be put at the disposal of the least prosperous countries by 1984.

Social and regional policies

(1) Social policy – the improvement of working conditions and the promotion of workers' rights, particularly in cases of collective dismissals, mergers or bankruptcies. In the past, national employment policies have been ineffective at finding solutions

to this problem, which constitutes a human nightmare and a considerable economic waste.

(2) Regional policy – increased efforts are required –
  (a) to stop or arrest rural population decline and conversely help resolve the problems of large industrial concentrations;
  (b) to assure a re-adaption in the declining regions;
  (c) to permit all member countries, current or future, to progress towards comparable economic and social positions, and
  (d) to modernise the Mediterranean regions for the enlargement of the Community with the addition of Greece, Portugal and Spain.

(3) Industrial policy – Europe can never be a hospital for sick industries: industry has to be redeployed towards growth sectors as this can be the only way to assure new and viable jobs. Such re-deployment has to be coordinated at Community level –
  (a) to guarantee the optimal use of available resources and avoid ruinous duplication of effort,
  (b) to safeguard the unity of the common market which could be compromised by divergent national policies, and
  (c) to develop on a more solid basis, industrial and commercial cooperation with third world countries. Rapid industrialisation in certain of these countries may cause problems, but the rising standard of living in these countries offer the possibility of increased exports, particularly capital goods.

(4) Energy policy – the EEC dependence on outside countries is heavy. Energy-saving measures need to be increased and new energy sources developed. The coordination of national policies is essential. Greater cooperation would permit –
  (a) the better exploitation of research investment, and
  (b) agreements with oil-producing countries to guarantee the volume and cost of supplies.

The future

Europe is no longer a matter for technocrats. It is Europeans themselves – all citizens of the Community – who have to answer the major questions of tomorrow:

(1) How far are we prepared to go to reduce social and regional inequalities in the Community and the countries that wish to become members, to enable all countries to become completely integrated in European economic and monetary unions?

(2) How can we guarantee jobs – and if possible jobs which satisfy

aspirations – for today's unemployed and for our children tomorrow? Must we share out the jobs which are currently available? Must we put more accent on greater competition in industry?

(3) What type of economic growth are we looking for, and based on what form of productive system? What objectives for consumption? What degree of intervention by public authorities? What sources of energy – nuclear or not? Are we ready in all these fields to pay the price of our choices?

(4) Just how far and at what speed do we want to move on the road to European Union? What form do we want this Europe to take, and what type of society and civilisation do we want?

(5) What sort of relationships do we want to have with the other major powers and with the countries of the third world? To what extent are we ready to extend our support to the latter?

How Europeans reply to these questions in the years ahead will determine the nature of the Community – our Community. The direct elections to the European Parliament in June 1979 were consequently vitally important. For the Community they are both a factor for democratisation and a factor of strength – through these elections the citizens of Europe were able to state how they wished to see the Europe of the future develop.

2. Some Statistical Details

Comparative statistics – Europe and the world

EEC: Area and Population

Country	*Area 000 sq. miles*	*Population M*
Belgium	12	10
Denmark	17	5
France	213	53
F. R. of Germany	96	60
Greece	51	9
Italy	116	56
Luxembourg	1	4
Netherlands	13	14
Republic of Ireland	27	3
United Kingdom	94	55
Europe Ten	640	269

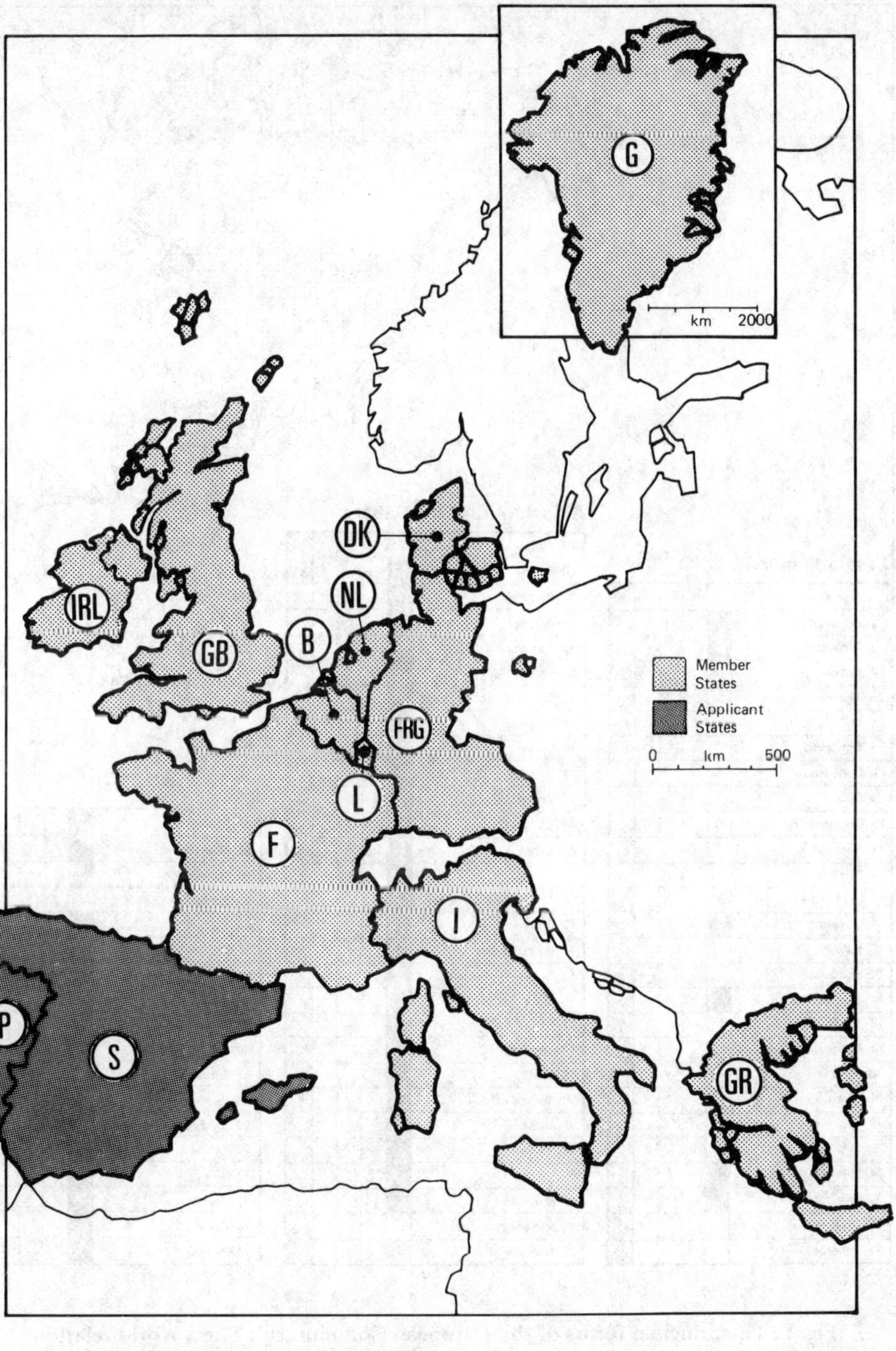

Fig. 1. The member countries of the European Community.

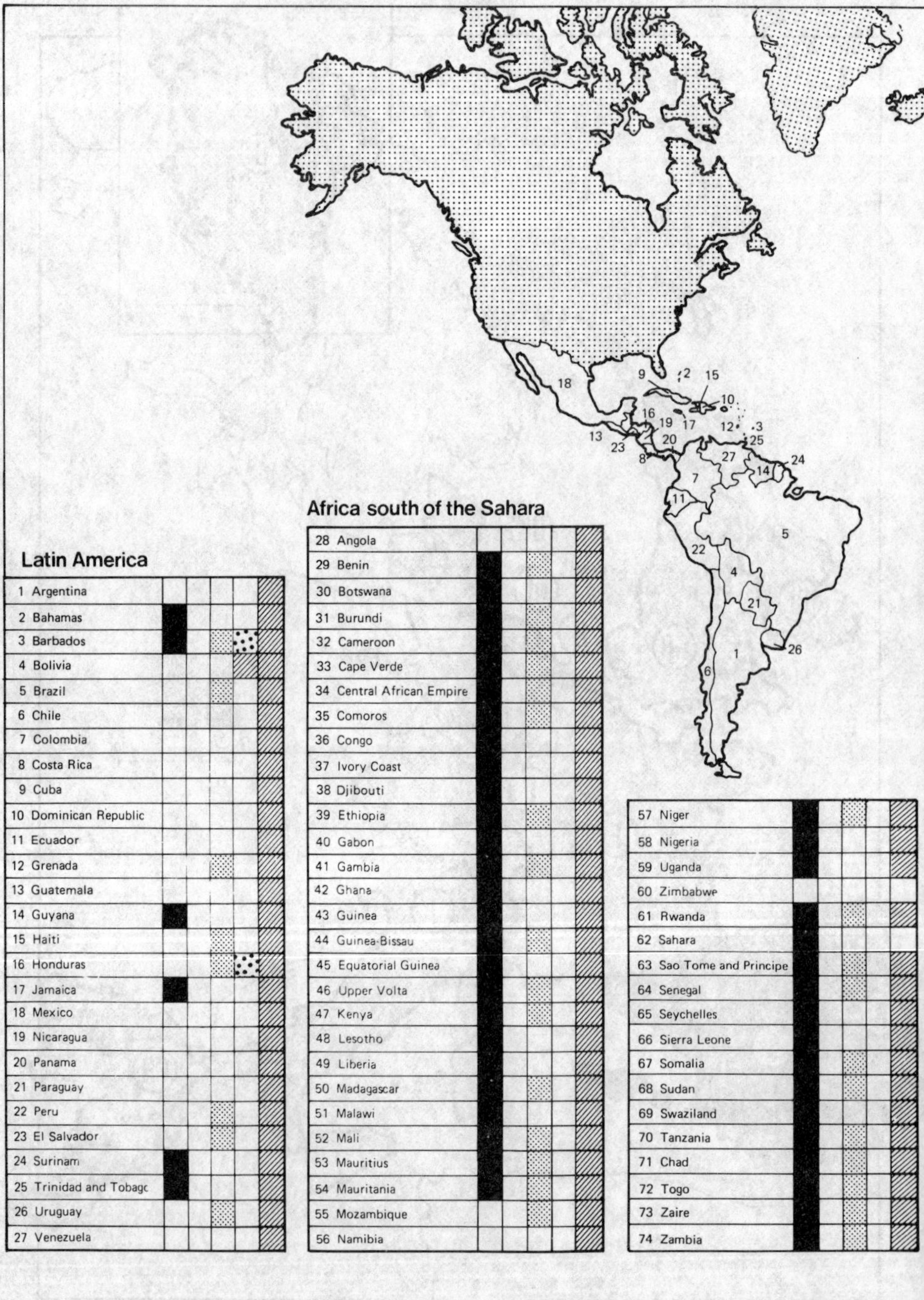

Fig. 2. The principal forms of the European Community's Third World relations

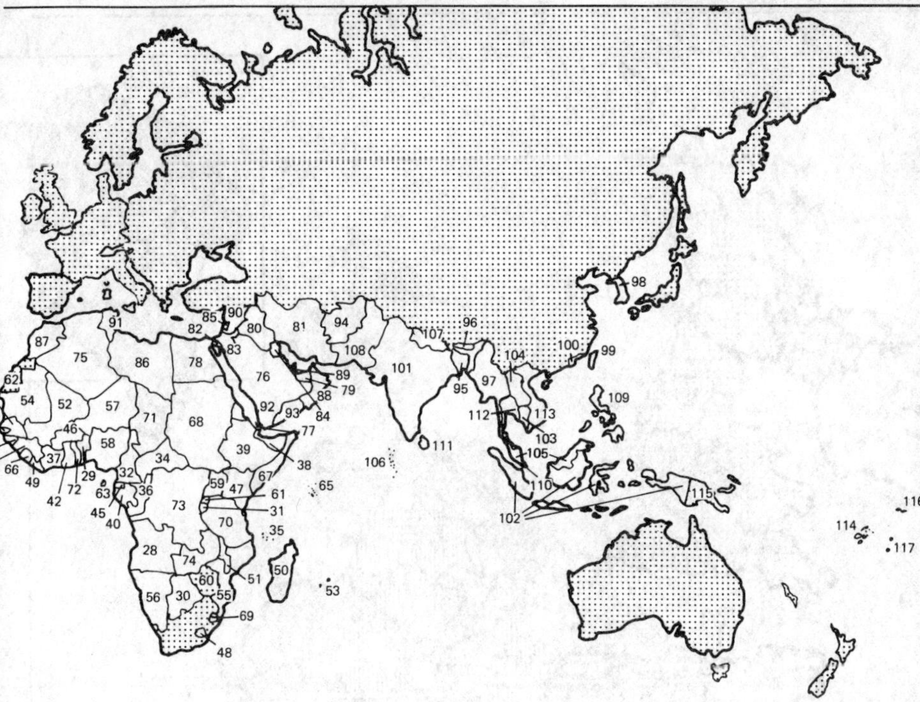

Mediterranean and Middle East

Country	Lomé Convention	Mediterranean Agreements	Food Aid	Financial Cooperation	Generalised Preferences
75 Algeria		X	X		X
76 Saudi Arabia					X
77 Bahrain					X
78 Egypt		X	X		X
79 United Arab Emirates					X
80 Iraq					X
81 Iran					X
82 Israel		X			
83 Jordan		X	X		X
84 Kuwait					X
85 Lebanon		X	X		X
86 Libya					X
87 Morocco		X	X		X
88 Oman					X
89 Qatar					X
90 Syria			X		X
91 Tunisia			X		X
92 Yemen (A.R.)			X	X	X
93 Yemen (P.D.R.)			X		X

Asia excluding Middle East

Country	Lomé Convention	Mediterranean Agreements	Food Aid	Financial Cooperation	Generalised Preferences
94 Afghanistan			X		X
95 Bangladesh			X	X	X
96 Bhutan					X
97 Burma					X
98 South Korea					X
99 Taiwan					
100 Hong Kong					X
101 India			X	X	X
102 Indonesia			X	X	X
103 Cambodia					X
104 Laos					X
105 Malaysia					X
106 Maldives					X
107 Nepal					X
108 Pakistan			X	X	X
109 Philippines			X		X
110 Singapore					X
111 Sri Lanka			X	X	X
112 Thailand				X	X
113 Vietnam			X	X	X

Key:
- Lome Convention (ACP States)
- Agreements with Mediterranean Developing Countries
- Food Act
- Financial Cooperation with other Developing Countries
- Generalised Preferences

Oceania

Country	Lomé Convention	Mediterranean Agreements	Food Aid	Financial Cooperation	Generalised Preferences
114 Fiji	X				X
115 Papua New Guinea	X				X
116 Western Samoa	X				X
117 Tonga	X				X

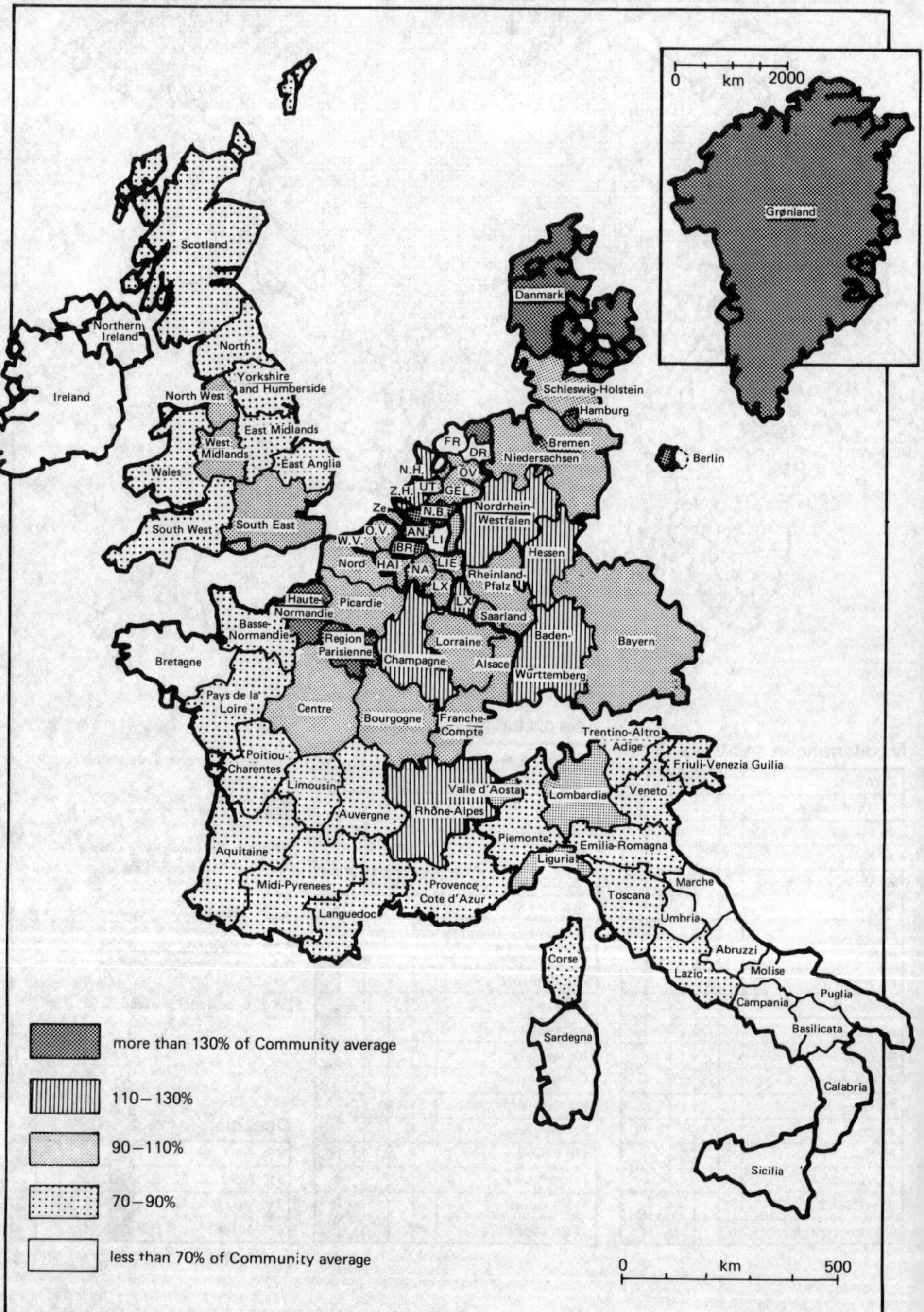

Fig. 3. Regional disparities within the European Community. Gross domestic product per inhabitant expressed in purchasing power parities.

EEC: Employment Categories and GDP

	Employment (in % 1979) A	B	C	Gross Domestic Product D(X)	E	Consumer Price Index F(X)
Belgium	3.2	36.7	60.7	2.3	7530	7.5
Denmark	8.3	30.2	61.5	1.9	8601	9.8
France	8.8	36.3	54.9	3.0	6960	10.1
F.R. of Germany	6.2	44.9	48.9	1.9	8186	4.2
Greece	30.8	30.0	39.2	3.6	2628	14.1
Italy	14.8	37.7	47.5	4.0	3602	15.8
Luxembourg	6.1	44.7	49.2	0.6	7821	6.9
Netherlands	4.8	32.7	62.4	2.6	7366	6.7
R. of Ireland	21.0	31.9	47.1	3.5	2899	14.5
United Kingdom	2.6	39.9	58.4	1.1	4345	15.5

Code: A = Agriculture; *B* = Industry; *C* = Services; *D* = Average Annual Growth 1973-1978 (%); *E* = Per inhabitant in 1978 (EUA); *F* = Average annual increase 1974-1979 (%).

Source: *Eurostat (except X: OECD 1980).*

EEC: Standard of Living

	Private Consumption per head in 1978 (EUA)	Per 1000 inhabitants: Cars 1978	Telephones 1978	Doctors 1977
Belgium	4604	302	322	2.2
Denmark	4781	276	569	2.0
France	4276	333	372	1.6
F.R. of Germany	4882	346	404	2.0
Greece	1827	80	266	2.2
Italy	2278	291	301	2.2
Luxembourg	4469	428	539	1.3
Netherlands	4261	295	453	1.7
R. of Ireland	1842	195	172	1.2
United Kingdom	2608	258	447	1.5

Source: *Eurostat.*

Future of European population

An average male living in the European Community can expect to live just over 68 years, according to the latest Eurostat figures – an improvement on twenty years ago when the figure stood at 64. The healthiest men appear to be in the Netherlands and Denmark where the average is 71. Women are more hardy: their average life expectancy is 75, with the Dutch and Danes again leading the field at 78 and 77 years respectively. Given that women tend to live some six or seven years more than men, it is not surprising that of the 269 million people in the Community 51.6 per cent are women.

But it is women who are more likely to have a wider choice of partners in marriage. Men are more numerous in the 0 to 44 age-bracket, and it is only thereafter that early male deaths bring women into the numerical ascendancy. This is particularly marked for senior citizens: 21 million women are over 65, while there are only 14 million men in this category, and women over 85 (1.5 million) outnumber men three to one.

Male supremacy in the early years is assured by 100,000 more boys being born than girls, but the number of births for both sexes combined has fallen from 4.1 to 3.2 million over the last twenty years. The highest birth rate in the Community is in the Republic of Ireland, where there are 21 babies per thousand of the population. Elsewhere it is around 12–14, except for Germany, where the current figure of 9 babies per thousand is only half what it was twenty years ago.

Another interesting statistic now appearing in demographic tables is the number of illegitimate births in a country. Denmark has the dubious honour of leading the field here. For every 1,000 babies, 259 are born out of wedlock. The next highest is the United Kingdom with 95, while in Belgium, the Netherlands and Italy the figure is nearer 30.

The population of the Community appears to be shrinking at both ends. Not only is the number of births decreasing, but the number of deaths is rising: in 1960, 2.5 million died, and by 1976 the figure had reached 2.8 million.

Different values and behaviour patterns are now reflected in the statistics on marriages and divorces. The marriage rate in the Community has fallen from 7.4 per thousand twenty years ago to 6.4 per thousand. But while weddings may be losing their attraction, those who do marry are just a little younger nowadays than their parents were – over the last quarter-century the average age for first marriages has dropped by one year, to 25 for men and 23 for women.

Divorces, on the other hand, have increased almost threefold since 1960, from a rate of 0.5 per thousand to 1.3 per thousand. The highest rates are in Denmark and the United Kingdom, where just over two people per thousand get a divorce.

3. People in the Community

The operation of the Community is important only insofar as it affects people – either directly or indirectly. While the free movement of goods is important, it is equally vital that citizens of the

Community should be able to move about freely whether they are travelling purely for pleasure or whether they want to move from one Community country to another to work.

However if all Community people are to be treated equally they must be allowed not only to travel freely to another member state but also to remain there and to work there if they wish. In addition, workers who move must have the same job security as workers native to their host country, and they must enjoy equal social security benefits.

Several million Community citizens now work in member states other than their own and the Community operates a European Co-ordination Office with the national employment services to match job offers throughout the Community with applications. This mobility has also been considerably facilitated by reforms which enable employed migrant workers and their families to benefit from social security protection in their adopted country.

While it is one thing for a building worker or a farmhand to slot easily into the workforce in another country, it is quite another matter in areas where precise academic or professional qualifications are demanded. Thus it was not until 1977 that doctors had the right to set up practice anywhere in the Community and later nurses were entitled to the same privileges. In 1979 lawyers were free to provide their services, though not to set up practice. Now that these precedents have been established, other professions have done so or will follow. Professional people are of course not all self-employed. Therefore not only they but the firms they work for must be free to offer their services anywhere in the Community and establish themselves. Community legislation has removed such restrictions from a wide variety of undertakings, among them aspects of insurance, banking, real estate farming and land purchase.

Three further aspects of Community life have been chosen for more detailed discussion. They cover the subjects of women's rights holidays, and retirement – all human aspects which are both topical and general, so that the sections which follow give a random but significant view of some human considerations which relate to a wide area of the population.

Women in Europe

To keep women better informed about Community activity the Directorate-General for Information has an Information Service for Women's Organisations, and publishes a journal *Women of Europe* in the six Community languages. The journal is designed to broadcast women's activities in the member countries and current news about the Community.

About one out of every three women in the Community believes that politics is better left to men; yet in the Community as a whole women form over half (51.6 per cent) of the total population, and of the 38 million women working outside the home the overwhelming majority are concentrated in low-paying industries, with limited prospects of promotion or training. Article 119 of the Treaty of Rome laid down the principle of equal pay for equal work as far back as 1957. It was included for economic rather than altruistic reasons, to ensure that free competition was not distorted by the employment of women at lower rates than men for the same work.

In the 1970s, however, influenced by militant feminist demands, the Community has taken a more positive and enlightened attitude to women. Throughout the Community it is now illegal *not* to apply the principle of equal pay for equal work, or to discriminate against women where training or promotion prospects are concerned. Practice tends to lag behind good intention, perhaps partly because of society's attitude, partly because of the attitude of women themselves.

Facts and figures

Of the 38 million women employed, more than two out of three are employed full time, with the rest employed part time or on a casual basis.

On average six to seven women out of ten are employed in the service industries, rising to over eight out of ten in the Netherlands. Although the situation varies from country to country, on average fewer than three out of ten (28 per cent) are engaged in industry and fewer than one in ten (7 per cent) in agriculture. Italy has the highest number of women working in agriculture (14 per cent) and the UK the least (1 per cent). A Commission survey of 1976 reported that 60 per cent would prefer to work outside the home. Asked what social reforms they thought the most important in improving women's status, one in three opted for a wage for work done in the home, two out of five wanted a more flexible working week and better child-minding services. Over 40 per cent considered family commitments hampered work opportunities for women.

There were national differences among those interviewed on the political role of women. Danish (78 per cent) and British (68 per cent) women led the field believing that women and men should play the same role in politics compared with their Luxembourg (47 per cent) and Belgian (45 per cent) sisters.

Community aims and legislation

Despite Article 119 of the Treaty of Rome, there was little advance on matters of equal pay or women's promotion prospects until the

1970s. In 1975 the Council of Ministers decided to reinforce the general legal provision of Article 119 by a specific directive on equal pay (75/117/EEC) which expressly excluded discrimination based on sex (in particular in job classification), provided for legal appeal for those who felt themselves discriminated against and gave protection against dismissal to workers who complained. This legislation was followed by a second directive (76/207/EEC) concerning equal treatment and non-discrimination on any grounds for men and women regarding employment, vocational training and promotion, and working conditions.

The equal pay principle is now part of Community legislation, but, as with the principle of non-discrimination, implementation is a slow process.

Training and family life

Sex discrimination, however, starts long before women enter the field of work. It is found, usually influenced by tradition rather than intent, in the schools and in opportunities for vocational training. Special emphasis has been laid on the need for change in educational attitudes, in particular on non-discriminating educational guidance in the choice of careers, and for teachers to be made aware of this. There must also be greater opportunity for girls to take up apprenticeship courses or vocational training schemes leading to well-qualified posts and the provision of special opportunities for education and training, enabling women to re-enter employment after a period of interruption. Family affairs must not be allowed to hinder but must be reconciled with their job aspirations. There should be paid leave available for either the father or mother when a child is ill, and extension of arrangements for workers responsible for sick or elderly dependants.

The European Social Fund, created by the Treaty of Rome, is used to further Community social policies, particularly today in the field of employment and training, and for helping special groups of workers such as those made redundant, migrants, the handicapped and young people. Since January 1978 the Fund has been operating under revised regulations, and one of the new priorities for assistance covers women over the age of 25, particularly the unskilled or semi-skilled, who have either lost their jobs, are seeking work for the first time or are coming back to seek a job after a long period of domestic responsibility. Due to economic recession, unemployment among women is high and many are handicapped by lack of earlier educational or vocational opportunity. Money from the Fund is available for approved training projects that seek to overcome these handicaps.

Women's Bureau

In November 1976 the Commission set up a Bureau for Questions affecting Women's Employment – an indication of the Community's desire to respond to needs in this area. The office is not intended to solve individual problems, but to work at Community level to achieve equal treatment for men and women at work. With this in mind the Commission have made a film – "Equal Chances, Equal Opportunities" – to illustrate the directives on equal treatment in the working world, and stressing the importance of wider choice of occupation for girls and women. The film is obtainable on loan from Guild Sound and Vision Ltd., Woodston House, Oundle Road, Peterborough PE2 9PZ, or from National Audio-Visual Aids Library, Paxton Place, Gipsy Road, London, S.E.27.

Holiday-makers

Membership of the Community offers to citizens certain advantages when visiting the member countries – reciprocal medical care is one of these advantages. In addition, travellers crossing internal Community frontiers may take in, free of tax, more goods in their personal luggage than those coming in from outside, while motorists are automatically guaranteed minimum legal insurance cover, according to the laws of the country visited, in case of accident.

Medical care

It can be expensive to be taken ill on holiday. Community citizens, however, provided that they are insured through their own national insurance schemes and follow certain procedures, are entitled to receive emergency medical care on the same terms as the people whose country they are visiting. This does not mean that treatment will always be free, as under the British National Health Service. It does mean, however, that through reimbursement or other arrangements only a small proportion of the costs should be borne by the visitor. Despite annual attempts by the European Commission to publicise the reciprocal arrangements available, many holiday-makers are unaware that they exist. The Community regulations have long applied to insured workers or pensioners and their families; since April 1978 certain categories of the self-employed and non-employed are also included in their scope. Self-employed people are eligible if at some time they have been insured in their own country as an employed person and have paid contributions within the current tax year as self-employed. People who are no longer working but have been insured as an employed person, and have paid sufficient contributions to enable them to draw a full-rate retirement pension, may also benefit.

Unfortunately, the procedure to be followed by holiday-makers who wish to insure themselves against trouble is not always perhaps as simple as it might be. British holiday-makers, for instance, must obtain, *before they go on holiday*, an Entitlement Certificate (Form E 111). This should be applied for on form CM1, to be found at the back of the DHSS leaflet SA28, available at local social security offices. The leaflet also provides full information about medical care in the Community countries. In the event of sickness or accident the visitor must apply to the nearest sickness insurance organisation and present Form E 111. (These organisations are listed on the back of the form.) UK citizens, however, do not need these forms if they are visiting Denmark or the Republic of Ireland.

Normally a visitor is entitled to treatment only for an ailment requiring immediate attention, though pensioners or those in receipt of industrial injuries benefit may be able to obtain a wider range of care. In some cases sickness benefit can also be claimed if application is made within three days to the local sickness institution.

Sickness expenses (medical care, medicines, hospital treatment, etc.) will be paid by the insurance organisation at the place where the insured person is staying, in accordance with the system in force in the country. Generally speaking, in Denmark, Germany, the Republic of Ireland and Italy medical care is given free by doctors approved by the insurance organisations. Medicines are also provided free in the Netherlands and in the Republic of Ireland. In other countries insured persons are required to make a (non-recoverable) contribution. In Belgium, France and Luxembourg the insured person must normally pay all or part of the costs incurred, and is then reimbursed by the competent local sickness insurance organisation in accordance with the scale applied to persons insured within the organisation.

If, during the stay, sickness or accident renders a person unfit for work, he may receive the daily benefits provided for under the regulations of the country where he is insured. He must inform the insurance organisation at the place where he is staying by submitting a medical certificate of unfitness for work, and must be examined by its medical adviser. This organisation will then request the organisation with which the worker is insured (in the UK the DHSS) for cash payments of the benefits. The latter, if the worker is so entitled, will pay him the benefits by international money order or through the organisation at the place where he is staying.

Information regarding medical treatment can be obtained from the following sources:

Belgium. Regional offices of the Auxiliary Fund for Sickness and Invalidity Insurance (Caisse Auxiliaire d'Assurance Maladie –

Invalidité), 10 Boulevard St. Lazare, 1030 Brussels.

Denmark. The social and health division of the local council, or the National Social Security Office (Sikring Sstyrelsen) Aebeløgade 1, Post Box 2566, 1000 Copenhagen.

France. (a) Outside Paris – Caisses Primaires d'Assurance Maladie. *(b)* In Paris – Service des Relations Internationales de la Securite Sociale, 84 Rue Charles Michel, St. Denis (93).

Federal Republic of Germany. Allgemeine Ortskrankenhausen (known as OAK), normally open Monday to Friday mornings only.

Greece. Social Insurance Foundation IKA, 8 Aghiou Constantinou, Athens.

Italy. Any of the local offices of the National Institute for Sickness Insurance (Instituto Nazionale per l'Assurazione Contra le Malatti (known as INAM).

Luxembourg. Caisse Nationale d'Assurance Maladie des Ouvriers, 10 Rue de Strasbourg, Luxembourg.

Netherlands. Algemeen Nederlands Onderling Ziekenfonds (known as ANOZ), Kaap Hoorndreff 24-28, Utrecht.

Republic of Ireland. The Health Board of the area in which the visitor is staying.

United Kingdom. Department of Health and Social Security, Overseas Branch, Newcastle Upon Tyne NE98 1YX.

Duty-free allowances

A member of the European Parliament, M. Dondelinger, suggested in a written question No. 623/77 in December 1979 that the "parsimoniously calculated" duty-free imports of cigarettes, alcohol and perfume allowed in by excise regulations in the member countries had a "deplorable psychological effect" on Community travellers, a quarter of a century after the creation of the European Community. The Commission pointed out in reply that several proposals it had sent to the Council of Ministers to ease the situation had yet to be implemented. The problem is that substantial differences exist between the excise duties on certain products transferred from one member country to another, and these have been widening in recent years. For this and other reasons it has not yet been possible to propose improvements in the duty-free import arrangements.

Insurance cover for motorists

Frontier officials no longer ask motorists to present their insurance "green card" when they cross the Community, or when they enter or leave Austria, Switzerland, Sweden, Norway and Finland. This is because insurance companies within the Community must provide third party cover for motorists travelling to other Community countries, and they have extended this principle to the other countries mentioned. It should be emphasised, however, that the automatic cover is only the *legal minimum* required according to the laws of the country visited and this differs from one to another.

The green card, therefore, is not legally essential, but motorists wishing to be fully insured against accident should make their own private arrangements.

Anyone taking a minibus to continental Europe should remember that passenger vehicles with seats for more than nine people, including the driver, require to be fitted with a tachograph for travelling in other Community countries, and in most non-EEC countries as well. For purely national traffic, governments may seek an exemption for vehicles of up to 13 seats (as the UK has done), but this does not affect anyone taking a minibus from the UK to another European country.

Attitudes to retirement

Europe faces a period of prolonged structural unemployment as a result of the introduction of new high technology industries. Among the ways increasingly canvassed to cope with this are early retirement and a shorter working week or day. A survey carried out in the Community at the request of the Commission's Directorate for Employment and Social Affairs on the attitude of the working population to retirement analyses European attitudes to these suggestions country by country. A sample of ten thousand was used, and the survey reveals considerable variation in views.

There are 100 million working people in the Community plus 40 million spouses, all sooner or later to be faced with the problem of retirement. Any prospect of Community harmonisation is rendered difficult by different presumptions about the age of retirement which now prevails. The Irish and the Danes, for example, believe in a highest retirement age around 65, in Luxembourg and Italy the norm is 60. Britain stands about half way between these figures, but for about 40 per cent of the Community's work-force the age of retirement is 60 or below.

Some 53 per cent of the work-force think about the prospect of retirement, though the prospect is viewed with satisfaction by only 40 per cent. The 50 to 54 age group views the prospect with greatest satisfaction. Among those who look forward least to retirement are women and the self-employed. It is men in the upper income brackets who look forward most. Satisfaction increases more with age among manual workers than it does among white-collar workers. Feelings about retirement vary from country to country, the least anxious being the Dutch (14 per cent) followed by the Irish (21 per cent), though the Irish have the largest proportion of "don't knows". The Danes express least satisfaction (27 per cent anxious, 44 per cent satisfied) and are most similar in this feeling to the Germans.

The question "When you get your pension will you stop working altogether or will you get a paid job?" elicited the answer that nearly 60 per cent intended to stop working altogether, while 24 per cent will try to get a paid job – 17 per cent of this number giving as their reason the desire to stay active; the wish to increase income was given by a mere 6 per cent. The relation between job satisfaction and a wish for early retirement appears to be tenuous: in answer to the question "If you had enough money to live as you wanted, would you still carry on working?" 60 per cent answered "yes," and less than a third said "no." Nationality produced far greater variations in intention: in the Benelux countries where people already look forward most to retirement, there is a greater degree of readiness to retire early; in Denmark, the United Kingdom and the Republic of Ireland the number of people wanting to carry on working after normal retirement is 26 per cent. An oddity in the Danish-Irish consensus is that both countries expect the highest retirement age in the Community, whilst the Irish have the lowest median income in the Community and the Danes the highest.

The poll went on to pose questions about attitudes towards the choice of shorter hours or better pay. The dominant trend was in favour of shorter hours with 51 per cent in favour and only 42 per cent for better pay. The bias in favour of shorter hours stretched right through the income ranges – 52 per cent of the lowest paid wishing for shorter hours as opposed to 43 per cent wanting more pay. The nationality divisions show the Danes heading the list of six countries opting for shorter hours, while a majority of the Irish, Italians and Luxembourgers called for more pay – the last with a massive 67 per cent, against a mere 20 per cent for shorter hours. In further analysis of ways to reduce the work-load by reductions in the working day or week, longer holidays or earlier retirement, the first option gained the most support (37 per cent) followed by the third (33 per cent). Only the Germans showed an appreciable leaning towards longer holidays. The Republic of Ireland, the United Kingdom and Denmark, in that order, were most in favour of a reduction in the working day or week. Luxembourg, France and Belgium were most in favour of early retirement.

The analysis concludes with the admission that research must be done into two separate notions which have a strong bearing on any policies designed to reduce working time and for a sharing of the work load: the age at which pension rights can be claimed, and the age at which the right to work may be lost. It is suggested that the dissociation in time of these two aspects, often confused at the moment, should calm the fears that many members of the working population have towards the end of their careers. Many Europeans would like to be free of the constraints currently imposed by the normal age of retirement, and many would be freed of a feeling of alienation if they knew they could stop earlier.

CHAPTER 2

ORGANISATION AND MANAGEMENT OF THE COMMUNITY

Introduction

As will have been seen from Chapter 1, the European Community was created by three Treaties:

(1) the Treaty of Paris was signed on 18 April 1951, which created the European Coal and Steel Community (ECSC),
(2) the two Rome Treaties signed on 25 March 1957, which set up the European Economic Community (EEC) and
(3) the European Atomic Energy Community (EAEC or Euratom).

Within the framework of these three Treaties the European Community is managed by four main institutions:

(1) *The Commission* – makes proposals for action and, when a decision to act has been taken, sees that it is carried out;
(2) *The Council of Ministers* – is the ultimate decision-taking body, representing the national governments of the Community, and through it each government is in a position to veto any proposal which conflicts with its vital national interests;
(3) *The Court of Justice* – is the final court of appeal in any case covered by the Common Market treaties, and
(4) *The Parliament* – whose function it is to exercise democratic control over this process by scrutinising legislation, by questioning both Commission and Council and by raising in debate matters of public importance.

Each of these bodies will now be considered in turn.

1. The European Commission

The present position

The Commission of the European Communities is composed of fourteen Members, two from each of the UK, France, Germany, and Italy and one from each of the other countries, each appointed for a four-year period by mutual agreement of the governments of the Community. The Members of the Commission act only in the interests of the Community: they may not receive instructions from any national government and are subject only to the supervision of the European Parliament, which alone can force them collectively to resign their responsibilities. Commission decisions are taken collegiately, even though each Commissioner is directly responsible for one or more portfolios.

The Commission's tasks are as follows.

(1) To ensure that Community rules and the principles of the Common Market are respected. As guardian of the Treaties the Commission is responsible for seeing that they are observed, and that decisions of the Community institutions deriving from the Treaties are correctly applied. The Commission decides on requests from member states to apply safeguard clauses and can, in exceptional cases, authorise temporary waivers (derogations) from the rules of the Treaties. It has investigative powers and can impose fines on individuals, particularly regarding violations of Community competition rules. States which do not respect their obligations can also be taken to the European Court of Justice by the Commission.

(2) To propose to the Community's Council of Ministers all measures likely to advance Community policies (in the fields of agriculture, energy, industry, research, environment, social and regional problems, external trade, economic and monetary union etc.).

(3) To implement Community policies on the basis of Council decisions or derived directly from the provisions of the Treaties.

  (a) The Commission has particularly extensive powers in the fields of coal and steel (investment co-ordination, price control etc.), competition (control of monopolies and public aid), nuclear energy (supply of fissile materials, control of nuclear installations etc.).

  (b) In other cases the Commission operates under a mandate from the Council – e.g., to negotiate trade agreements with third countries or to manage the agricultural markets.

  (c) The Commission also administers the funds of the common programmes which account for most of the Community budget and which aim –

    (i) to support and modernise agriculture (European Agricultural Guidance Guarantee Fund);

    (ii) to encourage industrial, vocational and regional change (ECSL appropriations, Social Fund, European Development Fund);

    (iii) to promote scientific research (the Joint Research Centres employ 2,500 people), and

(iv) to channel European aid towards the Third World (European Development Fund, food-aid programmes, etc.).

The Commission has an administrative staff – concentrated mostly in Brussels and to a lesser extent in Luxembourg – of 8,000 officials working in some 20 directorates-general (this is less than the staff of a good number of national ministries). One-third of the personnel is employed on linguistic work to ensure the equal recognition of the six Community languages.

The number of civil servants employed in member countries is almost one thousand times greater. For every 100,000 Europeans there are:

(1) 4,200 national civil servants; and
(2) 6 Eurocrats.

The Spierenburg Report

The success of the European Commission in fulfilling its duties under the Rome Treaty should not be underestimated, but this must not blind us to the fact that over the last ten years, sometimes for reasons outside its control, its influence, effectiveness and reputation have declined. This is the view of the Independent Review Body appointed by the Commission in January 1979 to examine the Commission's organisation and staff resources in the light of anticipated changes in the 1980s and to suggest ways in which to maintain a permanent Community civil service of the highest quality.

Chaired by Ambassador D.P. Spierenburg, and including Mr. Dick Taverne as one of its members, the Review Body has recommended a number of important changes in the Commission structure, not least that from 1981 only one Commissioner should be appointed by each member country, thus limiting the college to 12 when Portugal and Spain became members in the 1980s.

The Spierenburg report notes that the total number of Commission employees is smaller than is generally realised. Excluding research staff, it amounts to 8,000 officials, of whom some 40 per cent are directly or indirectly concerned with interpretation or linguistic work. Compared with national central administrations these numbers are hardly excessive. The problem is rather one of lack of cohesion within the college of Commissioners, an imbalance between portfolios, a maldistribution of staff between departments and shortcomings in the career structure of the civil service of the Commission.

These weaknesses have arisen partly from enlargement in 1973 and partly from the rather *ad-hoc* way Commission responsibilities have increased over the years. In addition, because of the accident of time at which they were recruited, very few top civil servants are expected to retire in the next six years, so that prospects for promotion are at present poor, and morale has inevitably suffered.

In its closely-argued report the Review Body recommends urgent action to make the Commission a more coherent and flexible college, while at the same time streamlining portfolios and encouraging greater horizontal and vertical mobility among staff.

The Commission: role and portfolios

The report stresses the need for the Commission to act as a college in maintaining its important position as initiator of action and guardian of the Treaties *vis-à-vis* the Council and the European Parliament. This requires strong co-ordination procedures and proper machinery for arbitrating between claims of competing sectors within the Commission. The Review Body believes that the college of Commissioners would be more effective if the President, assisted by one Vice-President, were actively responsible for directing co-ordination – at present, as one among equals, the President has no such overriding power.

The Review Body also queries the number of portfolios, each headed by a Commissioner, that now exist. It makes out a case for eight permanent portfolios, with a maximum of ten on enlargement, and suggests ways in which present portfolios could be amalgamated or changed. The aim is to give portfolios greater equality of importance and to spread the work of Commissioners more evenly. This is one reason why the report suggests the limitation of Commissioners to one from each member country (at present the larger states – Germany, France, Italy and the UK – appoint two Commissioners each).

The report also sees merit in keeping the college of Commissioners small if it is to act effectively with coherence and flexibility. The Review Body would like action taken on this matter before the appointment of the new 1981 Commission. If, however, the Commission is to remain as large as ever, it recommends that there should be four or five Commissioners without portfolio who would assist four or five of their colleagues in the management of portfolios with a particularly taxing workload.

Administrative structure

At present the Commissioners preside over 30 separate administrative units, most of which are Directorates-General divided into Directorates and Divisions. Some of these units have "horizontal" functions, such as the Legal, Budget and Personnel services, while others are "vertical," concerned with policy sectors such as agriculture and external relations.

The Review Body recommends the merging and streamlining of the D-Gs so that they have more relevance to its proposed portfolios. By 1981 it would like to see the vertical units regrouped into twelve Directorates-General corresponding to eight portfolios each covering a sector of Community policy, while the horizontal units should be put under the sole authority of the Presidency. Later, on the entry of Spain and Portugal, the number of D-Gs would be reduced to ten to coincide with the ten portfolios that would then form the final structure of the Commission. In line with such innovation the position of the Directors-General should be upgraded and they should be given considerably greater authority and responsibilities.

Turning to other staff, the Review Body was struck by the large number of Divisions (247) and Specialised Services (92) that make up the basic administrative structure of the Commission, many of which appear to have spawned haphazardly as the Community has developed. The report recommends a detailed review of existing units with a view to reducing their number, coupled with a package of proposals regarding promotion prospects and early retirement designed to offset any social dislocation arising from its recommendations.

In the wider field the Review Body proposes a number of ways for improving the recruitment, training and career prospects of all Commission staff. It also inserts a word of warning on the role of staff in the private offices or cabinets of Commissioners. While admitting that such cabinets are useful in helping the Commissioner do his work, the report points out that "some aspects of their operations are starting to cause difficulties and are even threatening to disrupt, quite substantially, the smooth running of Commission services." The role of the cabinet, the report suggests, is to act as trusted assistants to the Commissioner, help him with his personal political work, and ensure that he is fully briefed on other portfolios to enable him to meet the demands of collective responsibility. This role does not permit interference in policies and papers from Directors-General without consultation. The Review Body believes that if its recommendations for better streamlining, co-ordination and control of Commission portfolios are carried out, certain difficulties now apparent between cabinets and Commission staff would be eliminated.

2. The Council of Ministers

The Community's Council of Ministers, which meets usually in Brussels and less often in Luxembourg, is composed of ministers from each member state, and decides on the principal Community policies. It is the supreme executive and legislative authority in the European Community. Each member state of the EEC has one representative. Each country acts as president of the Council for a six-month period on an alphabetical rotation basis. Attendance at meetings is determined by the agenda: national agricultural ministers, for example, deal with agricultural prices and economics, and employment ministries deal with unemployment problems. The ten ministers for foreign affairs are responsible for co-ordinating the specialised work of their colleagues. The Council is assisted by –

(1) a committee of Permanent Representatives (COREPER) which co-ordinates the preparatory work of Community decisions and is assisted by numerous working groups of senior officials from member states, and
(2) a general secretariat of 1,500 persons.

Unanimity in the Council is required for certain important decisions. In practice it is frequently demanded by ministers even when not strictly necessary, which tends to slow down the Community's decision-making process. In recent times there has been more frequent recourse to the use of the qualified majority vote – 45 out of 63 votes, as instituted by the Treaties – France, Germany, Italy and the UK each have ten votes under this procedure. Belgium, Greece and the Netherlands have five, Denmark and the Republic of Ireland three and Luxembourg two.

3. The European Court of Justice

"There are judges in Luxembourg" ran the incredulous headline in a French newspaper when, nearly three years after the establishment of the first of the three communities, the Common Market's own court delivered its first judgment. Today even in the United Kingdom the European Court (as it is called for simplicity) is well known in the professional and business worlds and its 200 or so judgments each year have to be perused by lawyers, businessmen and government departments in a wide range of activities. It is true, however, that insofar as the intelligent man in the street is not affected by the European Court he would probably think it had something to do with the Human Rights Court in Strasbourg, or the International Court in the Hague.

The European Court in Luxembourg has ten judges, one from each of the member states of the Community. It is the final arbiter on what the Treaty and Community legislation mean. The European Community Treaties and their implementing legislation – Regulations, Directives and Decisions – impose obligations on member states, on the Community institutions, on trading companies and firms and, very rarely, on individuals. They also give corresponding rights to member states, to the institutions, and to individuals.

Like any other obligations, these obligations can be broken, and the Treaty lays down what is to happen if this happens. As we shall see, in the system of the Treaty three institutions are predominantly involved in the process of establishing a breach of the Treaty: the Commission of the European Communities, the European Court and the national courts. Here we are primarily concerned with breaches by a member state of its obligations under the Treaty.

Breach of obligations by a member state

It is the member state as such which joined the Community and it is the member state as such which can break its obligations. If the national Parliament refuses to pass a law necessary to give effect to a Community obligation it is the state which is in breach. If a local authority breaks a Community law the state again as such is responsible. If the Court of Appeal consistently breaks the rules of the Treaty, the member state is responsible.

The most serious breach of the Treaty occurs when a member state fails to enact legislation that it is obliged to enact or to repeal legislation it is bound to repeal. For example, Regulation No. 1463/70 of the Council required that as from 1 January 1978 the tachograph should be installed in certain goods and passenger vehicles. There was no choice left to member states, who were bound to inform the Commission in good time of the steps they had taken to implement the obligation and of what penalties they had laid down for breach of the Regulation. Although there are many examples of a member state failing to get the necessary implementing legislation through Parliament because of the government's inability to control Parliament, there are few examples of a member state refusing even to present the necessary Bill to Parliament.

The Treaty itself imposes a number of obligations on member states, the most important of which are, firstly, to take no measures which might impede the free movement of goods, persons and services throughout the Common Market, and secondly, to abolish any discrimination between imported and domestic goods and between national workers and workers from another member state of the Community.

Whereas by the end of the transitional period (31 December 1969 in the case of the old member states, 31 December 1977 in the case of the new member states) all traditional protective devices had been abolished (customs duties, quotas in the case of goods, work permits and employment quotas in the case of labour) old habits die hard, and other more subtle barriers have been revealed: subsidies and tax barriers, in the case of goods, educational qualification barriers in the case of people.

Ultimately, national indirect taxation, in so far as it obstructs the creation of a single market, will have to be harmonised (VAT is the first step along this road). For the present, however, member states are free to levy indirect taxes according to their own rules. The Treaty lays down two rules as to national taxes: tax on imported goods shall not exceed the tax on *similar domestic products*, and no member state shall impose on the products of other member states any internal taxation of such a nature as to afford *indirect protection to other domestic products.*

The Commission has for a long time considered that these rules have been broken by most of the member states in the case of their taxes on alcohol and it has now taken proceedings against four of them. The United Kingdom produces whisky, gin and beer from grain. France produces wine, brandy and liqueurs made from grapes and fruit. Italy produces wine and spirits from grapes (grappa). Denmark produces mainly vodka-like spirits from potatoes and grain (Aquavit and Schnapps); they all wish to protect their domestic production and also to export their excess. How can domestic taxation be used to do this? Well, Italy taxes grain-based alcohol (mostly United Kingdom whisky) at a rate six times higher than grappa. Denmark at the other end of the Continent taxes pure white spirits at roughly half the tax rate of whisky and brandy. The United Kingdom taxes wine at a rate five times higher than it taxes beer. France protects its market in a similar way (but in reverse). The interesting feature in common is that all these member states would claim that their tax system is non-discriminatory.

If whisky or brandy were produced in Denmark they would, say the Danes, be taxed in the same way as the imported product. The United Kingdom's miniscule production of wine is taxed in the same way as imported wine. Brandy is regarded as the beverage of the rich in England, whisky as the beverage of the rich in Italy.

Remedies for breach of community law

On the assumption that a member state has broken its obligations under the Treaty, what can be done about it? The Treaty provides three remedies. Firstly, one member state can bring an action in the European Court against another member state alleging that that state has broken the Treaty. This has happened on two occasions only, in the first of which the action was withdrawn when the Commission took over the "prosecution," and the second, which is still pending, will almost certainly go the same way because Article 170 of the Treaty lays down that "before a member state brings an action against another member state, . . . it shall bring the matter before the Commission." The Commission is then given an opportunity to take up the case after hearing the observations of both states and in practice the member states are only too willing to hand over the case to the Commission.

The second remedy, therefore, is for the Commission, either on its own initiative or on a complaint from another member state or even a private individual, to start proceedings against the offending member state. It is, however, always up to the Commission to decide whether to start proceedings or not. Until the end of 1976 there had been 40 such cases, more than half of which had been against Italy. Recently the Commission has opened further proceedings against France and the United Kingdom over their import restrictions on lamb and potatoes respectively.

The third way of remedying the breach is very different. It involves a private party starting an action in the ordinary national court.

Actions in the European Court against a member state

Under Article 169 of the EEC Treaty, if the Commission considers that a member state has broken the Treaty it must first inform the member state of its reasons for thinking so. This is to enable the member state to make representations to the Commission and to agree to remedy the breach. Only if the member state still resists may the Commission take the matter to the Court.

The Commission starts proceedings in the Court by application. This document sets out the Commission's arguments in fact and in law. If the Commission takes the view that it is urgent that the member state stop breaking the rules without waiting for the outcome of the case it may request the Court by a separate document to order the member state to take certain measures pending the outcome of the litigation. This was done, for example, when the United Kingdom introduced a subsidy to pig farmers but was told by the Commission to abolish it. When the United Kingdom refused, the Commission brought an action asking the Court to order the cessation of this aid forthwith, pending the outcome of the litigation. The Court, after hearing both sides, granted the order. The United Kingdom complied.

If no interim order is sought the defendant member state puts in a defence to which the Commission can reply. The defendant state can put in a further document, called a rejoinder. After all the written proceedings have been completed the case is set down for hearing before all ten judges of the Court. Evidence can be called, but this is rare because most cases turn on *law,* not *facts.* If evidence is necessary, procedure is very different from that followed nationally in most instances, for it is the Court and not the parties which decides which evidence is to be called, and, although the lawyers representing the parties may examine and cross-examine, there are no formal rules of evidence.

At the hearing the Commission is usually now represented by a practising lawyer. In an action against the United Kingdom, the United Kingdom would be represented by a British barrister. In such a case the official language would be English. About three weeks after the hearing the Advocate-General gives his opinion on the case. There are four Advocates-General at the Court, one from each of the large countries: Italy, Germany, France and the United Kingdom. One Advocate-General sits on every case. His role is to give an independent, impartial opinion as to how the case should be decided, and he is entitled to raise points that the Commission or the member state have failed to put forward.

The judgment of the Court must be unanimous. There is no dissenting judgment, which means that if a judge disagrees with the majority of his colleagues he must still sign the judgment.

Enforcement of the judgment

If the Court decides that a member state has broken its obligations under the Treaty, according to Article 171 the state shall be required to "take the necessary measures to comply with the judgment of the Court." But what can the Court do to enforce the judgment? The answer is nothing, but the position is exactly the same within most of the countries concerned. A court in the United Kingdom, for instance, cannot enforce a judgment against the government. The reason why the government complies with judgments of the court is not because it can be compelled to but because not to do so would bring about a collapse of the constitution.

Hitherto, member states have complied with judgments of the Courts, for not to do so would be tantamount to breaking the fundamental rule of the constitution of the Common Market. It is true that on one occasion Italy had to be brought back before the Court for failing to comply with the judgment of the Court, but it explained that it was doing its utmost to secure the passage of the appropriate legislation through the Italian Parliament.

Actions in the national court

One of the special features of Community Law, which makes it totally different from international law, is that obligations imposed on member states give rights to individuals. If, for example, it is unlawful under Community law to tax wine in the United Kingdom at a rate six times higher than the tax on beer, a shipper of wine from France could be entitled under Community law to claim back from the Customs and Excise the excess tax that he has paid. This he can do in the English High Court. The High Court would then have to interpret Article 95 of the EEC Treaty, that is, the taxation rule. In order to ensure that the Treaty is uniformly interpreted throughout the Community, the Treaty provides every court and tribunal of a member state faced with such a problem may ask the European Court to rule on the interpretation of the Treaty. Final Courts, e.g., the House of Lords and, in some cases, the Court of Appeal in England, have no discretion: they are obliged by the Treaty to refer such questions to the European Court for a ruling. If they fail to do so when they are obliged to do so the United Kingdom would once more be in breach of the Treaty. English courts are, however, not reluctant to refer questions of interpretation to the European Court, nor are they, it seems, reluctant to apply Community law. Thus, whether or not the United Kingdom complied with a judgment of the European Court in an action against the United Kingdom by the Commission, it might still find itself required by an English court to refund the excess tax that it had been charging. In the case of the tachograph it is more difficult to see how a case could be brought in the United Kingdom courts in that it is hard to see who may have suffered by the United Kingdom's failure to implement the Regulation – save, perhaps the manufacturers of tachographs. In most cases, however, anyone aggrieved by a member state's failure to comply with Community law can find an appropriate remedy in the national court.

Procedure

When a question is referred to the European Court, not merely the parties to the case but also all the member states and the Commission and Council are entitled to take part in the proceedings by putting in observations as to how the Court should interpret the Treaty. The procedure after the observations have been received is very similar to the procedure in a direct action against a member state. In its judgment the Court rules on the interpretation of the Treaty and then sends the case back to the national court, which must then apply the Treaty to the case. The ruling of the European Court is binding on the national court.

Conclusion

The Treaty provides three effective means for ensuring that its rules are complied with by member states. It relies on the vigilance of other member states, on the policing of the Treaty by the Commission, and finally on the vigilance of individuals in protecting their rights. The Commission is the principal guardian of the Treaty, but until recently it preferred to seek solutions along political lines. The recent actions by the Commission against four member states over taxation of alcohol, the increasing number of actions against states for failure to implement directives, and the action against the United Kingdom for failure to comply with the tachograph Regulation underline the growing importance of the European Court.

There is, of course, a possible problem that a member state might choose to disregard a judgment of the European Court. If that were to happen it might be resolved by the vigilance of an individual safeguarding his Community rights in a national court. A member state could not disregard a judgment of its own national courts without endangering not merely the Common Market but its own national constitution.

4.The European Parliament

The provisional headquarters of the Parliament is at Luxembourg, but, since direct elections, members have in the main met in the French city of Strasbourg, and in Brussels, where parliamentary committees meet. Committees and political groups also visit most other parts of the Community – the European Liberals have held a meeting in Aviemore, Scotland, and the Socialist Group in Newcastle. The Parliament's meeting place in Strasbourg was the Maison de l'Europe, which was built in 1949 as a temporary centre for the Council of Europe (an organisation of 18 member countries quite separate from the Common Market), and which the two institutions still share. On 7 March 1977 the Parliament met for the first time in its new £25 million headquarters in Strasbourg, "the Palace of Europe."

Election and membership

The European Parliament is the democratic voice of Europe. It is the forum in which individual members can stand up for the interests of their constituents – the general public. Polling day in the United Kingdom for the first direct elections was Thursday, 7 June 1979. Other countries of the European Community voted over the four-day period to Sunday, 10th June, and the results were known on Monday, 11th June.

The total membership is now made up as follows:

Belgium	24
Denmark	16
France	81
Germany	81
Greece	24
Ireland	15
Italy	81
Luxembourg	6
Netherlands	25
United Kingdom	81
	434

The next elections will be in June 1984. Until an elecion could be arranged in 1981 Greek MEPs were appointed by their national Parliament to the European Parliament.

The Parliament in operation

The Parliament does not sit in full continuous sessions —that is impossible so long as its members also have national parliamentary responsibilities. Instead plenary sessions are held, on average one week in every month. These *full* meetings however are only a small part of the work. The Parliament is organised in two key ways:

(1) specialised standing committees and
(2) political groups.

The major working unit is the specialised committee, each with a permanent staff in Luxembourg: its functions are as follows.

(1) Political Affairs.
(2) Legal.
(3) Economic and Monetary.
(4) Budgets.
(5) Social – Employment and Education.
(6) Agriculture.
(7) Regional Policy – Planning and Transport.
(8) Environment, Public Health and Consumer Protection.
(9) Energy and Research.
(10) External Economic Relations.
(11) Development.
(12) Rules of Procedure.

Committees work roughly on a 14-day cycle, and one committee or another is in session on almost every working day of the year. Like the USA Congressional committees they also hold special investigatory meetings on particular problems – e.g., the Regional Policy and Transport Committee has recently toured British Ports.

A visitor to the European Parliament in full session will find members seated not on opposite sides of the chamber, but in a continuous semi-circle facing the President's chair. This does not mean that there is no party system. An official political group within the European Parliament must consist of at least 14 members (or of 10 members provided they are drawn from 3 or more countries). There are at present six groups: Communist, Socialist, Christian Democrat, European Progressive Democrat, European Conservative and Liberal. Each political group has a permanent secretariat based in Luxembourg.

In addition there are a few independent members. During full sessions members sit in these party groups, *not in national delegations*, Liberals right and Communists left of the Speaker/President; the larger the group the greater the say it has – in, for instance, choosing chairmen of committees.

The agenda for plenary sessions is determined by a bureau consisting of the President, 12 Vice-Presidents (appointed on the basis of party balance), and the political group leaders.

A member of the public with a problem has several routes to the European Parliament.

(1) Communication with an individual Member of the National Parliament.
(2) Contact through the secretariat of a political group – virtually every point of view in the political spectrum is catered for.
(3) On specific matters, contact with the appropriate committee.
(4) Parliament may be petitioned by writing to its President. Any individual or group can petition – even those from countries outside the Community – if it deals with matters for which the Community has a responsibility.
(5) All full sessions of Parliament are open to the general public.

There are at least twelve vernacular languages within the Community. Fortunately only six are spoken within the Parliament: English, French, Dutch, Italian, German and Danish. For the record, 33 per cent of all speeches made at the European Parliament sessions in 1978 were in English, 18 per cent in German, 17 per cent in French, 15 per cent in Italian, 10 per cent in Dutch and 7 per cent in Danish.

However, simultaneous translation is provided. All documents are also translated into six languages recognised by a colour code.

Danish	–	Pink
French	–	Blue
German	–	Yellow
Italian	–	Green
Dutch	–	Orange
English	–	Purple

Community laws

The formal role of Parliament is for the most part consultative. Before reaching a final decision on a Commission proposal, the Council of Ministers almost always consults Parliament, but the Treaties do not oblige the Council to take any notice.

Parliament's real role in the legislative process is more influential than this procedure would lead one to believe. The Treaties enable the Commission to alter its proposals at any time before the Council has reached a final decision, so it is primarily through its influence over the Commission that Parliament is able to amend and even initiate legislation.

Community laws are made in five stages.

(1) Preparation of proposals – this is formally the prerogative of the Comission.
(2) Reference to the Parliament by the Council – when the Commission has drafted its proposals formally it submits them to the Council, which immediately forwards them to Parliament for its opinion.
(3) Committee stage – the proposal goes directly into one of the 12 specialised committees. This stage is remarkable for the detailed involvement of the Commission: on one side of the table sit the committee members, on the other the Commission officials and perhaps the Commissioner responsible for the subject.
(4) Report to the House – the proposals are debated and voted upon in the Parliament.
(5) Return to Council – the resolution of Parliament is then sent to the Council for approval.

This procedure is summarised in the chart shown on the facing page.

Powers of the European Parliament

National parliaments usually possess three main powers: to dismiss the government, to vote on the budget and to participate in law-making. The European Parliament, on the other hand, may dismiss

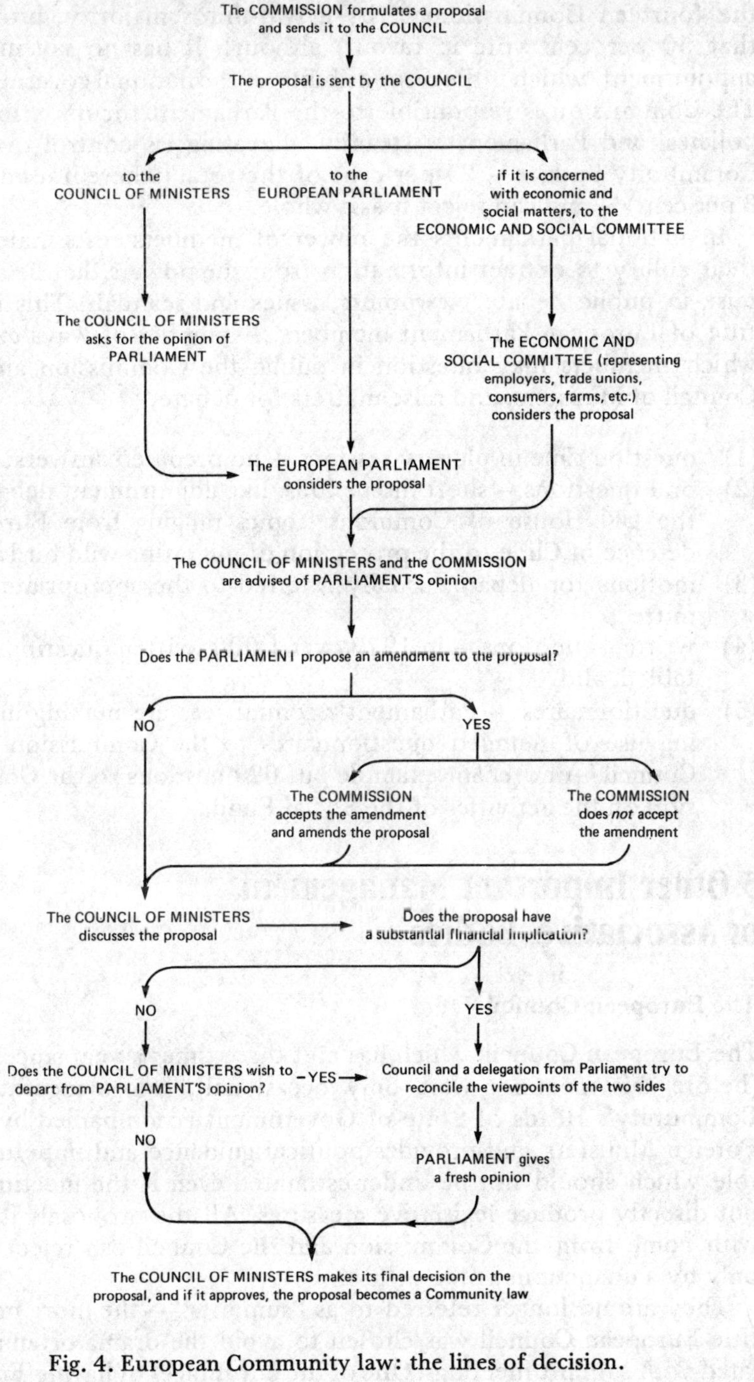

Fig. 4. European Community law: the lines of decision.

the fourteen Commissioners (by a two-thirds majority, providing that 50 per cent vote in favour) although it has no say in their appointment, which is the responsibility of the national governments. The Commission is responsible to the Parliament for its action and policies, and Parliament is steadily increasing its control over the Community budget – 25 per cent of the total (where it used to be 3 per cent) – and can reject it as a whole.

In national parliaments the power of members rests mainly on their ability to extract information from the powers that be and to raise in public debate viewpoints, issues and scandals. This is also true of European Parliament members. A number of ways exist in which members may question in public the Commission and the Council of Ministers, and raise matters for debate:

(1) question time in plenary sessions – no prepared answers;
(2) oral questions – short discussions, like adjournment debates in the UK House of Commons, topics ranging from European defence of Chile to the protection of migrating wild birds;
(3) motions for debate, usually referred to the appropriate committee;
(4) written questions – in 1979 over 1,000 written questions were tabled, and
(5) questionnaires – Parliament's committees are making increasing use of detailed questionnaires to the Commission or to Council – one recent example put 62 questions to the Commission on the activities of the Social Fund.

5. Other Important Management or Associative Bodies

The European Council

The European Council, which has met three times a year since 1975 (before this meetings were only occasional), brings together the Community's Heads of State of Government accompanied by their Foreign Ministers and provides political guidance and impetus – a role which should not be under-estimated even if the meetings do not directly produce legislative measures. All the proposals it deals with come from the Commission and the Council can reject them only by a unanimous vote.

They are no longer referred to as "summits" – the more modest title European Council was chosen to avoid the drama often associated with summit meetings. One of the advantages of having Foreign Ministers present is that it obviates constitutional difficulties for the Benelux countries where responsibility for foreign affairs is the exclusive preserve of the Foreign Ministers rather than the Prime Minister.

A number of politically and economically important matters which had reached deadlock in the institutions have been solved through the European Council. It was able to deal with the problems of direct elections to the European Parliament, for instance, and the European Monetary system was drawn up and adopted under its guidance. However, the European Council still has to streamline its working methods, stabilise its procedures and arrive at a clearer conception of its role in Europe's complicated mechanisms.

The Council of Europe

The European Council is not to be confused with the Council of Europe, an intergovernmental organisation of European states which came into being in 1949. There are at present 18 member states.

The founder members of the Council of Europe are ten in number: Belgium, Denmark, France, the Republic of Ireland, Italy, Luxembourg, the Netherlands, Norway, Sweden and the United Kingdom. Eight additional members joined in 1965: Turkey, Greece, Iceland, the Federal Republic of Germany, Austria, Cyprus, Switzerland and Malta.

Two institutions were set up under the Council's statute: an intergovernmental Committee of Foreign Ministers and a Consultative Assembly. In addition several committees of experts have been established to deal with matters of common interest to the member governments. The European Commission of Human Rights and the European Court of Human Rights were established following the signing of the European Convention of Human Rights in 1950.

The Council's stated aim is

> "to achieve a greater unity between its members for the purpose of safeguarding and realising the ideals and principles which are their common heritage and facilitating their economic and social progress."

The Council is specifically excluded from discussing matters relating to national defence.

The Economic and Social Committee

Before a Commission proposal can be adopted by the Council it is sent for the opinion not only of the European Parliament but also, in most cases, of the Community's Economic and Social Committee, a consultative body composed of 156 representatives from employers, trade unions and other interested groups in the Ten such as farmers and consumers. For questions dealing with coal and steel there is an advisory committee composed of representatives of producers, traders, workers, and consumers.

Many specialised bodies help associate professional and trade union interests in the development of the Community. The heads of their European federations are set up in Brussels and their experts are frequently consulted by the Commission before it adopts proposals in their definitive form.

The Court of Auditors

The Court of Auditors of the European Communities was created by the Treaty of Brussels of 22nd July 1975 and held its constituent meeting in Luxembourg (its provisional headquarters) on October 1977.

The Court of Auditors is responsible for the audit of the legality and regularity as well as the sound financial management of the resources levied from European tax-payers and manned by three communities:

European Economic Community (EEC)
European Coal and Steel Community (ECSC)
European Atomic Energy Committee (EAEC)

It has thus become the "financial conscience" of Europe.

The important powers of the Court of Auditors are rooted directly in a Treaty which has been ratified by the parliaments of all the member states. The dual function conferred on the Court by the Treaty – (1) to submit on its own initiative and at any time its comments on specific questions and (2) to give its opinion at any time at the request of one of the Community institutions – creates new possibilities of intervention for the external auditor.

The Court of Auditors consists of ten members appointed for a term of six years by the Council of the European Communities acting unanimously after consulting the European Parliament. The members of the Court elect the President from among their number for a term of three years.

The Court of Auditors divides the auditing responsibilities between its members. Each member has a direct responsibility to audit the expenditure/revenue of certain Community sections and a part of the Court's own activities.

The Court exists mainly because of the pressure exerted by the European Parliament to have set up an adequate body to support it in the exercise of its democratic control over Community expenditure and over the handling of European tax-payers' money. It has been described as the "Daughter of the Parliament."

The number of officers employed by the Court is 250, one-third being full time audit staff and two-thirds non-auditing. The apparent imbalance between vertical (on audit) and horizontal (administrative) staff must of necessity take into account the 25 personnel engaged in the translation service and the necessity for complete inter-member liaison accomplished by skilled assistants, so that each member is continuously informed of the activities of each of his fellow-members – an indispensable prerequisite to the Court's correct and successful functioning as a collegiate body.

CHAPTER 3

THE ECONOMICS OF THE COMMUNITY

Introduction

There now follows a short economic survey of the ten countries under the headings Domestic Economy, External Economy and Prospects. Readers should bear in mind that the economic survey of the Ten, as with all countries, is changing continually.

1. Economic Synopses of the Ten

BELGIUM AND LUXEMBOURG

Domestic economy

A resurgence in Belgium's principal industrial sectors, reflecting buoyant demand in both domestic and foreign markets, contributed to an upswing in economic activity in 1979. Following two years of sluggish growth – 1.2 per cent in 1977 and 2 per cent in 1978 – real gross national product (GNP) recorded a 3.3 per cent rise in 1979. Whilst the construction sector experienced a marked slowdown, industrial output rose by 4 per cent and an improvement was particularly noticeable in the steel and textiles sectors, although chemicals and foodstuffs also performed well.

By the turn of the year however it was becoming evident that the economy was entering a period of slower growth. It was forecast that real GNP would increase by only 1.5 per cent in 1980, with little improvement in the following year. The downturn is being experienced across the broad spectrum of Belgian industry, particularly in those areas which are sensitive to the current world recession, and industrial output is forecast to rise by only 2 per cent this year.

To assist the ailing steel sector the government and a group of the country's leading private financial and industrial interests agreed in April 1980 to establish a joint company – the Societe Financiere de la Siderurgie (SFS) – to help finance the restructuring of the industry. The company will raise between Bf 10 and Bf 16 billion towards the Bf 44 billion five-year investment plan. Additionally, in order to minimise unemployment in the textile industry the government proposed in August that Bf 35 billion should be spent on restructuring the sector over the period 1980-84.

Belgium's unemployment rate is one of the highest among EEC member countries and remains on a rising trend. At the end of July 1980 the number of people out of work numbered 313,264, which represented 7.7 per cent of the workforce, with little likelihood of any improvement in the short term. The numbers of unemployed were expected to reach 340,000 by the end of that year. The liberal nature of the social security system in Belgium poses a severe burden on government finances. Various efforts have therefore been made to alleviate the unemployment situation, including schemes for training young people, early retirement programmes and aid for enterprises which increase employment by reducing the length of the working week. However, employers are often deterred from hiring additional personnel by the high level of wages resulting from the indexation system, and by the substantial social security contributions currently payable.

Despite increases in commodity costs and substantial rises in imported energy prices, the rate of inflation in 1979 was maintained at the 1978 level, 4.5 per cent, which compares favourably with the country's major trading partners. Some increase in inflationary pressures was experienced in 1980 and the rate of increase for the year as a whole was forecast at 6.5 per cent. The fight against inflation is a major part of the Government's policy and strict price controls are in force; any increase must be justified to the Ministry of Economics and a period of notice is required before any adjustments can be implemented.

The Government has pursued a tight monetary policy with the twin objects of curbing inflation and maintaining the external value of the Belgian franc. By March 1980 the National Bank's discount rate had climbed to a peak of 14 per cent compared with 6 per cent a year earlier, which is very high in relation to the prevailing inflation rate in Belgium. Interest rates have subsequently eased but the National Bank's discount rate in 1980 still remained high at 12 per cent.

Fiscal policy has shown an expansionary trend in recent years and the central government borrowing requirement has risen substantially. The current administration is, however, committed to fiscal restraint and has already introduced some measures to this end. In the draft budget for 1981, announced in August of 1980, the borrowing requirement was to total Bf 242 billion, representing 6.4 per cent of GNP compared with 7.3 per cent in the 1980 budget. Overall current expenditure, at Bf 1,194.9 billion, was 7.6 per cent higher but did not exceed the expected nominal increase in GNP. The 1981 budget proposals also sought to curtail the increase in defence expenditure and to raise the prices and VAT on fuels. A lengthy period of fiscal restraint is now in prospect given the Government's overall target of a reduction in government borrowing to around 5 per cent of GNP by 1982.

External economy

Since 1976, when the current account of the BLEU (Belgium and Luxembourg Economic Union) slipped into deficit, the shortfall has widened considerably. A marked deterioration occurred in 1979 when the current account deficit reached $3.8 billion compared with $883 million in 1978. Despite a 23 per cent increase in exports by value in that year, this was more than offset by the rising costs of imports, particularly of energy. Belgium paid Bf 183.8 billion ($6.3 billion) for imported oil in 1979, compared with Bf 134.1 billion ($4.3 billion) a year earlier. Other factors also contributed to the worsening position, notably the reduction in the traditional surplus on service and transfer payments.

The economy of the BLEU is open and is largely export-orientated, and thus is often dependent on the economic performance of the Union's major trading partners. With the current global recession therefore, coupled with continuing high oil prices, the prospects for the BLEU's external economy are not bright and the current account deficit was expected to exceed $4 billion in 1980.

In the very recent past, the Belgian franc has periodically been one of the weaker currencies within the European Monetary System and in view of this, some observers have recommended a devaluation of the currency. However, the Belgian authorities are committed to the maintenance of a reasonably stable franc, and this policy has contributed to the present high level of interest rates. Over the short term the Belgian franc is expected to show some stabilisation around its current level and there seems little prospect of a devaluation in the immediate future, therefore.

Prospects

In common with most Western countries, Belgium is currently experiencing a marked downturn in most sectors of the economy. Stagnating industrial output, low domestic and foreign demand, together with the restrictive fiscal and monetary measures pursued by the government, were expected to result in low growth rates both in 1980 and in 1981.

Unemployment was expected to continue its upward trend and

the external position is unlikely to show any significant improvement while the recession in the West continues. Despite adverse pressures, however, the outlook for inflation remains fairly bright and should continue to compare favourably with most other OECD countries.

Luxembourg

Current economic indicators show that the general recession in the West is affecting business activity in Luxembourg. As a result of declining domestic and export demand and the tighter fiscal stance being adopted by the government, economic growth in 1980 was forecast at between 1.5 and 2 per cent compared with 2.7 per cent in 1979. Inflation, which was 4.5 per cent in 1979, continued to rise and was expected to exceed 6.5 per cent in 1980, largely as a consequence of higher costs of imported energy. Nevertheless, this still compared favourably with the performance of other OECD countries. Unemployment remains at a low level, currently at around 0.7 per cent of the workforce.

Arbed – Luxembourg's largest company, employing around 20,000 people and the fourth largest steel producer in Europe – was in 1980 undergoing its worst crisis since 1975. Over 90 per cent of its turnover is exported and the company was therefore severely hit by the fall in steel prices and the worldwide slump in demand. However, at the time of writing, the company was already undergoing a restructuring programme regarded by many as a model example for the rest of the ailing European steel industry. By 1983, Arbed was to employ only 16,500 people but planned to provide alternative employment for those made redundant. The cost over five years was originally estimated at Lux. F 23 billion, but in July of 1980 it was announced that the cost of the adverse economic conditions would amount to an additional Lux. F 13.5 billion. Arbed is vital to the Luxembourg economy and whilst the Government already provides some financial support it is unlikely that it would be able to withstand the disproportionate burden on public expenditure which substantial additional financing would involve.

Further expansion in the banking sector occurred in 1979. There was sharp growth in euromarket activities; by the end of that year banking assets in eurocurrencies rose to $79.6 billion from $58.3 billion at end-1978 while liabilities increased to $75.6 billion from $54.6 billion. Despite a slowdown in activity in 1980, the banking sector continued to play a major role in business activity in the Principality.

DENMARK

Domestic economy

Denmark has suffered in recent years from sluggish rates of growth, principally due to the need to restrain domestic demand. Gross national product (GNP) rose by 1.5 per cent in 1977 and 1 per cent in the following year. Although some improvement was evident in 1979, a relatively moderate rise of only 2.5 per cent was recorded. The need to correct the large external deficit on the country's balance of payments has been a key feature of government policy, although the OECD's latest survey on Denmark noted that fiscal restraint, high interest rates and incomes policies had all failed to achieve the desired results. The report suggested that a major improvement in international competitiveness was essential and suggested that the possibilities for changing the present system of wage bargaining, which relies heavily on indexation, should be investigated.

The continuing need to ensure a lasting moderation in costs, thereby maintaining competitiveness and controlling other adverse domestic trends, has prompted the government to persevere with existing policies. The relatively moderate controls implemented in the spring of 1979 were replaced in November by a stringent prices and wages "freeze." Although these measures are regarded as only temporary, pending the formulation of a long-term strategy, it is expected that a severely restrictive policy will be continued into 1981. For the time being, no price increases are permitted and the restrictions also apply to wages, salaries, fees, rents and dividends. In addition there are proposals to increase revenue and stabilise expenditure. These include an increase in corporation tax from 37 per cent to 40 per cent, a rise in wealth tax and a new tax on property. It is also proposed to abolish the current 10 per cent investment allowance for machinery and equipment.

The government hopes that these measures will contain inflation to within manageable levels. The figure of 10 per cent for 1978 was uncompetitive with the majority of EEC member states and the situation was not improved this year; a figure of 10.5 per cent or even more is expected for 1979. This is principally due to substantial wage increases earlier in the year as well as to considerable rises in the price of energy and other raw materials. The disparity with the inflation rate of the country's main trading partner, West Germany, is a particularly worrying factor.

However, in contrast with several EEC partner states, unemployment has shown an improved trend in 1979. The total out of work dropped by 30,000 over the year to June and at 136,000 (5.2 per cent of the working population), was at the lowest level since November 1976. This has been principally due to an early retirement scheme implemented at the beginning of 1979, although another contributory factor was the expansion of public sector employment. Nevertheless, the trend is likely to be reversed in 1980, as the expected cutbacks in public expenditure take effect and growth becomes more sluggish.

The need to maintain tighter control over fiscal and monetary developments has been emphasised in the policies introduced during 1979. It is a declared aim of the government to reduce the budget deficit in order to alleviate pressure on capital markets, money supply and interest rates. It was therefore hoped that planned expenditure cuts in the central government current and investment budget covering the fiscal year commencing January 1980, (together with a ceiling on local expenditure growth) would reverse the acceleration in public outflows. Figures revised in the light of the oil price increases suggest that the deficit for 1980 will be Kr 14.4 billion compared with a figure of Kr 12.5 billion for the previous year, representing 4.3 per cent of GNP in 1980 compared with 3.8 per cent in 1979.

The government's total borrowing requirement (which includes borrowing to cover loan redemption) is expected to rise from Kr 39 billion this year to Kr 42.8 billion in 1980.

Interest rates have shown a marked rise during the latter half of 1979. Against a background of growing external imbalance and a relatively weak current account, the official discount rate rose by 3 per cent to 11 per cent in the period June – September, although this was in line with a generally rising trend throughout Western Europe. The necessity of financing the country's burgeoning deficit and maintaining the krone's position on foreign exchange markets is likely to result in continued high interest rates and further strict controls on lending through the use of ceilings on bank advances.

The various sectors of industry, which consists mainly of medium-sized firms producing a limited range of goods, achieved only slow growth in the year to August 1979, of 1.6 per cent. Agriculture, which has been for long an important element in Danish prosperity, has benefited considerably in the last few years from a combination of high levels of investment and recent good harvests. While the sector has made an important contribution to the country's export performance, and despite the impressive rate of modernisation, there is now some evidence of discontent among farmers who consider that the current high level of costs and new restrictions on investment allowances may adversely affect their standard of living.

The shipbuilding sector continues to face severe difficulties in spite of substantial government support whilst the fishing sector is suffering from the imposition of stringent regulations regarding the size of fishing grounds and levels of catches.

External economy

In recent years Denmark's over-riding economic problem has been its rapidly expanding trade deficit and the heavy external borrowing required to finance it. A substantial deficit of $2.9 billion in 1976 was followed by shortfalls of $2.7 billion and $2.4 billion in 1977 and 1978 respectively. Current indications suggest that a further large deficit will be recorded this year, possibly exceeding $3 billion, and if the position remains unchecked, there may be severe consequences for the Danish economy. Whilst both agricultural and industrial exports have shown a healthy increase this year, contributing to an expected overall rise in value terms of 10 per cent, the increase in imports has been 15 per cent.

The principal difficulty facing the country is its vulnerability to the rapid increase in the cost of imported energy. The fuel import bill increased by 45 per cent in the first eight months of the year (although there were also substantial rises in the cost of imported agricultural, industrial and consumer goods). This situation has prompted the government to give urgent attention to the question of alternative sources of supply.

Development of gas fields in the Danish sector of the North Sea is also at present under consideration. A Kr 3 – 8 billion development plan has been submitted to the Ministry of Commerce, and the consortium involved is under contract to deliver gas to the state distribution company by October 1984. This is likely to make only a marginal contribution to the country's energy needs and it appears likely that Denmark will continue to rely on imported fuels to a large extent for the forseeable future.

External borrowing has for long been a feature of financing the heavy current account deficits and the net debt has now been estimated at Kr 65 billion ($12.5 billion) with annual loan repayments and interest amounting to Kr 7.7 billion ($1.5 billion). Although Denmark's creditworthiness is relatively good, it has been forecast that if present trends continue, the terms of borrowing abroad may become prohibitive. In this event it is not inconceivable that IMF assistance would be required with its consequence of some external control over government policy.

An associated problem has been the weakness of the krone. Since the inception of the European Monetary System (EMS) the Danish krone has been one of the weakest participating currencies and market pressures necessitated an adjustment of 2 per cent against the deutschemark. Since the German currency was revalued by 3 per cent at the same time, the effective devaluation of the krone against the mark was 5 per cent.

It was hoped that this would be sufficient to restore Denmark's competitiveness in its principal export market. The krone again came under pressure as the deutschemark strengthened against the dollar and the government announced a further 5 per cent devaluation against all currencies. Two devaluations of this magnitude raises the question of Denmark's continuing membership of the EMS.

Prospects

It was expected that 1980 would be a significant year for the Danish economy. Forecasts produced before the prices and wages "freeze," suggested that the current account may deteriorate still further next year with adverse consequences for the country's reserves, creditworthiness and currency stability. Great importance is therefore attached to the ability of the new measures to restore balance of payments equilibrium.

Economic growth will be still more sluggish in 1981; indeed, GNP may show nil growth. In any event the short-term improvement in the level of unemployment will be reversed and forecasts suggest that the total could rise in 1981.

Union co-operation, which is crucial to the effective implementation of government policy, may well be adversely influenced by any deterioration of unemployment figures; any overt opposition to a severe and long-term incomes policy could result in a crucial test for the government.

FRANCE

Domestic economy

The French economy experienced solid growth of almost 4 per cent in real terms during 1979, stimulated by sustained expansion in the external sector, buoyant public sector investment and a modest revival of private investment in the second half of the year. However, under the impact of higher oil prices and the depressed international environment, short-term prospects have become much less favourable. Economic activity slowed to below 2 per cent in 1980 and export growth weakened, contributing to a pronounced swing into current account deficit. At the same time inflation is accelerating and unemployment has resumed an upward trend. Although external influences will remain a problem — notably the high cost of imported oil on which France is highly dependent – longer-term prospects for the economy are more encouraging since French industry seems reasonably well equipped to cope with international competitive pressures.

Economic policy in recent years has been conducted within the framework of a three-year strategy introduced in September 1976 – the Barre Plan – with the short-term objective of reducing inflation and unemployment as well as restoring equilibrium to the external sector. In 1978 emphasis was also given to improving the financial position of companies to provide a sound foundation for the future of the French corporate sector. It was considered that a restoration of profitability was essential to stimulate investment and thereby ensure the long-term prosperity and competitive position of the French economy. The government therefore introduced a policy of deregulating industrial prices during this period.

The balance of payments on current account registered a significant improvement during the three-year period covered by the plan (see External economy) but the inflation targets have not been met, and indeed the rate is now higher than in 1976 when the plan was introduced. Apart from the inevitable pressure resulting from increased oil prices, the growth of wages has consistently been above the rate of inflation and personal consumption, fuelled by a reduction in savings, has also risen steadily. In addition, the removal of controlled prices for many industrial products in the second half of 1978 added to inflationary pressures during the year. Consumer prices in 1979 were 10.8 per cent higher than in the previous year and rose further in 1980, but pressures could moderate in 1981.

Despite the healthy growth of the economy in 1979, which included a 3.5 per cent increase in industrial production, unemployment has remained on a rising trend. An overall policy of restructuring and rationalisation in the declining areas and sectors of French industry, notaby steel and shipbuilding, was one reason for the lack of improvement in 1980; the declining impact of the government-sponsored youth employment scheme was another. Although the government's regional development agency, DATAR, helped to create 60,000 jobs in 1979, various adverse factors resulted in an increase in the level of unemployment to 1,370,000 (6.4 per cent of the labour force) compared with 1,238,000 twelve months earlier. This trend continued in 1980. On a seasonally adjusted basis the number of unemployed rose for the fifth successive month in March, to reach 1.4 million – an increase of 100,000 over the March 1979 figure. In view of the slowdown in growth expected this year, there is a strong possibility that the number out of work will rise by a further 100,000.

While the unemployment figures give cause for concern, the need to adhere to an austere policy to attain other economic objectives has led to a generally restrictive fiscal and monetary stance.

A budget deficit of Ffr. 3.1 billion is projected compared with a shortfall of Ffr. 37.5 billion in 1979. The 1979 figure represented no more than 1.8 per cent of GNP, a slightly smaller proportion than in 1978 and a much lower figure than the ratios in other EEC countries – for example West Germany (3.4 per cent) the UK (5.1 per cent) and Italy (12.0 per cent).

Monetary policy is also restrictive and the trend of accelerating inflation has given further impetus to the need to maintain strict credit ceilings. The target for overall money supply growth (M2) was 11 per cent in 1979, although this figure was exceeded by 2 per cent. The 11 per cent target was maintained in 1980 and the authorities have recently announced that several sectors of credit which until now have been free of restrictions (including export credit) will be closely monitored to ensure that the targets are adhered to. In addition lower limits for bank lending have been set for the second half of 1980. For the large banks, for example, the credit ceiling for the end of 1980 is 103.5 (end 1979 = 100). The commercial banks' base lending rates have shown further regular increases.

In keeping with the administration's policy of removing government controls, increasing competition in industry and stimulating private investment the "Loi Monory" was introduced which, with tax incentives, encouraged and substantially increased investment on the Bourse. A further plan has recently been implemented with the aim of giving private investors a bigger stake in government-controlled companies, thereby, it is hoped, encouraging efficiency and competitiveness. Initially the scheme is to be confined to state-owned banks and insurance companies with the most successful of the nationalised banks, Société Générale the first to offer shares to the public.

An increase in private investment is, however, only one of the government's priorities over the next five years. A new economic plan, the eighth since the war, is being formulated for the period 1981–86. Although its aims are likely to be less clearly defined than those of previous plans, it is expected that priority will be given to developing a programme to reduce the country's dependence on oil, continuing the process of increasing competition within the manufacturing sector, improving the efficiency of agriculture and reducing unemployment.

External economy

The impact of higher imported energy costs was reflected in the deterioration in the external position in 1979. Following a trade surplus of $700 million in 1978, a substantial increase in import costs, particularly in the second half of the year, meant that the trade account reverted to deficit and only substantial net revenue from the invisible account produced an overall current account surplus of $1.4 billion.

The principal reason for the rise in imports was the cost of imported oil which rose to $19.3 billion compared with $13.2 billion. Thus although exports registered strong growth during the year, the benefit was more than offset by the growing energy burden which contributed substantially to the overall import figure of $94.4 billion and resulted in a trade shortfall of $1.9 billion. As in the previous year the invisible account produced a substantial surplus; net inflows from the EEC, and continued high revenue from tourism accounted for a surplus in excess of $3 billion.

The improvement in the balance of payments during 1978 and 1979 contributed to a large increase in the value of international currency reserves. France's large gold holdings had an even greater impact, benefiting from the massive increase in gold price during the year; their contribution raised the value of the total reserves of $57 billion.

The French franc has been a strong member of the European Monetary System (EMS) since its inception in March 1979. Despite the deterioration of the economy, the franc remains at the top of the EMS and has shown an unexpected resilience overall. The stabilising effect of EMS has undoubtedly been a factor although high interest rates have also contributed to the present situation; during the last twelve months the franc has shown little variation against a strong pound on a trade-weighted basis, and its performance is regarded as one of the successes of the Barre plan.

The continued strength of the currency is dependent upon a successful external performance, a factor that is threatened once again by the increasing burden of imported energy costs. France is making a determined effort to reduce its dependence on oil and is rapidly expanding its nuclear energy capacity. In 1979 approximately 17 per cent of the country's needs were supplied from ten nuclear reactors and the proportion will have increased to 55 per cent by 1985. The government is not allowing any environmental opposition to its programme (particularly apparent in Brittany) to deflect it from its aim to make France the most advanced nuclear nation in the world, particularly since the oil bill is expected to rise from the 1979 figure of $19.3 billion to $26.2 billion.

Prospects

With a persistently restrictive economic policy and a depressed trade outlook for 1981, slackening growth, perhaps to 2 per cent or even lower, is expected; in these circumstances a further rise in unemployment is likely. Consumer prices have recorded sharp increases in the first quarter of the year, influenced by rises in the cost of raw materials and oil imports. Despite the expected slowdown in the economy, inflation is expected to reach 13%, while the current account will swing into deficit forecast at $5 billion. These indicators are likely to show some improvement in 1981 and the longer-term outlook for the French economy is not discouraging given the capacity of industry to compete in world markets.

Political considerations will assume more importance in the run-up to the 1981 presidential election. It appears likely that M. Barre will remain in office for the time being, continuing to pursue restrictive policies. The President has indicated strong support for M. Barre but the possibility of a replacement cannot be ruled out.

FEDERAL REPUBLIC OF GERMANY

Domestic economy

The government's expansionary economic policy has resulted in an upswing, particularly apparent towards the end of 1978 and continuing into 1979. Rising domestic demand and output contributed to a continued improvement in activity and GNP growth of some 4 per cent is expected in 1979/80 compared with the increase of 3.4 per cent registered in 1978. This level of economic expansion compares favourably with West Germany's major trading partners whose average growth for 1979 was 3 per cent. The difficulties experienced during the early part of 1979, namely the industrial dispute in the steel industry, shortages and price rises in oil products, and the severe weather conditions created only short-term uncertainty amongst producers and consumers, and by the end of the first quarter, business activity had shown an overall increase of 4 per cent.

This renewed confidence has resulted in increased capital spending, particularly investment in new equipment, which rose by 8.2 per cent in real terms in 1978 and is expected to show a further increase of 7–8 per cent in 1979/80. Increased investment has been stimulated by the substantial expansion in manufacturing output which is reflected in the highest level of capacity utilisation seen since 1973. The intention is to increase production levels still further in the light of the currently high order levels. New orders in 1979/80 have shown a rise of 9 per cent compared with the same period in 1978 and are expected to remain at a high level during the rest of the year.

The steel sector, in particular, is expected to register a good performance in 1979/80 despite the difficulties earlier. The automotive, electrical and mechanical engineering sectors are also benefiting from full order books although the chemical industry has experienced some fall in demand and the paper sector is beset with supply difficulties. This problem is also apparent in the construction industry where, as a result of delays due to the severe winter, orders in hand amount to 3½ months work. Some strain has since become evident, with orders exceeding capacity in an industry already suffering from a shortage of skilled labour.

In 1978 unemployment averaged less than a million for the first time in four years. The target for 1979/80 was to maintain unemployment below 3.5 per cent of the workforce and by June the level had already fallen to 763,000 (3.3 per cent) with a corresponding fall in short-time working. A significant feature of the West German economy is the existence of a large proportion of "gastarbeiter" or foreign workers principally from Turkey, Yugoslavia and Italy. In total they represent 9 per cent of the workforce and despite the social problems created by their presence, constitute an essential element in maintaining the country's prosperity.

Fiscal policy has been designed to support the expansion of demand and thereby aid sustained economic growth. Costs in direct taxation have been somewhat offset by indirect increases in revenue in the form of higher VAT. Nevertheless, the measures are expected to result in net borrowing of over DM 31 billion although the outline forecasts set a somewhat reduced borrowing requirement of DM 28 billion.

The government's measures have caused some concern to the banking authorities. In the six months to April 1979, an expansion in money supply on the broad (M3) scale amounted to an annualised rate of 9.3 per cent (exceeding the annual target figure of 6–9 per cent). Continuing demand for credit in order to maintain the recovery of the domestic economy has contributed markedly to this situation and the Deutsche Bundesbank has become concerned that inflationary pressures will be exacerbated. According to the Bundesbank, the strength of monetary expansion compelled the Bank to adopt a firmer monetary stance during the first five months of 1979, by raising interest rates and divesting the commercial banks of a large part of their free liquid reserves. This action highlights the difference in current emphasis between the Bank's policy and that of the government.

Despite their efforts however, it is evident that in common with most European economies, West Germany is experiencing a reversal of the trend of declining inflation. Although the rate is still one of the lowest amongst member states of the EEC the country is not immune to the pressure created by the recent oil price rises, and since the cost of many other consumer durables and services has risen faster this year it is expected that the overall increase will be in the order of 4–5 per cent compared with a 2.6 per cent rise in the previous year. Settlements in the current wage round should not contribute to the acceleration, although the unions' increasingly intransigent attitude could have a material effect in the longer term. For many years West Germany has benefited from excellent industrial relations but the seven-week strike in the steel sector suggests that the traditional spirit of compromise may now be at an end.

External economy

Following several years of substantial trade surplus, there have been some indications that a downward trend is now in progress. In 1978 West Germany benefited from strengthening foreign demand as the economies of the country's principal trading partners continued their recovery. Despite a sharp appreciation of the deutschemark against the dollar (12.5 per cent in 1978) and other leading European currencies, favourable terms of trade also contributed to a substantial trade surplus for the year, of $25 billion.

The situation in the first half of 1979 was less encouraging. The trade surplus for the period January–June totalled $8 billion compared with $9.4 billion registered in the same period in 1978. Whilst exports and imports continued to expand during the first six months the rise in export revenues was more than offset by a sharp increase in import prices, particularly due to the upward price spiral of crude oil and petroleum products.

The narrowing trade surplus is likely to be more than offset by substantial outflows on invisibles; tourism will, as usual, account for a large proportion of the deficit but the Federal Government's net transfer to the Community Funds have also shown a large increase. It is expected that present trends will be maintained for the period 1979/80 and an overall current account deficit for the same period of $1 billion is forecast.

In recent years West Germany has had to overcome the recurring problem of maintaining its export competitiveness in the face of the deutschemark's continued strength, though the European Monetary System (EMS) has proved to be an important stabilising influence. Nevertheless continued success depends on the maintenance of moderate wage increases and a healthy flow of export orders resulting from consistent investment activity in Western Europe; current indications suggest that these factors may not be evident in 1981, with a consequent adverse affect on the West Germany economy.

Of more immediate significance is the increasing problem of rapidly rising energy costs. In common with other European economies West Germany imports a substantial amount of its energy needs and it is estimated that the Federal Republic will have to spend DM 1.6 billion more on crude oil imports in the second half of the year than in the first. For this reason the Chancellor outlined certain measures which will place emphasis on voluntary energy conservation.

At the same time the government intends to provide subsidies for the mining industry, support increased production and importation of coal in order to encourage the accelerated development of coal-fuelled power plants, and phase out the power stations which still use oil. West Germany's nuclear power stations produce about 10 per cent of the total electricity output and the current construction and planning programme will double the output in the next few years.

Prospects

Over the years the West German economy has proved to be more resilient than most of its European counterparts and it is therefore unlikely to be as severely affected as others by the current evidence of a downturn in world economic activity. Nevertheless the country is not insulated from world problems and the current high level of business confidence is unlikely to be maintained in 1980/81. Further rises in oil prices and weakening export demand for German goods will adversely affect the country's external performance.

The authorities' concern at the rising level of inflation seen in the period 1979/80 is expected to ensure that strong emphasis, in the form of a tighter monetary policy, is given to restricting any further increase. This policy many result in some curtailment in the rate of growth, perhaps of the order of 3 per cent; a consequent rise in unemployment is therefore anticipated. The trends of prices and employment may prove to be important factors in the level of co-operation received from the trade union movement and could prove to be significant in 1980, an election year.

GREECE

Domestic economy

A slowdown in economic growth to 3.5 per cent was experienced in 1979 compared with the annual average of 5.1 per cent recorded in the period 1970 to 1977 and the very satisfactory 6 per cent growth achieved in 1978. The 1979 result was affected by rising energy prices, a downturn in the world economy and the impact of unfavourable weather on Greece's important agricultural sector. A further slowing of growth to about 2.0 per cent is forecast for 1980 as government measures to reduce inflation take their effect on the economy.

Greece's economic growth performance has in recent years consistently exceeded the average for OECD member countries. The government has committed the economy to fast growth in order to bring about structural adjustments prior to accession to the EEC on 1 January 1981. This has, however, created problems and the economy has suffered from high levels of inflation and increasing balance of payments deficit (see **External economy** below).

A serious deterioration in the inflation performance became evident during 1979, with consumer prices in November 1979 standing 22.8 per cent over the level of a year earlier. In 1978 inflation had been restricted to 12.6 per cent. Higher oil prices contributed to the acceleration but large wage increases and a growing budget deficit have also been responsible. In an attempt to reverse this adverse trend, the government announced a package of counter-inflationary measures in September 1979 which included the introduction of price controls, an increase in interest rates and the imposition of restrictions on bank lending. In addition, public sector investment was cut by Dr 16 billion and no further wage increases were allowed during 1979. The government's target is to bring inflation down to 15 per cent by the end of 1980 and below 10 per cent by 1981. A series of short strikes in protest against the austerity measures has caused widespread disruption to the economy.

According to official figures unemployment stands at 2.5 per cent of the working population though many observers believe that a more realistic figure would be in the region of 5 per cent. However, unemployment in Greece is relatively low by European standards and in some industries there is a labour shortage. Employment has been increased at the expense of productivity in many sectors protected from foreign competition. Import tariffs are to be dismantled over a five-year period and this is likely to result in some shedding of surplus labour, which could lead to a rising trend in unemployment.

Heavy industry in Greece is confined to shipbuilding and steel production. Manufacturing, which accounts for 20 per cent of gross domestic product (GDP), comprises largely consumer and intermediate products should as foodstuffs, beverages, tobacco, textiles, carpeting, clothing, footwear and non-metallic minerals. Manufacturing production has been increasing at an annual rate of about 7 per cent over the past two years. There is also a flourishing cement industry and a well-established chemical industry based on plastics, fertilisers and pharmaceuticals. The exploitation of mineral deposits, notably bauxite, has increased the importance of mining and has led to the establishment of an aluminium processing industry.

Agriculture provides work for about 40 per cent of the population. Agricultural products, including drink and tobacco, contribute 30 per cent of total exports and account for 14 per cent of GDP. The government's policy continues to be to improve productivity, restricting production of low yield crops and stimulating the growing and marketing of crops with export potential.

External economy

Greece's external economy has been characterised in recent years by an increasingly adverse trade account and for 1979 this is expected to amount to a record $5 billion compared with $3.5 billion in 1978. Although the government has sought to curb buoyant domestic demand, imports are estimated to have risen by about 39 per cent during 1979. Higher import prices for oil and stockbuilding by importers have been major factors contributing to this rise. Export receipts rose by some 33 per cent in 1979, but it is estimated that oil imports accounted for approximately half of total export revenue in this period.

A substantial contribution to the balance of payments is derived from service and transfer payments especially of tourism, shipping and workers' remittances. Tourism has shown the most rapid expansion in recent years and during the eleven months to November 1979 revenue from this source was over $1.5 billion. Emigrant remittances have continued to increase since 1974 to exceed $1 billion in 1979. Shipping remittances recovered strongly after a poor performance in 1978, increasing to over $1.3 billion in the eleven months to November 1979. While net receipts from invisible earnings amounted to an estimated $2.7 billion in 1979 the current account deficit almost doubled to $2.3 billion.

The large current account deficits of recent years have precluded any major build-up of international reserves. However, as a result of a higher valuation of gold, component reserves increased to $2.2 billion in November 1979, sufficient to cover 2.7 months' imports. Recourse to international markets for loans has been largely to finance investment programmes. Total public external debt, at $3.1 billion at end-1978, is not unduly large and debt service during the year was a manageable 10.0 per cent of earnings from the export of goods and services. During 1979 a high rate of capital inflow-deposits in foreign exchange, supplier credits, entrepreneurial capital and inflows for the purchase of real estate enabled government borrowing on external markets to be reduced to $500 million.

In an attempt to reduce the growing current account deficit, the government imposed severe restrictions upon imports in December 1979. Basic items of foodstuffs, raw materials and fixed asset equipment for agriculture, fisheries, mines, industry and handicrafts are exempt from these restrictions. For other items, importers are required to place a deposit of 75 per cent of the value of imported goods with the Bank of Greece for a six month period. Luxury commodities and other non-essential imports are also subject to an additional 25 per cent consumption tax. These measures will remain in force until 30 June 1980.

The EEC is by far Greece's major trading partner and there is a growing balance in the Community's favour. This has arisen largely because of increased Greek imports of capital goods for mining, the chemical industry, and electrical and telecommunications projects.

Prospects

The outlook for 1980/81 is for much reduced growth of only 2.0 per cent, a figure which is in line with the expected average for EEC member countries. In the past Greece has regularly achieved considerably faster expansion than the EEC. The forecast rate of growth is well below the target set in the present development plan, and following only moderate expansion in 1979 it now seems unlikely that the plan's overall growth target can be achieved.

Inflation and an increasing current account deficit continue to be major constraints on the economy. If the authorities adhere to their intention of cutting public expenditure sharply, and achieve success in moderating pay increases, the inflation rate could be reduced to around 15 per cent in 1980. The austerity programme involving reduced private and public consumption should also benefit the balance of payments, but despite this and the imposition of import restrictions, no significant improvement can be expected in view of

Greece's vulnerability to the adverse oil price developments of recent months.

ITALY

Domestic economy

For several years Italy has shown a remarkable resilience in overcoming economic problems in the face of a continuing political stalemate. High growth, a healthy current account balance and a steady reduction in the level of inflation have characterised the country's economic performance. However, long-standing difficulties have re-emerged following an encouraging performance in 1979 and a decline in growth and an increase in inflation are expected in 1980.

Growth in GNP registered a substantial rise approaching 5 per cent in 1979 after a somewhat sluggish performance with growth at 2.6 per cent the previous year. The expansion was the fastest of any major West European country and was based on an impressive rise in industrial production (6.5 per cent) resulting from buoyant private consumption, continued industrial stock-building and sustained foreign demand.

A major contribution to this performance came from the many small and medium-sized companies which represent an important element in Italian industry. Their efficiency, high productivity and relative financial self-sufficiency at a time of record interest rate levels, have enabled them to flourish while larger corporate groups in both the private and state sectors are facing serious problems of labour unrest, high wage costs and, this year, increasing export difficulties. Small companies have traditionally made a substantial contribution to the country's export performance, particularly in the clothing and textile sectors where the emphasis is on small scale but high quality products, and in the engineering industry. Much of Italy's output among the smaller companies involves the so-called "black economy," and the employment of secondary, unregistered labour has been estimated to be worth 15–20 per cent of the country's overall GNP. At the same time the large nationalised sector has experienced difficulties, particularly in the steel, electronics and car sectors. To overcome these problems and improve profitability and international competitiveness, vigorous efforts have been made to increase investment while at the same time pursuing a policy of restructuring and rationalisation.

In a broader context, attempts continue to diversify industry from the relatively affluent North and attract investment to the depressed areas of the country, notably the Mezzorgiorno where unemployment, at 11 per cent of the workforce, remains well above the national average and incomes compare unfavourably with the rest of the country. Priority has been given to encouraging expansion from both domestic and foreign concerns and the steel and car sectors have been prominent with development programmes.

A further boost to the industrial sector should emanate from the recently implemented "reconstruction and reconversion" law which will make the equivalent of £2 billion available in the form of subsidised loans to companies which aim to rationalise, modernise or relocate plant while maintaining employment levels. The need to restrict the level of unemployment remains a priority for the government. Although there was an increase in job vacancies during 1979 as a result of the upswing in activity, the large rise in the available labour force, particularly first-job seekers, resulted in an increase to 1.8 million (over 8 per cent of the workforce), at the beginning of this year. Current indications suggest that there will be a further increase during 1980.

Inflation also remains on an adverse trend with the "scala mobile" system of wage indexation fuelling further increases in labour costs and consumer prices. By February 1980 inflation was rising at an annualised rate of 21.7 per cent, compared with the overall increase for 1979 of 14.7 per cent. Sharp increases in oil prices have contributed substantially to the acceleration, a factor which is harming Italy's international competitiveness.

The situation has prompted a further tightening of monetary policy. Interest rates have shown a steady increase during the last six months, with the official discount rate now standing at 15 per cent. With money supply expanding at an annual rate of 24 per cent the Bank of Italy has taken steps to restrict credit growth by introducing penalties for excessive bank lending.

Fiscal policy for 1980 reflects the need to respond to the slowdown in growth while at the same time attempting to curb inflationary pressures. Tax revenue in 1980 is forecast to rise by 20.3 per cent (with indirect taxation showing the most substantial increase). The authorities are also attempting to direct the emphasis of their spending programme towards the stimulation of public investment, involving the implementation of programmes of communications. In a further attempt to counter the expected recession this year, the authorities have now completed a system of export credit facilities combined with a rationalisation of the system of granting State insurance guarantees which should enable exporters to compete more effectively in world markets.

External economy

Italy derives much of its economic strength from the performance of the export sector. During the period 1975–9 growth was vigorous, with the volume exported last year about 45 per cent higher than in 1975. This was an important factor in the transformation which was achieved on current account, where a deficit of some $3 billion in 1976 became a surplus of around $6 billion in 1978 and 1979. However, the current slowdown in world trade combined with Italy's declining international competitiveness will be reflected in little volume growth of exports. At the same time import payments will be substantially higher (the energy bill rose from $2.5 billion in 1978 to $10 billion in 1979, and is expected to show a further rise to $17 billion in 1980). As a result there will be a much reduced current account surplus – in the region of $1.5 billion – and in 1981 there may well be a small deficit.

The invisible sector traditionally produces substantial revenue, and in 1979 net income was particularly high at $6.5 billion. Tourist receipts have been on a rapidly rising trend in recent years and are expected to have reached $6.7 billion (net) in 1979 compared with $5.1 billion the previous year. The importance of the contribution of the tourist sector to the balance of payments is illustrated by the fact that only the US derives more in gross earnings from this source.

Since the inception of the European Monetary System (EMS) the lira has proved to be one of the more stable member currencies, although some weakening has been evident. Over 1979 as a whole, however, the currency has shown little variation in its trade-weighted value. The band remains at 6 per cent, compared with 2¼ per cent for other members.

The greater flexibility granted to the lira's exchange rate movements at the inception of EMS enabled the authorities to adjust the currency in the light of the declining US dollar and the stronger West European currencies. The adverse effects of inflation on competitiveness in West European markets were therefore largely offset by the lira's strength against the dollar (the currency in which much of Italy's raw material imports are settled). It appears increasingly unlikely, however, that the flexibility within EMS will be of help to the lira if inflation continues to show a wide disparity with the economies of Italy's principal trading partners.

The healthy external performance in 1979 combined with the sharp increase in the value of gold towards the end of the year contributed to a substantial rise in the value of Italy's international reserves. An increase of over 76 per cent was registered in the twelve months to the end of March 1980, when reserves (including gold valued at market prices) amounted to $53.8 billion.

In the light of the expected deterioration of Italy's trade balance the country's dependence on oil assumes increasing importance. Italy relies more heavily than any other major western industrialised nation on oil imports; approximately 75 per cent of overall energy requirements come from abroad. In these circumstances the government has given high priority to conservation measures and has announced a ten year plan aimed at doubling the country's electricity capacity by 1990. The programme includes extensive construction of hydro-electric, thermal and nuclear plants. Despite substantial opposition to further development of nuclear capacity the government appears determined to proceed. The results of this programme will however be felt only in the long term. In the meantime the government is attempting to diversify its oil supply base away from dependence on uncertain Middle East supplies. To this end the administration has recently reached an agreement with Venezuela to increase its level of oil shipments substantially.

Prospects

The slowdown in activity now apparent in most major West European economies will be reflected in Italy's growth rate, which is not expected to exceed 2 per cent in 1980/81. The recession will be particularly evident in the second half of the year with weakening domestic demand resulting in a further increase in unemployment.

In view of the continued rise in the cost of imported energy the trade deficit must be expected to widen in 1980 as the country's terms of trade deteriorate. Buoyant tourist earnings will, however, ensure that the current account remains in surplus – around $1.5 billion – but this will probably disappear next year.

The need to restrain inflation, which could exceed 20 per cent in 1980, necessitates adherence to restrictive monetary policies. The effect of the wage indexation system is generally felt to be adverse but in the light of the sensitive political situation it is unlikely that the government will introduce any revision for the time being.

NETHERLANDS

Domestic economy

The Netherlands' economy registered moderately satisfactory growth in 1979. The increase in gross national product (GNP) of 2.7 per cent was a slight improvement on that recorded in the previous two years. A rise in business activity, apparent towards the end of 1978, continued for the greater part of 1979; however, the trend was reversed in the final months of the year as a decline in world trade growth adversely affected the country's volume of exports and correspondingly reduced the demand for manufacturing output.

The short-term outlook is not promising with GNP growth for 1980/81 forecast at below 1.5 per cent. Expectations of a further weakening of economic activity have been reflected in moderate levels of investment. Confidence has been affected by a combination of factors; the recent wage freeze, a continuing deterioration of export prospects and the authorities' adherence to a restrictive monetary policy involving very high interest rates.

The level of industrial production reflected the somewhat variable economic performance during 1979 and there were marked differences in individual sectors. A clear improvement was evident in the chemicals industry after several years of decline and the shipbuilding sector also reflected the benefits of a comprehensive programme of restructuring and rationalisation. The textile industry on the other hand has shown a continued decline and the regions involved have suffered accordingly; aggressive competition from cheaper Far East and East European products largely accounts for the current difficulties being experienced by this sector.

Faced with a downturn in the economy the government decided, despite the inflationary dangers, to introduce a somewhat expansionary budget, including a spending programme which signifies a marked change of emphasis from the principles outlined in Bestek (Blueprint) '81. This was an economic plan designed to reduce public spending over a three-year period by $5 billion while at the same time stimulating and reducing inflation and unemployment. It became increasingly clear, however, that the programme's overall objectives were irreconcilable. For example, the commitment to reduce unemployment has necessitated the inclusion of a specific job creation allocation of Fl 12 billion in the 1980 budget which will result in an increase rather than a decrease in government spending. Government estimates in September postulated total budget expenditure of Fl 114.9 billion, an increase of Fl 10.8 billion (9.4 per cent) over the 1979 figure. Subsequent estimates have suggested that this figure may be much higher despite economies in the public sector. It seems probable that increased expenditure will not be offset by the extra income derived from increases in natural gas prices (an anticipated additional revenue of Fl 1.7 billion) and a rise in indirect taxation; further public sector economies may be necessary.

It remains to be seen whether the government's regional development programme will be affected by the present circumstances. Several areas have suffered from a severe decline, notably the Limburg region in the South East where 45,000 jobs, lost as a result of the closure of coal mines between 1965 and 1975, have proved difficult to replace. While a concerted effort has been made to provide new employment, a range of regional incentives and investment aid, the job creation process here and elsewhere is proving essentially ineffective. Unemployment has remained at the persistently high level of 200,000 (5 per cent of the labour force) and little improvement will be seen this year despite the government's original commitment to reduce the level to 150,000 by 1981.

Inflation in the Netherlands over the past two years has been very moderate by current international standards. At an estimated 4.3 per cent, the increase in consumer prices was only slightly above that for 1978 (4.1 per cent) and less than half the average for other OECD or EEC member states. The government has continued to apply fairly stringent price controls on domestic sales and although the cost of fuel imports has risen sharply, the effect has been limited in the Netherlands where domestic gas production accounts for nearly 60 per cent of energy requirements. The rate of inflation in 1980 is, however, expected to deteriorate as higher prices for imported consumer goods and oil accentuate domestic pressures on wage costs stemming from increased union militancy. The increase in consumer prices could be almost 7.0 per cent, but this rate of inflation is still little more than half that expected for the OECD countries as a whole.

The achievement of tight monetary targets has been a further factor accounting for the low rate of inflation in recent years. Growth in the M2 money supply was restricted to 7.5 per cent in 1977, 4.3 per cent in 1978 and no more than 2.2 per cent in the 12 months to September 1979, although there has subsequently been a marked rise in the rate of monetary expansion. The central bank discount rate was raised five times during 1979 and now stands at a record 9.5 per cent, giving the highest real interest rate amongst members of the European Monetary System (EMS).

External economy

The progressive deterioration of the Netherlands' balance of payments, apparent in 1977 and 1978, was partially reversed during 1979. The improvement was wholly attributable to the return to surplus on net service and transfer payments, for the trade gap widened from $0.6 billion to an estimated $1.4 billion. The current account deficit, at $700 million marks a significant reduction on the previous year's figure although a return to the customary surplus enjoyed prior to 1978 was not achieved, and seems unlikely in the foreseeable future.

In recent years the import bill has been boosted by a high propensity to import consumer goods. Exports on the other hand have been affected by the appreciation of the guilder and self-imposed restrictions on the volume of gas exports. The overall trade position is again likely to deteriorate in 1980 as exports decline in a contracting world market and despite a further positive contribution from invisibles the current account deficit could reach $2 billion this year.

Despite a technical devaluation against the deutschemark within EMS in September 1979, the guilder remains one of the strongest participating currencies. The effects of the authorities' restrictive monetary stance, the relatively low inflation and the continuing benefit of gas export revenues have offset the growing current account imbalance. According to National Westminster Bank's trade-weighted calculations the guilder's appreciation at end January 1980 was 27.3 per cent above the end 1971 level, compared with 26.4 per cent at end 1978. The guilder could well appreciate slightly during 1980 against most major currencies, but is unlikely to keep pace with the deutschemark.

The substantial size of gas resources and their contribution to the Netherlands' primary energy supplies has insulated the country from the worst effects of the substantial oil price rises seen in recent years. It has been estimated that the Netherlands has reserves to meet domestic requirements for another 45 years. The authorities place great importance on husbanding the country's resources since a steady decline would necessitate increased reliance on oil imports. In 1978 the authorities foresaw the need to conserve reserves of natural gas and for a policy of reducing annual production by 5 per cent per annum over the next twenty years. To complement this the government announced a wide-ranging programme of energy savings in September 1979, involving investment of Fl 60 billion over a twenty-year period. A further area of crucial decisions involves the use of nuclear power. Potential sites for power stations are limited in view of the country's high population density; in addition there is considerable environmental opposition to any further development of the present limited facilities, and it seems likely that for some years at least, the Netherlands will be relying heavily on its own declining indigenous resources complemented by a higher proportion of imported oil.

Prospects

Recent economic indications confirm that the downturn, evident towards the end of 1979, continued into 1980. A decline in world trade and increased import prices will adversely affect the balance of payments, and a larger current account deficit, possibly reaching $2 billion, can be expected this year.

It appears likely that consumption and investment will remain at a low level in 1980 and current forecasts suggest that GNP will increase at a much slower rate – perhaps in the order of 1.0 to 1.5 per cent. In these circumstances unemployment will not show any decline from its present level. Much will depend on the government's ability to formulate an effective overall strategy during the period of the current wage freeze. The evidence suggests that a stringent prices and incomes policy will be pursued throughout the year, combined with a concerted effort to restrict the level of public spending. Nevertheless, international trends will undoubtedly affect the level of domestic prices and despite the current wage freeze it is estimated that the rise in consumer prices will approach 7 per cent.

REPUBLIC OF IRELAND

Domestic economy

For several years Ireland registered the fastest rate of growth in Western Europe. Sustained domestic demand and a consistent government policy of stimulating investment, both domestic and foreign, resulted in a period of fairly rapid expansion, with real gross national product (GNP) growth of 5.5 and 7 per cent in 1977 and 1978 respectively. This expansionary phase did not, however, continue as the authorities were forced to adopt restrictive measures in view of the deteriorating external position and a more modest growth rate of 3 per cent was recorded in 1979.

Little stimulus may be expected in the Irish economy in the short term in view of the fall in personal consumption and weak investment demand, coupled with the current world recession. GNP growth of 0.5 per cent is forecast for 1980. The slowdown in the domestic economy has become apparent across the broad spectrum of Irish industry. Industrial production registered a 6.8 per cent growth rate last year but the final out-turn for 1980 is forecast at no more than 3 per cent. An even sharper downturn is being experienced in the construction sector where a volume fall of some 5.5 per cent is expected this year.

As a consequence of the worsening external position (see **External economy** below) and a wider-than-forecast budget deficit for 1979, the government introduced a much more restrictive budget in February 1980. Following several years of high levels of public spending the overall public sector borrowing requirement for 1980 was cut from IR £1 billion to IR £896 million. Whilst the burden of direct taxation was slightly reduced for the PAYE sector, large increases in direct taxation were introduced including a 5 per cent rise in the VAT rate, which now stands at 25 per cent.

Following the rapid expansion of credit in 1978, particularly to the private sector, the government embarked upon a fairly stringent monetary policy but, as a result of an acceleration in the growth of the money supply early in 1979, the authorities adopted a much tighter stance and in the first half of 1980 further restrictions have been imposed. The Central Bank of Ireland had introduced an 18 per cent ceiling on the growth of bank credit to the private sector in the twelve months ending February 1980 and this limit has been reduced to 13 per cent for the period 1980–81 with even more stringent guidelines for personal lending and hire purchase. The year on year rise in the broadly-defined money supply (M3) was 9.4 per cent compared with 34.6 per cent for the same period a year earlier. Although the degree of slowdown is, to some extent, exaggerated by the exceptionally high level of the monetary aggregate in the first half of 1979, some underlying improvement is nevertheless apparent. Additionally, it appears that demand for credit by the private sector is sluggish at present and if this continues it seems likely that the government's 13 per cent target could be achieved.

Consumer prices, which were restricted to a 7.6 per cent increase in 1978, rose by 13.2 per cent last year compared with the OECD average of 9.9 per cent. This downturn stems largely from higher energy costs although substantial rises in food, public service costs and wages also contributed. The increases in indirect taxation have inevitably pushed up the cost of living in 1980 and the oil price rises of 1979–80 continue to have an adverse effect. It is expected therefore that the consumer price index for 1980 as a whole will have risen by around 19 per cent. In the opening stages of talks on the new wage round, the unions have demanded rises of 20 per cent against government guidelines of only 7–8 per cent which suggests that pressures on labour costs and, hence, inflation could remain a significant factor in 1981, with consumer prices rising by a further 15–16 per cent.

The generally depressed level of economic activity, coupled with the cuts in public spending and the slowdown in the number of those leaving Ireland to take up employment elsewhere, have resulted in a rising trend in unemployment. Latest government figures show that 9 per cent of the workforce of 1 million are unemployed. However, excluded from this figure are certain categories of unregistered unemployment and the true figure may be well in excess of 12 per cent.

The problem of high unemployment and the need for job-creation have been a priority of the Irish government for several years and was one of the main aspects of Fianna Fail's manifesto when the party was returned to power in 1977. The country's Industrial Development Authority (IDA) places great emphasis on job-creation as part of its overall plan to promote growth and investment. By utilising financial incentives in the form of grants and tax relief, it hopes to capitalise on the country's existing strengths, develop Ireland's natural resources and attract substantial overseas investment. In its Industrial Plan, which covers the period 1978–82, the IDA aims to create and fill an average of 15,000 jobs each year though, after a successful start, it seems that this objective may not now be achieved.

Despite the fact that the volume of net output by the agricultural sector decreased by 8 per cent in 1979 and the value of farm incomes fell by 12 per cent, agriculture remains a highly productive and profitable sector. In the period 1970–78 output rose by some 35 per cent, considerably more than the average for Europe as a whole, and during the same period farm incomes rose by 75 per cent. This prosperity is undoubtedly due to the opportunities presented by the Common Agricultural Policy of the EEC which provides ready access to large markets and guarantees secure price levels. National policies designed to improve efficiency have also contributed, but have only marginally increased employment opportunities. Little change in farm incomes is expected, though net output is forecast to rise by some 7 per cent.

External economy

The high levels of economic growth experienced in the latter half of the 1970's were accompanied by a series of moderate current account deficits, which in the period 1976–78 stablised at around $300 million a year. In 1979, however, a marked deterioration occurred and the deficit widened to an estimated $1.5 billion despite a substantial improvement on invisibles. A deficit of this magnitude is expected for 1980, and no substantial reduction seems likely next year.

The worsening position is attributable principally to the large increase in the import bill associated with the oil price rises. Ireland is dependent on oil imports for over 70 per cent of its total energy requirements; the bill has risen from $640 million in 1978 to around $1 billion in 1979 and is forecast to exceed $1.6 billion shortly. In 1979 it was estimated that energy demand would double by 1990 and the government is looking for a greater diversification of supply sources. The Electricity Supply Board is expanding its coal and gas-fired generating capacity and is considering building a nuclear power station despite intense opposition. Offshore hydrocarbon exploration has been continuing for some time and the recently reported oil discoveries in the Porcupine Basin have led to some cautious optimism that Ireland could reap substantial benefits from this by the mid-1980s.

Exports by value are expected to rise by 22 per cent in 1980. Whilst agricultural exports should remain buoyant, it is doubtful whether industrial sales will regain the strength shown at the beginning of the year in view of the recession being experienced in Ireland's major markets. A marginal decline is anticipated in the volume of imports in 1980 but the import bill is forecast to rise by some 14.5 per cent.

The net position on invisibles should remain around the 1979 levels despite the downturn in the tourist sector. The prospects of a significant improvement on current account are, therefore, not encouraging and the eventual outcome should prove little different from last year's.

Whilst the UK remains Ireland's principal trading partner the country is pursuing a policy of export diversification – particularly to partner EEC countries. Membership of the Community has brought considerable financial benefit in the form of grants and loans from the European Investment Bank and Ireland now maintains a considerably more independent stance from the UK. This development has been consolidated by the country's membership of the European Monetary System (EMS) which resulted in a break in the historic link between sterling and the Irish punt.

After more than a year of membership of EMS the performance of the punt has been fairly satisfactory although some questions have been raised as to the currency's underlying strength in view of the current account and budget deficits together with the high rate of inflation in Ireland. The Bank of Ireland intervened in the early months of 1980 to support the punt, although recently it has shown more resilience. The Central Bank of Ireland lists three main reasons for this improvement: payments from the EEC; heavy borrowing abroad by both the public and private sectors; and the seasonal pattern of Ireland's balance of payments. The IR £700 million current account deficit which is forecast for 1980 as a whole was largely recorded in the first half of the year, and the authorities anticipate that the rest of the year will be roughly in balance.

Foreign investment has long been welcome in Ireland. The US remains by far the most important source, accounting for over 51 per cent of new overseas investment negotiated by the IDA since 1960; British firms account for 10.5 per cent followed by West German firms with 8.4 per cent. According to the US Department of Commerce, Ireland is the most profitable location for US manufacturing investment. Over the period 1974–79, American firms with a presence in Ireland earned an average return on investment of 29.9 per cent which compares with 14.2 per cent for the EEC on average, and 12.9 per cent worldwide.

Considerable incentives are offered for foreign investors. The IDA is empowered to offer grants of up to 60 per cent of capital costs for new projects as well as training grants of up to 100 per cent. Tax incentives, including 100 per cent tax depreciation allowances and tax relief on export profits, are also available. After 1 January 1981 the latter will not be available to new companies. It will be replaced by a 10 per cent tax rate applicable to all manufacturing companies irrespective of whether they sell within Ireland or overseas. This new concession will last for 20 years.

Prospects

There seems little prospect of any significant improvement in the problems facing the conomy in the short term. The deflationary budget has meant that growth in 1980 has been revised downwards to less than 1 per cent and forecasts for 1981 are only marginally better. Again, little improvement is anticipated in the external position in view of the downturn being experienced by Ireland's major trading partners coupled with continuing high oil prices. Some reduction in the rate of inflation may become apparent in 1981 but the increase in consumer prices is thought likely to remain in double figures until 1983–84. The rising trend of unemployment continues to give cause for concern but it is questionable whether a significant reduction in the numbers of unemployed can be achieved considering the cutbacks in public expenditure following from the 1980 budget.

UNITED KINGDOM

Domestic economy

Although the annual rate of inflation now appears to have peaked in the United Kingdom, attempts to reduce cost pressures continue to dominate the economic scene. The real money supply has fallen rapidly in recent months and the continued high level of interest rate implies a severe squeeze on the economy. However, only a limited reduction in inflationary pressures can be expected with the scope for further reductions in 1981 being critically dependent upon the response of pay negotiators to the tight monetary conditions.

In the March 1980 budget the government reaffirmed its commitment to contain public expenditure in the context of a medium-term financial plan. The economic policy of the authorities is based on a tight monetary policy which is seen as a necessary prerequisite to reducing inflation and providing an environment in which economic growth can eventually be encouraged. In the interim, the prospects are for falling demand and higher unemployment.

The continued increase in earnings above the rate of inflation, together with direct tax reductions granted during 1979, permitted real incomes to increase by 6 per cent in 1979 compared with the previous year. Despite the increase in the savings ratio over the same period consumers' real expenditure grew by 4 per cent.

However, by the end of the year it was clear that real incomes were coming under increasing pressure as the gap between prices and earnings was largely eroded. The extent to which consumers' expenditure has responded to this pressure is unclear as the picture has been distorted by the payment of tax rebates towards the end of 1979. In the first quarter of 1980, consumers' expenditure was 2.9 per cent higher than in the latter half of 1979. Much of this may be accounted for by pre-budget sales of spirits and tobacco, and the extension of retailers' January sales further into the New Year. More recent figures for the volume of retail sales indicates a decline from the high pre-budget February level.

The timing of the recession does not depend upon a decline in consumer demand. Other components of demand were weak in 1979 and are likely to decline further into the 1980s. Government consumption increased only slightly in real terms during 1979 whilst fixed investment by both the public and private sectors fell by over 2 per cent. The severe financial squeeze on the corporate sector has forced companies to postpone or cancel capital investment programmes. The reduction of stocks from the exceptionally high levels of 1979 was a key factor in triggering the recession. In the first three months of 1980 the volume of stocks fell by over £600 million (at 1975 prices) and is likely to accelerate in the coming months.

Despite the substantial increase in domestic demand in 1979 output was largely unresponsive. Gross Domestic Product (GDP) increased by only 1.7 per cent in 1979 compared with the previous year, of which nearly half was attributable to North Sea oil and gas production. This disparity was largely accounted for by a massive deterioration in the UK's overseas trading position, from a £800 million surplus on current account in 1978 to a £2.3 billion deficit in 1979. Import volume increased by 11.6 per cent and export volume by only 3.6 per cent over the same period whilst the terms of trade were virtually unchanged.

With little prospect of a significant increase in domestic demand and a depressed overseas market, the prospects for output are discouraging. A 0.75 per cent decline in output has already been recorded in the first quarter of the year compared with the previous quarter, and a 2–3 per cent fall is likely for 1980 as a whole, a more severe decline than in the 1975/76 recession. This suggests a gloomy outlook for unemployment, with more than 2 million adult unemployed by the end of 1980, an increase of over one-third compared with the corresponding period in 1979. This is the highest level of unemployment for nearly half a century.

External economy

The United Kingdom's current account position deteriorated by some £3 billion during 1979. Over the same period the balance on oil account improved by £1.2 billion. The recent strength of sterling (derived in part from its status as a "petrocurrency") has created difficult trading conditions for manufacturing industry in overseas markets. In addition, the strong exchange rate together with a high level of consumer demand encouraged a substantial increase in imports, with trade in invisible goods (excluding oil) deteriorating by £3 billion. The accustomed large surplus on invisible account has also been eroded through higher interest, profit and dividend payments abroad by foreign oil companies operating in the North Sea together with increased net contributions to the EEC. The authorities have recently negotiated reduction in the latter for 1980, although the stage at which this will be reflected in the invisible balance is uncertain. Overall, some further deterioration in the invisible account is expected during 1980. The expected improvement in the visible account is limited, despite the movement into surplus of trade in oil and the effects of the recession upon import growth. Thus only a modest improvement from 1980's current account deficit of £2.3 billion can be expected as the problems of trading in a depressed world market are exacerbated by the continued strength of sterling.

The United Kingdom's approaching self-sufficiency in oil, together with the movement of international interest rate differentials in sterling's favour have been important factors in sterling's recent strength. However, the latter is only a temporary advantage and much of it may be eroded as UK interest rates fall towards the end of 1980. Moreover, the high relative level of inflation in the United Kingdom continues to be of concern.

The authorities maintain a basically non-interventionist approach towards the exchange rate. The strength of sterling combined with high domestic costs have been a source of concern to manufacturing industry, as it has been increasingly difficult to compete in overseas markets. However, a high exchange rate can play an essential role in the fight against inflation as it tends to moderate the costs of imported goods and materials and limits the ability of companies to grant large wage increases.

Prospects

Monetary policy is now the main weapon in the authorities' fight against inflation. The current money supply target range is for a 7–11 per cent annual rate of growth of sterling M3 in the fourteen months to mid-April 1981. Although the growth in the money supply on a monthly basis has been volatile, there has been a moderation in monetary growth in recent months. In the six months to May, sterling M3 increased at an annual rate of about 8.5 per cent compared with 14 per cent in the previous six months.

During the first quarter of 1980 unusually tight money market conditions developed as the public sector moved into surplus. Short-term interest rates rose to over 18 per cent for 3 months' paper in March and April, despite substantial assistance from the Bank of England. Conditions have since eased somewhat as Exchequer flow returned to a more normal pattern. The desire now is to wait until there are clear signs that the monetary situation in general is finally under control and within the current target range. Some of the recent moderation in monetary growth has been due to exceptional conditions during the first quarter, when tax payments pushed the public sector into surplus. There has also been little indication of a moderation in corporate sector loan demand despite the de-stocking recorded in the first quarter of 1980. Furthermore, the removal of the "corset" is likely to result in a surge in monetary growth as commercial bills held outside the banking system reappear on the banks' balance sheets, which in turn will tend to obscure the underlying demand for bank credit. There may also be some reluctance to reduce MLR significantly before it is clear that the rate of inflation is falling, as this might be interpreted as an easing of the authorities' resolve to defeat inflationary pressures.

In the medium-term financial plan announced in the budget the government reaffirmed its commitment to reduce public sector pressures on monetary growth. As the first stage in this plan the Public Sector Borrowing Requirement target was set at £8.5 billion for 1980/81 compared with an out-turn of £9.8 billion in the previous financial year.

Although the timing of interest rate reductions is uncertain, the severity of the recession should reduce the demand for bank finance and allow the monetary targets to be achieved. A steady reduction in money supply growth should therefore be compatible with a general lowering of interest rates in 1981.

2.The Central Banks

Introduction

Accurate comparisons between countries are difficult to make because of the variety of arrangements in aspects of central bank establishment, ownership and control.

Apart from the personalities involved there are two considerations which seem to determine the role assigned to a central bank in monetary policy. One is how far the determination of monetary policy, or simply the quantity of money, should be placed beyond the reach of government in its day-to-day control of the economy. The other is how important is the contribution that a central bank can make to the formulation of national economic policy and to the choice of application of monetary instruments through the special knowledge and relationship it can develop in the monetary sphere. The bank will need to keep itself informed independently of current developments in the economy, requiring the employment of high quality research staff.

All the Community central banks are publicly owned except for the Banque de Belgique (where the State has only a 50 per cent interest) and the Banca d'Italia (where capital is held by a group of financial institutions, some of which are themselves publicly owned).

BELGIUM

Banque Nationale de Belgique SA,
Boulevard de Benlaimont 5,
B1000 – Bruxelles.

The National Bank of Belgium (Banque Nationale de Belgique) was created by the Act of May 1950 on the initiative of the then Minister of Finance. Originally it had three basic functions:

(1) the issuing of bank notes,
(2) credit activity proper and
(3) cash service for the state.

Of these functions that of direct dispenser of credit has by now lost all significance, while that of lender in the last resort has become more and more important, especially in the field of monetary policy, since it has enabled the central bank to act directly on the liquidity of financial intermediaries. Originally it had the privilege of note issue, though not the monopoly, since Parliament could not authorise private bankers and cooperative societies to issue bank notes.

The central bank, set up in the form of a joint stock company of which the state holds 50 per cent of the capital, is controlled by the provisions of a Royal Decree in August 1939, relating to the activities, the organisation and the attributions of the National Bank adopted in fulfilment of the law of May 1939, whose provisions were modified by the Act of April 1975.

Another Act of considerable importance is that of December 1973, which ascribed to the National Bank, apart from the authority to fix its own interest rates, also the right of initiative in proposing measures of monetary policy. In particular this latter Act ascribed to the central bank the power to make "recommendations" to financial intermediaries and has increased the means of action traditionally at the disposal of the central bank so that the banks, private savings banks, and financial intermediaries of the public sector may be subject to the obligation –

(1) to respect a given relation between the different elements of their assets and liabilities;
(2) to respect given limits for certain elements of their assets and liabilities which offer the central bank the possibility of setting up a form of quantitative credit control;
(3) to place special deposits with the central bank which allow for the direct "sterilisation" of the liquidity of financial intermediaries when this is judged to be excessive, and
(4) to respect the maximum interest rates applicable to the various categories of funds collected by the public.

The Governor of the National Bank is nominated by the King for a period of five years and presides over the board of directors, the governing council, the general council and the general assembly. The board of directors has a number of members varying between four and seven including the governor. All the members are nominated by the King for a period of six years on the proposal of the governing council and the board devotes itself to the running of the bank. The governing council, set up in 1926, deliberates on general questions relating to the bank, to the currency, to credit and to the economic development of the country; apart from the members of the board of directors, it also includes representatives from the world of industry, commerce and agriculture, from trade-union oranisations as well as from financial institutions of public interest. The general council is composed of the governor and directors, the members of the governing council and the auditors: it devotes itself mainly to questions relating to the general organisation of the bank and to the remuneration of the governor and the directors. The college of auditors has between eight and ten members who are elected by the general assembly.

The National Bank also functions as State cashier, and in this respect is subject to the control of the Court of Auditors.

Amongst the principal services of the National Bank that of a centre for risks should be underlined. This was set up on the basis of a voluntary agreement between the National Bank and the other banks in 1965 and its activity was officially recognised and extended by virtue of the Royal Decree of October 1967. The centre for risks centralises all information which the banks are required to communicate to the National Bank relating to the granting, increase, reduction and suppression of credit above one million francs as well as the use to which this credit is put.

DENMARK

Danmarks Nationalbank,
DK. 1093 Copenhagen K,
Harinegade 5.

It is the responsibility of Danmarks Nationalbank as the central bank of Denmark to maintain a sound monetary system and to facilitate and regulate money transaction and lending activities. The Nationalbank is thus the central monetary authority of Denmark. The bank discharges its responsibilities in cooperation with the government, notably the Royal Bank Commissioners, who supervise the performance of the duties assigned to the bank under Danish law. The basic statutes governing the banking system are the Bank Act of 1930 and the Danmarks Nationalbank Act of 1936.

The Nationalbank enjoys the sole right of note issue. The bank holds the government account and provides short-term finance when necessary. The above-mentioned Danmarks Nationalbank Act changed the status of the bank from that of a joint-stock company to a self-governing non-profit institution.

The bank is managed by a board of directors, a committee of directors and a board of governors. The Nationalbank is also the registration authority for commercial banks and savings banks and has the usual central banking responsibilities in relation to them.

The central bank has a statutory duty –

(1) to maintain the domestic value of the currency,
(2) to control the external value of the currency and
(3) to control credit expansion.

The central bank must report to government via the Minister of Economic Affairs on major changes in monetary policy. The Annual Report is published but not submitted to Parliament. The bank is an official government body and no private body has a share in the general capital fund.

The governor is appointed by the Monarch (i.e., the government), and remains in office until seventy years old. Two deputy governors are appointed by the board of directors. None of the governors are members of the board, consisting of 25 directors, 8 with seats in the

Folketing, 2 appointed by the Minister of Trade, Industry and Shipping (who is the board's presiding officer) and 15 elected by the board.

FRANCE

Banque de France,
F75049 Paris CEDEX 01,
Boite Postale NO 140-01.

The institutional and structural framework of the French banking system is formed not only of banking and financial institutions properly so called but also of bodies charged with the realisation of credit policy, i.e., the Bank of France, the National Credit Council and the Commission for Control of the Banks.

The Banque de France was created by Napoleon in 1800. Originally it was a private bank functioning as a discount and deposit bank without any special privileges. The Act of December 1945 nationalised the Bank of France, transferring its shares to the State. The management of the bank is entrusted to the governor who is nominated by decree of the President of the Republic passed by the Council of Ministers and is assisted by two vice-governors, similarly appointed. The deliberating body of the bank is the General Council, formed of the governor, the vice-governors and ten councillors, nine of whom are nominated by a decree passed by the Council of Ministers: seven of these are appointed by the Ministry of Finance to represent different economic ministries.

The Bank of France as affirmed by the statutes of January 1973 "receives from the State the general task of supervising currency and credit"; the application of the State's monetary policy is therefore its responsibility. The bank has the exclusive and unlimited privilege of issuing bank notes for all the metropolitan territory. There are five categories of productive operations for the issue of notes which are expressly indicated by the bank's status, being the operations in –

(1) gold and currencies;
(2) discount operations;
(3) advances on public bills and stocks and shares;
(4) advances to the state, and
(5) operations of acquisition and sale of public and private bills on the open market.

The bank also carries out a certain number of operations deriving from its qualities or resulting from various assignments amongst which are the central service for risks and credits which exceed a given amount, the central archive for unpaid cheques and the special service for the transfer of funds between banks. Lastly the bank is the administrative organ of the National Credit Council. There is no provision for the direct intervention of the state in the running of the banks' business and although there are solid traditions of close collaboration between the government and the management of the bank, formally it enjoys full independence.

The Bank of France as an enterprise in which the state is the sole stock-holder is obviously subject to the control of the latter. This control is exercised permanently by auditors and periodically by the Commission for the Auditing of the Accounts of Public Enterprises, which, however, according to the decree of January 1966, "is not competent to examine and to judge the monetary policy and the credit policy followed by the bank."

FEDERAL REPUBLIC OF GERMANY

Deutsche Bundesbank,
D 6000 Frankfurt,
Postfach 2633.

In West Germany responsibility concerning monetary policy is in principle the competence of the central government, but in fact it is shared between the government and the German Federal Bank (the Deutsche Bundesbank). The latter has greater responsibility concerning credit policy, while the control of the banking profession is the competence of the Federal Office for Control of the Banks, which acts in close collaboration with the Bundesbank.

The Deutsche Bundesbank, set up by the Act of July 1957, is the central institution of banking organisation in West Germany. It has progressively taken over the functions of the Reichsbank, has the privilege of issuing bank notes and the duty of watching over the stability of the currency both at home and abroad, conserving its power to acquire the currency and regulating the circulation of paper money and the granting of credits. As for the principal means at the disposal of the bank for the fulfilment of its duties, it is necessary to mention the fixing of the discount rate, the obligatory reserves on credit institutions and open-market operations.

Since its origin the bank has been an institution under public law of which the state holds all the capital, but it carries out its assignments in full independence of the orientations of the federal government since it has only the obligation of upholding the general economic policy of the government, so that it may be considered as being the most independent of the European central banks.

The Bundesbank holds the accounts of the federal Treasury and of the Treasuries of the Länder as well as those of the public administrations and local collectives. Another of its assignments is the service of inter-bank clearing.

The Central Council is the body which determines the general policy of the bank, while the directorate is charged with its execution. The Council is presided over by the President of the Bundesbank and is composed of the members of the directorate and the presidents of the Länderszentralbanken. All members of the Council are nominated by the president of the Federal Republic, the members of the directorate on the proposal of the federal government, and the presidents of the Länderszentralbanken on the proposal of the Bundesrat, which is the parliamentary representation of the Länder. Members of the federal government have the right to participate in meetings of the Central Council of the bank. As against this, the president of the Bundesbank must be invited to participate in all meetings of the Council of Ministers in which questions relating to monetary policy are discussed.

GREECE

The Bank of Greece,
Athens,
Greece.

The central bank of Greece was founded in 1928, and despite the major setback as a result of the military campaign in Asia Minor, the country made great strides towards social and economic development. These were combined with political and institutional changes, such as the establishment of the central bank and of two specialised credit institutions, the Agricultural Bank, and the National Mortgage Bank. The decision to set up a bank of issue had been made in the context of the effort to ensure monetary stability and improve the structure and functioning of the Greek credit system.

By the end of World War II the ideas expressed during the inter-war period by J.M. Keynes had gained ground and had started having a decisive influence on economic policies in the industrial countries.

In that climate the views about the role of central banks took a different form. It was now felt that they had to adjust their policies —targets and instruments — to the main objectives of economic policy, namely the attainment of high rates of economic growth and employment levels as close as possible to full employment. In particular monetary policy which is implemented by central banks, aims at supplying the economy with credit in such a way as to facilitate the attainment of the desired rates of economic growth without disrupting monetary equilibrium.

An important event in the context of cooperation between the government and the central bank was the establishment of the Currency Committee in 1946, which provides a forum for the analysis and assessment of the monetary impact of general economic measures and ensures harmony between monetary and fiscal policies to serve short and long term economic objectives.

Over the past fifty years there have been certain outstanding achievements of the bank.

(1) In 1944 monetary stabilisation was taken with the introduction of the new drachma equal to 50 billion old ones. The note of exchange was fixed at 600 drachmas per pound and the Bank of Greece undertook to exchange the drachma for British military pounds convertible into pounds sterling on a one-to-one basis.

(2) In 1953 there was a readjustment of the exchange rate. The devaluation of the drachma by 50 per cent and import liberalisation were bold steps which proved very successful and led to the final restoration of the country's monetary equilibrium. The rate of inflation slowed down and the balance of payments showed a considerable improvement. Thus the year 1955 marked the beginning of a long period of monetary stability.

(3) After the restoration of monetary stability the bank attained another important goal: the attraction of private savings into the banking system.

(4) The bank played an important role in founding and financing new development agencies and in carrying out new projects assigned to it by the state.

ITALY

Banca d'Italia,
I–00184 Roma,
Via Nazionale 91,
Casella Postale 2484.

As far as the credit sector is concerned the Interministerial Committee for credit and savings (CICR) is the body responsible for tracing out the broad lines of monetary, credit and exchange policy. The CICR was created in July 1947 to replace the old Committee of Ministers provided for by the Banking Act 1936 and suppressed in 1944. The Committee, in whose meetings the governor of the Bank of Italy participates by right and in fact very actively and often very decisively, is composed of the Treasury Minister, who presides over it, and the Ministers of public works, of agriculture, of industry and trade, of foreign trade, of the budget and economic programming and the Minister charged with state participations. The Banking Act stipulates that the Committee has recourse to the Bank of Italy for controls within its competence and in order to carry out its decisions. Within the framework of the Directives issued by the Committee which mark out general principles, the Bank of Italy plays a decisive role in choosing appropriate instruments and means to achieve the defined objectives: furthermore the governor of the bank may take initiatives in order to facilitate the application of the measures decided on by the Committee.

The Bank of Italy, which was created by an Act of August 1893, and which has been the only bank of issue since 1926, had undergone, as a result of the provisions of the banking act, important modifications which have transformed it from a joint-stock company into an institution under public law whose activities are limited almost exclusively to relations with credit institutions. Its capital, divided into 300,000 nominal shares of 1,000 lira each, can be held only by savings banks, credit institutions under public law and banks of national interest, social security organisations and insurance companies.

The Higher Council of the bank, composed of 12 members chosen by the General Assembly with the approval of the President of the Republic, is charged with the nomination of the governor (who enjoys complete freedom of action and full independence), the director-general and the deputy director-general, but still with the approval of the President of the Republic.

The bank is subject to the control of the state in consideration of the fact that it exercises functions of public interest and administrative services on behalf of the state. This control is exercised by a permanent commission presided over by the Treasury Minister, which at the request of the latter expresses opinions on measures concerning banknotes, modifications made to the Statute of the Bank and on the application of laws concerning the bank of issue.

LUXEMBOURG

There is no Central Bank as such in Luxembourg. BLEU, the Belgo-Luxembourg Economic Union was formed in 1921; these countries pool their foreign currency holdings, operate a single balance of payments regime and combine their foreign trade statistics.

NETHERLANDS

De Nederlandsche Bank NV,
NL–1017 ZM Amsterdam,
Westeinde 1.

The Dutch Central Bank (De Nederlandsche Bank NV) was created in 1814 on the initiative of King Williem I. Because of its origin as a private enterprise the central bank is still organised as a form of a joint-stock company, but all the shares were nationalised in 1948. Since 1904 it has enjoyed the privilege *de facto* of issuing banknotes while in 1948 it gained the privilege by law (Art. 10 of the Banking Act 1940). It has its headquarters in Amsterdam and a separate office in Rotterdam as well as 15 branches and 39 agencies scattered about the rest of the country. Unlike other central banks, its capital belongs entirely to the state.

The direction of the bank is entrusted to two bodies:

(1) the board of directors, which consists of the president, the secretary and from three to five directors, and whose members are all nominated by the Crown, and
(2) the Council of the bank, composed of 17 members.

The Central Bank acts as a "bank of banks" – i.e., as a lender of last resort and as a supervisory body for the private banks. According to the Banking Act of 1948 it has the duty of regulating the value of the Dutch monetary unit in the most favourable way for the prosperity and welfare of the country and as far as possible of stabilising its value.

The Central Bank is therefore responsible for the monetary policy of the country but maintains its autonomy with respect to the state: it also acts as an exchange office, i.e., as a supervising body for currencies according to the terms of the regulation of currencies established by a decree of October 1945.

The Banking Act of 1945 reserves for the Minster of Finance the power to give instructions to the Central Bank in certain cases, but up to now this power has never been exercised.

The Central Bank has a statutory duty –

(1) to maintain the domestic value of the currency;
(2) to control the external value of the currency;
(3) to supervise the banking system, and
(4) to facilitate money transmission.

The exchange rate is fixed by the Minister of Finance with Central Bank advice. In other respects the bank is independent although its actions must not conflict with government objectives. The governor is appointed by the Queen on the advice of the Minister of Finance for seven years, but he may be reappointed.

At least 3 and not more than 5 directors are similarly appointed for seven years. 12 members of the Board of Commissionaries are appointed by the Queen from a short list of 3 for each place for a four-year term. 17 members of the Bank Council include a Royal Commissioner representing the Government and 4 Commissaries; the other 12 members must legally include representatives of the government, commerce (including transport), industry and agriculture, labour unions and the monetary and credit sector.

REPUBLIC OF IRELAND

Central Bank of Ireland,
PO Box No. 559,
Jamie Street,
Dublin 2.

The Central Bank of Ireland came into existence in 1943 as a result of the Central Bank Act of 1942, and took the place of the Currency Commission which had been set up under the Currency Act of 1927. The issuing function was transferred to the Central Bank on its formation.

The 1942 Act empowered the Central Bank to act as a lender of last resort but the liquidity of the system was such that this power was not used until 1955. The bank was also empowered to take deposits from banks. The Exchequer account was formerly kept at the Bank of Ireland (one of the leading commercial banks founded in 1783) but was transferred to the Central Bank under the 1971 Act, though some public accounts are still held by the Bank of Ireland.

The monetary policy function of the Central Bank is set out in section 6 of the Central Bank Act of 1942, which gave the bank "the general function and duty of taking (within the limit of the powers for the time being vested in it by law) such steps as the board may from time to time deem appropriate and advisable towards safeguarding the integrity of the currency and ensuring that in what pertains to the control of credit, the constant and predominant aim shall be the welfare of the people as a whole." This statement of the general functions and duty of the bank is followed in the Act by a subsection empowering the Minister of Finance wherever he thinks proper to require the governor of the bank or the board "to consult and advise him in regard to the execution and performance by the bank of the general functions and duty imposed on the bank."

The Central Bank Acts of 1942 and 1971 in effect give the Central Bank a large measure of autonomy.

Under the 1971 Act the Central Bank was made the licensing authority for banks, and formal powers were given to the bank to require a holder of a banker's licence to maintain a specified ratio between assets and liabilities. These powers strengthened the position of the bank, particularly by providing an alternative instrument of monetary control in addition to those of moral suasion and quantitative guidelines formerly employed by it.

UNITED KINGDOM

Bank of England,
Threadneedle Street,
London, EC2.

The Bank of England has perhaps the widest range of responsibilities of any bank in industrialised countries, but it does not have as much independence of action or such formal obligations in monetary policy matters as some of the others. It has no overriding statutory obligation to maintain the value of the currency, but it does have other roles apart from the execution of monetary policy, such as acting as banker to the government and some private customers, the printing and issuing of banknotes, issuing and registering government stock, management of foreign reserves, and the supervision of commercial bank liquidity and solvency. In some countries such functions are performed by government agencies other than central banks. It is the Treasury ministers who have to account to Parliament for monetary policy. The bank is accountable to the Chancellor and Prime Minister for providing advice and for acting as the government's banker. It lays its annual report before Parliament, but the report has never been debated.

The Bank of England's governor has said "that the bank's independence is much better seen as independence within government freely – and forcibly on occasions – to express its view to government." The lack of parliamentary accountability in the United Kingdom can create situations that would be unlikely to arise elsewhere. For example, what other financial centre could have instituted such a fundamental change as Competition and Credit Control (1971) not only without needing statutory authority but also without any parliamentary discussion? It must be remembered that the bank, founded in 1694, was a private concern until taken over by the government in 1945.

One important advantage the United Kingdom enjoys is the special relationship that has developed between the Bank of England and the financial community. The relationship provides the authorities with a valuable and indeed unique source of guidance. It is a measure of the bank's status that British financial institutions continue to prefer to accept the discretionary form of control it exercises rather than be tied down by rigid legal requirements imposed in many other countries.

The governor is appointed by the Crown for five years and has a deputy governor and 16 directors, of whom not more than 4 may be full time executive directors. The 12 non-executive directors are appointed from a wide variety of interests in industry and commerce, trade union affairs and banking (they may not be members of the House of Commons, Ministers of the Crown, or working in a government department).

3. Stock Exchanges

Introduction

The tasks of a stock market are:

(1) to enable investors to buy or sell securities regularly and expeditiously;
(2) to determine and publish prices of a certain quality;
(3) to improve the liquidity and marketability of securities and to improve the depth of the market;
(4) to protect investors and to put all users of the market on an equal footing;
(5) to keep the cost of security-transaction services as low as possible, and
(6) to reduce the difference between the cost of capital to issuers or borrowers and the yield to investors.

When an issue is placed parts of it will normally be taken up by three groups of investors:

(1) those who are certain that they will hold the bond until maturity;
(2) those who much expect to have to sell before maturity because they may need cash, and
(3) those who will hold the investment until such time as in their opinion a favourable situation for switching their investment has arisen.

The investors' decision will be influenced by –

(1) the type of security (especially the terms of issue and the maturity date);
(2) the minimum rate of interest which investors require from bonds of this type;
(3) the financial standing of the issuer;
(4) the net sales proceeds expected, and
(5) the cost of obtaining continuous information.

The objective of the issuer is easier to ascertain than that of the investor: his aim is the lowest possible cost of capital. The cost of capital to the issuer, or the cost of capital raised, is determined initially by the issue price and by the amount of the interest and redemption payments.

The securities markets, whatever their structure, have substantial achievements to their credit. Their contribution to the financing of industry is obvious.

In countries with well-developed financial markets, all that can be expected from any effort to improve the efficiency of secondary stock markets is a minor reduction in the cost of capital and a modest increase in the yields from securities.

Stock markets do not exist for their own sake, and in the member states of the European Communities there are both fragmented stock markets and integrated markets. There can be different interpretations of what constitutes an integrated secondary stock market and what constitutes a fragmented one.

An integrated secondary market would in general be one that was a single uniform entity covering all dealings in certain securities already in circulation. Admittedly even in this straightforward case one could distinguish between functional sectors (such as the information and decision-taking sphere, the execution sphere and the settlement and custody spheres), but procedures within these sectors would follow a single pattern.

In the straightforward case the fragmented secondary market can be defined as the opposite of the integrated market. Some aspects always suggest that a market segment belongs to a certain system of security dealing, while others suggest the opposite. For this reason it is not possible to draw a sharp dividing line between integrated and fragmented stock markets.

BELGIUM

Although the role of the banks in Belgian investment is now very marked, this is a comparatively recent development and was led by the National Savings Bank rather than the commercial banks. The regulations governing bank investment activities were only relaxed in 1967 to allow permanent portfolio holdings covering issues by other companies. Although the main stock exchange (Brussels) is governed by a Council, the main regulatory body is the Commission Bancaire (CB). The function of this commission is to coordinate the approach of commercial companies to the capital market and to protect prospective investors against false information.

DENMARK

The only stock exchange in Denmark is the Københauns Føndsbors. It has two sections, the "Main" Exchange and the "After" Exchange. There are 33 stock exchange members spread over 24 member firms.

They are appointed by the Economics Minister and come under a special Ministry supervisory authority which has no officials engaged full-time.

The securities subject to the trading procedures of the Main Exchange (Honerdbønsen) are the major shares and almost all bonds.

The shares admitted to the Efterbørsen are those which have not qualified for admission to the Honerdbønsen. A stock may be traded here provided that the related share capital of the issuing company amounts to DKR 1 million at par value. The majority of stocks (about 180) are quoted on the Efterbørs. In addition small bond issues are traded.

FRANCE

Despite a boom in the French economy and demands by industry for funds, the stock exchange is prevented from realising its potential by the numerous controls exercised over the various institutions by the government through the Bank of France. Two events are, however, significant.

(1) The formation in 1967 of La Commission des Opérations de Bourse (COB or Stock Exchange Commission, which was set up to improve the standing and efficiency of the Paris stock market by checking the truth and completeness of information provided.

(2) The Baumgartner Commission, instigated by the Minister of Finance to investigate the possibility of reforming the financial institutions. This Commission reported in 1972 on the structure and functions of the Stock Exchange, and suggested –
- *(a)* the granting of tax credits to foreign investors;
- *(b)* lower taxes on dividends;
- *(c)* changes in the stockbroking system allowing limited liability status and the establishment of "contrapartistes" or jobbers;
- *(d)* the introduction of block trading of shares to promote institutional business, and
- *(e)* easing the rules covering new issues.

Some of these recommendation have been implemented either as they are, or after amendment.

FEDERAL REPUBLIC OF GERMANY

The granting of a stock exchange quotation is subject to legislation contained in the Stock Exchange Act, as amended, and the rules of the Stock Exchange Admissions Office. This office ascertains the completeness of the information without investigating its accuracy. Certain reporting requirements exist, but these are more than covered by the statutory requirements for interim profit figures; these are often provided by the larger groups on a half-yearly or even quarterly basis in a voluntary but frequently not consolidated manner.

New laws are currently under preparation which will encourage increased stock exchange activity, and improve the information available to the public about quoted companies.

GREECE

Stock exchanges may be established in Greece only by law, and at present only one stock exchange exists.

The listing of corporate shares and bonds on the stock exchange and their removal therefrom are governed by law.

All companies limited by shares (corporations whose registered capital is at least ten million drachma) may have their shares and bonds listed on the stock exchange. An application has to be filed with the stock exchange by the interested corporation together with a visaed excerpt of the minutes of its board of directors and with certain supporting documents and data concerning the establishment and operation of the corporation.

A removal of listed corporate securities from the stock exchange board occurs when there is –

(1) reduction of the capital stock below the statutory limit of 10 million drachma;
(2) a limited volume of transactions in corporation securities over a long period of time;
(3) a drop in the demand for securities;
(4) non-compliance of the corporation with the general or special decisions of the Capital Market Committee or with the Stock Exchange Regulations.

The Greek Capital market is in a stage of full development especially since the promulgation of EMER Law 148 of 1967 which has furthered considerably the demand for securities. The number of persons interested in stock and bond investments is steadily growing, the volume of stock exchange transactions is expanding and stock quotations are improving.

The Stock Exchange hopes to benefit from the general expertise of the EEC countries on entering the Community.

ITALY

Italian stock exchanges are controlled and run in the style of public service industries. Consequently they operate within a rigid framework. The market is narrow and imperfect, and there is no compensation fund for the protection of investors. There is also broker competition and a fair amount of dealing carried on outside the market. In fact there would seem to be a considerable need for extra-statutory controls.

The standard of reporting depends almost entirely on the company involved and there is a wide variation in quality. The minimum standard of reporting is governed by the Civil Code.

LUXEMBOURG

Investment is largely handled by the banks or by the state institutions. The Commissaire au Controle des Banques exercises a supervisory role with regard to stock exchange listings. There are no formal requirements concerning published financial information other than that contained in company legislation.

NETHERLANDS

Although the dealings of the Amsterdam Stock Exchange are similar to those of the London Stock Exchange – involving a broker/jobber type transaction and high voluntary standards – there the similarity ends. The Dutch market is dominated by the six Dutch international companies whose standard of reporting is generally in the forefront of the best practice. Apart from these companies, capital requirements are almost always met by private loans rather than debentures or by internal financing. Consequently there is a marked lack of new issues. A new feature of the Dutch capital market is the increasing role being played by the institutions, such as pension funds, which are tending to create a closed market between themselves and the state and/or industry.

In general the requirements of the stock exchange regarding published information over and above the statutory requirements are laid down as a condition of obtaining a quotation by the Stock Exchange Society (Vereeniging voor den Effecienhandel).

UNITED KINGDOM AND REPUBLIC OF IRELAND

An establishment of one stock exchange for Great Britain and the Republic of Ireland was instituted in 1973, although the London exchange had been in existence for over two centuries, and some provincial exchanges for a century or more.

The stock exchange has evolved its requirements regarding both financial reporting and listing and prospectuses within the framework of the Companies Acts. In most instances the Council's requirements supplement the current Companies Act.

CONCLUSIONS

There are two closely related questions which should be taken into account when considering stock markets in the EEC.

(1) Is a similar form of organisation for the secondary stock markets of the individual member states desirable in the interests of a proper functioning of the Common Market?
(2) Which is the better form of organisation – an integrated market or a fragmented market?

The five factors determining the appropriate degree of segmentation of a secondary market vary from country to country:

(1) the turnover characteristics of the securities traded in a country;
(2) the dealing procedures actually in use in the country and the dealing procedures capable of being introduced;
(3) the state of communications technology and the cost of data transmission;
(4) the nature and extent of the demand from various groups of investors for transaction services, and
(5) the number and structure of business and financial centres in a country.

Since the Community is expected to continue to develop more in the direction of a uniform economic and monetary area, the disadvantages of parallel markets will come to outweigh the advantages, but at the same time there will be a gradual transmission from parallel markets to competing markets and the market organisers will inevitably find themselves exposed to even more intensive competition.

CHAPTER 4

ECONOMIC AND MONETARY UNION

1. The Need for a Coordinated Monetary Policy

In its most extreme form, economic and monetary union means a single economy, a single currency, with centralised economic decision-making. The architects of the European Economic Community who drew up the Treaty of Rome in 1958 believed that free trade between the member countries would lead progressively to greater economic union, but they made no specific provision for its attainment. Instead they concentrated on achieving a customs union and drew up a twelve-year stage-by-stage plan for the dismantling of intra-Community customs barriers. But it soon became clear that the Community could not stop at free trade and that for their own sakes, the member states would have to look beyond their customs union as growing economic interdependence pointed to the need for greater economic and monetary integration.

The customs union, achieved ahead of schedule in July 1968, was a resounding success and intra-Community trade in goods and services expanded rapidly – now accounting for half of member state's foreign trade as against one-third in 1958. During the same period member states' foreign trade increased 275 per cent in real terms and now accounts for no less than one quarter of gross Community product (i.e., one quarter of the aggregate amount of all services supplied and goods produced in the nine countries). In some member countries (Ireland, Belgium, the Netherlands and Luxembourg) the share of foreign trade actually exceeds 50 per cent, while the figure for Denmark is 33 per cent. In the Federal Republic of Germany and the United Kingdom, the share has risen from 20 per cent to just under 30 per cent, while in Italy and France the figures are around 25 and 20 per cent respectively.

The EEC customs union has eliminated the fear that tariff barriers between Community countries might be restored overnight against member countries' goods, perhaps depriving entire industries of their export markets. However, it has not managed to prevent excessive exchange rate fluctuations which can have a similar, if not greater, disruptive impact on trade than customs duties. As a result, intra-

Community trade is still fraught with uncertainty despite the fact that the customs union has brought about an unprecedented degree of interdependence between the member states of what is a highly industrialised Community. The fact that member states already carry out 50 per cent of their foreign trade with one another reflects a degree of mutual reliance never before witnessed in history. Indeed Ireland and the three Benelux countries carry out between two-thirds and three-quarters and France, Italy, Denmark and the Federal Republic of Germany half of their trade with other member countries. The United Kingdom is the exception, transacting two-thirds of its foreign trade with non-member countries.

Given this high degree of interdependence a customs union alone cannot provide the necessary long-term security: one pillar cannot suffice indefinitely to support the edifice formed by the objectives laid down in the Treaty, namely improvement and alignment of living standards and uniform development of all regions without structural imbalances and distortions to competition. To this end, what is needed is the economic union which is advocated in the Preamble to the Rome Treaty and which itself cannot be attained without monetary union. Only within such a union can the convertibility of all member countries' currencies at fixed exchange rates be guaranteed, thus preventing money market fluctuations distorting competition and intra-Community trade.

The authors of the Treaty were quite content initially to urge in general terms coordination of monetary policy "to the full extent needed for the functioning of the common market" with each member state undertaking to pursue the economic policy needed to ensure the equilibrium of its overall balance of payments and to maintain confidence in its currency, while taking care to ensure a high level of employment and a stable level of prices. In addition each member country was to regard its exchange rate policy "as a matter of common concern." It was only at the summit conferences of the Heads of State or of Government held in the Hague in December 1969, and in Paris in October 1972 that the objective of creating an economic and monetary union within ten years and also of striving to achieve European Union was discussed in concrete terms.

Growth and full employment

This major venture had, however, to be embarked on in the midst of a major crisis in the international monetary system by a Community that was also preparing for the accession of Denmark, the United Kingdom and Ireland. With little or no synchronisation of national economies and no Community exchange rate system to ensure monetary cohesion, the currencies of the nine member states making up the newly enlarged Community also diverged in the wake of the successive international monetary crises. Those states whose currencies were substantially revalued were compelled to adjust their economies to the higher rate, to neglect branches of the economy with lower value added and to undertake as much rationalisation as possible. As a result they now possess an efficient and modern industrial structure but for the time being there is a serious shortage of customers for their sophisticated products and services. The member states whose currencies lost ground during the international monetary crises found that, on an international comparison, they had become poorer in that they had to pay more for their imports and received less for their exports. Some of them found that they could no longer earn sufficient foreign exchange to purchase the tempting goods and services their partners had to sell. Consequently they were also unable to press ahead with investment and rationalisation schemes, having instead to tighten their belts even when their partners granted them credit. The result was that strong-currency and weak-currency countries hit the trough of the recession together. They have striven in vain – ever since to get their economies back on to a secure and steady growth basis.

For the surplus countries to help pull their partners out of the recession, they need to be able to count on sustained expansion in demand at least within a Community which at the same time is not continually being wrecked by monetary upheaval. Accordingly economic and monetary policies need to be worked out in common in order to achieve growth and stability within a wider economic framework than the purely national one. Because of the Community's substantial involvement in international trade, greater growth and stability within the Community would not only help its component member countries but would also benefit the rest of the world.

The existence of an economic and monetary union requires joint control of the money supply, that is to say of the bloodstream that feeds the circulatory flow of economic activity. It also implies joint management of the exchange rate which governs the competitiveness of Community exports and which in turn determines the Community's economic relations with the rest of the world. Were each member state to regulate its money supply as it saw fit, no common economic policy would be possible. The paths of the economies would be bound to diverge, and any common front shown towards the rest of the world would then certainly be more apparent than real.

Studies have shown that economic and monetary union in an

advanced phase would be viable in the Community with a budget of between 5 and 7 per cent of the combined national products and indeed in the pre-union phase with one of between 2 and 3 per cent of the aggregate. A budget of this size would provide sufficient resources to finance the transfers necessary to guarantee a more consistent development of economically backward regions and thus ensure more consistent development of economically backward regions and thus ensure more rapid growth for all. There would, moreover, be no need to pursue the ambitious objective of a federal state modelled on the United States, where, for historical reasons, many responsibilities have been centralised and the federal budget accounts for as much as 20 per cent of the national product. Clearly much would depend on the economically stronger member countries being willing to pay more into the common budget than they get out of it so as to assist the weaker members. The latter understandably are unlikely to be enthusiastic about a Community that lacks this kind of solidarity.

Strengthening the international monetary system

In its still incomplete form there is another field in which the European Community is failing to play the role that other industrialised countries and developing countries are entitled to expect of a grouping with such lofty political and economic objectives – that of external relations. The reform of the international monetary system still left the dollar as the sole world currency. Less than 4 per cent of the world's foreign exchange reserves are held in the form of the Special Drawing Right, the neutral and jointly administered world currency of the International Monetary Fund. However the dollar is no longer sufficiently strong to shoulder alone, on behalf of the rest of the world, the responsibilities associated with a key reserve currency in which all countries can safely denominate their assets. On the other hand the Community as a whole is big enough to create a second strong world currency that can help to underpin the international monetary system. The Nine constitute an entity that is of the optimum size advocated by economic theorists for a single currency area. Together the member states could develop into one of the major currency areas in a future world economic system that has a stronger regional bias.

If there were a strong well-managed reserve currency in Europe other than the dollar, industrialised countries, oil-exporting countries and developing countries would no longer need to fear the depreciation of their foreign exchange reserves. They would be able to choose the currency in which to hold their reserves and this would afford them a greater degree of certainty as regards the long-term planning of their development and investment programmes. Their orders would with greater regularity be channelled to the established industrialised countries. The United States and Europe would be compelled to manage their currencies properly since the other countries would have a choice of reliable reserve currencies, in contrast to the present system of narrow-biased national currencies. The policy of "benign neglect" of which the US monetary authorities have been accused in recent years as regards the dollar would no longer be conceivable. If the exchange rates of the major world currencies could no longer fluctuate as widely as they have done of late, this would create conditions much more favourable to long-term export business and investment decisions, thereby enhancing appreciably the prospects for continuing steady growth in a world economy free from the recessions suffered in the last few years.

Enlargement of the community

As more countries join the Community, the more difficult it will be to hold together a customs union that has not graduated to the status of an economic and monetary union. The Community, which has set itself the task of admitting as members in the first half of the decade three Southern European countries (Greece, Portugal and Spain), must take the equivalent leap forward towards a monetary union if enlargement is not to result in the achievements made so far being watered down or forfeited altogether. A currency mechanism attempting to equalise the daily fluctuations of twelve currencies would have little in common with a genuine customs union and would be virtually impossible to manage. The prospective member states hope to gain much from membership of the Community but their hopes are likely to be disappointed. In their own interests and in those of the existing member countries the prospective members must join a fully operational Community that has set itself definite objectives and gives the member countries definite objectives as well.

Barriers to the attainment of economic and monetary union

In its member states' interests and in the interests of the world economy, the Community must evolve into an economic and monetary union, but this cannot be imposed overnight. As past events have shown it cannot even be achieved by way of detailed stage-by-stage plans laid down in advance.

The governments and political parties of the member states still remain responsible for the formulation of national economic policies and remain answerable to their respective electorates for the consequences, especially if these include unemployment and inflation. Before they can transfer responsibility for economic and monetary policy to European-level bodies, governments must be certain that these bodies can and will discharge these responsibilities properly. The man in the street must know for certain that his democratic rights will be safeguarded at European level too.

For this reason, direct elections to the European Parliament and a European Monetary Union are conditional upon one another. An economic and monetary union comprising states grouped together on the basis of freedom is inconceivable in the absence of direct legitimacy conferred by a body having power of democratic control. On the other hand, a directly elected European Parliament would in the long term be relegated to a position of impotence if it has no scope for influencing the key issues of economic and monetary policy. This does not detract from the need for a European Central Bank that enjoys a sufficient degree of independence *vis-à-vis* the political authorities. The European Central Bank and the bodies responsible for economic policy must be established in such a way that they are able to operate at Community level as effectively as the most efficient national authorities.

Economic disparities

In addition to gradual development of democratic structures a further *sine qua non* for economic and monetary union is a basic consensus on the external and economic ends to be pursued and on the means to be employed for this purpose. Achieving such a consensus is not a straightforward matter in a Community which is marked by wide regional disparities as regards development, where member states have such different historical backgrounds and in which the role played by government in the economy also varies very widely from country to country. Recollecting the past, people in some countries take fright at the thought of unemployment while at the same time they take a dose of inflation fully in their stride. By contrast people in other countries are from experience allergic to a rate of inflation running at more than 3 to 4 per cent.

The countries that have already brought inflation under control are reluctant to enter into any commitments *vis-à-vis* the countries that are still fighting two-figure or high one-figure rates of inflation. Indeed they are anxious lest, as part of union, they should catch the same disease. By contrast the countries with high rates of inflation are afraid that they might be forced too abruptly into a stable-price Community within which they would have to sacrifice their growth prospects. Their fear is that a monetary union might dash their chances of catching up economically with other countries by imposing the same pace of development for all and thus freezing existing economic disparities. It is, however, common knowledge that high rates of inflation do not lend themselves to coordination. Nor are they – to say the least – conducive to steady growth in the long term. Therefore there must be no slackening in the successful efforts made in recent years to bring down the rates of inflation that got out of hand during the oil crisis. The higher rates must be slowly and cautiously eased back to the average level of inflation in the stability-conscious member states. Inflation rates can be aligned, but only downwards, on the rates recorded in the low-inflation countries. As a root cause of disease, inflation must like any other inflammation be attacked and cured without damaging healthy parts of the patient's body by unduly drastic action.

Once inflation has been contained and the conditions created for hastening balance of payments equilibrium, the achievement of more vigorous growth in the less developed countries will no longer be hampered by the fact that, after each promising upswing these countries have been obliged many times to take deflationary action.

Mr. Roy Jenkins, the past President of the European Commission, drew attention to the necessity of interrelationships when delivering the Jean Monnet lecture to the European University Institute in Florence in October 1977. However, it was only in the following year that his urgent appeal to member states' governments to set out with determination along the road to economic and monetary union met with a response. Economists who had been asked by the Commission in 1975 for their views on the obstacles to economic and monetary union laid the blame on the governments' lack of political will – like showjumpers, however, governments shy away from fences that seem too high for them. They were all the more cautious because of the failure of the first attempt made in the 1960s to achieve economic and monetary union by way of a stage-by-stage plan. While member states' economies could not be brought more closely into line and while growth and inflation rates diverged so widely, the governments would not attempt to clear the major fence in front of them. They were afraid that another refusal would pose a major threat to what had been achieved so far and could cost the Community a good deal of its credibility. Any new initiations contemplated by policy-makers on the monetary front require very careful preparation and adequate safeguards ensuring support and cooperation from the "real" economy. This is because nothing is more sensitive to inadequate improvisation than a currency. But in April 1978, with efforts to bring member states' inflation rates more closely into line beginning to produce effects, the President of the French Republic and the German Chancellor at the meeting of the European Council in Copenhagen put forward their own proposals for the establishment of a new European Monetary System (EMS) which would again embrace all member states and with each of them playing a full part.

Although the attempt to create an economic and monetary union by way of the ten-year plan ended in failure, it would be a mistake to belittle what had been achieved even prior to the launching of the European Monetary System. In the four strategic areas of

monetary policy
economic policy
building of a common capital market
tax harmonisation

substantial progress had already been made and important work carried out with a view to further development.

2. Steps towards an Integrated Monetary Policy

European exchange rate system

The Monetary Committee which was set up in 1959 and the Committee of Governors of the Central Banks which came into being in 1964 are the specialist bodies responsible for coordinating monetary policy within the Community. They are essential components of the first major attempt to create an economic and monetary union launched in 1969.

At the request of the member states' governments, a group of experts chaired by the then Luxembourg Prime Minister for Finance, Pierre Werner, produced in 1970 a stage by stage plan for economic and monetary union based on a blue-print previously drawn up by the European Commission. In March 1971, the governments adopted the main short-term proposals put forward by the group without, however, endorsing its more far-reaching longer-term political implications. The approach advocated in the Werner plan and in the two ensuing Council Resolutions dated March 1971 and March 1972 centred on the gradual reduction of exchange rate fluctuations between member states' currencies.

While the major world currencies were preparing in 1972/3 for the changeover to unrestricted floating, the member states of the Community were keen to limit the margin within which their currencies were allowed to deviate from one another to 2.25 per cent. The intention was to underpin monetary cohesion within the Community. The member states were to be given a yardstick against which they would be able to assess their economic policies.

A coordinated stabilisation policy was to be pursued to ensure that the margin of 2.25 per cent was observed against a background of a generalised floating of currencies. Provision was made for coordinated intervention to support currencies that were temporarily in danger of being unable to keep within the lower limit of the margin of fluctuation. The central bank of a country whose currency found itself in this precarious position was to sell other currencies and purchase its own currency on the foreign exchange markets in order to hold its rate steady. The central banks in the other member countries were also committed to purchasing the threatened currency in order to support it. In the normal course of events there was to be an unlimited obligation to intervene on the exchanges. The currency credits granted to the country with the threated currency by its partners were as a rule to be paid back within four to eight weeks – unless, that is, they were consolidated for longer periods under the support mechanism available. If the day-to-day fluctuations in the exchange rates of the currencies taking part in the Community exchange rate system are plotted on a graph, they produce a snake-like ribbon the width of which varies depending on the gap between the strongest and weakest currency. Hence the Community exchange rate system is referred to as "the snake".

In practice, however, not all the member states were able to line up the highly ambitious objective underlying the Community exchange rate system at a time of hectic fluctuation in the world's currencies, particularly the dollar. In the course of time the United Kingdom and Ireland (June 1972), Italy (February 1973), France (January 1974 and, after re-entering for a short while, again in March 1976) and the associated non-member countries Sweden (August 1977) and Norway (December 1978) withdrew from the snake. The member countries that belonged to the snake on the eve of the changeover to the EMS were the Federal Republic of Germany, Denmark, Belgium, the Netherlands and Luxembourg.

Despite all the monetary pressures it has encountered, the Community exchange rate system has not deviated from its objectives and has ensured that these will also be adhered to within the EMS. Admittedly the central rates of the currencies remaining in the snake have had to be adjusted on several occasions. The requirement that they must endeavour at all times to remain within the margin of fluctuation prescribed has been a great help to the countries participating in the system in their efforts to achieve their stabilisation goals. At the same time it has made for close economic policy coordination between the countries able to keep their exchange rates in step without unduly large adjustments. This has been particularly true of the Federal Republic of Germany and the Benelux countries.

Establishment of the main monetary cooperation mechanisms in the Community – including the European Monetary Cooperation Fund, the European Unit of Account and the monetary support mechanism – was attributable directly or indirectly or linked to the European Exchange rate system (the snake).

European Monetary Cooperation Fund

The European Monetary Cooperation Fund was set up in April 1973 and since then has been concerned primarily with managing the Community exchange rate system (the snake) and the Community's short-term monetary support mechanism. It is through the Fund and the currency credits made available by member states that currency support measures are settled.

Under the new European Monetary System (EMS) agreed in December 1978, the Fund will continue in the initial phase, to settle balances connected with intervention and short-term monetary support. In addition it will issue European Currency Units known as ECU against deposits by member states of a given proportion of their gold and foreign exchange reserves. After two years, it is to be gradually consolidated into a genuine European Monetary Fund which will manage part of member states' gold and foreign exchange reserves on behalf of the Community.

Short-term monetary support and medium-term financial assistance

Close cooperation between member states on the monetary policy front requires financing mechanisms that provide short-term support for action taken to maintain the cohesion of the European exchange rate system and that provide medium-term relief for member countries with balance of payments problems. At times of nervousness on foreign exchange markets the exchange rates of the member states' currencies can be kept within the desired narrow margin of fluctuation by intervention on the part of the monetary authorities. Under a system of short-term monetary support set in place as early as February 1970, the Central Banks grant one another three-month credits for the purpose of financing such support measures or helping member countries cope with temporary balance of payments deficits. These credits are renewable for a further three months.

A system of medium-term financial assistance under which foreign currency credits are granted to a country for a period of between two and five years to help it overcome balance of payments deficits was adopted in March 1971.

While short-term support is granted unconditionally, medium-term balance of payments assistance is conditional upon the recipient member state taking steps to tackle effectively the causes of its payments deficit. In December 1977, when the volume of credit available under this system was doubled, measures were also taken to ensure closer supervision of compliance with the economic policy conditions laid down in connection with the grant of credits. Credits are granted in instalments or *tranches* and the Council announces the release of each new *tranche* only after it has been shown that the debtor country has, in the preceding period, complied with the economic policy conditions set. This procedure is designed to foster the adjustment process in member states which, for balance of payments reasons, have sought assistance for their partners.

Member states have not the slightest intention of operating the two support mechanisms described above in isolation from the solidarity arrangements that have been made at international level whenever the Community's support mechanisms are to be used: account is taken of the forms of assistance that may be available from other sources – e.g., the International Monetary Fund. Member states' contributions to the Community support mechanisms is restricted to a specific amount. Each country is allocated quotas within which it can count on support (debtor quotas), or is itself required to provide support (credit quotas).

A further instrument for assisting countries in balance of payments difficulties was introduced in February 1975, when in the wake of the oil price increases, some member states were forced to run up substantial current account deficits. Acting on a proposal from the Commission, the Council of Ministers decided to authorise the issue of Community loans on the international financial markets. Italy and Ireland received additional balance of payments assistance financed out of the yield from these loans. The Commission has also requested authorisation from the Council to issue Community loans, the proceeds of which will be used to tide member countries over balance of payments difficulties even where these are no longer directly attributable to the oil price increases.

European unit of account

Since its inception the European Community has had to calculate member states' payments to the Community budget and their reciprocal commitments and obligations by reference to a unit of account. At the time when exchange rates between member states were fixed and based on a gold parity the unity of account could be expressed by an amount fixed once and for all in terms of national currencies. But once the leading industrialised countries decided to allow their exchange rates to fluctuate on a day-to-day basis the Community was compelled to devise a unit of account that took account of changes in the currencies' effective values.

Since 1975, therefore, the Community has been in the middle of switching from one financial unit for use in Community affairs, the old "unit of account" (UA) to the new European Unit of Account (EUA). The old unit of account had a gold-based value at pre-1971 parities, and it was necessary to move to a unit based on a more up-to-date and meaningful foundation. Under the new European Monetary System (EMS) agreed in December 1978, the EUA was renamed the ECU and assigned new functions. The name ECU goes back to the old gold and silver coins, the Ecu, that were in circulation in France for several hundred years.

Following the entry into force of the European Monetary System in 1979, the ECU/EUA is now used in all areas of Community activity without exceptions, the decision to apply the ECU provisionally in the common agricultural policy having been extended. The Community has thus returned to using a single unit of account after a period of several years during which units of account of very different kinds had existed at the same time. Since it was devised in 1975 the EUA has been phased into use in the various areas of Community activity.

1975 ACP–EEC Lomé Convention, balance sheet of the European Investment Bank
1976 ECSC operational budget
1978 General budget of the Communities
1979 Establishment of the EMS: custom matters: European Monetary Cooperation Fund: provisional introduction for three months into the common agricultural policy (EGU).

The EUA may also be used in the fields of banking and commerce and various banks offer arrangements for deposits denominated in EUA – annual interest rates on bank deposits.

Definition
The ECU is identical with the EUA though unlike the EUA it provides for a revisions clause enabling changes to be made to its composition. It is a "basket" unit made up of specific amounts of member states' currencies determined by reference to the size of each member state's economy.

The ECU, like the EUA, is made of the following amounts

Belgian franc	3.66
Danish krone	0.217
French franc	1.15
Deutschemark	0.828
Italian lira	109.00
Irish punt	0.00759
Luxembourg franc	0.14
Dutch guilder	0.286
Pound sterling	0.0885

The equivalent of the ECU/EUA in any currency is equal to the sum of the equivalents of the amounts making up the unit. It is calculated each day on the basis of representative rates for each Community currency against the dollar which is used as a common reference for expressing exchange rates.

The rates are established on each exchange market at 14.30 hours by the relevant central bank. On the basis of these rates the Commission establishes an ECU/EUA equivalent on the Community currencies and in the other major currencies. These equivalents are published each day in the *Official Journal of the European Communities* ("C" Edition) and may also be obtained from the Commission via the telex automatic answering service; they are also reported by the main European press agencies and are published in many newspapers. The ECU is discussed further on p. 114.

Value in National Currencies of one ECU/EUA

National Currency	*Rate at 31 October 1980*
Belgian franc and Luxembourg franc	41.0534
Danish krone	7.87681
French franc	5.90795
Deutschemark	2.56459
Italian lira	1213.74000
Irish punt	0.672290
Dutch guilder	2.77505
Pound sterling	0.558709

Although under the Common Agricultural Policy common support price levels for farm products are set throughout the Community in terms of units of account, the actual prices received by the farmers are calculated not by their national currencies' normal exchange relationships to the unit of account but by special exchange rates called the Green Currencies; so the farm prices received by farmers vary between countries when measured in normal exchange rate terms.

The Community possesses, in the shape of the EUA, a practical accounting instrument that enables it to evaluate member states' commitments and obligations according to their real value. Slowly but surely, use of the EUA as an accounting device is being extended to an increasing number of fields. Since 1975 it has been applied in connection with the European Development Fund, set up to assist the 53 African, Caribbean and Pacific (ACP) countries that are signatories with the Community to the Lomé Convention. The European Investment Bank in Luxembourg also uses the new unit for its balance sheet and for its loan operations. In 1978 the Community drew up its own budget for the first time in EUA.

Although at present the EUA is first and foremost an accounting instrument, the Commission maintains interest-bearing balances expressed in EUA in banks in several member states with a view to maintaining the value of its budget resources.

The EUA is not yet used as an instrument for effecting payments.

Coordination of economic policy

Although currencies and the exchange rates between them determine trade relationships they are necessarily in their turn a reflection of underlying economic realities. The Community endeavours to influence the exchange rates that obtain between member state currencies in such a way as to bring about a greater degree of convergence between national currencies. Thus monetary policy is not an end in itself but an instrument for working towards the real objective – closer alignment of national economies and removal of regional and structural disparities where the latter are incompatible with an economic union. To further this aim, the Commission began issuing annual economic policy recommendations to member states as early as the 1960s. Moreover, as from July 1969, a member state contemplating important short-term economic policy decisions or measures likely to have a substantial impact on the economies of other member countries or on the situation in the member state concerned has been required under a Council decision to hold prior consultations.

Since 1971 the Council has carried out a twice-yearly examination of the economic situation in the Community, based on communications from the Commission and has drawn up short-term economic policy guidelines to be observed by the Community and by each individual member state in the interests of harmonious economic development. Each year the Commission presents a report on the economic situation which is adopted by the Council and is intended as a guide for member states' economic and budgetary policy decisions.

In 1974 the objectives underlying economic policy convergence and the resulting economic policy requirements imposed on member states were given clearer shape in a basic directive on stability, growth and full employment and in a decision concerning the convergence of economic policies. To promote closer economic policy coordination a special Coordinating Group was set up within Council in 1972 which brings together Commission representatives and representatives of the competent ministry in each member state. Moreover, in 1974 the three separate committees responsible at the time for short-term economic policy, for medium-term economic policy and for budgetary policy were merged into a single committee with sub-committees with a view to promoting more effective coordination.

Despite these more sophisticated arrangements, the goal of improved coordination of economic policies could not be achieved during the troubled economic times that came in the wake of the oil crisis. Inflation got out of hand in 1974 and 1975 in several member states, and it was only during 1977 and 1978 that efforts made to narrow the span of inflation – which had ranged between 6 per cent and 25 per cent – were successful enough to halve this gap. In addition, reducing the current account disparities between the strong-currency and the weak-currency member countries is proving to be a laborious process and also a painful one in that it had to be launched in 1975 at a time of declining growth rates throughout the world and had to be supported in the ensuing years when economies were recovering only at a faltering pace.

Structural policy

(a) Medium-term programmes (covering five years)

From 1964 onwards the Community's medium-term and long-term economic policy objectives have been formulated by a Medium-term Economic Policy Committee and submitted by the Commission to the Council for approval in the form of programmes. The programmes have contained not only quantitative growth targets but also qualitative structural and social policy objectives.

This has been by no means a simple matter in a Community in which some member states placed their faith first and foremost in market forces whereas others advocated a greater degree of economic planning. Thanks to the medium-term programmes drawn up, economic forecasting techniques applied in member states have become more comparable. Indeed the planning work and the associated coordinating work have forged closer cross-frontier links between government departments and promoted mutual understanding of the different concepts and methods applied. By contrast, it has not been possible in all member states to put fully into practice at economic policy level the objectives laid down in the medium-term programmes, and as a result, these have been implemented only in piecemeal fashion.

(b) Regional and industrial policies

The major structural disparities between the national economies and the major regional development disparities within the individual member states can be remedied neither by a coordinated short-term economic policy nor by a medium-term programme alone. What is needed is a genuine transfer of resources from the richer to the poorer regions of the Community.

The key instrument for equalising regional disparities is intended to be the Regional Fund, which, however was only set up in 1974, and has since had to be content with an admittedly growing but as yet modest budget.

The Fund was allotted a budget of 1,500 million EUA in its first three years of activity from 1975 to 1977 and has a budget of 1,850 million EUA for its second three-year period of activity from 1978 to 1980. In the Fund's early years Community funds could normally be granted only in the form of back-up assistance for member states' existing national development programmes. It is only in the next few years that specific measures are to be taken at Community level to improve regional structures which take greater account than in the past of the Community's objectives and needs.

Industrial policy as well as regional policy has an important contribution to make to structural improvement. A common market signifies change and renovation. Industries that have found themselves isolated without a future behind national frontiers must adjust to a wider, unrestricted market and encouragement must be given to the creation of new, forward-looking industries and service branches. The Community must foster the continuing adjustment process without which uncompetitive industries would be kept artificially alive. The Community must, however, see to it that redundant workers are reabsorbed into the economic system with the help of the Social Fund and the provisions laid down in the Treaty establishing the European Coal and Steel Community. The Community has in fact already done a great deal to help redeploy hundreds of thousands of workers who had lost their jobs and has also helped to make life easier for workers retiring early.

(c) Financing intruments

Financing new jobs and promoting structural change requires large amounts of investment credits which in the normal cause of events are provided by existing financial institutions and the financial markets. The Community, however, must proffer its assistance and help finance the creation of new jobs at least in those areas where the Common Market is speeding up the pace of structural change and contributing to the more rapid closure of obsolete plant.

The European Investment Bank was set up in 1958 primarily with a view to helping to develop the Community's less favoured areas. It is designed as an instrument for financing plant modernisation or conversion schemes or job-creation schemes and for providing member states with financial assistance for joint projects of Community interest. Since its inception the EIB has granted credits of more than 10,000 million EUA and has in recent years stepped up its lending operations to an annual rate of around 1,500 million EUA.

Under the Treaty establishing the European Coal and Steel Community, which came into force in 1952, the then High Authority and the present Commission as its successor have made available to the coal and steel industry credits amounting to over 4,500 million EUA. The coal industry had to contend with major conversion difficulties in the early years, just as the steel industry also now faces a major over-capacity problem.

In 1976 the Council authorised the Commission to issue loans totalling 500 million EUA each year for the purpose of financing the construction of nuclear power stations and thereby going some way towards meeting the Community's future energy requirements.

In mid-1978 as its contribution towards combating economic stagnation and resolving the structural crises affecting several industrial sectors, the Council of Ministers authorised the Commission to float loans amounting to over 1,000 million EUA on the international financial markets. The European Investment Bank is responsible for managing the credit operations on behalf of and in connection with the Commission. This has provided the Community with a further – admittedly limited – source of funds to promote and facilitate structural change.

Through the Guidance and Guarantee Sections of the European Agricultural Fund the Commission each year allocates some 1,000 million EUA to improving agricultural structure. This makes it easier for farmers to change over to modern production methods and to the kind of high-value products for which they are ready markets.

Free movement of capital

There can be no economic and monetary union or common market without the free movement of capital, allowing investors to move funds at will to the places where the best yields are available. In a large free-enterprise economic entity with balanced structures maximum returns on investment should reflect maximum economic utility. The Community however still has a long way to go before it can be described as a common market with balanced structures. The countries with the weaker structures and currencies thus attempt to curb the outflow of domestic savings by imposing bans and controls on such movements of capital. Their currencies and economic prospects are not sufficiently sound and attractive to encourage an inflow of enough private capital from other member states. Since it has not been possible to bring economic structures more closely into line, the liberalisation of capital movements has also not proceeded much beyond the initial measures provided for in the two relative directives adopted in 1960 and 1962. Although these directives have facilitated trade between member states, cross-frontier payment of wages and salaries and of fees, cross-frontier payments effected in respect of services rendered and the granting of short-term and medium-term trade credits by prohibiting restrictions on such capital movements, the granting of financial credits for industrial investments, capital investments and cross-frontier dealing in quoted securities have still not been entirely liberalised.

Instead of forming a common capital market on which surplus savings in the richer countries and regions are transferred to the poorer countries and regions, national markets are still isolated from one another. As a result the so-called Euromarkets on which operations involving international foreign currency credits are transacted have become the main channel for capital movements. On these markets however, weak-currency countries have to borrow in hard currencies since their own vulnerable currencies are not acceptable to the market. Further progress towards liberalisation of capital movements will be achieved only gradually as progress is made in the other fields appertaining to economic and monetary union.

Tax harmonisation

In the field of tax harmonisation too there has really been one important milestone, namely the abolition of the cumulative turnover tax, the full burden of which fell on every product at every level of distribution and which served to restrict and distort most drastically not only free movement of goods but also competition. The cumulative turnover taxes have been replaced by value added tax systems in all member states. Value added tax (VAT) is levied at each distribution level only on the increase in value contributed at that level and the overall burden of taxation is no longer a function of the number of distribution levels a product passes through before reaching the ultimate consumer.

There are a large number of disparities as regards exemptions, reduced rates for essential goods and increased rates for luxury goods. These remaining disparities and the various excise duties, particularly on spirits, tobacco and oil, continue to hamper the free movement of goods. They are the cause of the queues of lorries one sees at the Community's internal frontiers and of the customs checks imposed on travellers, since these tax differentials must be accounted for at frontiers by tax funds in the exporting country and taxation in the importing country. For revenue purposes some member countries prefer to rely most on indirect taxes on consumption and apply correspondingly high VAT and excise duty rates, while others derive the bulk of their revenue from high direct taxes on income and wealth. These differences of emphasis are determined by deep-rooted historical and psychological considerations. They can be remedied only if economic structures are gradually brought more closely into line.

No action has yet been possible as regards harmonisation of direct taxes on companies, particularly corporation tax and depreciation rules. The Commission has had to concentrate first of all on those direct taxes that constitute substantial barriers to the free movement of capital and investment. For this reason it is focusing its efforts on abolishing forms of tax discrimination between parent companies and subsidiaries operating in different member countries, on the special form of withholding tax and on combating tax avoidance and evasion in so far as such efforts can assist in helping to complete a customs union which has still not been taken to the stage of economic and monetary union.

The new European Monetary System (EMS)

Return to monetary cohesion

Implementation of the stage-by-stage plan for creating an economic and monetary union out of the Community as it stands at present has not proved possible during the 1970s. The difficulties the individual member states have had to contend with have shown that economic and monetary union is now neither less important nor less essential than before. With half of their imports and exports coming from or going to their Community partners, and with their foreign trade accounting for one-quarter of the Community's national product, the member countries are already heavily dependent upon one another and the interpenetration of their economies is far advanced. The Community's internal trading area, the future of which is in our own hands, must now be made secure and the danger of a retreat into protectionism within Europe, which looms larger with every day of delay, removed once and for all.

The Community must return to a path of growth and price stability. Without stability member states will struggle along divergent paths as inflation increasingly undermines the prosperity of some of them without the others seeing any improvement in their situation. This is because without adequate growth the weak-currency countries are unable to purchase enough goods and services from their partners to prevent the mass of unemployed expanding throughout the Community. In recent years, time and time again, some member countries have had to cut back on the orders they placed with their partners because they were running out of the currency reserves needed to settle invoices. Workers in other member countries lost their jobs. Member countries could, simply by pooling part of their reserves, avert the most damaging consequences of permanent stop-go policies as a result of which several member countries are in effect having to live from hand to mouth.

The year 1977 brought a renewal of interest in the objective of economic and monetary union – an ambition which had appeared to have been shelved. Following the speech by Commission President Roy Jenkins in Florence, which was designed to remind member states' governments of the merits of a single currency, the Commission laid before the Council at the end of 1977 an action programme for the years ahead. This programme was aimed at steering the Community back on to a path of growth and stability – the prerequisites for any monetary union – by way of closer coordination of economic and monetary policies.

The year 1978 then saw the launching of a practical but limited initiative by the French President and German Chancellor to set up a European Monetary System. All three meetings of the European Council of Heads of State or Government held in 1978 were dominated by this subject. At the April meeting in Copenhagen, the plan was discussed for the first time. At the July meeting in Bremen basic features were approved and at the December meeting in Brussels, the resolution was adopted in which the Heads of State or Government of all nine countries expressed their support for the new system.

The new European Monetary System which came into force on the 13 March 1979 must not be confused with the projected economic and monetary union, let alone with a common currency. Its immediate limited objective is to create a zone of monetary stability in Europe by closer monetary policy cooperation. It will initially be used like the European exchange rate system as an instrument of combating excessive fluctuations in exchange rates and hence for reducing a factor of uncertainty in trade and payments between member states. In addition, through a more stable exchange rate policy it will endeavour to create room for an economic policy geared to achieving a greater measure of internal and external stability for both deficit and surplus countries.

The ECU as the pillar of the system

The system combines well-tried practices from the currency snake and a new ECU-based procedure for keeping currencies more closely in line than previously and for avoiding divergencies. The ECU which lies at the centre of the European Monetary System will be used as a denominator or *numéraire* for the exchange-rate mechanism, as the basis for a divergence indication, as the denominator for operations in the intervention and credit mechanisms and as a means of settlement between monetary authorities. It will thus become the new European Unit of Account, which is not yet a generally accepted means of payment but is intended to be used increasingly as a means of payment initially between member states' central banks and subsequently perhaps in connection with international capital movements.

The ECU is a basket of the member states' currencies, with the amount of each currency in the basket corresponding to the economic importance of the country in question. In this way the weight of each currency influences the value of the ECU basket, which is calculated each day by the Commission on the basis of quotations on the relevant national foreign exchange markets. As in the snake a grid of bilateral exchange rates has been established restricting the margin of fluctuation to 2.25 per cent either way. Only Italy opted to apply initially a wider margin of 6 per cent. When a currency is threatening to leave the grid as its exchange rate fluctuates by more than 2.25 per cent (or 6 per cent in the case of Italy), this currency must be supported through intervention, i.e., it must be bought by the central bank responsible for the currency which has risen to the upper limit of its margin.

In addition to the conventional policy of intervention, provision has also been made for preventative measures where a currency deviates unduly (by more than 75 per cent of its margin) from its average EUC rate. When this threshold of divergence is crossed the country concerned is expected to correct the situation by taking appropriate measures which can cover intervention in various currencies, domestic economic policy measures (e.g., in respect of interest rates), other economic measures (e.g., in the field of taxation or incomes policy) and lastly changes in the central rates themselves.

Changes in the central rate must not become the rule when a country experiences difficulties. Such changes should be carried out however where underlying economic circumstances have altered – they should not be delayed or ruled out for reasons of prestige.

The system will be reviewed at intervals. This is important because the United Kingdom has approved, and belongs to the new system, but declined to take part in the intervention mechanism from the start; it has, however, agreed to pursue an exchange policy which would assure the stability of the pound in relation to other Community currencies. The funds available for defensive action have been increased significantly under the new system. Moreover central banks' currency debts arising from intervention need now be settled only after 45 days rather than 30 days required before. At the same time short-term monetary support can now be extended for two further three-month periods instead of one, with the result that such support can now be granted for nine months in all. The amount available for short-term support has been increased to 14,000 million ECU and that for medium-term financial assistance granted for between two and five years to 11,000 million ECU. This means that the potential volume of credits available under the support mechanisms for defending currencies' central rates against speculation has been increased almost three-fold. It is now easier to repay currency credits, since all participating member states have agreed to deposit with the European Monetary Cooperation Fund, on loan, 20 per cent of their gold and 20 per cent of their dollar reserves and receive in return a corresponding amount of ECU. They can use the latter to repay 50 per cent of their debts while the remainder must be covered from national reserves.

The pooling of 20 per cent of member states' gold and dollar reserves is intended as an initial step towards a European Monetary Fund proper, to be set up two years after the establishment of the EMS. The reserves in this Fund, which remain the property of member states' central banks, are available to the Community without any restrictions for use as reserve assets and as a means of settlement. One part of the currency reserves is managed jointly; the Community will also have to pursue a common foreign exchange policy towards non-member countries' currencies, in particular the dollar. In this way ECU will gradually help the Community to play an enlarged role in the field of international monetary policy and in the world economy.

The time remaining before enlargement of the Community must be used to ensure that the Community in the 1980s not only becomes a geographically larger entity but is also strengthened internally. The Community must develop the structures that will permit it to pursue a short-term economic policy of its own and to combat both the present unwillingness to invest and the current level of unemployment. The rest of the world expects the Community to play an active part in helping the world economy to climb out of recession.

The system in operation – 12 months after

Initially the Danish crown and the Italian lira appeared to be relatively strong currencies. In the former case a combination of high interest rates and support for the Danish crown by the German Central Bank appeared to give the Danish currency some advantages over other currencies. In the case of the Italian lira the basic fluctuation of 6 per cent for the Italian currency – plus the improved Italian balance of payments – made the lira initially more attractive *vis-à-vis* other EEC currencies.

The Commission has individualised both the Maximum Divergence Spread and the Divergence Threshold *vis-à-vis* the ECU for each of the participating countries. It is possible that this action by the Commission has been to some degree responsible for the relative stability of the EMS during the first six months of the operation of the system. Nevertheless, on 23 September 1979 some technical adjustments were made to the parities of the participating currencies. The Council Resolution of the 5 December 1978 (Establishment of the European Monetary System and Related Matters) stated "The weights of currencies in the ECU will be re-examined and if necessary revised within six months of the entry into force of the system and thereafter every five years or on request if the weight of any currency has changed by 25 per cent."

The Commission gives external forces as being the real reasons for the changes. These forces, despite changes in American domestic monetary policies have included sales of dollars and purchases of deutschemarks on the international currency markets. Also the position of the pound sterling has caused some tensions within the EMS. Although the pound is one of the composite national currencies of the ECU, the UK was not a participant, but sterling's position as a component has caused problems for the system since at the beginning of the period the pound was tending to increase in value, both against the dollar as well as against other Western currencies, whilst at the end of the period the British currency was declining in value. The influence of both the dollar and the pound on the EMS underline two basic problems. These problems are outside influences and the composition of the ECU. The main outside influence at a strict monetary level would seem to be the position of the dollar since this is a currency of intervention. It seems, therefore, that this problem will remain both until American domestic policies begin to bite and some form of international funding operation is mounted to stabilise the dollar. In the latter case the EEC is likely to play a major role.

The problem of the composition of the ECU appears to imply that even if and when the UK should participate in the EMS, further individualisation by the Commission of Maximum Divergence Spreads and Divergence Thresholds *vis-à-vis* the ECU for participating currencies may be necessary. Even with such "individualisation" further coordination and/or convergence of the economic and monetary policies of the member states of the EEC will most probably be needed.

Individualisation of Maximum Divergence Spreads and Divergence Thresholds

Currencies	*Maximum Divergence Spread vis-à-vis the ECU* *per cent*	*Divergence Threshold vis-à-vis the ECU* *per cent*
Belgian/Luxembourg franc	2.03	1.52
Danish krone	2.18	1.64
French franc	1.80	1.35
German deutschemark	1.51	1.13
Italian lira	5.43	4.07
Irish punt	2.22	1.67
Dutch guilder	2.01	1.51
Pound sterling	—	—

The United Kingdom

The position of the United Kingdom is somewhat complex. Following the unhappy UK experience of her short-lived participation in the "snake" system in 1972, the UK has given the impression of viewing participation in the EMS with some degree of reserve. However, the Conservative Government elected in 1979 expressed interest in EMS, and in June 1979 it was stated that the UK would participate in the embryonic European Monetary Cooperation Fund. Shortly afterwards the UK exchanged 20 per cent of its reserves of dollars and gold against ECUs. However, a decision regarding the UK's participation in the EMS itself has been shelved.

Unless the pound sterling is relatively stable in the foreign exchange markets and until the UK rates of wage inflation *vis-à-vis* productivity increases and approaches those of other participants in the system, it would seem to be premature for the UK to participate. Unless the UK manages to satisfy these two requirements then she would have to take drastic economic and monetary measures should she wish to participate in the EMS. However, should the two criteria be met with, the UK's participation would further extend the existing zone of international monetary stability. Further, should it be necessary, the UK could, like Italy, request a 6 per cent margin of fluctuation for her currency, and would be eligible for receiving loans made on special conditions and interest rate subsidies of up to 3 per cent for these loans.

The European Monetary System is a complex one which presents a zone of monetary stability in a turbulent international monetary sea. It marks the first really serious effort at achieving an economic and monetary union through an attempt at coordination and/or convergence of the economic and monetary policies of the participating member states.

3. The European Investment Bank

The European Investment Bank (EIB) was created by the Treaty of Rome establishing the European Economic Community, which came into force on 1st January 1958. The Bank is an independent public institution within the Community and operates on a non-profit-making basis. Its essential function is to contribute to the balanced development of the Common Market.

For this purpose, it grants long-term loans or gives its guarantees to enterprises, public authorities and financial institutions to finance investments contributing to the solution of regional problems, promoting industrial conversion or the creation of new ventures, or serving the interests of several member states or the Community as a whole.

Organisation

The members of the EIB are the member states of the Community, who have each subscribed a specific share of the Bank's capital, which totals 3,543.75 million units of account. The Bank is directed and managed by a board of governors, a board of directors and a management committee. Accounts are submitted to an audit committee.

The board of governors consists of Ministers nominated by the member states, one for each country, usually the Minister of Finance. Its functions include the appointment of members of the board of directors, management committee and audit committee of the Bank, approval of the balance sheet and the annual report, and laying down general guidelines for the credit policy of the Bank.

The board of directors takes decisions in respect of granting loans and guarantees and raising loans. It fixes interest rates on loans and commission on guarantees. It sees that the Bank is properly managed in accordance with the provisions of the Treaty of Rome and the Statute and with the general directives laid down by the board of governors.

The management committee is responsible for the current business of the Bank; it prepares the decisions of the board of directors and ensures that these decisions are implemented.

The audit committee verifies annually that the operations of the Bank have been conducted and its books kept in a proper manner.

Projects financed by the EIB

Projects furthering the development of the common market

Article 130 of the Treaty of Rome prescribes that the purpose of finance provided by the European Investment Bank shall be to aid –

(1) projects for developing less developed regions;
(2) projects for modernising or converting undertakings or for developing fresh activities called for by the progressive establishment of the Common Market, and
(3) projects of common interest to several member states.

In practice, EIB financing in member countries may cover –

(1) projects in regions qualifying for support under national regional aid schemes, provided they contribute to the economic development of their region;
(2) projects involving the modernisation or conversion of enterprises, or the creation of new activities made necessary either by the structural difficulties affecting some sectors or by the presence of obsolescent, declining industries in certain regions (e.g., those beset by serious unemployment stemming either from the state of the market or from failure to keep abreast of technology, such as the textiles, iron and steel or shipbuilding industries), or
(3) projects of common interest to several member states or the Community as a whole, either because they serve the purposes of European economic integration (communications infrastructure – roads, railways, inland waterways and telecommunications, improving intra-Community relations, and projects involving close technical and economic co-operation between companies from different member countries) or because they pursue the implementation of Community policies or the realisation of common aims (e.g., protection of the environment and advanced technology, especially in the energy supply sector – nuclear power stations, gas-lines, development of oil and natural gas deposits, energy-saving installations).

Projects within the community

To qualify for finance, projects should normally be implemented in the European territories of the member states (or be registered in the member states in the case of transport projects).

If, however, its board of governors unanimously so agrees, the Bank may, under its Statute, provide finance for projects located outside the Community, a faculty it has for the most part exercised in favour of projects of common interest (e.g., projects in the oil and natural gas sectors) and operations under association or co-operation agreements between the Community and various non-member countries.

Fixed investments

In pursuit of the aims already described, the Bank provides credit for planned investment projects, financing the fixed investments and similar elements of fully specified projects pursuing a definite objective and capable of being carried through within a set period of time. It does not advance funds to meet the general cash requirements of companies or public undertakings nor for the acquisition of intangible assets or securities.

Projects for all sectors of the economy

The Bank finances public infrastructure and investment projects in the various sectors of production, not only industrial but also agricultural development and projects in the services sector.

These include buildings and installations for industry and mining, transport infrastructure, telecommunications, energy production and transmission facilities, transport equipment, irrigation schemes, water supply and treatment plants, effluent disposal and the provision of industrial zones, vocational training centres and housing as adjuncts to investment projects in production sectors.

The Bank may lend only for projects that make a direct or indirect contribution to improving economic productivity in general, always looking closely at the economic justification of projects and in particular their impact on employment.

Where projects are mounted by firms operating in the production sector, debt-servicing payments must be met out of operating profts. With other types of project, e.g., infrastructures showing an indirect or long-term return, debt-servicing payments may be covered by an undertaking on the part of the government on whose territory the project is located, or the equivalent, in which case the overriding consideration is the general economic benefits offered by the project.

Borrowing from the EIB

Enterprises

Private or public enterprises can obtain loans from the European Investment Bank regardless of their legal status, provided that their projects conform with the above criteria.

The Bank does not make the granting of its loan dependent on the nationality of the borrower. Not only enterprises in member countries, but also enterprises from other countries or their subsidiaries may obtain funds from the Bank.

Public authorities
The Bank can also lend to states and financially autonomous public authorities (e.g., German Länder, French departments and Italian regions).

It does not make loans for local authority services such as health, welfare or urban roads.

Financial institutions
(a) The European Investment Bank may grant *indirect loans* through the intermediary of banks or financial institutions in support of projects which comply with the above-mentioned criteria. The intermediary then becomes the contractual borrower.
(b) The indirect lending technique has made great strides where *global loans* have been granted for financing *small and medium-scale ventures*. These loans are granted to banks or financial institutions and the proceeds on-lent as suggested by the intermediary and with EIB approval for financing economically beneficial ventures meeting the Bank's criteria, but of too small a scale to allow of an individual loan operation.

Allocations from global loans are reserved for small and medium-scale ventures, the amount of each sub-loan ranging in practice between 50,000 and 4 million units of account, while the investments it goes to finance may not exceed a total cost of 12 million EUA.

Types of loans obtainable from the EIB

Amount of loans
Although it has not laid down any absolute minimum figure, the European Investment Bank generally prefers to make individual loans of not less than 1 million EUA per project. As already explained, it may also provide finance for smaller ventures through the global loan system.

Bank funding for a given project should not normally exceed the equivalent of 80 million EUA, although for certain major projects of common interest mounted by a number of promoters a series of loans, for a higher aggregate total, may be granted.

The Bank's loans cover only part of the cost of projects, supplementing the borrower's own funds and other sources of finance. The amount of the loan is determined in each individual case, after appraisal of the financing plan. The Bank rarely lends more than 50 per cent of the cost of the fixed assets involved.

Currencies
The Bank's loans are usually disbursed in several currencies (those of the member states of the European Community and others, in particular the US dollar). The Bank selects its currencies of disburse-

ment according to its holdings at the time and after consulting borrowers as to their preferences, although where transfer of the funds is to take place shortly after conclusion of the contract the actual currencies of disbursement are agreed before signature.

Interest rates

As the European Investment Bank finances its loans mainly by borrowing on the capital markets inside and outside the Community and operates on a non-profit-making basis, rates of interest on its loans approximate closely to the cost of its borrowings on the markets.

These rates are set periodically by the Bank for each of the currencies in which it disburses loans to its borrowers, to take account of the cost of its resources.

The Bank's rates are in no way determined by the type of project financed, its location or the status of the borrower. The rate charged on each loan is generally established at the date of signature of the contract and is not subject to revision. Loans are paid out at par, so that the borrower receives the whole nominal amount of the loan. The rate of interest applying to loans disbursed in several currencies is equal to the average rate fixed by the Bank for each of the currencies of disbursement, weighted to take account of the proportion of each payment made in each currency and also, where appropriate, of differences in the time allotted for repayment of each currency.

Repayment of loan: grace period

Repayment of principal can be deferred to start from the time when the project reaches completion and comes on stream, normally a period of between two and four years. Thereafter, the loan is generally reimbursed in equal six-monthly instalments covering both principal and interest, payments in respect of which must be made by the borrower in the currencies originally received.

In certain cases and where its resources allow, the Bank may consider granting loans repayable in full at term.

Security

Like any forward lender whose resources consist of funds borrowed on the market, the Bank must have appropriate security for its loans. It requires its borrowers to provide customary banking security, preferably a guarantee from the state in whose territory the project is being carried out, a public authority with first-class credit standing, a major bank, or a major industrial or financial group associated with the project. Charges on specific assets, sufficiently liquid to cover the balance outstanding at any time, may also be accepted in certain cases.

Use of loans

The currencies disbursed by the Bank may be used for payments in any country subject to such restrictions as may apply in the borrower's country. The Bank requires that orders, supply contracts and works relating to projects which it helps to finance be open as far as possible to international competition, including at least the member countries of the European Economic Community.

The EIB as guarantor

The European Investment Bank can also help to finance projects which comply with its eligibility criteria by guaranteeing loans contracted directly by enterprises or public authorities with financial institutions or on the market.

The information given in the preceding pages applies *mutatis mutandis* to the guarantees given by the European Investment Bank. In return for its guarantee, the Bank requires that its risks be covered by the customary security and a small commission.

Approaching the EIB

Initial approaches may be quite informal. Any enterprise, authority or financial institution wishing to contact the European Investment Bank (in any of the Community languages) should telephone, telex or write directly to the Head Office:

2, place de Metz – Bôite Postale 2005,
Luxembourg.
Tel. 435011 – Telex 3530 bankeu lu

or to its Office for Operations in Italy:

Via Sardegna, 38,
1-00187 Rome.
Tel. 483651 – Telex 62130 bankeuro.

Contact with the EIB may also be made through the promoter's banker.

Documentary material to be supplied

After initial contact and confirmation that the project seems likely to prove eligible, and that the current EIB terms are likely to be acceptable, the applicant should provide the Bank with documentary material. This need not follow any standard form but should contain the usual information on the activities and financial situation of the borrower. In particular, it should offer a description of the investment project to be financed: nature and cost (including working capital requirements, if any), financing plan, utilisation programme, employment to be created/safeguarded and economic benefits offered by the project with respect to the financing criteria mentioned above. The documentary material should also include the most recent annual reports, with balance sheets and profit and loss accounts and cash-flow forecasts, assessments of prospective markets and the likely return on the project. Finally, it should specify the amount and the term of the loan sought and the security proposed.

All these points may be presented in summary form. They will be dealt with in greater detail subsequently, when the Bank comes to appraise the application, assuming that the initial information provided justifies investigation in depth.

The Bank's appraisal

The aim of the Bank's appraisal is to ensure –

(1) that all projects conform with the Bank's lending criteria, are technically viable, offer economic benefits and comply with national and Community legislation;

(2) that projects promoted by enterprises in production sectors are backed by financially sound borrowers whose financing plans ensure that implementation of the projected investments will not jeopardise their financial stability, and whose debt servicing payments will be covered out of operating profits;

(3) that other projects (infrastructural works showing an indirect or long-term return carried out by a public agency or the concessionnaire of a public authority) are accompanied by assurances that servicing of the debt will be backed by a government guarantee or the equivalent.

This appraisal is carried out in contact with the borrower by the Department of Operations in the Community assisted by technical advisers specialising in the various sectors and by economists and lawyers, all of whom are members of the Bank's staff.

The granting of a loan is submitted for an opinion to the state in whose territory the project is carried out and to the Commission of the European Communities. The Bank asks directly for these opinions without the borrower having to intervene. This procedure, like the other stages of the appraisal, is naturally covered by strict rules of banking secrecy.

Applications for loans are submitted to the board of directors which meets regularly, at least six times a year. Once the approval of the board of directors has been given, a finance contract is drawn up in compliance with the national law applicable, in an agreed form, and signed.

4. The EEC Savings Bank Group

Savings Banks Group of the European Community,
92-94 Square E Plasky BTE 1,
B.1040 Brussels.

The EEC Savings Banks Group was set up in 1963, and the subsequent years of collaboration between associations has developed from modest beginnings into its present position, where it is recognised by the European Communities as the spokesman for the EEC savings banks. The present-day role which it has adopted as the spokesman for more than 137 million savers who have entrusted their savings deposits to its over 1,500 member institutions has transformed the EEC Savings Banks Group into a "lobby for the saver," a title which it in no way regards as degrading, but on the contrary as a title of honour and a commitment. Europe – and also the Europe of the savings banks – does in effect become a reality through the extension of Community Law.

In general the EEC Savings Banks Group made its appearance unnoticed through the back door in a series of small steps. In the first years of its existence from 1963 to 1967, the EEC Savings Banks Group was not "an association of associations" but to a large extent an information and representation office. At the time one of its main tasks was the provision of information on the European Communities and on the savings banks in neighbouring countries. The foundation of the association work of the EEC Savings Bank Group was laid between 1967 and 1970 (in 1967 the Savings Banks Group was set up under Royal Decree under Belgian Law) as this was the time when step-by-step plans for economic and monetary union and for the attainment of a European capital market were being discussed and work began on coordinating banking access and supervisory provisions in the EEC.

The EEC Savings Banks Group has taken over a special role in Brussels to correspond to the way in which its sees the challenge to the savings banks in the EEC; it has also developed a working style to exploit this role to its best advantage. For the past five years, for instance, this has included the division of the internal information service into two areas: technical documentation, and the provision of information to the savings banks about the credit sector of the EEC.

Dr. Klaus Meyer Horn who has been Secretary-General of the EEC Savings Banks Group from the very beginning, maintains rightly that it is part of the social responsibility of the savings banks to look after and advise workers and families on money matters. In the dual role as spokesman for the savings banks and the saver the opinions of the association are paid particular attention by the Commission, because unlike those of several other associations the Group does not reflect a restricted sectoral point of view but takes the interests of the general public into account.

One of the difficulties is the fact that the business structures of the savings banks are still different, and consequently they are not all affected in the same way by the proposals of the EEC Commission nor by the access to the common banking market. EEC rules on export credits, interest subsidies for agricultural credit, or municipal loans secured by mortgages in other countries do not affect the savings banks which do not – or do not yet – carry out such transactions.

One of the special characteristics arises from the fact that the membership circle of the EEC Savings Banks Group is formed from the national savings bank organisations, rather than from the individual savings banks. The EEC Savings Banks Group has a General Assembly – composed of 58 delegates from nine countries – a board of administration composed of two members from each country, and nine advisory committees in whose work over two hundred experts from the savings banks organisations of the nine countries participate. All of the working papers, minutes of meetings and reports are produced in at least three languages at the group, and some publications are published in five languages.

The Community imposes a challenge, because 140 million customers of the savings banks in the EEC expect a uniform business policy and it is only by collaboration across national frontiers that the savings banks will be in a position to meet the requirements of their customers, with a network of over 34,000 branches and a balance sheet total of 160,000 million pounds.

CHAPTER 5

THE COMMUNITY BUDGET

1. Introduction

Every spring in Brussels and Luxembourg the various institutions of the European Community prepare their estimates for the succeeding year. Those of the Commission cover the costs of Community policies, agriculture, regional and social spending, industrial and energy policies and aid to developing countries. The budgets of the other institutions – the Parliament, the Council of Ministers, the Court of Justice and the Court of Auditors – are largely administrative, the money needed for salaries, publications and administration.

By early summer all these estimates of expenditures, and of the revenues needed to finance them, are published by the Commission. This is known as the first draft of the European Community Budget. The Community's year runs from January to December. The first draft of the budget, therefore, is only the first stage in a process of political and economic decision-making which continues until mid-December. Only on the 1st January following does the budget come into effect.

A balanced budget

In the modern national economy, the aim of continuously balancing the budget is no longer a dominant objective of fiscal policy. Moreover, financing public expenditure is only one of the criteria involved.

As important in the modern national economy is whether the budget is to be "reflationary" (i.e., revenue to be less than expenditure) or "deflationary" (i.e., revenue to be more than expenditure), and how much the government thinks it can finance out of borrowing.

By contrast, the Community budget is "balanced:" expenditure and revenue must always come to the same total. The Treaties envisage neither deficit financing (a "reflationary" budget), nor the piling up of unspent revenues (a "deflationary" budget). If it turns out that there is not enough money to meet expenditure, a supplementary budget has to be introduced.

The Community budget is therefore presented primarily in terms of expenditure. It follows automatically that revenue will be raised to finance all those items of spending which are eventually approved.

The size of the budget

The 1978 Community budget came to 12,362 million EUA. In terms of total public finance it is equivalent to about 2.5 per cent of the combined national budgets of the Nine. It corresponds to 0.8 per cent of total Community production (GDP). Of course, such fields as defence, education and social security, which make up the bulk of national budgetary expenditures, are wholly or almost entirely excluded from the Community budget.

It would be a mistake to think, however, that the budget itself is the only area of public finance affected by the activities of the Community. In some spheres the full impact of the Community policy is reflected, not in the Community's own budget, but in the budgets of the nine separate member states themselves. This is the case where the Community coordinates national policies (for example, in the field of coal and steel), or where schemes are jointly financed by Community and national funds (for example, in the field of industrial re-training).

About three-quarters of the Community budget is accounted for by the Common Agricultural Policy: furthermore, the determining factor in relation to most of this spending is not so much the budget itself as the level of agricultural prices guaranteed to Community farmers at the Spring Price Review. Partly for this reason, agricultural price guarantees are classified as "compulsory" – they arise necessarily out of a policy which has to be carried out under the Treaties, as described later in this chapter. The rest of the Community Budget is divided between social spending, financing the regional fund, research, energy, industry and transport, aid to developing countries, staff and administration. Community staff totals some 15,000 persons, a substantial number of these being linguistic staff.

Main elements of expenditure in 1978 budget, adopted by European Parliament on 15 December 1977 (in EUA)

Sector	*Appropriations*	%
Agriculture	9,131,743,000	73.87
Social Sector	559,107,000	4.52
Regional Sector	525,000,000	4.25
Research, Energy, Industry and Transport	294,255,303	2.38
Development co-operation	380,942,000	3.08
Staff	387,433,000	3.13
Administrative expenditure	105,740,200	0.86
Information	13,018,000	0.11
Aids and Subsidies	45,308,100	0.37
Miscellaneous	694,600,000	5.61
Other Institutions	224,857,289	1.82
Total	12,362,003,892	100.00

Breakdown by Institution

Institution	*Appropriations*	*%*
European Parliament	100,424,612	0.8
Council	97,117,002	0.8
Commission	12,137,147,303	98.2
Court of Justice	17,332,920	0.1
Court of Auditors	9,982,055	0.1
Total	12,362,003,892	100.0

2. Revenue

Own resources revenue

The first Community budgets were those of the European Coal and Steel Community (ECSC) established under the Treaty of Paris in 1951. Under this Treaty the ECSC was self-financing: the High Authority was empowered "to procure the funds it required to carry out its tasks by imposing levies on the production of coal and steel and by contracting loans." This remains the position with regard to ECSC expenditure today. The EEC and Euratom Treaties of 1957 (the Treaties of Rome), however, contained different financial arrangements. Once the amount of spending was established the costs were shared out amongst the member states on the basis of national quotas (under EEC Article 200 and Euratom Article 172, Germany, France and Italy paid 28 per cent each, Belgium and the Netherlands 7.9 per cent and Luxembourg 0.2 per cent). During the 1960s moves were made to establish total financial autonomy for the Community, and agreement was eventually reached in April 1970: instead of relying on money transferred from national budgets, the Community was to have its "own resources" – revenue which was automatically at the Community's disposal irrespective of where it was levied.

A ceiling on expenditure

One of the fundamental changes arising from the transition to complete financing of the EEC from "own resources" is that the Community is gradually bringing expenditure into line with revenue. This was not the case as long as the member states were under a virtually unlimited obligation to provide funds to fill the financial gaps remaining beyond the proceeds from customs duties and levies which they handed over to the Community. Only since 1970 has this obligation been restricted by complicated rules whereby financial contributions could change only within relatively narrow margins. In theory since 1978 and in practice since 1979 expenditure passing through the Community Budget can be drawn solely from the available proceeds from customs duties, levies and VAT.

The Commission commented in its three-year financial forecast for 1978, 1979 and 1980 (Annex to Volume 7 of the 1978 Preliminary Draft Budget) that "since the maximum VAT assessment basis was set up at 1.0 per cent there would be a surplus of about 3,400 million EUA above expenditure for 1979 and 4,000 million EUA left over for 1980." These figures give a rough idea of how expenditure can be increased further and how, therefore, Community policies can be extended.

A document drawn up by the German Ministry of Financial Affairs in April 1978 states that "the financial autonomy granted to the Community by the ratified Council Decision of 1970 means that the Community must match its budgetary requirements to its own resources." The consequent volume of revenue would not be static; rather would this arrangement enable the Community to extend its financial activities each year in step with economic growth.

Value added tax as a source of community funds

Only the VAT component of own resources is "dynamic". It alone is a true function of growth since, regardless of the (varying) VAT rates in the member states, VAT revenues rise along with the nominal increase in turnover.

This does not, however, apply to customs duties and levies.

Revenue from customs duties

In recent years customs duties have increased very regularly by an average of 10 per cent. Nevertheless, the abolition of customs duties between the six original member states and the three new member states acceding in 1973 (who were granted the benefit of transitional periods) and between the Nine and the EFTA countries could have a very clear impact – i.e., could slow down the increase in revenue from customs duties. To this must be added the tariff reductions under arrangements with other countries. The Commission estimates that the resultant drop in revenue from customs duties could nevertheless be compensated by the real and nominal growth in imports.

Structure of EEC Revenue in 1978

	%
Customs duties	39.53
Agricultural levies	13.79
Sugar levies	3.08
	56.40
Financial contributions	43.60
12,226,300,000,000 EUA =	100.00

The effects of further tariff reductions under the GATT Tokyo Round, cannot be assessed until the multinational negotiations have been concluded. Provision has, however, been made for a tariff-cutting plan extending over eight years.

Agricultural and sugar levies

Revenue from agricultural levies is considerably less predictable. The amount depends on the common threshold prices, the level of imports from non-member countries, world market prices and currency fluctuations against the representative ("green") rates applied to agriculture. Roughly 70 per cent of levies are derived from grain, 45 per cent of which consists of maize. Owing to a number of uncertain factors the prediction of revenue from levies can only be incomplete; theoretical and actual values differ by up to 20 per cent. Unlike customs duties, agricultural levies cannot be regarded as a relatively stable form of own resources for the Community. Between 1968 and 1974, for instance, they fluctuated between 810 million EUA and 211 million EUA and rose again to 1,066 million EUA in 1976.

Sugar levies – a further source of rvenue for the Community – greatly depend on the decisions reached by the Council of Agricultural Ministers. The levy paid by the undertakings is used to finance the refunds associated with the sale of sugar on the world market (production levy) and to finance the storage costs aimed at maintaining a regular flow of sugar to the market (storage cost levy). Roughly 63 per cent of all levies are assigned to Germany and France.

Miscellaneous revenue

To the sum of revenue shown in the table (12,226.3 million EUA) which constitutes 98.9 per cent of total revenue, are added the tax yield from salaries, wages and other deductions from staff remunerations (72.1 million EUA) and staff contributions to the pension scheme (24.3 million EUA) plus various receipts bringing total revenue for the 1978 Budget to 12,362,003,892 EUA.

3. Budgetary Institutions

The Treaties of Paris and Rome which established the ECSC, the EEC and Euratom gave the European Parliament (described in the Treaties as "the Assembly") the right to be consulted on budgetary matters. On ECSC spending, the last word resided with the High Authority (now the Commission). On EEC and Euratom spending the Council of Ministers had the last word.

The move to "own resources," however, implied a change in this distribution of power. The taxation financing the Community Budget was no longer to be paid through the separate national budgets, but was automatically to become Community revenue. In consequence, the national parliaments were to lose part of their power to tax.

Such a loss of parliamentary control at national level could only be justified if it could be restored at Community level. When, therefore, agreement on "own resources" was at last reached in 1970, it was accompanied by an agreement to increase the budgetary powers of the European Parliament. The changes were incorporated in the Treaty of 21 April and the decision of 22 April 1970.

The intention in these measures was to introduce the new system in two stages. During the period 1970–75, when only the customs duty and levy part of "own resources" had been introduced, the 1970 revision of EEC Treaty Article 203 gave the Parliament additional, if limited, new powers. The second stage was supposed to run from 1975, with the remaining contributions from national budgets being replaced by the 1 per cent VAT.

However, 1975 came without the vital agreement on the VAT base. This did not materialise, in fact, until the following year; it was then expected that the system would be in effect from the beginning of 1978. This time, it was the failure of national parliaments – in fact, all except Britain and Belgium – to adopt the necessary measures which held up full introduction of "own resources" for at least one more year.

Meanwhile, however, a new Treaty – that of 22 July 1975 – increased the budgetary powers of the Parliament still further. Parliament's right to reject the budget was recognised; powers to amend the budget were increased, and Parliament acquired the last word in completing the audit procedure. It also provided for a new Court of Auditors to be set up to assist Parliament in its control work.

The Budgetary Authority

These changes to the Treaties have resulted in budgetary powers being shared by two Community institutions, the European Parliament and the Council: together they are called the Budgetary Authority.

The Committee on Budgets

Throughout the budgetary procedure, the principal Parliamentary body involved is the Committee on Budgets. This is one of the

Parliament's twelve specialised committees, and currently consists of 35 Members, selected in such a way that each of the political groups and each of the nine member states is represented. It has its own permanent secretariat of European Parliament officials.

This committee has three broad functions:

(1) On the budget itself, it is the committee with primary responsibility for producing the draft reports for debate by the full Parliament. Each of the other committees produces opinions in its own field of competence which are taken into account by the Committee of Budgets.
(2) Through its Control sub-committee it examines the accounts of the Community, and prepares the annual decision on the discharge to the various Community institutions with respect to their expenditure in previous years.
(3) As well as examining the budget itself, the Committee examines *all* proposals made by the Commission which have financial consequences. Usually the Committee draws up an opinion which is sent to whichever specialist committee is considering the substance of the proposal.

The Budget Council

On the Council side, the main body involved is the Budget Council. This consists of the nine ministers from the separate national governments with particular responsibility for Community finance.

This Budget Council is chaired by a "President-in-Office:" the Minister from the country which at that time holds the Council presidency. This presidency changes every six months – countries take it in turns by alphabetical order (in the languages of the countries themselves).

Within the structure of the Council there is a Budgetary Committee (*not* to be confused with the Committee on Budgets of the Parliament). This consists of officials, mostly drawn from the nine national Treasuries or Ministries of Finance.

4. The Budgetary Procedure

The best way to understand how the European Parliament's budgetary powers work in practice is to follow, in detail, how the Community Budget is established. The procedure is complex and is indeed still evolving steadily. There are also several "grey areas" where the precise competences of the different institutions are still in dispute.

Preparatory steps

The first stage is the preparation by all the Community's institutions and services of draft estimates for the next financial year. This takes place in the opening months of the preceding year. All these estimates are collated into the "preliminary draft budget," by the Commissioner responsible, and are discussed by the Commission as a whole.

Meanwhile the Council holds a special meeting with both the Finance Ministers and the Foreign Ministers present. The objective is not, at this stage to put a ceiling on the budget, but rather to establish priorities and examine the technical problems of the budgetary procedure itself.

Following this meeting, the President of the Council of Ministers attends a meeting of the Parliament's Committee on Budgets to report on the Council's thinking.

In March the Committee on Budgets appoints a "rapporteur" for the next year's budget, with the role of drawing up and presenting the Committee's reports on the subject and suggesting suitable amendments, drawing together the various opinions of committees, political groups and outside bodies. The objective is to reach a consensus – to find a common Parliament view. Also in March, the Commission sends Parliament a "communication" on general policy guidelines for the budget. The rapporteur then drafts a report on the document and presents it for debate by the full Parliament in April or May. The report will indicate Parliament's own priorities for spending as well as recommendations on procedure. Also during the Spring the Commission notifies the other institutions of the *maximum rate* for the increase in non-compulsory expenditure.

"Compulsory" and "non-compulsory" expenditure

The expenditure side of the Community Budget is divided into *compulsory* and *non-compulsory* spending. On this distinction turns much of Parliament's budgetary power.

Compulsory expenditure is that which arises directly from the Treaty or from Acts adopted by virtue of it. A clear and undisputed example of this kind of spending is the Guarantee section of the European Agricultural Guidance and Guarantee Fund (EAGGF). The purpose of this Fund and the Common Agricultural Policy are laid down in the Treaties. The Regulations drawn up on the basis of the Treaty, and setting up common market organisations for certain sectors (beef, veal, milk, etc.,) envisage Community intervention automatically under certain price conditions. Therefore, the amount of expenditure is a consequence of the regulations themselves and of factors (harvests, climate, world prices) outside the control of the institutions. Compulsory spending, subject to some relatively minor disagreement about classification, amounts to approximately three-quarters of the budget.

Non-compulsory expenditure refers to the rest: mostly finance for policies adopted in accordance with Article 235 of the EEC Treaty (i.e., new policies, not already laid down in it). The precise definition of non-compulsory expenditure is vague, as is the method of resolving disputes between the institutions as to the appropriate classification. The Belgian delegation, which held the presidency of the Council during the budgetary procedure of 1970, published the so-called Harmel list[1] which sought to name all the items to be included as non-compulsory expenditure. Since then, various other attempts have been made to define the distinction. The Commission provides a proposed breakdown line-by-line in the preliminary draft each year.

In practice, there is broad agreement between the Council and Parliament as to the classification of expenditure. Appropriations for social policy, energy and research, administration, industrial and transport policy are all, by common agreement, classified as non-compulsory. Parliament, supported by the Commission, contended that the Regional Fund set up in 1975 was non-compulsory: at the time, the Council argued that, because the three-year endowment had been fixed by a European Council,[2] the expenditure was compulsory by nature.

Following a preliminary conciliation meeting in April 1975 between Council and Parliament, an "agreement to disagree" was reached as far as the first three-year endowment was concerned. However, it was agreed that Regional Fund expenditure from 1977 onwards was to be classified as non-compulsory.

In general, however, Parliament and its Committee on Budgets have sought to move the institutions away from technical disputes over the meaning of and distinction between compulsory and non-compulsory expenditures. In Parliament's view, the Council and Parliament should try to make a general agreement on the shape of the budget, and only use their respective powers to overrule each other in cases of conflict.

Issues still unresolved

Most of the remaining points of dispute relate, in effect, to "financial cooperation" expenditure – that is, expenditure to cover the costs of the financial cooperation agreements with third countries: for

1. After the name of the then President of the Council.
2. At the meeting of the Heads of Government in Paris 9–10 December 1974, it was decided that they should meet accompanied by the Ministers of Foreign Affairs three times a year: these meetings are known as the European Council (*see* p.40).

example, the Maghreb and Mashrak groups. This part of the budget – a growing part – is considered compulsory by the Council and by the Commission because of the international agreements involved. Parliament maintains that the expenditure does not arise directly from the Treaty, and therefore cannot be considered compulsory or automatic. Despite these differences, no important conflict has arisen on this complex issue of classification since 1975 – both sides preferring a pragmatic approach.

Practical significance

What is the significance of the distinction between the two types of expenditure and how does the maximum rate affect the budgetary powers of the Parliament? The reason for the controversy over what might seem to be abstruse technical details lies in the fact that the Treaties give Parliament far greater powers over non-compulsory expenditure than over compulsory expenditure.

For compulsory expenditure, Parliament can propose "modifications" to the Council. If these involve an increase they have to be *positively* accepted by the Council, acting by a qualified majority. If they involve no increase or a decrease they are accepted, unless rejected by a qualified majority in the Council.

For non-compulsory expenditure, Parliament has the last word over the individual items. Even if the Council rejects or modifies Parliament's amendments, these can be re-tabled and, provided they obtain a three-fifths majority with at least half the members voting in favour, the budget is accordingly amended – either increased or decreased.

The maximum rate

The maximum rate refers to the amount by which, in principle, the non-compulsory items in the budget can be increased in any one year over the previous year's level. It is based on three factors:

(1) the rate of growth of Community production (GNP);
(2) the trend of member states' own budgets, and
(3) the Community rate of inflation.

Going on data for previous years, the Commission calculated an overall percentage rate: in recent years it has fluctuated between 10 per cent and 15 per cent (thus broadly reflecting the average Community rate of inflation).

The size of the maximum rate can clearly have an effect on the balance of the budget. If it is set at a rate which will result in non-compulsory expenditure rising more slowly than compulsory, the proportion accounted for by agriculture will rise; if it increases faster, the agricultural proportion will fall.

Both the Council and Parliament can propose increases in non-compulsory expenditure. If the maximum rate, for example, were 10 per cent and the non-compulsory total for the previous year were 2,000 million EUA, the two institutions could, in principle, increase the non-compulsory expenditure by 200 million EUA between them. The position is not quite as simple as this, however. It has been generally agreed that Parliament has the right, irrespective of action by the Council, to increase non-compulsory spending by half the maximum rate (i.e., in the example above by 100 million EUA): in this event, however, the Council is not limited to only 100 million in its turn – it can still go up to the whole 200 million EUA.

In these circumstances the maximum rate is not really the true maximum. The true maximum is the "maximum rate × 1½ (i.e., in the example above, 300 million EUA).

Even more complicated is the position if the Council does *not* increase non-compulsory spending by even half the maximum rate. In this case can Parliament take over some of the Council's slice? For example, if Council's increase comes to only 50 million EUA, can Parliament go up to 150 million EUA – and what happens if the Council actually proposes a decrease of, say, 100 million EUA? Can Parliament then make up the reduction and add on top the full maximum i.e., vote for 300 million more than the Council?

In neither of these cases is the situation entirely clear. Parliament has taken the view that on top of its own automatic half of the maximum rate, it can indeed take over any unused slice of the Council's half.

All these limitations can, in practice, be overcome if Parliament and the Council are in agreement. The maximum rate can be increased provided Parliament votes to do so by a three-fifths majority, and Council by a qualified majority.

The draft budget

The preliminary draft budget prepared by the Commission is presented to Parliament. Grouped together in seven volumes are the estimates of each institution, as well as the staff plans of subsidised organisations. Against any item where there is a change over the previous year there is an explanatory statement.

A full debate on the preliminary draft is held at Parliament's July sitting. Almost simultaneously the Commission draft is sent to the

Council which starts work immediately on the draft budget. This work takes place in three stages.

(1) The Budgetary Committee of the Council draws up an interim report where a certain number of minor and technical points are usually agreed.
(2) This report is examined by the Committee of Permanent Representatives (COREPER) where most of the routine matters are decided.
(3) All unresolved questions are dealt with at the Budget Council of Ministers.

The Commission is represented at all these meetings.

During this procedure the first formal contacts are made between Council and Parliament (the procedure for cooperation between Council and Parliament is set out in an exchange of letters between the two Presidents and the two institutions dated November 1971). A delegation from Parliament, composed of its President and representatives of the Committee on Budgets, discuss the evolving budget with the Budget Council, which then draws up the Draft Budget, which is transmitted by Council to Parliament before the end of August – Parliament's Committee on Budgets and its rapporteur then begin work on the preparation of the draft amendments and modifications.

While the Committee on Budgets is examining the budget as a whole, other Parliament committees will be examining in detail those aspects relating to their special field of competence. These are the "spending committees," e.g., regional policy (Committee on Regional Policy, Regional Planning and Transport) or social spending (the Committee on Social Affairs, Employment and Education). Each of these will appoint a rapporteur of its own – actually called a "draftsman," since the document produced is an "opinion" rather than a full report.

The Committee on Budgets' meeting in October is devoted to a detailed examination of the draft budget. All the draft amendments at this stage are discussed and voted on. Amendments (called modifications where they apply to compulsory expenditure) can be tabled by –

(1) the Committee on Budgets;
(2) other committees;
(3) any of the political groups, or
(4) any five Members of Parliament.

In addition the opinions (i.e., reports) of the spending committees are taken into account – these committees' draftsmen attend the meeting. Also present are the President-in-Office of the Budget Council (i.e., the Budget Minister of the country currently in the chair) and the Budget Commissioner, who take full part in the meeting.

The result of this meeting is the report of the Committee on Budgets. This consists of a resolution which sets out the main political observations, and the bulk of the report itself, which includes a considerable amount of explanatory material. It includes an opinion on the amendments and modifications to the draft budget which have been examined by the Committee as well as those amendments which it has adopted itself.

This meeting of the Committee is generally a marathon – in 1977 it had to consider three hundred amendments. It may extend over several days.

Parliament's "first reading" of the budget takes place at a special sitting of the House at the beginning of the last full week in October. The exact format of this session tends to vary, one of the main considerations being the availability of the President-in-Office of the Budgets Council. The main elements, however, do not vary.

Firstly, the report of the Committee on Budgets is presented to the House by the rapporteur. There follows a two-day debate, which includes speeches by the "spending committee" draftsmen; spokesmen for each of the political groups and the independents, and other Members. Both the Budget Commissioner and the President-in-Office of the Council reply to the debate.

The political groups usually meet to table last-minute amendments, which are examined by the Committee on Budgets on the second day.

On the third day, the Committee on Budget's rapporteur presents an oral supplementary report. There then follows the lengthy procedure of voting on all the amendments and modifications, both those with the approval of the Committee, and those which have not been accepted by the Committee, but which groups and other committees or Members wish to press all the same.

The rules for voting are different depending on whether the amendments are in respect of compulsory or non-compulsory expenditure.

Non-compulsory items. For amendments to non-compulsory items to be adopted it is necessary for them to obtain not merely a majority of those voting but a majority of all Parliament's members – i.e., 206 or more since the 1979 direct elections.

Compulsory items. For amendments to compulsory items only an absolute majority of those voting is needed. At this stage it is easier for Parliament to amend agricultural spending than other items.

Finally Parliament votes by simple majority on the resolution contained in the Committee on Budgets' report, and all adopted amendments and modifications together with this resolution are sent to the Council.

Final examination and voting

At the beginning of November the Council of Budget Ministers begins its second (and final) examination of the budget. This takes place in four stages:

(1) The Budgetary Committee examines Parliament's amendments and modifications.
(2) COREPER does the same.
(3) At a meeting of the Budget Council in mid-November an exchange of views takes place with a delegation from the Parliament. This meeting can be resumed after further Council examination.
(4) The Council reaches its final decisions on the budget.

Parliament's Committee on Budgets meets at the end of November to examine the Council's decisions. On the basis of a proposal by the rapporteur it can then decide to re-table certain amendments to non-compulsory expenditure.

At the same time the spending committees also meet and may re-table their amendments, as also can the political groups.

The Committee on Budgets meets again at the beginning of December. It decides its attitude to the other committees' amendments, and may also adopt, on a provisional basis, a resolution and report for debate by the next full sitting of Parliament. On the Thursday of the December sitting a vote is taken on all amendments on the Committee on Budgets' Report and on the budget itself.

For any amendment to be adopted it must receive *(a)* the votes of a majority of Parliament's members (206 or more since direct elections) and *(b)* three-fifths of the votes cast.

As each amendment comes up, the rapporteur gives a brief recommendation as to how the House should vote. Finally comes the vote on the budget as a whole.

Rejection of the budget

At this stage, Parliament has the ability to exercise one of its two fundamental powers: to "refuse supply" by rejecting the budget *as a whole*. (The other fundamental power is to sack the Commission *as a whole*.)

Under the conditions of the 22 July 1975 Treaty, Parliament rejects the budget *(a)* if a majority of its Members (i.e., 206 or more) vote against, and *(b)* if it does so on the basis of a stated reason or reasons. This is to prevent a situation in which a budget could be rejected by a coalition of totally divergent interests: for example, one group voting against because agricultural spending was too high, another because it was not big enough.

If either of these conditions is unfulfilled, the budget is declared adopted (i.e., the budget is adopted even if the vote in Parliament is, for example, 50 in favour, 90 against).

If the budget is actually rejected, it is probable that the new financial year will begin, on 1 January, without any expenditure having been authorised. In this event, the "system of twelfths" is introduced to cover immediate expenditure. A sum equal to one-twelfth of the preceding year's expenditure can be spent in each month for any chapter or item of the budget.

Meanwhile, the Commission begins the preparation of a new draft budget, and the procedure begins again (though probably at an accelerated pace).

Raising the maximum rate

It is always possible – and, indeed, according to the record likely – that the increases in non-compulsory expenditure agreed by the Council and Parliament will exceed the maximum rate notified by the Commission at the beginning of the budgetary procedure. In this event, the maximum rate itself has to be raised.

This can be done *(a)* if the Council votes to do so by a qualified majority, and *(b)* if Parliament votes to do so by a majority of its members and three-fifths of the votes cast.

It seems unlikely that either institution would reject an increase in the maximum rate made necessary by increases in spending which both have agreed.

The financial regulations

Anyone not accustomed to the complexities of the Community Budget is likely to be puzzled by a number of features. First many items will have entered against them two figures:

(1) Payment Appropriation, and
(2) Commitment Appropriation.

Other items will appear to have no actual sums of money against them at all – only the expression "Token Entry".

The details of the budget cannot be fully understood without reference to the Financial Regulation. The Financial Regulation is a document which is provided for in Article 209 of the EEC Treaty. It lays down the rules for the preparation of the budget, its presentation, implementation, auditing and control. It describes in broad terms what the layout of the budget should be. Furthermore it spells out the procedure for the closing of accounts, the making of cash advances, and the implementing of appropriations – in fact, it conditions the whole budgetary procedure.

Commitment appropriations are the sums of money *voted* to cover the legal obligations entered into in that financial year. This makes it possible to sign contracts for long-term projects, some of the spending under which will arise in future years, e.g., research projects.

Payment appropriations cover the sums of money which will actually be spent in the financial year. The corresponding commitments will partly be those in the same budget, but also, of course, commitments from previous years' budgets which now come up for actual payment.

Parliament's budgetary powers are similar in relation to both commitments and payments: for example, there is a maximum rate in relation to each. As far as revenue is concerned it is clear that only payments need to be covered for the budget to balance.

Carry-overs. When the financial year ends it is possible that certain appropriations voted by the Budgetary Authority have not been spent. The procedures for dealing with these unspent sums are described in Article 6 of the Financial Regulation.

Structure of the Budget. The way in which the budget is to be presented is dealt with in Articles 11 to 16 of the Financial Regulation. Article 15 provides for separate sections of the budget dealing with the respective revenues and expenditures of the Parliament, the Council, the Commission, the Court of Justice and the Court of Auditors. The budgets of most subsidiary bodies are contained in the Commission section. The budget of the Economic and Social Committee, however, is to be found within the Council section – it is to the Council that ECOSOC has to submit its budget at the beginning of the year before it goes to the Commission.

Nomenclature. Article 15 also deals with budgetary nomenclature. The budget as a whole is broken down into items each of which can be the subject of a separate vote. These items are grouped under "titles," "chapters" and "articles."

Token entries. When the Budgetary Authority wishes to indicate the intention to undertake a particular activity as soon as possible, but at the time of drawing up the budget is unable to estimate the level of expenditure, a separate item is included in the budget without any actual sum being allocated to it. This is a token entry. This does not necessarily mean that nothing can be spent on the activity during the year: sums can in fact be allocated later in the year either through transfers or supplementary budgets.

Transfers. When the budget is adopted it contains the best estimates available at the time of the costs of the various policies. However, as the year progresses changes may have to be made. In these circumstances Article 21 makes it possible to transfer appropriations from one line to another.

Supplementary budgets

Article 1 makes provision for supplementing or amending budgets to be proposed by the Commission, in the event of unavoidable, exceptional, or unforeseen circumstances.

The detailed arrangements contained in the Financial Regulation for the handling of carry-overs and transfers, however, do not solve one major budgetary problem: how far does the inclusion of a line on the budget oblige the Commission actually to spend the money? The problem can arise in two forms, one purely technical, the other fundamentally political. In the first case the Commission can fail to spend money duly included in the budget – because for instance, applications for aid under the Regional Fund have not been processed fast enough. In the second case an appropriation can remain unspent because the Council has failed to adopt the legislative instrument under which the expenditure is to be incurred.

A situation of this kind places the Commission in something of a dilemma. As a general rule – for example in the energy and industrial sections – the Commission has been unwilling to spend money for which no legislative (as opposed to budgetary) basis exists. In one notable case, however (aid to non-associated developing countries in the 1976 budget) – the Commission spent the money despite the failure of the Council to adopt the relevant overall regulation. It is now suggested that where disagreement arises as to whether the Commission should implement a budgetary line in the absence of a separate legislative basis the conciliation procedure should be activated.

The conciliation procedure

Conciliation is one of the more institutional developments within the European Community of recent years. It was brought into existence by joint declaration of the Community institutions on 4 March 1975 and by a change of Parliament's own Rules of Procedure on 16 December 1976.

The conciliation procedure can be activated by either side. It takes place in a committee formed especially on each occasion, consisting of the nine ministers from the relevant Council and a delegation of nine from the European Parliament. On the Parliament's side the rules call for a delegation having a balanced representation of political tendencies and including the relevant committee chairman and rapporteur. A three-month time limit is set for agreement to be reached, though a lesser period can be fixed in cases of urgency. The final decision of course, is still reached according to the provisions of the Treaty. In effect, however the procedure gives Parliament a suspensive veto for a certain period.

The steps in the procedure are as follows.

(1) The Commission makes a proposal with budgetary consequences, indicating that this can be the subject of conciliation if necessary.
(2) Council asks Parliament for its opinion.
(3) The relevant Parliament committee prepares its report. The Committee on Budgets, if not principally concerned, will give its opinion on the financial implications. This is approved by Parliament as a whole, which sends it in the form of a resolution (i.e., opinion) to the Council.
(4) Council rejects the whole or part of Parliament's proposals.
(5) Either Council asks Parliament whether it wishes to activate the conciliation procedure, or Parliament itself asks for conciliation.
(6) Parliament appoints a delegation consisting of, for example, the Parliament's President, the Chairman of the Committee, the Committee's rapporteur and the spokesmen for each political group.
(7) Meetings are held between this delegation and the nine appropriate Ministers on the Conciliation Committee.
(8) Before three months (or any shorter time period) are up, outline agreement is reached.
(9) This agreement is incorporated in a new report from the Committee which is adopted in the form of a new resolution by Parliament as a whole.
(10) This new opinion is accepted by the Council which takes the final decision on implementation.

One example of how the conciliation procedure has worked in practice is provided by the revision of the Financial Regulation during 1977. The previous Regulation had been adopted by the Council in April 1973. Various developments (in particular the Treaty changes of July 1975) made a revision necessary, and at the request of Parliament the Commission put forward 89 proposed amendments on 19 May 1976. These were examined by Parliament's Committee on Budgets, which rejected or altered some of them, and proposed 42 amendments of its own. The Committee report was voted through Parliament in December 1976, and virtually all Parliament's changes were accepted by the Commission. The document was then sent to the Council of Ministers.

After examination the Council adopted a common position on the Regulation, and this was found to be unsatisfactory by Parliament's Committee on Budgets. To avoid a major confrontation between the two parts of the Budgetary Authority, the conciliation procedure was invoked.

Parliament approved the results of the conciliation on 13 December 1977 and the new Financial Regulation was adopted by the Council on 21 December 1977.

Summary of budgetary procedure

	Key events in the budgetary procedure	*Statutory dates (Article 203 and Financial Regulation) amended by inter-institutional agreements 1976 onwards*
I	*Preparatory stage*	*January – April*
	1. Commission's communications on global budgetary problems	Before April (Council resolution of 1975)
	2. Joint Council consideration of Commission's document	Not specified (but usually takes place during early April)
	3. Parliamentary guidelines – plenary debates	Not specified (but usually in the April or May part session)
	4. Council/Committee on Budgets discussion of guidelines (presence of President-in-Office)	Not specified (but usually takes place in April)
II	*Preliminary draft budget*	*May – July*
	5. Information by the Commission to Council and Parliament on the maximum rate	Before 1st March (inter-institutional agreement)
	6. Transmission to the Commission of the draft estimates of the different institutions	15 May, but 20 June for European Parliament
	7. Public presentation of the preliminary draft budget to Committee on Budgets	Not envisaged (but usually takes place towards the end of May
	8. Transmission of the preliminary draft budget by the Commission to Council and Parliament	Before 1 July
	9. Internal Parliamentary consideration of preliminary draft	Not specified (but, in practice during June)
	10. Presentation of the preliminary draft budget to Parliament with debate	June or July part-session
	11. Meeting of Parliamentary delegation with Council prior to establishment of draft budget	Before 10 September

III	*Draft budget*	*July – September*
12.	Establishment of the draft budget by Council	Before 10 September
13.	Transmission of the draft budget by Council to Parliament	10 September
14.	Presentation of the draft in plenary session of European Parliament and debate	September part-session
15.	Internal Parliamentary consideration of draft budget	Not specified (but, in practice, takes place during September/October)
IV	*Possibly, letter of amendment*	*September – October*
16.	Deadline for Commission transmission to the Council of letter of amendment to the preliminary draft	30 days before the first reading of the draft budget by the European Parliament
17.	Deadline for transmission of letter of amendment to the draft budget to the European Parliament	15 days before the first reading of the draft budget by the European Parliament
	Parliament	
V	*The draft budget amended by Parliament*	*October – November*
18.	Transmission to the Council of the draft budget amended and modified by Parliament	28 October
19.	Meeting between Council and Parliamentary delegation on Parliament's amendments to the budget	Before 20 November
20.	Council deliberation on the draft budget as amended by Parliament	29 October – 20 November
21.	Transmission by Council to Parliament of the budget modified by Council following the reading by Parliament	23 November
VI	*Second reading of the draft budget by Parliament and adoption of budget*	*November – December*
22.		Not specified (but, in practice, is completed in the December part-session)

5. The 1979 Budgetary Procedure

Preparation of policy guidelines

In the March and April part sessions, the European Parliament adopted its guide-lines for the budgetary and financial priorities of the Communities in 1979 and called for a major increase in the budget as necessary to transform the Community's economic and social influence into reality; in particular it high-lighted the need for a major increase in the Regional Fund, placing special emphasis on structural policy.

The Commission submitted to Parliament and Council a communication containing a global appraisal of the budgetary problems of the Community in March. This document was examined by a joint meeting of the finance and foreign ministers of the Community whose President, Mr K.B. Anderson, reported to the Committee on Budgets and Parliament in April.

The budgetary procedure begins

On 20 June 1978, the Commissioner responsible for the budget presented the preliminary draft to the Committee on Budgets. The formal presentation to the plenary session of Parliament took place on 3 July 1978. This preliminary draft was judged not to be a significant step towards the achievement of the priorities established by Parliament. Above all, Parliament was disappointed that the Commission had provided for no increase in the Regional Fund beyond the figures put forward by the European Council in December 1977.

A delegation from the European Parliament met Council on 18 July 1978. This delegation informed Council that Parliament did not consider it appropriate that the 1979 budget should be one of "austerity." Several national delegations reacted favourably to the position of Parliament. However, in drawing up its draft budget, the Council reduced the provision for appropriations to a level below that proposed in the preliminary draft budget and reduced payment appropriations to a level lower than that in the 1978 budget.

Parliament's first reading

The various parliamentary committees then considered the draft budget as well as the draft letter of amendment, submitted by the Council on 9 October, which concerned almost exclusively agricultural spending.

The Committee on Budgets, in the presence of the representatives of the Commission and Council, met several times in September and October to examine the draft amendments and proposed modifications, and at its meeting on 16 and 17 October 1978 adopted a report drawn up by the rapporteur from the 1979 budget, Mr Martin Bangemann.

He then reported to Parliament in budgetary plenary session which took place on 23–25 October and at which a large number of amendments were adopted. In summary, Parliament increased the draft of the Council by 847 million EUA as regards payments and 2,308 million EUA as regards commitments. The largest single item within this increase was accounted for by two amendments for the Regional Fund, increasing commitments from 620 million EUA to 1,100 million EUA and payments from 320 million EUA to 553 million EUA. Other amendments increasing energy, development and social spending, and providing special reserves – both for general purposes and for the consequence of enlargement – were also adopted. The Budget thus amended was transmitted to Council which, at its meeting of 20 November 1978, made further changes.

Closing stages of the procedure

At this meeting, Council accepted amendments adopted by Parliament to the value of 322 million EUA in payments and 628 million EUA in commitments.

The major amendment of a somewhat controversial nature which Council accepted concerned the Regional Fund: here, whilst it is understood that some members of the Council were not favourably disposed, the Council did not find the qualified majority necessary under Article 203 of the Treaty to reject this amendment. Other amendments accepted increased the provisions for the energy and social sectors.

Council contended that, even though it had accepted the Regional Fund amendment, this would require a new agreement between the institutions on setting a higher maximum rate for increase in non-compulsory expenditure. Parliamentarians, however, maintained that, under the Treaty itself, such an agreement was implicit in the formal decisions on the specific amendments.

The Committee on Budgets had a meeting subsequently and, in examining other amendments which had *not* been accepted by Council, decided to re-table a considerable amount to restore appropriations in the social, industrial and development sectors, as well as for extra staff needed to implement new policies and to conduct audit work. However, when the December plenary met to adopt these amendments, the necessary majority for them was narrowly missed, a sufficient minority believing that the budget, as amended by Council on 20 November, should be adopted without any change, so that there would be no political or legal uncertainty in proceeding to a definite adoption of the budget. The adoption of the 1979 budget was formally declared by the President of Parliament on 14 December.

Various comments on the position were made by Ministers in certain member states, and Council left the door open for possible further discussions.

Following the adoption of the budget, it therefore became incumbent on the Commission to implement the budget and all the indications are that it will discharge its responsibilities in this matter. Moreover, the institutions will have an opportunity for discussions in the future, as the Commission will present a supplementary budget in early 1979 to restore some of the essential items lost because of the votes of Parliament on 14 December which resulted in not changing Council's budgetary decisions of 20 November in any way.

Influence of the European Parliament on the procedure

The 1979 budgetary procedure represents a new development consistent with the traditions that have built up since the coming into effect of the 1970 Treaty. Each year, Parliament has sought to give to the budget, and through it to the Community, a greater capability for economic and social intervention. All the institutions are constrained by the terms of Article 203 of the Treaty. For example, more than a clear majority of members of Parliament is necessary to restore amendments in the last stage of the procedure. Similarly, by analogy, more than a straight majority – a qualified majority – is necessary for Council to reject Parliament's amendments to non-compulsory expenditure when it modifies the amended budget in November. Nonetheless, the terms of the Article give to both institutions a reasonable degree of influence over the development of budgetary policy.

By concentrating on the Regional Fund as the priority for 1979, the European Parliament was able, following strictly the provisions of Article 203, to increase this Fund by nearly 100 per cent in relation to both the preliminary and draft budgets and to the 1978 budget. In other words, through the normal exercise of its budgetary powers, Parliament was able to increase the effectiveness and scope of a major instrument of Community policy, despite the reluctance of both the Commission and Council. This responsible act does not represent an increase in Parliament's powers, merely a rational application of existing Treaty provisions. These powers are severely limited because they require the mobilisation of a very broadly-based political will within the institution. Furthermore, they require Parliament to concentrate its efforts on one, or maybe two, key priorities if a major qualitative change is to be achieved.

6. The 1980 Budget

By rejecting the 1980 Budget on 13 December 1979 the European Parliament created an unprecedented situation. The Rome Treaty makes provision for such an eventuality by allowing a monthly appropriation equivalent to one-twelfth of the previous years (1979) budget for current payments.

Parliament objected to the budget on three main grounds –

(1) lack of action to control agricultural expenditure;
(2) reductions which it considered unjustifiable in non-obligatory expenditure covering regional and social policies, energy, help to industry and research;
(3) failure to indicate in the budget the cost of aid to developing countries and of the Community's lending and borrowing transactions.

The budget was eventual approved.

7. United Kingdom – Contribution Adjustments

At its meeting on 29–30 May 1980, the Council of Ministers agreed a three-year formula for reducing Britain's contribution to the Community budget. The formula is in two parts: adaption of the financial mechanism adopted in Dublin in 1975 to limit gross contributions, and supplementary measures for extra Community spending in the UK. Reimbursements from these two sources are expected to total £1,577 million for 1980 and 1981.

	Estimated £M	*Reduced* £M	*Difference* £M
1980	1,088	371	717
1981	1,305	445	860
Total	2,393	816	1,577

Supplementary measures should take the form of investment expenditure in the United Kingdom designed to contribute to improvement in its economic performance. Nearly half would come through the amended financial mechanism, with the balance from the special measures.

The revised financial mechanism

The financial mechanism, adopted in 1975, was basically concerned with gross contributions to the Community budget rather than net contributions. According to present criteria governing the mechanism, the UK would be eligible for reimbursements of only £114 million in 1980. In accordance with the Council formula of May 29–30, the Commission has proposed amending the mechanism so that in 1980 this sum could be raised to £285 million, assuming estimated payment is based on this year's new budget proposals.

The main changes involved are the abolition of the tranche system of payments, and the deletion of limitations on reimbursement because of balance of payments surplus, or a ceiling of 250 million EUA, £152 million, or 3 per cent of budget expenditure whichever is the less.

Instead the Commission proposes a safeguard (unlikely to be reached in the foreseeable future) that reimbursement must in no case exceed the smaller of the following amounts –

(1) net payments from the member country during the current financial year, exluding payments made under the new Regulation, but including monetary compensatory amounts (MCA);
(2) contributions to own resources from VAT (i.e., payments made to the Community after deduction of customs duties and agricultural levies).

The Commission also proposes some technical amendments to Regulation 1172/76 relating to the currency rate of the EUA, and substitutes the term "gross domestic product," the latter a concept no longer used in statistical and economic analysis. The statistics to be used for calculations will be the most recent ones compiled by the Community Statistical Office.

Supplementary measures
The Commission notes that the Community aim is for a "convergence of the economies" of the member countries. The Community can best help, therefore by strengthening British economic potential through investment in areas hit by industrial decline, and by exploitation of coal resources. This would involve a rolling programme to which the Community could contribute up to 70 per cent of the cost of approved schemes.

The Commission emphasises that any such investment must be consistent with the Community's existing policies for economic development.

Projects eligible for assistance could cover a wide range:

(1) economic and social development in transport and communications, telecommunications, transmission of energy, water and sewerage, advance factories and public housing;
(2) urban renewal programmes;
(3) investment concerned with exploitation of coal resources.

Help for infrastructure development would normally be confined to assisted areas and must be consistent with Regional Development Fund programmes, though exceptions might be made in special circumstances outside these regions.

The UK would submit the appropriate programmes to the Commission; when approved each special programme would be published in the Community Offical Journal, and the UK would be expected to give suitable publicity to the Community contribution.

Financing

Once approved the Commission would make an advance payment of 90 per cent of the amount of the Community share of the cost, and the balance would be paid as soon as the work is certified as finished.

Normally credits would be entered in the Community budget of the year following the year to which they apply. But, subject to Council agreement, if the UK so requests, implementation of the supplementary measures may be credited in advance, with consequent financial benefit. When the Regulation enters into force it will be applicable retrospectively from 1 January 1980.

8. The 1981 Budget Proposals

The budget was prepared so that when the farm ministers met in the spring of 1981 they would do so with their heads firmly pressed against the VAT ceiling, the present limits of the Community's own resources.

If they did that, and if they perceived a real need to spend more money on some agricultural purposes, then they would have to make a corresponding economy in some other agricultural sector, and that is a state of affairs that the Commission has always wished to see (European Democratic Group spokesman). This view has now emerged as a consensus view of Parliament.

The implications are clear: the Community's own resources are rapidly becoming exhausted. Only a small fraction of the 1% VAT rate now remains unused and this could well prove insufficient during 1981. From 1975 to 1979 Community revenue (customs duties, levies and VAT) increased at an annual rate of 12.5%, but in the same period agricultural market guarantee expenditure increased from about £2,800 M (equivalent) in 1975 to £6,500 M, an average annual increase of 23%, or nearly twice the rate for total revenue.

In 1981 available revenue was to total about £13,000 M (equivalent). The Commission in drawing up the preliminary draft budget for 1981 allowed £346 M for contingencies, including the 1981 agricultural price review, harvest uncertainties and other measures.

The time when the Community could spend its way out of politically embarrassing decisions has come to an end.

The table below compares the level of spending proposed by the Council for 1981 with spending planned by the Commission and with the previous year's Budget. Figures are for payment appropriations (i.e. money actually paid or to be paid during the year). Figures are given in Sterling calculated at the rate of 1 EUA = £0.62935. Major items of expenditure are also given as a percentage of the total budget.

The EEC Budget for 1981

	Final Budget for 1980 £	%	*Commission's preliminary draft for 1981* £	%	*Council's Draft for 1981* £	%	*Council's cuts in Commission's 1981 proposals* £	%
TOTAL BUDGET	9,870m		12,619m		12,109m		–510m	–4.0
Of which:								
CAP Total	7,511m	76.1	8,565m	67.9	8,535m	70.5	–30m	–0.4
inc. Guarantee	7,229m		8,144m		8,131m			
Guidance	282m		421m		404m			
Regional Fund	254m	2.6	485m	3.8	315m	2.6	–170m	–35.1
Social Fund	235m	2.4	447m	3.5	352m	2.9	–95m	–21.1
Special item for UK*	–	–	614m	4.9	614m	4.9	0	0

*Note: Total repayments in UK to 1981 were expected to be about £1,007m, 8.3% of the Draft 1981 Budget.

CHAPTER 6

THE COMPANY IN EUROPE

1. Company Legislation

Introduction

The typical form adopted by most of the important industrial and commercial enterprises in the Community is that of a corporation with limited liability and a share capital.

These enterprises are the main producers of wealth and as employers they have an impact on the lives of a large number of Community people. They are institutions of strategic importance in relation to the economic and social systems of the Community. They are incorporated under the separate laws of the ten member states, whose national laws vary widely especially in relation to the internal structure. This situation creates a barrier to cross-frontier activities of both the company and those with whom it deals. Efforts to overcome this barrier are detailed in Part 2 of this chapter under the heading "Harmonisation of company law." First, though we look at the framework of the existing law in each of the countries making up the Community.

BELGIUM

Belgian company legislation has been introduced by several laws co-ordinated by the Royal Decree of 30 November 1935. This Royal Decree has been incorporated in Title IX of Book 1 of the Commercial Code. It has been subject to many revisions, of which the Law of 6 March 1973 and the Law of 24 March 1978 are the most recent: the former is based on the EEC's First Directive of 9 March 1968, the latter on its Second Directive of 13 December 1976, both dealing with the harmonisation of the company law of the member states.

Special additional rules exist for some insurance companies and some investment companies, and banks are subject to Royal Decree No. 185 of 9 July 1935 with respect to the control of banks and the issuing of securities.

Belgian commercial law recognises several forms of business enterprise. The most important types of company are the corporation (*naamloze venootschap/société anonyme – NV/SA*) and the private limited liability company (*personenwennootschap mit beperkte – aansprakelykheid/société de personnes à responsabilité limitée – PVBA/SPRL*).

Both the NV/SA and the PVBA/SPRL have legal personality. The shares of NV/SA may be quoted on the stock exchange: those of PVBA/SPRL may not, since it is essentially a private company and may not offer its shares to the general public.

The shareholders of an NV/SA may be both individuals and legal entities, the Partners of an PVBA/SPRL may only be individuals. Both types of company have a limited life of 30 years, but renewal is allowed.

The corporation (NV/SA)

The basic requirements for the formation of an NV/SA are as follows.

(1) A minimum of seven founding persons, who may be individuals or legal entities, residents or non-residents, citizens of Belgium or of a foreign state. After the creation of the NV/SA the number of shareholders may not become less than seven during more than six successive months; if it does, anyone whose direct interests are prejudiced may request the court to declare the company dissolved.
(2) A minimum capital of Bf 1,250,000.
(3) The full subscription of the authorised capital: if a part of the capital has not been subscribed, liability rests with the founding persons and they are, by law, deemed to be the subscribers for the amount involved.
(4) At least 20 per cent of each share or stock representing the authorised capital must be paid in.

The following is a more detailed statement of the formal requirements.

The NV/SA must be created by means of a notarial instrument or it fails to qualify as a legal entity. This authenticated document must, in accordance with the regulations of linguistic law, be drawn up and executed in German, Dutch or French depending on the location of head office.

The following must be included in the notarial instrument.

(1) A statement concerning the fulfilment of the basic requirements ((1) – (4) above),

(2) The name and the purpose of the corporation,
(3) The amount of the subscribed capital,
(4) Information concerning the contribution in cash (i.e., the credit institution in which the contribution in cash has been deposited) – credit institutions are mentioned in Article 1 of the Royal Decree No. 56 of 10 November 1967 with respect to the promotion of the use of near-money,
(5) Information concerning contributions in kind such as –
 (a) the extent and the conditions of the contribution in kind, the names of the contributors and the conclusions of the accountant who is appointed by the court to draw up a report on the valuation of the contributions;
 (b) the charges connected with contributions of mortgaged or pledged assets;
 (c) the realisation prices of the contributed immovables which were transferred during the five years preceding their contribution, and
 (d) the conditions to which the exercise of a contributed option is subect,
(6) The extent and justification of the special benefits granted to the founding persons,
(7) The amount of the costs related to the formation of the NV/SA (e.g., notary's fees, registration duties, research),
(8) The place, date and time of the shareholders' general meeting.

An abstract of the notarial instrument must be deposited at the record office of the Commercial Court within 15 days of its being drawn up: the application for entry in the Commercial Register can be made simultaneously. The abstract must also be published in annexes of the Belgian Official Gazette within 15 days of the above deposit.

The private limited company (PVBA/SPRL)

The basic requirements for the formation of a PVBA/SPRL are as follows.

(1) There must be at least two and not more than fifty founding persons (though a minimum of three shareholders is required if the company is formed by spouses).
(2) Only individuals may become shareholders.
(3) The purpose of a PVBA/SPRL may not consist of savings, insurance (including life insurance) or exchange of securities abroad.
(4) The authorised capital must be fully subscribed.
(5) A minimum capital of Bf 250,000 is required, and it must be fully paid in.

The formal requirements are as follows.

(1) The PVBA/SPRL must be created by means of a notarial instrument.
(2) The instrument must include the same statements as are required for the notarial instrument of an NV/SA.
(3) An abstract of the instrument must be deposited at the record office of the Commercial Court within 15 days, and must be published in the Belgian Official Gazette within 15 days following this deposit.

Other forms of business organisation

Other forms of business organisation under Belgian law include the following.

(1) General partnership regulated by Articles 15–17 of Title IX of Book 1 of the Commercial Code. Although the general partnership has legal personality the partners' liability is unlimited.
(2) Limited partnership regulated by Articles 18–25 of Title IX of Book 1 of the Commercial Code. The limited partnership has legal personality, and two types of partners can be distinguished:
  (a) the *active* partners, whose liability is unlimited, who are engaged in the management of the organisation, and
  (b) the *non-active* partners whose liability is limited to their contribution if they do not participate in the management of the organisation.
(3) Limited partnerhip with shares under Articles 105–115 of Title IX of Book 1 of the Commercial Code. The limited partnership with shares has legal personality.
(4) Cooperative regulated by Articles 141–166 of Title IX of the Commercial Code. The cooperative has legal personality and is formed by at least seven shareholders whose liability may be limited or unlimited.
(5) There are two types of business organisation which do not have legal personality under Article 3 of Title IX of Book 1 of the Commercial Code:
  (a) the temporary association, and
  (b) the association in participation.
  Both these are forms of joint venture.

DENMARK

Danish law permits any type of association unless contrary to good morals or the public interest. The types of companies which attract the most interest are the joint-stock company (Aktieselskab – A/S) and the limited liability company (Anpartsselskab – ApS). These two types of company are separate legal persons and are solely liable to their creditors.

The laws relevant to A/S were revised as a result of Denmark's entry into the European Economic Communuty; the ApS is a new form previously unknown in Denmark.

The joint-stock company – A/S

The characteristics of an A/S are as follows.

(1) The company must be incorporated under the rules of the Law A/S.
(2) The company must be registered in the Register of Companies.
(3) The minimum capital must be Kr 100,000 divided into at least three shares.
(4) The company must be engaged in business for the purpose of making profit to be distributed among the shareholders in proportion to their respective shares (Law A/S, Section 1(4)). Profit to be distributed does not necessarily mean that a yearly distribution of profit must take place, but also covers the right of the shareholders to the proceeds of liquidation. If both these rights have been denied to the shareholders however, the entity will not be an A/S. The means employed to pursue this economic gain are irrelevant.

The incorporation of a joint-stock company is effected by means of a charter drawn up between at least three incorporating parties (founders). This charter must meet the requirements of the Law A/S on several points. The charter, along with a draft of the by-laws, will subsequently be subject to approval by the incorporating shareholders' meeting. After approval by this meeting all the relevant documents are filed with the Registrar of Companies, which has the right to deny registration if there has been a failure to comply with the Law A/S. The procedure takes four months. Registration of the company is a pre-requisite for its existence as a legally recognised entity.

The period between the approval of the charter of incorporation and the completion of registration is a period of transition generally referred to as the incorporation period. The name of the company must indicate the fact that incorporation is in progress by adding "under incorporation" to its name; if not, a party to a contract may withdraw therefore (Law A/S, Section 12(3)). During this transitional period the founders are personally liable for the company's legal and financial transactions and the company may not appear as a party in court (Law A/S, Section 12).

The Charter of Incorporation must be signed by at least three persons of which at least two must be Danish residents unless otherwise permitted by the Minister of Commerce or according to the EEC Treaty. The parties may be natural or legal persons, the Danish State or a municipality (Law A/S, Section 3).

The Charter must contain the following details (Law A/S, Section 5):

(1) subscription price of the share capital;
(2) rules pursuant to which the capital must be contributed;
(3) date of the incorporating shareholders' meeting;
(4) assessment of the maximum costs of incorporation, and
(5) draft of the by-laws.

If the company plans to acquire assets through the issue of shares, the charter must contain –

(1) the basis of valuation of these assets;
(2) the name and addresses of the parties involved in the transaction, and
(3) information as to which part, if any, of the acquisition value will be paid in shares and other conditions pertaining to the acquisition.

The acquisition value may not exceed the value allocated to the assets on the opening balance sheet of the company.

If the company takes over a going concern, the charter must be accompanied by balance sheets and profit and loss accounts of the going concern for the two years preceding the takeover, and a profit and loss account for the period between the last closing of the financial year and the date of the takeover.

Law A/S, Section 4 contains the minimum provisions to be included in the by-laws of the company:

(1) the company's name;
(2) the statutory seat of the company;
(3) its corporate purpose;
(4) the amount of its share capital;
(5) the denomination of the shares and the voting rights attaching to them;
(6) whether the shares will be bearer shares or registered shares;
(7) whether the shares are to be incorporated in negotiable documents;
(8) if special rights will be attached to certain classes of shares;
(9) any limitation on the free negotiability of the shares;
(10) notice requirements for a shareholders' meeting, and
(11) the accounting period of the company.

The limited liability company (ApS)

The limited liability law (Law ApS) was effective from 1 January 1974. This type of company is closely related to the joint-stock company but the following main differences should be noted –

	ApS	*A/S*
(i)	Minimum capital Kr 30,000	Minimum capital Kr 100,000
(ii)	Minimum number of incorporating parties: 1	Minimum number of incorporating parties: 3
(iii)	Founders must subscribed to the full amount of capital	Founders need not subscribe to any amount of capital
(iv)	Application for registration to be filed within 2 months after signing the charter of incorporation	Application for registration to filed within 6 months after after signing the charter of incorporation
(v)	Shares are all registered and need not be issued if so decided by the by-laws	Shares may be registered or bearer shares
(vi)	Banks and financial institutions may not use the ApS form	A/S forms can be used by banks and financial institutions

Other forms of business organisation

Other frequently used types of association in Denmark are –

(1) the Cooperative society;
(2) the General Partnership;
(3) the Limited Partnership;
(4) the Partnership limited by shares.

FRANCE

The most important types of company in France are the corporation (*Sociétě Anonyme* – SA) and the limited liability company (*Société à responsabilité limité* – SARL). Since foreign companies generally prefer to operate in France through a subsidiary, SA or SARL are the two most important forms of company, and are governed by the 1966 Company Law which codified the many provisions previously contained in various laws, decrees and jurisprudence.

The corporation (SA)

The SA must have at least seven shareholders, who may be either French or foreign individuals or legal entities. The duration of an

SA's legal existence must be set at no more than 99 years in the articles.

A minimum capital of Ffr 500,000 for a public SA and Ffr 100,000 for any other SA is required. Shares must have a nominal value of at least Ffr 100 and may be in registered or bearer form.

As a rule shares of an SA are freely transferable, but the articles may require formal approval by the company for the transfer of registered shares. Such approval is deemed to be given if not refused within three months and, if approval is refused, the directors must cause the shares to be bought by the SA within three months after such refusal. Some additional extensions of time may be granted by the court.

The ordinary general meeting must be held at least once a year and not later than six months after the end of the financial year, unless it is postponed through an application to a commercial court by the board of directors.

The limited liability company (SARL)

An SARL must have at least two and not more than fifty shareholders, who may be either French or foreign individuals or legal entities. Legal duration is the same for the SA – a maximum of 99 years.

It must have a minimum capital of Ffr 20,000 which must be fully subscribed, issued and paid in on formation. SARL shares may not be negotiable and public offerings of SARL shares, bonds and other securities are not allowed. Shares are, however, freely transferable among shareholders and between them and their ascendants, descendants, spouses and heirs unless the articles provide otherwise. Consent is assumed to have been given if not refused within three months of a transfer.

An annual general meeting must be held at least once a year, not later than six months after the close of the financial year.

Disclosure and reporting requirements for SARLs concern mainly their shareholders. SARLs are restricted in several ways by the 1966 Company Law: they cannot issue bonds, be quoted or carry on banking, insurance, savings and loans or public show (other than film) activities.

Other forms of business organisation

Other forms of business organisation under French law include the following.

(1) General partnership (*société en nom collectif*).
(2) Limited partnership (*société en commandité simple*).

(3) Limited partnership with shares (*société en commandité par actions*).
(4) Sole proprietorship (*enterprise individuelle*).
(5) Civil companies (*société civiles*) used for real estate and construction holdings.
(6) Joint venture (*société en participation*).
(7) GIE (*groupement d'interêt économique*).
(8) Branches of foreign companies.
(9) Special purpose companies which have a special legal and tax status (e.g., open-end investment companies, chartered export or regional development companies).

FEDERAL REPUBLIC OF GERMANY

German commercial law gives legal recognition to a variety of incorporated and unincorporated forms of business. The two important types of incorporated business enterprise are the corporation (*Aktiengesellschaft* – AG) and the limited liability company (*Gesellschaft mit Beschränkter Haftung* – (GmbH)).

The shares of an AG can be dealt in on the stock exchanges upon application and following the publication of a prospectus: those of a GmbH may not. Unless it is intended to raise funds on the German stock markets, the GmbH will as a rule be a more convenient form of organisation than the AG. The great majority of foreign-owned businesses in Germany are operated in the form of a GmbH. Indeed, due to the low minimum capital requirement, the flexibility of the 1892 GmbH Law and its position between corporations and unincorporated bodies the GmbH is by far the most popular form of incorporated business domestically as well.

The corporation (AG)

The German Stock Corporation Law of September 1965 regulates the rights and duties of AGs and their shareholders. This Act introduced major reforms concerning, inter alia, shareholders' rights *vis-à-vis* those of management, control of management, full disclosure of profits and reserves, detailed regulations for related enterprises, especially combine (*Konzerne*) and mandatory provisions as to consolidated financial statements, annual reports and corporate accounting.

An AG is defined as an association with an independent legal personality whose capital is divided into shares. Creditors have recourse only against the AG's assets, the shareholders' liability being limited to delivery of the amount of their subscriptions to the AG's capital.

Formation of an AG involves two procedures.

(1) Drawing up the Articles of Incorporation (*Satzung*), subscription of shares, appointment of the first Supervisory Board (*Aufsichsrat*) and Auditors by the AG's founders. The Supervisory Board in turn appoints the first Managing Board (*Vorstand*).

(2) Application for registration in the Commercial Register.

To form an AG the Articles must be signed by at least 5 persons (individuals, or legal entities, resident or non-resident, German or foreign nationals) who must also subscribe the entire share capital. The articles include the by-laws and must be authenticated by judicial or notarial record. The record must specify the amount of the founders' shares, the amount at which they were issued and the class of shares.

The application for registration is then filed in the Commercial Register, The local court examines the application and if everything is in order, orders registration of the AG and publication in the Gazette of the Federal Ministry of Justice (*Bundesanzeiger*) and at least one local newspaper.

The limited company (GmbH)

The German law concerning companies with limited liability (*GmbH Gesetz*) of April 1982, as amended, governs the rights and duties of GmbHs and their shareholders. It has proved a remarkably flexible law and the GmbH form is by far the most popular in Germany, especially for foreign and smaller firms.

A reform of the GmbH Law is under review, and the draft leaves unchanged the basic structure of the GmbH. At present the EEC is considering the coordination of laws relating to limited liability companies and the GmbH law may have to take the Community legislation into account.

A GmbH is defined as an independent legal entity established for any legally permissible purpose. Only the GmbH's assets are accountable for liabilities of the company to creditors, the members' liability being limited to the amount of their agreed subscriptions to its capital according to the Articles.

In practice the GmbH comes nearest to the closely-held corporation, and is favoured by small and medium-sized firms owing to the many options in structure, low minimum capital and minimal requirements concerning publicity and accounting. The Publicity Law of 1969 requires certain business enterprises, including the larger GmbHs, to publish annual financial statements and group accounts (where applicable) and have them examined by independent public accountants (*Wirtschaftsprufer*). GmbHs affected are those with 5,000 employees or annual sales of over DM 250 million or over DM125 million in assets.

The capital of a GmbH must be at least DM 20,000 fully subscribed and 25 per cent paid in at formation.

Other forms of business organisation

Between the company and the limited partnership is the rarely-used partnership limited by shares (*Kommanditgesellschaft auf Aktien* or KGaA), the General commercial partnership (*Offene Handelsgesellschaft* or oHG), the Limited Commercial Partnership (*Kommanditgesellschaft* or KG), the Sole Proprietorship (*Einzelfirma*) and the Branch (*Zweig nieder lassung*) of a foreign corporation.

The Limited Partnership in the form of the GmbH & CoKG is a hybrid consisting of a limited commercial partnership (KG) with a GmbH as the general partner and the GmbH's shareholders, their families or others as limited partners. A genuine business purpose is essential, but if accepted the form may serve as a means of preventing double taxation of distributed profits to both the GmbH and its members.

GREECE

The most important types of company in Greece are the corporation (*anonymes eteria* – SA) and the limited liability company (*Eteria Periorismenis Efthinis* – EPE). Since foreign companies generally prefer to operate in Greece through a subsidiary SA or EPE, only these two forms will be discussed.

The corporation (SA)

The company must have at least two shareholders: they may be physical persons or legal entities, and may be either Greek or foreign. The company's Articles of Association must be drawn up before a Greek notary and must then be filed with the Ministry of Commerce. They must be approved by the Ministry and then published in the official Government Gazette. The total time required for the establishment of an SA is three months.

What is included in the Articles of Association is spelled out in Law 2190/1920 as amended subsequently by LD 4237/1962.

(1) The name of the company and the nature of its business.
(2) The legal seat of the company, which must not be outside Greece.

(3) The duration of the company which must be for a definite period of time.
(4) The amount of share capital (not less than Dr 5,000,000) and how it is to be paid. This minimum capital must be fully paid up at the time of formation.
(5) The number of shares and how they are to be issued. Shares may be either registered or bearer, and not less than Dr 100 nor more than Dr 30,000 per share.
(6) How the board of directors will be composed and what powers it will have (the board should convene at least monthly in Greece, or, with prior permission of the Ministry of Commerce, abroad).
(7) How the shareholders' general meeting will be composed and what powers it will have.
(8) Distribution of profits and shareholders' rights.

The limited liability company (EPE)

The procedure for establishing an EPE is similar to that for an SA, except that it is generally less costly and the time required is shorter. As in the case of an SA the EPE charter must be drawn up before a notary. A copy is then deposited with the Court of First Instance and a summary is sent for publication in the official Government Gazette. The time required for establishing a Greek EPE is less than that for an SA, usually taking less than one month.

Distinctions between the SA and the EPE

(1) Loans may be made to partners or administrators of an EPE but may not be made to directors of an SA or persons related to them.
(2) An EPE does not require a compulsory distribution of profits while for an SA there is a minimum distribution of 6 per cent required by law.
(3) Undistributed as well as distributed profits are taxed to the partners of an EPE: undistributed profits are taxed to the company in the case of an SA.
(4) The appointment of auditors for an EPE is not mandatory, but such appointments must be made by an SA.
(5) Effective control requires a majority of both capital and partners in an EPE while a majority of capital is enough in an SA.
(6) Impairment of capital (net worth less than 50 per cent of paid-up capital) in an EPE leads to a compulsory additional contribution of capital or to a decrease in capital which may not, however, be less than Dr 200,000, this does not become necessary in an SA.

Other forms of business organisation

Other legal forms of business enterprise include –

(1) The general partnership *(Omomythmos Eteria)*.
(2) The limited partnership (*Eteromythmos Eteria*).
(3) The silent commercial partnership.
(4) The sole proprietorship.
(5) The joint venture (*Kinopraxies*) often used by technical companies for large-scale projects or between Greek and foreign industrial companies.
(6) The civil company (*Astike Eteria*) used for real-estate ventures and governed by the provisions of the Civil Code and not the Commercial Code.
(7) Branches of foreign companies, where local Greek incorporation is not desired by foreign parents.

ITALY

The Italian Civil Code gives legal recognition to a variety of incorporated and unincorporated forms of business enterprise. The two most important forms of incorporated businesses are the corporation (*società per azioni* – SpA) and the limited liability company (*società a responsabilità limitat* – SrL). The SpA is the most popular legal form for larger enterprises, although the SrL is often used if a limited number of people and a modest capital are sufficient for business purposes.

The corporation (SpA)

An SpA can be formed by a minimum of two persons through a public deed drawn up by a notary, containing the information required by Article 2328 of the Civil Code. The statutes (by-laws) represent an integral part of the incorporation deed. The notary is responsible for carrying out the formalities for the registration of the company with the court and with other public bodies and for paying the relevant taxes and dues.

An SpA may be managed by a single director (*amministratore unico*) or by a board of directors (*Consiglia di Amministrazione*) appointed by the shareholders: there is no limit to the number of directors or to their nationality.

The SpA is the classic type of corporation, whose members are liable only to the extent of their unpaid shareholdings. The participants' equity is represented by shares, which are nominative; bearer shares may be issued only in certain regions as an aid to industrial development. The minimum share capital is L 200 million: the par value per share can be of any amount. Before the company is incorporated at least three-tenths of the share capital must be paid up and lodged with the Bank of Italy and may not be withdrawn until the incorporation of the SpA has been approved by the Court. The company is then registered in the Register of Business Enterprises.

In order to form an SpA with a share capital of L 2 billion or more, appropriate authorisation must be obtained from the Ministry of the Treasury.

The limited liability company (SrL)

The members of such companies have limited liability, as in an SpA. This form is generally used where there is a limited number of participants and where a low capital is sufficient. The participants' equity is represented by quotas recorded in the register of quotaholders and not by shares as in the case of SpA.

The minimum quota capital is L 20 million. Before the company is formed three-tenths of the quota capital must be paid up and lodged with the Bank of Italy and may not be withdrawn until the incorporation of the SrL has been approved by the Court. The company is then entered in the Register of Business Enterprises.

Other forms of business organisation

Other forms of Italian business enterprise include the following.

(1) *Società in accomandita per azioni* (SApA) – a company in which at least one member is unlimited, the liability of the remaining members being limited to the unpaid nominal value of their shareholdings.
(2) *Società cooperativa a responsabilità Limitata* (*Società coop a.r.L*) Limited Liability Cooperative.
(3) *Società in nome collettivo* (Snc) – a general partnership.
(4) *Società in accomandite Semplice* (SAS) – a partnership in which the liability of certain partners is limited by agreement.
(5) *Società semplice* – civil law association.
(6) *Società cooperativa – a responsbilità illimitata (Società coop a.r.i)* – an unlimited liability cooperative.

LUXEMBOURG

Luxembourg company law has been much influenced by the commercial laws of the neighbouring countries. Luxembourg formed part of France from 1795 to 1815, and during this period the Code Napoleon was introduced, remaining in force throughout the nineteenth century. During the Second World War Luxembourg was treated as a part of Germany and this in turn influenced fiscal laws of the country.

The Section of the Code Napoleon dealing with companies remained in force until the promulgation of the Law on Commercial Companies in 1915. The law of 1915 is still in force today although it has been amended on a number of occasions through the years.

Luxembourg commercial law distinguishes between commercial entities and civil entities. As a general rule Luxembourg law recognises freedom of enterprise in whatever form and for whatever purpose. The freedom is limited only if the entity is either contrary to public policy or in conflict with the interests of third parties.

The most important types of corporate entities are the corporation (*Société Anonyme* – SA) and the limited liability company (*Société à responsabilité limiteé* – SARL).

The corporation (SA)

The Law of 1915 regulates the rights and duties of SAs and their shareholders. The SA is defined as an association with independent legal personality whose capital is divided into shares. The liability of the shareholder is limited to their shares in the SA. Such shares are negotiable on the stock exchange or elsewhere.

An SA can be incorporated in either of two ways – *(a)* the direct method, or *(b)* the subscription method.

In the case of the *direct method* the incorporation must be recorded by a notary: failing this the SA will be considered a nullity. This nullity can only be the subject of an appeal by third parties to the company and not by the company against third parties.

The following steps must be taken in order to incorporate as SA:

(1) Seven persons must underwrite the Articles.
(2) The capital must be completely subscribed.
(3) At least one-fifth of the face-value of every share must be paid-up; such payment must amount to at least Lf 50.

The document containing the Articles drawn up by the notary must be lodged with the Registrar within one month after signature, and must be published (together with the necessary information regarding the appointment of the directors and supervisors and of officers with signing powers) in the Supplement to the Official Gazette (*Récueil Special du Mémorial du Grande-Duché de Luxembourg*) within one month of registration.

The subscription method whereby an SA may be incorporated is rarely employed.

Incorporation is effected by the following three steps:

(1) The draft Articles of incorporation are published.
(2) One of the parties signs a subscription form and thus participates in the act of incorporation.
(3) The first general meeting of shareholders takes place in the presence of a notary: if the majority of subscribers have no objection, the incorporation of the SA becomes a fact.

A legal reserve to protect shareholders and creditors is required of every SA. An annual allocation of 5 per cent of the year's profits is prescribed by the Law of 1915, Article 72: this allocation is no longer obligatory when the reserve equals 10 per cent of the capital.

The life of the company cannot exceed 30 years.

The limited liability company (SARL)

The limited liability company was introduced on 18 September 1933 as an amendment to the Law of 1915. The 1933 provisions were patterned on those contained in the French Law of 7 March 1925.

The limited liability company is a commercial entity incorporated by a limited number of participants.

As distinct from the SA, the SARL has several advantages:

(1) Only two members are required for incorporation.
(2) There is no publication requirement with regard to financial statements unless the company is engaged in banking activities.
(3) The structure of corporate management is simple.
(4) The prerequisites of incorporation are less costly.

The maximum number of members of an SARL is 40, though in certain cases the number may be exceeded.

The capital must be at least Lf 100,000 divided into shares of Lf 500 or multiples of Lf 500 (Article 182).

Legal entities other than SA or SARL include –

(1) general partnerships;
(2) limited partnerships without share capital;
(3) limited partnerships with share capital, and
(4) cooperatives.

NETHERLANDS

Civil law in the Netherlands recognises a number of incorporated and unincorporated forms of business enterprise. Forms recognised by law as legal entities include the following:

(1) The corporation (*naamlose vennootschap* – NV).
(2) The limited liability company (*besloten vennootschap met beperkte aansprakelijkheid* – BV).
(3) The foundation (*stichting*).
(4) The association (*vereniging*), the most important of which are the cooperative association (*cooperatieve vereniging*) and the mutual insurance association (*onderlange waarborgmaatschappij*).

The corporation (NV)

(1) The NV must be created by a notarial instrument or the company may be declared void. The instrument of incorporation must be drawn up and executed in the Dutch language, either by a Notary Public who is a resident of the Netherlands or by an authorised Dutch consul abroad. (In the Netherlands a notary public is appointed by the Crown.)
(2) The Minister of Justice must declare that he has no objection to its formation.
(3) The managers must register the corporation with the Commercial Register and deposit an authorised copy of the instrument of incorporation at the Registrar's Office.
(4) The founders must jointly participate for at least Fl 35,000 (the minimum capital to be paid in) and 20 per cent of the authorised capital.

The limited liability company (BV)

The BV differs in only three respects from the NV. Firstly, the shares of the company cannot be evidenced by certificate and, secondly, the shares are not freely transferable. Since the BV cannot issue share certificates the register of the company becomes vitally important: the BV itself is obliged to keep an up-to-date register with the names and addresses of all of its shareholders. The third distinction between NVs and BVs is in regard to the publication and contents of the annual report: the general rule is that within 5 months of the close of the financial year of an NV or BV, the management must draw up and submit to the annual meeting of the shareholders a report containing a balance sheet, profit and loss statement and explanatory notes. The report must be signed by all the general managers and by the members of the Supervisory Board if such a board exists, and it must be certified by a Registered Auditor. Under certain conditions an NV or BV is not obliged to draw up its annual report –

(1) if it belongs to a group of companies;

(2) if the relevant data are included in the consolidated report of another group member;
(3) if all the shareholders before the close of the financial year agree that the annual report need not meet the requirements of the Second Book of the Civil Code;
(4) if the NV or BV is not a bank, insurance company or assurance company, and
(5) if no bearer shares, bearer debentures, or bearer certificates of registered shares or debentures are either in circulation or listed on the stock exchange.

If the NV or BV is required to publish its annual report, deviation from the general rules of the Second Book of the Civil Code is possible only if the parent which publishes the consolidating report guarantees all the debts of that NV or BV, or if the NV or BV is active mainly outside the EEC.

Other forms of business organisation

In addition to the incorporated bodies mentioned earlier, unincorporated business forms are also widely used in the Netherlands. The most important of these are the following:

(1) The general partnership (*vennootschap onder firma*).
(2) The limited partnership (*commanditaire vennootschap*).

THE REPUBLIC OF IRELAND

Irish law gives legal recognition to a variety of incorporated and unincorporated forms of business. The two important types of incorporated business enterprise are the public limited company and the private limited company. The shares of a public company may, upon application and following the publication of a Prospectus, be dealt in on the stock exchanges; those of a private limited company may not. Unless it is intended to have funds on the stock market, the private limited company will as a rule be a more convenient form of organisation than a public limited company.

The public limited company

Irish public limited companies are regulated by the Companies Act, 1963. The basic requirements for the formation of a public limited company are as follows.

(1) Preparation of a Memorandum of Association which contains essential facts about the company, including its name, objects and share capital.

(2) Preparation of Articles of Association which regulate the relationship between the company and its members, including the appointment and powers of the directors for the conduct of the company's officers. Table A in the First Schedule to the Companies Act, 1963, may be adopted by a company as its Articles and will apply so far as it is not excluded or modified by special articles.
(3) Signature of the Memorandum of Association by seven persons (the subscribers), each of whom must agree to take at least one share in the capital of the company and express a wish to be formed into a company in pursuance of the Memorandum.

The following must be included in the Memorandum of Association.

(1) The name of the company with Limited (or the Irish equivalent *Teoranta*) as the last word of the name.
(2) The objects of the company.
(3) A statement that the liability of the members is limited.
(4) The amount of the share capital with which the company proposes to be registered and its division into shares of a fixed amount.

The private limited company

A private limited company is governed by the same legislation as the public limited company and most of the provisions of that Act apply to it. The basic difference between the two types of company is that a private company must by its Articles restrict the right of members to transfer their shares, limit the number of members (excluding employees and ex-employees) to fifty and prohibit any invitation to the public to subscribe for shares or debentures.

A private limited company must have a minimum of two members. Another distinction between the two types of company relates to the publication of annual accounts. At least once in every calendar year every company must file an Annual Return with the Registrar of Companies within 60 days after the annual general meeting, made up to a date 14 days after the meeting. The Return must contain a list of shareholders, particulars of directors and secretary and the amount of the company's indebtedness in respect of mortgages and charges which are required to be registered with the Registrar of Companies under the Companies Act, 1963. In the case of a public company the Return must contain a copy of the Audited Accounts, Directors Report and Auditors Report laid before the Annual General Meeting: this does not apply to the private company.

UNITED KINGDOM

The principal forms of business enterprise apart from concerns owned by the government are:

(1) companies, including branches of foreign corporations, and
(2) partnerships and sole proprietorships.

The limited liability company

The most important and common type is the limited liability company having a share capital. This type of company may be either private or public. The company limited by guarantee is another form of limited liability company, but is rarely found in business undertakings. The distinctive feature of a limited company is that it has a legal entity separate from that of its members. Creditors have recourse only against the company's assets, the shareholders' liability being limited to the amount of their subscription to the company's capital.

Most United Kingdom companies are formed by incorporation under the appropriate statute. The Companies Acts contain detailed sections dealing with incorporation including rules relating to the issue of shares, management and administration and mandatory provisions concerning the issue of and disclosure of information in financial statements.

The document by means of which a company is incorporated is the Memorandum of Association, which must contain the following.

(1) The name of the company, with "Limited" as the last word.
(2) The domicile of the company, that is the country in which the registered office is to be situated.
(3) The objects of the company.
(4) A statement of the limitation of the liability of members.
(5) The amount of share capital divided into shares of a fixed amount.

The Memorandum must be signed by each subscriber. The Articles of Association regulate the relationship between the company and its members, including the appointment and powers of directors for the conduct of the company's affairs. Under the European Communities Act, 1972, when any amendment is made a printed copy of the amended Memorandum and Articles must be filed with the Registrar of Companies. This requirement is retrospective.

Once the required documents have been delivered the Registrar will issue a Certificate of Incorporation, and will publish a notice of its issue in the *London Gazette*. When a Certificate of Incorporation has been issued the company becomes a body corporate with perpetual succession, and if it is a private company it may commence business immediately: a public company must first obtain another certificate called a Trading Certificate before it can commence business or exercise its borrowing powers.

The public limited company

A company may be incorporated either as a public or as a private company. A public company is one whose Articles do not contain the provisions detailed under the heading The Private Limited Company.

It is simpler to form a private company and subsequently to convert it into a public company than to form a public company.

Conversion may be effected under the terms of the Companies Act 1948 by altering the Articles of Association by special resolution which requires the same majority as is required for the passing of an extraordinary resolution.

The private limited company

The Companies Acts state that a private company is one whose articles impose the following restrictions.

(1) The right to transfer its shares is restricted.
(2) The number of its members is limited to 50 (excluding employees and former employees).
(3) Any invitation to the public to subscribe for any shares or debentures of the company is prohibited.

The other respects in which a private company differs from a public company include the following.

(1) The minimum number of directors is one, as against two for a public company.
(2) Two or more directors can be appointed by a single resolution at a general meeting.
(3) There is no statutory age limit on the directors unless the company is a subsidiary of a public company.
(4) A director holding office for life on 18 July 1945 cannot be moved by ordinary resolution.
(5) Neither a prospectus nor a statement in lieu of prospectus is required when capital is issued.
(6) The company can commence business immediately on registration and requires no trading certificate.
(7) A proxy may speak at general meetings.

Partnership

A partnership may not consist of more than 20 persons but exceptions are made for the purpose of carrying on practices of solicitors or accountants or business as members of a recognised Stock Exchange or for any other person specified by the Department of Trade. There is no requirement that all or any of the partners should be British subjects and a body corporate may be a partner.

Other legal forms of doing business include:

(1) companies limited by guarantee;
(2) bodies incorporated by royal charter or by special statute;
(3) unlimited companies;
(4) branches of foreign companies, and
(5) sole proprietorships.

2. Harmonisation of Company Law

Harmonisation of company law is a long and complex business, but after ten years the Community programme has begun to gather some momentum. By the end of 1978 the Community had four directives affecting company law on the statute book, with another four awaiting decision. The Commission is currently preparing Ninth and Tenth Directives. The directives flow from Article 54(3)(g) of the Rome Treaty. The object of the harmonisation programme is both to facilitate freedom of establishment of companies in member countries in accordance with the Treaty, and to protect the interests of members and third parties. It aims to encourage the free movement of capital by providing common safeguards and removing obstacles to cross-frontier co-operation throughout the Community, thus enabling investors to make investment decisions without their choice being affected by differences in national laws.

Progress Chart

Directive	*Commission*	*Economic and Social Committee*	*European Parliament*	*Redraft*	*Adopted by Council*
First	*	*	*	*	9–3–68
Second	*	*	*	*	13–12–76
Third	*	*	*	*	9–10–78
Fourth	*	*	*	*	25–5–78
Fifth	*	*			
Sixth	*	*	*		
Seventh	*	*	*		
Eighth	*				
Ninth					

As will be seen from the chart, however, progress on the programme has been slow. The First Directive on disclosure of information was adopted by the Six in March 1968, but it took over eight years before the Second Directive was adopted in 1976. There was better progress in 1978, when the Third and Fourth Directives, both submitted to the Council in 1978 were adopted in October and July respectively of that year.

The improvement in the adoption rate in 1978 probably reflects the growing realisation of governments and business that the divergence and complexity of national company laws can be counterproductive to intra-community trade, while proposals awaiting decision concerning groups of companies reflect the political desire for more concrete information on the activities of the multinationals.

The Convention on mutual recognition of companies, firms and legal persons adopted by the Six in 1968 is still a matter of negotiation between the Six and the new members. Amendments to the Convention are still being discussed, and it could be several more years before negotiations are complete.

The four directives already adopted are concerned *inter alia* with disclosure of information by companies and technical aspects of company law, such as nullity; measures to increase the security afforded to creditors and shareholders; certain safeguards concerning mergers, and the establishment of minimum standards for company accounts by prescribing obligatory items for the balance sheet and profit and loss account.

FIRST DIRECTIVE

This directive sets out certain requirements for the publication of accounts and restricts the grounds on which a court can declare a company null and void.

It provides

(1) that a company is liable to third persons for the acts of its directors and agents, even if these acts are outside the objects of the company, and
(2) that companies must insert details of their registered number and country of incorporation on letter-headings and other forms.

SECOND DIRECTIVE

Public companies are required to have a minimum subscribed capital of 25,000 EUA. Other changes concern specific responsibility for pre-incorporation liabilities, a virtual prohibition on the issue of shares at a discount, and stringent controls on the issue of shares for consideration other than cash. The payment of dividends and interim dividends is also subject to some restriction.

THIRD DIRECTIVE

This directive is concerned with harmonisation of national rules affecting domestic mergers of public liability companies, where one company acquires all the assets and liabilities of another, and the latter is dissolved without liquidation. The aim of the directive is to co-ordinate the procedures for and effects of mergers and similar operations in order to arrive at an equivalent degree of protection throughout the Community for the members, creditors and employees of companies involved in such operations.

The provisions of the directive, which must be converted into national law within three years, define what is meant by a merger; stipulate those companies which may be merged; lay down minimum requirements for the content, publication and supervision of the draft terms of mergers to be drawn up by administrative or management bodies, and determine the powers of general meetings and the rights of individual shareholders and of minority shareholders.

The protection of employees in the event of mergers and similar operations was dealt with in a specific directive, adopted in 1977, on the maintenance of employees' rights in the event of transfers of undertakings. In view of the degree of protection afforded by this directive and the short space of time that has elapsed since it was adopted, the present directive reaffirms the existing protection by referring to the previous legislation.

The directive also governs the grounds and detailed procedures for rendering mergers void; such nullity may only be ordered under certain conditions. The directive also applies in the case of merger by the formation of a new company.

In adopting this directive, the Council of Ministers thought that it might also forward negotiations on a convention, currently being prepared by an inter-governmental group of experts, on mergers between public limited liability companies of different member states.

FOURTH DIRECTIVE

This directive is concerned with the harmonisation of the annual accounts of both public and private limited companies. Its effect is to make annual accounts (particularly balance sheets and profit and loss accounts) comparable throughout the Community. From now on their physical presentation will have to conform to prescribed layouts; assets and liabilities will have to be set out in accordance with fixed rules, and annual accounts will be subject to audit.

The main purpose of the directive is to protect members, employed persons, creditors and other third parties, although its scope is more extensive. It means that more than a million companies in the Community will, in future, be presenting comparable annual accounts which will make co-operation between undertakings in different countries easier, and should stimulate trans-frontier investment. At the same time the public will have more information about company acitivities and thus economic activity as a whole.

Because of the difficulty of determining the extent to which a company must comply with the requirements of the directive to publish particulars without reference to its size, the legislation distinguishes between small, medium-sized and large enterprises; for small and medium-sized undertakings there are a number of derogations concerning the drawing up, publication and checking of annual accounts.

The adoption of this directive was expected to improve progress on the Seventh Draft Directive concerning annual accounts of groups of companies and multinationals now being considered by a Council of Ministers' working party.

The directive has been welcomed, particularly as it is expected to bring about a considerable improvement in the standards of reporting and disclosure.

The expected impact of this important directive on member states varies, but there will of necessity be changes in national legislation in order to conform with the mandatory provisions of the directive.

Although there are a considerable number of options left open to member states, many of these options are in the form of possible concessions for particular classes or types of company. The concessions require specific inclusions in the national legislation, failing which they will be inoperative.

Member states are free to take advantage of the concessions and exercise other choices within the limits provided in the directive. They are free to set *more* restrictive conditions for the operation of any particular concession than those permitted by the directive but may not set *less* restrictive conditions. They are also free to ignore any of the concessions in the directive. The options may be exercised by member states deciding to carry the options into national law, so allowing companies some freedom of choice in selected matters. Member states need not apply the provisions of the directive to banks and other financial institutions or to insurance companies.

They need not apply the directive to companies which are not for profit within the meaning of Article 58 of the Treaty of Rome. The member states likely to be most affected by the directive fall into two largely complementary groups, affected either by the new requirement to give a true and fair view and discretion on disclosure or by the mandatory formats of accounts.

The following tables shows the expected changes in national legislation, and it will be seen that Belgium, Denmark, Germany, Ireland, the Netherlands, and the UK appear to be the least affected, whilst Luxembourg, Italy and France seem harder hit.

	Number of requirements giving rise to			
	Extensive Change	*Some Change*	*Minor Change*	*No Change*
Belgium	5	4	3	41
Denmark	8	6	3	36
France	7	19	–	27
Germany	8	5	5	35
Greece	–	–	–	–
Italy	12	14	2	25
Luxembourg	21	11	2	19
Netherlands	5	7	1	40
Republic of Ireland	3	8	1	41
UK	–	10	–	43

(Figures for Greece not available at the time of printing.)

There are three requirements requiring some degree of change in all member states:

(1) breakdowns of turnover by activity and geographical market;
(2) breakdown of the number of employees by category, coupled with information on wages, social security costs and pensions, and
(3) disclosures required in the annual report of information as to the development of the company, important events *after* the financial year-end, the company's likely future development and research and development activities.

Six or more member states are affected to some degree by –

(1) the disclosure requirements for participatory interests;
(2) the need to disclose debts becoming due by the company after five years and the security given by the company in respect of all debts;
(3) the requirement to disclose deferred taxes, and
(4) the writing-off of formation expenses over not more than five years and prohibition of the distribution of profits until available reserves are at least equal to unamortised expenses.

BELGIUM

The Belgian law of 17 July 1975 on accounting records, coupled with the subsequent Royal Decrees on the annual accounts of companies (principally the Royal Decree of 8 October 1976) anticipated substantially the requirements of the directive.

DENMARK

The minimum requirements for the form and content of the balance sheet and valuation principles as well as the types of income and expense which must be shown separately in the income statement are set out in the Companies Act. However, a high degree of flexibility exists under this Act as regards the presentation of accounts and accounting information. Thus the directive's requirement for mandatory formats are likely to necessitate extensive change in the manner in which accounts are presented.

FRANCE

Impact has been assessed against the background of requirements applied to public limited companies (SAs). Account has also been taken of recommendations of professional organisations.

Accounts in France are already subject to some uniformity of presentation.

FEDERAL REPUBLIC OF GERMANY

The change likely to arise in Germany has been based on a comparison between the directive's requirements and the stipulations of the German Stock Corporation Law (*Aktiengesetz*) applicable to German stock corporations (AG). Limited liability companies (GmbH), which will also be covered by the directive but which do not fall under the Stock Corporation Law, have not been considered. At present the majority of the GmbHs are not regulated by detailed accounting rules, nor do their financial statements have to be published or audited. For GmbHs, therefore, almost all of the directive's requirements mean an extensive change as compared with the present position. At present the concept "notes on the accounts" is unknown in Germany. German stock corporations (but not GmbHs) have to prepare a directors' report which is subject to audit and comprises two sections: one comments on the business situation in general, and the other gives additional information and explanations regarding certain financial statement terms. The directors' report has to be filed with the Trade Register whereas the financial statements are published in the *Federal Gazette*. When summarising expected impact it has been assumed that the explanatory section of the directors' report is in effect equivalent to the "notes" referred to in the directive. The requirement to present accounts following mandatory formats will necessitate relatively little change in Germany as far as AGs are concerned.

GREECE

It is not yet established what changes will be necessary, but it is anticipated that the implementation of the directive will present very few problems toward uniformity.

ITALY

Italian law does not require "notes on the accounts". In some cases information disclosed in the directors' report is equivalent to the note disclosure required under the directive: the Italian Civil Code contains a mandatory format for accounts. Nevertheless the directive formats will require change in Italy.

Because of the absence of any generally accepted financial accounting and reporting practices in Italy, the comments on present practice are based on legal requirements.

LUXEMBOURG

The change in Luxembourg on the implementation of the directive has been made against the background of the law on commercial companies (*sociétés commerciales*). Account has not been taken of the specific legislation applicable to holding companies (*Sociétés Holding*).

Luxembourg companies are likely to be significantly affected by the directive's mandatory formats for the annual accounts.

NETHERLANDS

The basic requirement is for accounts to present a true and fair view and to be prepared in accordance with accounting principles generally accepted in the Netherlands. However, the law does not set out in detail how the foregoing is to be achieved and consequently there is a considerable freedom available to adopt principles and forms of presentation best suited to specific circumstances. The introductions of mandatory formats will be the most striking change in Dutch financial reporting.

REPUBLIC OF IRELAND

Because the law in Ireland tends to do no more than provide an overall framework for accounting and reporting, considerable account has been taken of the requirements of professionally established accounting principles when assessing the directive's impact.

The overriding requirement in Ireland is that accounts shall present a true and fair view. However, the law does not set out in detail how this is to be achieved, and there is considerable freedom to adopt a form of presentation best suited to the individual company's circumstances. For this reason the directive's requirements for mandatory formats will require extensive change.

The public filing and availability of the accounts of private limited companies and extensive proft and loss account disclosures, including (subject to possible concessions) disclosure of gross profit margins, will also be extensive changes.

UNITED KINGDOM

The comments for Ireland apply equally to the United Kingdom except that the accounts of private limited companies in the United Kingdom are at present filed and publicly available.

As regards Northern Ireland the progressive implementation of the Companies Order (Northern Ireland) 1978 between 1980 and 1982 will eliminate significant differences between Northern Ireland and the rest of the United Kingdom. By 1982 when the directive is expected to come into effect, its impact will be uniform throughout the United Kingdom.

Account layouts

The balance sheet may be presented in either a vertical or a horizontal form. The profit and loss account may be drawn up in either of two forms, one of which analyses costs by *type of expense* while the other analyses costs by the *purpose of expenditure*. Both forms of profit and loss account may be presented either vertically or horizontally. Member states may prescribe one of the formats for the balance sheet and profit and loss account or allow companies to choose between two for the balance sheet or at most four for the profit and loss account.

Medium-sized companies may *publish* an abridged balance sheet although they must *prepare* a full balance sheet, four examples are given below.

(1) A vertical balance sheet showing the minimum amount of information.

(2) A horizontal balance sheet showing the full detail that must be given by large companies.
(3) A horizontal profit and loss account prepared on "the type of expenditure" basis giving all the detailed items.
(4) A vertical profit and loss account prepared on the operational basis showing the purpose for which expenditure was incurred with all detailed items.

Code for Examples

XX Represents main balance sheet captions (those preceded by letters in the directive's accounts layouts) which must be shown on the face of the balance sheet of all companies.

X Secondary balance sheet captions (those preceded by Roman numerals in the directive's accounts layouts) which must be shown on the face of the balance sheet of all companies.

00 Represents detailed balance sheet or profit and loss account captions (those preceded by Arabic numerals in the directive's accounts layouts) which must be shown separately unless immaterial, in the published accounts of large and medium-sized companies. Disclosure may be on the face of the balance sheet or profit and loss account or in the notes on the accounts.

0 Detailed balance sheet or profit and loss account captions (those preceded by Arabic numerals in the directive's accounts layouts) which must be shown separately, if material for the purposes of giving a true and fair view by large companies. Disclosure may be on the face of the balance sheet or profit and loss account or in the notes on the accounts.

EXAMPLE 1
Minimum Vertical Balance Sheet (Article 10)

C Fixed Assets		XX
(i) Intangible assets	X	
(ii) Tangible assets	X	
(iii) Financial assets	X	
D Current Assets (showing separately for debtors amounts due in more than one year)		XX
(i) Stocks	X	
(ii) Debtors	X	
(iii) Investments	X	
(iv) Cash	X	
F Creditors (due within one year)		XX
G Net Current Assets		XX
H Total Assets less Current Liabilities		XX
I Creditors (due in more than one year)		XX

J	Provisions for liabilities and charges		XX
L	Capital and Reserves		XX
	(i) Called-up capital	X	
	(ii) Share premium account	X	
	(iii) Revaluation reserve	X	
	(iv) Reserves	X	
	(v) Profit or loss brought forward	X	
	(vi) Profit or loss for year	X	
			XX

NOTES

1. The above layout assumes that national law provides that called-up capital (as opposed to subscribed capital) is shown at L(i) and capital called but not paid is shown at D(ii).
2. The above layout assumes that national law provides that formation expenses (to the extent that they are allowed to be shown under assets) are shown under C(i).
3. For larger companies the above layout assumes that national law requires or allows all items preceded by arabic numerals to be shown in the notes on the accounts.
4. The above layout also shows the form of balance sheet that would be published by small companies if all possible concessions relating to the balance sheet were granted to them (and making assumptions 1 and 2 above).
5. Net current assets will include amounts due from debtors after more than one year.

EXAMPLE 2

Horizontal Balance Sheet (Article 9)

Assets

A	Subscribed capital unpaid			XX
B	Formation expenses			XX
C	Fixed assets			XX
	(i) Intangible assets		X	
	1 Costs of research and development	0		
	2 Concessions, patents, licences, trade marks and similar rights and assets	0		
	3 Goodwill	00		
	4 Payments on account	0		
	(ii) Tangible assets		X	
	1 Land and buildings	00		
	2 Plant and machinery	00		
	3 Other fixtures and fittings, tools and equipment	00		
	4 Payments on account and tangible assets in course of construction	00		

(iii) Financial assets		X	
1 Shares in affiliated undertakings	00		
2 Loans to affiliated undertakings	00		
3 Participating interests	00		
4 Loans to undertakings with which the company is linked by virtue of participating interests	00		
5 Investments held as fixed assets	0		
6 Other loans	0		
7 Own shares	00		
D Current assets			XX
(i) Stocks		X	
1 Raw materials and consumables	0		
2 Work in progress	0		
3 Finished goods and goods for resale	0		
4 Payments on account	0		
(ii) Debtors (Amounts becoming due and payable after more than a year must be shown separately for each item)		X	
1 Trade debtors	0		
2 Amounts owed by affiliated undertakings	00		
3 Amounts owed by undertakings with which the company is linked by virtue of participating interests	00		
4 Other debtors	0		
5 Subscribed capital called but not paid (unless under A-Assets)	0		
6 Prepayments and accrued income (unless under E-Assets)	00		
(iii) Investments		X	
1 Shares in affiliated undertakings	00		
2 Own shares	00		
3 Other investments	0		
(iv) Cash at bank and in hand		X	
E Prepayments and accrued income (unless under D(ii) 6-Assets)			XX
			XX

Liabilities

A Capital and reserves			XX
(i) Subscribed capital (unless called-up capital shown under this item)		X	
(ii) Share premium account		X	
(iii) Revaluation reserve		X	
(iv) Reserves		X	
1 Legal reserve, in so far as required	0		
2 Reserve for own shares, in so far as required	0		
3 Reserves provided for by the articles of association	0		
4 Other reserves	0		

(v) Profit or loss brought forward	X	
(vi) Profit or loss for the financial year (unless under F-Assets or E-Liabilities)	X	
B Provisions for liabilities and charges		XX
1 Provisions for pensions and similar obligations	0	
2 Provisions for taxation	0	
3 Other provisions	0	
C Creditors (Amounts becoming due and payable within one year and after more than one year must be shown separately for each item and in total)		XX
1 Debenture loans, showing convertible loans separately	00	
2 Amounts owed to credit institutions	00	
3 Payments received on account of orders in so far as they are not shown separately as deductions from stocks	0	
4 Trade creditors	0	
5 Bills of exchange payable	0	
6 Amounts owed to affiliated undertakings	00	
7 Amounts owed to undertakings with which the company is linked by virtue of participating interests	00	
8 Other creditors including tax and social security	0	
9 Accruals and deferred income (unless shown under D-Liabilities)	00	
D Accruals and deferred income (unless shown under C9-Liabilities)		XX
		XX

EXAMPLE 3
Profit and Loss Account

Type of Expenditure basis – horizontal (Article 24)

A *Charges*	
1 Reduction in stocks of finished goods and in work in progress	0
2 *(a)* Raw materials and consumables	0
(b) Other external charges	0
3 Staff costs	
(a) Wages and salaries	00
(b) Social security costs, with a separate indication of those relating to pensions	00
4 *(a)* Value adjustments in respect of formation expenses and of tangible and intangible fixed assets	00
(b) Value adjustments in respect of current assets, to the extent that they exceed the amount of value adjustments which are normal in the undertaking concerned	00
5 Other operating charges	00

6	Value adjustments in respect of financial assets and of investments held as current assets	00
7	Interest payable and similar charges, with a separate indication of those concerning affiliated undertakings	00
8	Tax on profit on ordinary activities	00
9	Profit on ordinary activities after taxation	00
		00
10	Extraordinary charges	00
11	Tax on extraordinary profit	00
12	Other taxes not shown under the above items	00
13	Profit for the financial year	00
		00

B *Income*

1	Net turnover	0
2	Increase in stocks of finished goods and work in progress	0
3	Work performed by the undertaking for its own purposes and capitalised	0
4	Other operating income	0
5	Income from participating interests, with a separate indication of that derived from affiliated undertakings	00
6	Income from other investments and loans forming part of the fixed assets, with a separate indication of that derived from affiliated undertakings	00
7	Other interest receivable and similar income, with a separate indication of that derived from affiliated undertakings	00
		00
8	Profit on ordinary activities after taxation (brought down)	00
9	Extraordinary income	00
		00

EXAMPLE 4

Profit and Loss Account

Operational basis – vertical (Article 25)

1	Net turnover	0
2	Cost of sales (including value adjustments)	0
3	Gross profit or loss	00
4	Distribution costs (including value adjustments)	00
5	Administrative expenses (including value adjustments)	00
6	Other operating income	0
7	Income from participating interests, with a separate indication of that derived from affiliated undertakings	00
8	Income from other investments and loans forming part of the fixed assets, with a separate indication of that derived from other affiliated undertakings	00

9.	Other interest receivable and similar income, with a separate indication of that derived from affiliated undertakings		00
10	Value adjustments in respect of financial assets and of investments held as current assets		00
11	Interest payable and similar charges, with a separate indication of those concerning affiliated undertakings		00
12	Tax on profit or loss on ordinary activities		00
13	Profit or loss on ordinary activities after taxation		00
14	Extraordinary income	00	
15	Extraordinary charges	00	
16	Extraordinary profit or loss		00
17	Tax on extraordinary profit or loss		00
18	Other taxes not shown under the above items		00
19	Profit or loss for financial year		00
			00

FIFTH DIRECTIVE

This draft directive is concerned with employee participation and company structure in the Community.

Originally submitted in 1972, negotiations have hitherto foundered over a definition of uniform guidelines concerning worker participation in company management. In November 1975 the European Commission published a discussion document or "green paper" giving an account of the principal positions and trends discernible in the Community and suggesting some solutions. The European Parliament, however, has not adopted a position on either the draft directive or the green paper. The Commission is aware that the directive will have to be revised, but it does not intend to take any further action until it has had the Parliament's opinion.

SIXTH DIRECTIVE

The draft directive submitted to the Council on 26 September 1972 deals with the contents, verification and distribution of the prospectus which is published when securities issued by companies are admitted to official stock exchange quotations. An amended draft is at present under consideration by the Council Working Party on Economic Questions which has completed the third reading.

SEVENTH (DRAFT) DIRECTIVE (AS AMENDED)

This proposal complements the Fourth Directive, in that it seeks to ensure comparable accounting procedures for groups of companies, whether national or international. The harmonisation process would ensure that multinational companies, with registered offices in the Community, would have to publish group accounts relating to all their subsidiaries throughout the world and make clear the relationships and activities within the group, while those with head offices outside the Community would be subject to the same rules as apply to activities carried out by companies established within the Community. The draft defines the vertical and horizontal company network that would be affected by the directive.

The Commission has pointed out that if the directive is adopted the principle of a "true and fair view" of company activity would no longer be a formality but have full legal effect. Thus the directive clearly sets out the principles that would apply in drawing up group accounts. These must not be merely a group consolidated profit and loss account, but must give a true and fair view of the group's assets, liabilities, financial position and results. The methods of consolidation must not be changed from year to year.

EIGHTH (DRAFT) DIRECTIVE

The Commission presented the Council with the Eighth Draft Directive on the 24 April 1978. The aim of the proposal is to harmonise the minimum qualifications required in Community countries to audit the annual accounts of limited companies.

The content of the examination is specified in the proposal. Special provisions are included to allow persons already practising as auditors, who do not fulfil the conditions laid down in the directive, to be exempted from the need to pass the examination of professional competence. The possibility of recognising equivalent overseas qualifications is also provided for.

The Commission is now awaiting the Opinions of the Economic and Social Committee and of the European Parliament.

NINTH AND TENTH (DRAFT) DIRECTIVES

The Commission is currently preparing proposals for a Ninth Directive concerning the structure of groups of companies and for a Tenth Directive concerning the winding up and liquidation of companies with share capital.

3. Establishing a Business in EEC Countries

Introduction

This section refers to the establishing of a business in EEC countries. It is not a substitute for a legal treatise but rather an indication of essential points so that instructions to establish business can be adequately given and received.

BELGIUM

In accordance with Article 197 of Title IX of Book I of the Commercial Code, all companies which have their main office in Belgium are considered to be Belgian companies and are therefore subject to Belgian Law.

Foreign companies are those which have their main offices abroad: they are entitled to do business in Belgium and to appear before the Belgian Courts. If foreign companies set up a Belgian subsidiary, the legal requirements referred to in paragraphs 5ff and 21ff of the Commercial Code must be complied with.

The formation of a Belgian branch of foreign company is subject to the following requirements.

(1) Deposit of the Articles of the foreign company at the record office of the Commercial Court (*Rechtbank van Koophandel/Tribunal de Commerce*). The application for entry in the Commercial Registry (*Handelregister/Registre du Commerce*) will be made simultaneously.
(2) Publication of the Articles of Association in the Annexes of the Belgian Official Gazette (*Belgisch Staatblad/Monitor belge*) within 15 days following the above deposit.

Foreign companies establishing a Belgian branch are subject to the same rules as Belgian companies as regards publication of the balance sheet and profit and loss account.

The responsibilities of branch managers are the same as those of the managers of Belgian companies:

(1) they are responsible to the NV/SA for proper performance of their mandate;
(2) they are jointly liable to the corporation and to third parties for all violations of the Articles of Association or of company law, and
(3) the directors are also personally responsible for certain special infractions defined by company law with respect to the forming of the NV/SA, to management, to book-keeping and the distribution of its profits.

DENMARK

A foreign enterprise may conduct its activities in Denmark through a subsidiary created under Danish Law or through a registered branch. Both Law A/S and Law ApS recognise branches of foreign companies. A branch may be established in Denmark by foreign companies incorporated under their own national law if permitted by Treaty or by the Minister of Commerce (Law A/S, Section 147).

The prerequisites for establishing a branch are as follows.

(1) The branch must be registered in the Register of Companies in Copenhagen.
(2) Together with the application for registration, the company must submit –
    (a) an official document stating that the company was incorporated under and in accordance with its national laws;
    (b) a statement that the branch will comply fully with Danish law;
    (c) a mandate for the management of the branch;
    (d) the by-laws of the company, and
    (e) proof that the management of the branch is of age and that at least one of them is a Danish resident.

The Registrar of Companies will terminate the registration under the following circumstances:

(1) at the request of the company;
(2) at the request of a creditor, if he can show that the branch can no longer meet its financial obligations, or
(3) if the company fails to appoint a branch management within the time limit set by the Registrar.

After termination of the registration the branch will no longer be allowed to do business in Denmark.

The law attaches the following legal consequences to the establishment of a branch.

(1) The branch must use the name of the company with the addition "filial" (branch) and with a clear indication of the nationality of the company.
(2) The branch stationery must contain information with regard to the company's name, its statutory seat and registration number (if the amount of shares is listed, a distinction must be made between capital paid-in and unpaid).
(3) The branch must be managed by one or more managers who must have the authority to bind the branch legally.
(4) The company will be subject to Danish law for all actions undertaken in Denmark.

FRANCE

If a foreign company, entity or individual sets up a French subsidiary (SA or SARL) the normal legal requirements for the establishment of a company apply, but in addition a direct investment application must be filed with the Ministry of Economy and Finance.

The formation of a French branch of a foreign company is somewhat less complicated than the setting up of a company. The basic steps are as follows.

(1) The filing of a direct investment application with the Ministry of Economy.
(2) The depositing of two copies of the translated Articles of the foreign company with the clerk of the Commercial Court.
(3) Application for entry in the Commercial Registry (*Registre de Commerce*) presenting at this point a number of documents, including the translated birth certificates of the foreign company's directors, the reference (*gérant*) of the branch if he is a non-EEC national and the certificate of deposit of the lease or rent agreement of the French branch office.
lease or rent agreement of the French branch office.
(4) Upon entry in the Commercial Registry, declarations of existence to direct and indirect tax authorities and procurement of a statistical SIRENE number (*Systéme Informatique pour le Raportoire des Enterprises et Etablissements*
(5) For branches of foreign banks or insurance companies, negotiations with French regulatory authorities are necessary, especially as regards capital structure.

Branches of foreign companies are managed by one or more managers, whose powers are granted – and may be limited – by the foreign company's directors. There are in fact few specific French legal rules governing the powers of responsibilities of branch managers.

FEDERAL REPUBLIC OF GERMANY

Foreign enterprises wishing to start up business operations in Germany are not required to obtain permission unless –

(1) the business is one for which a licence is prescribed under the trade regulations (e.g., banking, insurance, mortgage banking and certain other activities) or
(2) the German operation is to be in the legal form of a branch and the head office is a foreign corporation with its domicile in a country outside the EEC.

The application to do business in Germany through a branch of a foreign company is made to the Ministry of Commerce of the State where the branch office is to be opened. It must be accompanied by certified copies of the following documents relating to the foreign company.

(1) Certificate of Incorporation.
(2) Articles and By-laws or Memorandum and Articles of Association.
(3) Published accounts (if the accounts have not been published, audited financial statements must be submitted).
(4) A list of members of the board of directors and their addresses.

These documents must be certified by the German consulate in the country in which the foreign company has its registered office. The Ministry of Commerce may require the submission of certified translations of the documents if it sees fit, but it does not normally do so if they are in the English language. (The purpose of these provisions is to ensure that adequate protection is granted to German creditors of the enterprise).

Normally a period of two to three months elapses between the date of the application and the date on which permission to do business is granted. It is, however, possible to commence business pending approval of the application.

A branch of a foreign company is normally required to maintain complete accounting records and supporting vouchers in Germany.

The branch may do business throughout the Federal Republic once permission is granted. Permission may be denied for several reasons.

(1) Lack of share capital – under DM 100,000 in the case of a foreign company without limited liability or under DM 200,000 in the case of a foreign limited liability company.
(2) A branch of a foreign corporation in the form of a "Zweigniederlassung" must also register on the Commercial Register through the local court. Non-resident companies prefer the GmbH form for German operations as a rule, but the branch form has been employed by foreign banks, insurance companies, film distributors, ship and air-transportation companies and in cases where start-up losses can be set off against the foreign corporation's profits until the German operation is profitable.

Where the foreign company wishes to establish a German enterprise in the form of an AG, GmbH, KG, etc., the normal domestic rules apply. Where a foreign company wishes to become a general partner in a partnership or maintain a liaison office of its own, a permit is required as in the case of setting up a branch.

Some general rules of German law apply to all new businesses, regardless of legal form.

(1) All new businesses in whatever form must register with the Trade Office (*Gewerbeamt*) and the tax authorities in the town or district in which their office is situated.

(2) Merchants – including individuals – carrying on one of nine basic commercial activities listed in HGB enterprises requiring a commercial organisation due to volume or type of transaction carried out, and enterprises organised under the Commercial Law (AG, GmbH, KG, etc.,) must be entered in the Commercial Register.

GREECE

If a foreign company, entity or individual sets up a Greek subsidiary (SA or EPE) the general requirements for forming a company in Greece apply. In addition the foreign company, if it wishes to have its investment under the umbrella of the Foreign Investment Law 2687/83 (for the attraction of foreign capital in productive investments), must apply to the Ministry of Coordination and Planning (Foreign Investments Section) for a Joint Ministerial Decree, signed by the Ministers of Coordination and Planning, Finance and Industry, granting approval under Law 2687. The principal advantages of investment under this law are the repatriation rights of capital, dividends, and interest, and certain tax and other duty benefits. It should be pointed out that the capital used for the establishment of the subsidiary must be imported from abroad and evidenced by bank remittances of foreign exchange from abroad. This foreign exchange evidence is required both by the notary and by the Bank of Greece, which controls the import of foreign capital.

The formation of a Greek branch is less complicated than setting up a Greek company. The interested foreign parent company files a petition to the Ministry of Commerce requesting the establishment of a Foreign Branch in Greece according to Article 50 of Law 2190/1920, and submits the following documents.

(1) Articles of Association and statutes showing that the company has been established in accordance with the laws of the country in which it is registered.
(2) A certificate from the Chamber of Commerce of the city in which the company is registered, stating that the company is currently operating and giving the amount of its paid-in capital and year of formation.
(3) A statement prepared by the company giving the names of its directors and/or officials having authority to bind the company.
(4) Power of Attorney in favour of a local representative, including power to accept service of process and legal documents.

All these documents must be notarised by the Greek Consul of the country in which the company is registered and be translated into Greek by the Ministry of Foreign Affairs in Athens. The approval of the Ministry of Commerce is then published in the Official Gazette, and as of that date the branch is legally established in Greece.

The foreign parent is obliged to file its annual balance sheet with the Ministry of Commerce, as well as a financial statement of the Greek branch activities.

It should be noted that in order for a foreign parent to set up a Greek branch, the foreign parent must have as capital in the case of an SA, an amount in foreign currency equivalent to DR 5,000,000 and in the case of a limited liability company an amount in foreign currency equivalent to DR 200,000. This capital amount is determined by the Ministry of Commerce.

ITALY

A foreign enterprise desiring to establish a place of business in Italy may choose either a subsidiary in the form of an incorporated entity (SPA or SRL) or a branch.

A strict application of the tax regulations should result in the same consideration and treatment being given to both a limited company and a branch, but in practice a separate legal entity such as subsidiary company is preferable from a tax point of view. Although a branch files a tax return based on its accounts, it is always regarded with a certain amount of suspicion by the tax authorities, who may request the financial statements of the head office to be produced with a view to determining that the arms-length concept has been adhered to. For this reason and also because a subsidiary can be charged by the parent company with interest, royalties and other charges whereas a branch cannot, a subsidiary is usually preferred to a branch. In the case of branches some uncertainties exist in this respect.

Dividends from an Italian company received by a non-resident company having a permanent establishment in Italy are included in the permanent establishment's income and are subject to the corporate income tax, but an amount equal to one-third of the amount of dividend may be credited against the income tax due, thus effecting a tax-free receipt of these dividends. A tax advantage of a permanent establishment as opposed to a subsidiary is that when the former remits profits to its head office there is no withholding tax.

There are no specific procedural difficulties in establishing a subsidiary company. The certificate of incorporation must be drawn up by a notary, and if not drawn up in the Italian language must be accompanied by a sworn translation. It should contain the following:

(1) name;
(2) address of the legal office;
(3) brief description of the purpose;
(4) duration (which may be any number of years);
(5) amount of the share capital (or quota capital in the case of a SRL), description of the shares and the names of the subscribers;
(6) names of the first board of directors;
(7) names of the first board of statutory auditors, and
(8) date on which the first financial period will end.

The subsidiary acquires its judicial personality when the Court has approved its Certificate of Incorporation.

As a branch of a foreign company it is not a legal entity, it is not necessary for a notary to assist in establishing it. It is, however, necessary to file certain documents with the office of the court having jurisdiction over the place where the branch office is opened. These are as follows.

(1) A notarised copy of the Certificate of Incorporation and By-laws of the company.
(2) A notarised copy of the resolution of the shareholders or of the board of directors of the foreign company to open a branch in Italy, which must also state where the branch is to be located, the name of the person appointed manager of the branch and the powers which are conferred on the said manager.
(3) A notarised power of attorney to the manager.
(4) A certificate of an officer of the foreign court (or company registry) stating that the foreign company is a company organised under the law of the state and that the documents indicated under (1) and (2) above have been filed there in accordance with the law of the state.
(5) The signature of the manager of the Italian branch.

The documents indicated above have to be duly certified and legalised by the Italian consular authority and by the Ministry of Foreign Affairs in Rome and, if not drawn up in the Italian language, must be accompanied by a sworn translation in Italian. The signature of the manager of the branch, who need not be an Italian citizen, must also be certified. Once the Court has approved the setting up of the branch it becomes part of the foreign company.

LUXEMBOURG

Foreign enterprises wishing to start business operations in Luxembourg require the same permission as inland enterprises (Law of 1915, Article 158).

If a foreign enterprise has its main place of business in Luxembourg, it will be subject to the Laws of the Grand Duchy, i.e., be regarded a Luxembourg company (Law of 1915, Article 159). If a foreign enterprise establishes a branch (*succursale*) or a place of business (*siège d'opérations*) the enterprise is obliged to publish the same information as a Luxembourg company (Law of 1915, Article 160).

The name and legal form must be printed on all documents, invoices and letters issued by or on behalf of the foreign company. The manager and other officers of the branch are subject to the same duties and liabilities as in the case of any Luxembourg company (Law of 1915, Article 160).

NETHERLANDS

A foreign enterprise may conduct its activities in the Netherlands through a subsidiary created under Dutch law or through a branch. The internal organisation of a subsidiary would be governed by the law of the Netherlands. Shares of a subsidiary may be issued publicly or privately, and the issue of stock for foreign subsidiaries is treated in exactly the same way as for Dutch companies. Shares may be listed on the Stock Exchange if the sum total of the par value of issued shares is at least DLF 500,000, subject to the approval of the Stock Exchange authorities. Both subsidiaries and branches must comply with provisions of the Dutch law dealing with matters other than the actual establishment of the company, e.g., social security law.

Generally, Dutch law recognises the legal status granted by the country of origin of a foreign company doing business in the Netherlands, and accords these companies the same treatment as that given to similar organisations created under Dutch law. Therefore the law of the place of incorporation is utilised to determine the rules applicable, for example, to the internal organisation of the branch or the authority of the manager of a branch. Due to the present socio-economic situation in the Netherlands, the establishment of a foreign branch or subsidiary of a foreign company does require the special approval of the Minister of Economics if that branch or subsidiary is to engage in industrial activity. Foreign branches or subsidiaries engaged only in sales or other service activities are not subject to this rule, since their influence on the labour market is considered to be comparatively minor. The foreign *industrial* investor must supply the following information to the Ministry of Economics:

(1) the legal form and objectives of the enterprise;
(2) the type of products to be manufactured;
(3) estimated total values of sales and exports expected in the near future;

(4) the amount and origin of the capital;
(5) financial statements;
(6) a description of the type of capital to be furnished – i.e., cash or in kind, share or loan capital, and
(7) the number of employees expected to be employed in the near future, distinguishing between males and females.

Both industrial and service enterprises must also secure an Exchange Licence from the Nederlandsche Bank (the Central Bank) so that funds can later be transferred outside the Netherlands. To protect the right to this licence certain requirements must be met. With respect to industrial enterprises all relevant information is considered to be provided when an investment permit is granted by the Minister of Economics; in the case of non-industrial enterprises, the application procedure is usually handled by the enterprise's commercial bank, which forwards all necessary information to the Central Bank.

REPUBLIC OF IRELAND

A foreign company wishing to set up a place of business in Ireland must comply with the provisions of Sections 352–357 of the Companies Act 1963. The more important provisions of these sections are that the company shall, within one month of the establishment of the place of business in Ireland, deliver to the Registrar of Companies for registration the following documents.

(1) A certified copy of its charter, statute, Memorandum and Articles or other instrument constituting or defining the constitution of the company, and if the instrument is not written in the English or Irish language a certified translation of it.
(2) A list of the directors and secretary of the company, indicating in relation to each director his Christian name and surname and his usual residential address, and in relation to the secretary his Christian name and surname and his usual residential address, nationality if not Irish, his business occupation and particulars of any other directorship held by him in bodies corporate in Ireland.
(3) The names and addresses of one or more persons resident in Ireland authorised to accept on behalf of the company service of process and any notices required to be served on the company, and also the address of the company's principal place of business in Ireland.

UNITED KINGDOM

There are no specific regulations relating to the establishment of a business in the United Kingdom by a foreign company. Foreign companies which establish a place of business within Great Britain must comply with the provisions of the current Companies Act. These require the filing with the Registrar of Companies of certified copies of the documents of constitution, particulars concerning the directors and secretary and certain other information. Where the required documents are not in the English language an English translation must be filed. An overseas company is obliged to file such accounts as it would have been required to file were it incorporated in Great Britain, subject to any exceptions which the Department of Trade may prescribe. In most cases, it is possible to obtain a dispensation which will permit the filing of the accounts published in the country's own country, or an English translation of those accounts if they are not in the English language.

4.Working with Europe

Business Cooperation Centre

Director,
Business Cooperation Centre,
Rue Archimedes 17,
B 1049 Brussels,
Belgium.

The aim of the Business Cooperation Centre is to encourage cooperation between firms in different member states of the European Community, with a view to increasing their competitiveness and helping to adjust to the expanded market. The Centre was set up by a decision of the Commission of the European Communities on 21 June 1973 and is a department of the Commission, by which it is financed, but it enjoys considerable autonomy in carrying out its functions. Its services are free of charge.

The function of the Centre is to try to find partners for firms interested in cooperation, to provide firms with information and advice and to keep the Community informed on obstacles of a general nature encountered by firms in their desire to cooperate or to merge.

Partner search

Liaisons of the kind which it is the Centre's role to encourage should be understood to mean long-term reciprocal ties which go beyond the stage of purely commercial relations. The cooperation agreements may involve any of the following:

(1) R & D (joint research, exchange of licences and know-how);
(2) purchasing (joint buying of raw materials, reciprocal supplying of primary products);
(3) production (specialisation agreements, joint production of a product, standardisation of products);
(4) marketing and sales (joint market research, joint trademarks, reciprocal use of sales networks, joint organisation of sales in a market outside the Community), and
(5) management (joint use of management facilities).

Cooperation initiated by the Centre may also take the form of financial link-ups between firms –

(1) setting up of a joint subsidiary;
(2) acquisition of a minority holding;
(3) mutual acquisition of holdings;
(4) setting up of a joint holding company, and
(5) mergers and takeovers.

On the other hand, the Centre plays no part in relations of a purely commercial nature or where no mutual long-term reciprocal link is involved. Thus the following are excluded: subcontracting, offers of or requests for commercial agencies and ordinary licensing agreements.

The Centre offers its services to all business firms of whatever legal form, financial structure or branch of activity (production, distribution or services). It was created primarily to meet the needs of small and medium-sized firms: large undertakings will naturally have little or no reason to make use of the Centre, since they have their own economists, lawyers and tax experts who can solve the problems of international cooperation.

The Centre can deal only with cooperation between firms from the Ten. The partner firms must be of different nationalities, nationality being determined by the location of the Head Office. The cooperation may, however, cover activities outside the Community (e.g., joint exports to non-member countries or the establishment of a joint production subsidiary in a non-member country).

When a firm asks the Centre to help it to find a partner with whom it can cooperate, the Centre will ask the firm to provide details about itself, and to specify what type of partner and what kind of cooperation it is looking for.

Supplying information to firms

As a rule the Business Cooperation Centre takes no part in negotiations between firms or in the conclusion of agreements, but is always prepared to attend as a neutral third party and to provide information or advice on the opportunities for and limitations on international cooperation.

The questions may deal with areas such as company law, right of establishment, rules relating to foreign investment, exchange control and tax arrangements applying to foreign shareholders.

European Patent Office

New technologies are responsible for 75 per cent of industrial growth. If new technology enjoys the protection of a reliable patent, inventions will stimulate expansion. Patents are a weapon in the struggle for new markets and can form a basis for cooperation between undertakings and for licensing agreements.

Prior to the establishment of the European patent anyone wanting to obtain a patent in several countries in Western Europe had to file a patent application in the language of each national office. He had to have a professional representative entitled to act before the authorities of the countries concerned. He had separate correspondence with each office and he had to know the different patent laws and the procedures in each country.

Since June 1978, however, it is possible to obtain an examined patent for most West European states by filing a single patent application in one language (English, French or German) at the European Patent Office.

The protection of inventions afforded by the European patent is thus (1) less expensive; (2) less complicated, and (3) more reliable. For its proprietor, the European patent will have the same effects as a portfolio of national patents granted in each state which has ratified the European Patent Convention. In fact the European patent will cover a market comprising 290 million people.

Organisation

The European Patent Office was first opened in Munich in 1978; it was established in the Convention on the Grant of European Patents signed in 1973. The Office has approximately 1,000 staff, including the highly qualified search examiners of the former International Patent Institue at the Hague and of the Berlin Annexe of the German Patent Office.

The European Patent Convention is linked to the world-wide Patent Cooperation Treaty (PCT) which came into force in 1978. European patents can be granted on the basis of an international application filed in accordance with the PCT in any state party to the PCT. The objective of the PCT is to centralise part of the patent grant procedure in the countries which have ratified the Treaty by entrusting searching, and to a certain extent examination, to a limited number of major offices (e.g., those of the USA, Soviet Union, Japan and the European Patent Office).

Procedure for obtaining a European patent

A European Application can be filed in Belgium, France and the Federal Republic of Germany, Italy, Luxembourg, The Netherlands, and the United Kingdom. Sweden and Switzerland are the non-EEC countries allowing an Application.

Other states which have signed the European Patent Convention and for which it will therefore in all probability be possible in future to file a European Patent Application are Denmark, Greece and the Republic of Ireland. Austria, Liechtenstein, Monaco, and Norway are the non-EEC countries in the same position.

Any legal or natural person regardless of nationality, residence or place of business can apply for a European patent. The procedure is as follows.

(1) Patent applications must be filed with the Receiving Section in the branch at The Hague or with the office in Munich.
(2) The next step is the allocation of data, filing, payment of fees and formalities examination.
(3) Then the search and forwarding of the search report together with all documents cited therein to the applicant.
(4) Publication of the application and the search report.
(5) Substantive examination for novelty inventiveness and the possibility of industrial application of the invention.
(6) Grant of patent.

The fees payable in the European grant procedure have been so calculated that the cost of obtaining a European patent, taking into account the cost of representation – before the EPO or national patent offices – and translation will normally be less than the cost of obtaining three national patents.

In many cases the European route will be worthwhile even if the applicant seeks protection in only two contracting states on account of the advantages of the uniform grant procedure, and the uniform title to protection.

The following sources of information will be useful to anyone wishing to make use of the European Patent System.

(1) The Official Journal (published monthly).

(2) The European Patent Bulletin, which publishes information about the progress of application every two weeks. It is the key document for finding out about published applications and granted patents.

(3) Patent documents – the office publishes patent applications and specifications of granted patents.

(4) Information about applications – The Information Department provides information on the content of the Register of Patents and handles the opening for public inspection of the content of European patent applications.

(5) Libraries – there are libraries in both Munich and The Hague.

(6) Addresses:

European Patent Office,
Erhardtstr 27,
Munich.

Post Bus. 5818,
2280 Hvirkswijk ZH,
Netherlands.

Gitschiner St 97-103,
D-1000 Berlin 61.

CHAPTER 7

THE ACCOUNTANT IN EUROPE

1. The Accounting Profession

Introduction

There are differences both attitudinal and conceptual in the accounting professions of the member states of the European Economic Community. There are differences in the exclusiveness of the work performed by the members of the profession, and in their organisation, status, training and numbers.

In most countries the audit of larger quoted companies must be undertaken by state-authorised professional people. Many countries do not limit auditing exclusively to the professionally qualified person – in France, for instance, where auditing is regarded and organised as a less rigorous profession, and Italy where there is no national organisation at all. In most countries theoretical training, concentrating on legal aspects applies. Denmark, Germany and the Netherlands require both theoretical and practical competence, whereas in the UK the accent is on professional practice and experience. In most countries the status of the qualified accountant is high, but the status of the auditor is not always as well regarded. Lack of status applies in Italy and Belgium, and a further factor contributing to this lack of status is often the absence of any developed equity market.

When comparing the accounting professions in the Community, the audit field is limited to a certification programme as determined by statute rather than the passing of an opinion as to the clarity and fairness of the financial statements.

The potential development of the accountancy bodies appears to be tied to the amount of autonomy and independence allowed to the members.

Where representatives are allowed to participate in legislative reform as in the UK, Denmark, Germany and the Netherlands, and in recent years France and to a lesser extent Belgium, one can see the emergence of standards, initially in the form of recommendations but eventually becoming mandatory, governing the accounting, auditing and reporting functions.

BELGIUM

The accounting profession is divided into the auditing and accounting functions. The auditing profession is governed by the Institut des Réviseurs de Banque (IRB) and the Institut des Réviseurs d'Enterprises (IRE). The former body was founded in 1935 and is regarded as the premier of the two Institutes. However, its members specialise in the fields of banking and insurance, although they may be appointed as a réviseur d'enterprises. Appointment has to be made by the Banking Commission and membership of the Institute is less than 50.

Members of the IRE are primarily involved in the audit of commercial firms. There are about 400 members concerned with this type of work. Qualification as a member of IRE, which dates from 1953, is obtained by completing a three-year training period and either graduating with a university degree in economics or business administration, or passing the Institute's own examinations.

Most qualified accountants are members of the College National des Experts Comptables, but the designation "Expert Comptable" has no legal status. Membership of the College is obtained in a similar manner to that of the IRE, by undergoing a five-year training period with a member of the College followed by a professional examination.

Both professions, auditing and accounting, are governed by codes of ethics, that of the IRB being particularly restrictive.

DENMARK

The accounting profession in Denmark is organised within the Foreningen af Statsautoriserede Revisorer (FSR) the Institute of State authorised Public Accountants, founded in 1912. A licence to practice as a state-authorised public accountant is granted by the Ministry of Trade, Industry and Shipping and is dependent upon an applicant being qualified by examination, experience, and other requirements. The qualification can also be obtained by completing a five-year full-time course culminating in the Master of Commerce degree in auditing.

FRANCE

In 1966 the auditing and accounting activities were separated, the auditing profession being organised under the Ministry of Justice and the accounting profession coming under the auspices of the Ministry of Economics and Finance.

The main body within the accounting profession is L'Ordre des Experts Comptables et des Comptables Agrèes established in 1942, and subsequently amalgamated with a number of different accounting bodies. As a result of laws passed in 1968 L'Ordre combines with L'Institut Francais des Experts Comptables to form a unified accounting profession. Part of the unification procedure is that the Comptables Agrèes part of L'Ordre (who could be regarded as bookkeepers) should cease to be eligible for recruitment to L'Ordre from 1968. A number of Experts Comptables are also separately qualified and authorised to undertake statutory audits. Membership of L'Ordre does not carry any right to perform audits and is restricted to qualified accountants actually in practice and working as principals.

Current membership of the accounting profession i.e., L'Ordre and L'Institut is approximately 1,400. In order to qualify as a member of L'Ordre a person must pass examinations – exemptions from some papers are granted to graduates. A student must also undergo a three-year articleship with at least one of those years in the office of an approved accounting topic. In practice most applicants to membership of L'Ordre are 30 years of age, but the minimum age of admittance is 25 years.

The auditing function originated in 1867, but in 1966 the Companies Act extended the statutory requirement to large SARLS, created the profession of Commissaires, fixed minimum fees, and laid upon the Commissaire the duty of certifying the truth and fairness of the accounts, assets and liabilities, and forming an opinion on certain management activities.

It is significant that although an Expert Comptable can be registered as a Commissaire aux Comptes the reverse is not true. Commissaires aux Comptes must be members of La Compagnie Nationale des Commissaires aux Comptes who number about 7,000.

The profession in France is clearly divided into accounting and auditing functions, and both professions have codes of ethics.

FEDERAL REPUBLIC OF GERMANY

Accounting in Germany is undertaken by Wirtschaftsprüfer (WP) whose position and profession is protected by law in the Wirtschaftsprüferordnung, 1961. This law set up the Chamber to regulate the profession to amalgamate the oldest body of public accountants – Vereidigte Buchprüfer (VBP) – with the WP dating from 1931 and to delegate the technical, practising matters to the Institute WP. The title of WP is restricted to those qualified and in practice; a WP who ceases to practise, say to enter business, loses the title.

The 1961 Act licensed the profession of tax adviser (Steuerberater – SB) and tax assistant (Steuerbevollmächtiger – STBEV). There are about 5,000 WPs, some of whom would rank among the 7,500 STB and a further 25,000 STBEV. Only a WP can audit the AG, KGaA, the larger GmbH, insurance companies, banks, savings institutions, cooperatives and public utilities. The method of becoming a WP is to graduate before obtaining six years' business experience (at least four of which are with a WP) and passing the Institute's professional examination. The usual age for admittance is 35 years.

The qualifying requirements for a STB are of a similar nature subject to specialisation in taxation theory and practice. The WP is engaged, in addition to statutory auditing work, on investigations and consultancy. A WP would not undertake book-keeping, company registrar or secretaryship work. There is a detailed code of ethics, which places great stress on his independence, issuing rules as to occupations and relationships, and requiring him to take an oath on admission concerning the exercise of his professional duties.

GREECE

There are three accounting organisations in Greece.

(1) *Institute of Certified Public Accountants of Greece (SOL).*
Set up in 1955, this is the only body recognised by the Greek Government for carrying out audits. It is however virtually a closed shop (limited to 45 members) and controlled by the government.

(2) *Institute of Incorporated Accountants in Greece (EPEL).*
This rival body was set up in 1968 claiming to establish an independent profession. There has been a bitter argument between SOL and EPEL ever since as to who represents the Greek profession. Both bodies have from time to time circularised the Presidents of leading accountancy bodies in Europe and around the world to put their case for recognition.

(3) *Association of Certified Accountants and Auditors of Greece (SELE).*
This body was formed in May 1980, by a group of Accountants who were anxious to see a body of Accountants formed in Greece that would be independent and structured along the lines of the Institutes and Societies of those Countries that have developed accounting profession and whose membership would be of the highest calibre. One of the primary objectives of forming the Association was to enable people who wish to make a career in accounting to obtain a professional qualification.

ITALY

The accounting profession in Italy is regulated under the Ministry of Justice which stipulates the regulations. The profession is also influenced to some degree by the Civil Code as regards the auditing function. Instead of being organised at national level, the profession tends to be administered on a regional basis. There are two types of professional accountant, both governed by laws passed in 1953: Doctors of Commerce, and Accountants and Commercial Experts. Doctors of Commerce (*Ordine dei Dottori Commercialisti*) represent the academic wing of the Italian profession. Qualification is through a four-year university course in economics, accountancy, banking, public, civil and commercial law. The requirements also include a doctoral thesis followed by a state examination. There is no requirement for practical experience and a Dottori Commercialista does not have to practise to retain the title.

The Accountants and Commercial Experts (*Collegio dei Ragioneri e Perite Commerciali*) are qualified to a greater extent by practice and experience. Membership of the Collegio is by passing the accounting diploma examinations. At least two years' practical experience must be obtained with a member of the Collegio or the Ordine in public practice, and a state examination must be passed in the provisions of the Civil Code. The work that the Collegio or the Ordine are empowered to undertake is identical and both are held competent to carry out the statutory audits of companies. Any company must have a Collegio Sindacale (Board of Auditors).

Practising Dottori or Ragionieri usually do so as sole practitioners. There are about 17,000 Dottori, of whom about 50 per cent are in practice, and 8,000 Ragionieri, of whom 90 per cent are in practice.

LUXEMBOURG

The Accounting profession is principally carried on by L'Ordre des Experts Comptables Luxembourgeois, which has about 40 members. Members must be Luxembourg nationals, and qualify by becoming graduates and then completing a three-year period of articles under a member of L'Ordre.

Unlike his counterpart in Belgium, the professional Expert Comptable in Luxembourg must be in practice. The type of work undertaken includes audit and accounting work generally, tax and business consultancy, formation and liquidation work. A member of L'Ordre practices as a sole practitioner or in partnership.

All partnerships limited by shares, and limited companies, must undergo an annual statutory audit. The persons entitled to carry out the audit are not specified by law and therefore it is not necessarily the prerogative of the Expert Comptable. Lawyers, employees, or relatives may carry out the function of the statutory examiner (Commissaire). The change to Expert Comptable is under consideration.

NETHERLANDS

The profession of accounting is an amalgamation of the Nederlands Instituut van Accountants (NIVA) formed in 1895 and the Vereniging van Academisch Gevormde Accountants (VAGA) dating from 1927. Until the 1960s VAGA formed the academic but not necessarily professionally experienced body. In 1962 the Registered Accountants Act was passed,

(*a*) safeguarding the interests of qualified and experienced accountants, and
(*b*) ensuring adequate standards of training and education.

Company law reform was followed by the unification of the Dutch accounting profession in the Nederlands Instituut van Register Accountants (NIVRA) formed in 1967 from the membership of the NIVA and the VAGA. Although there are other organisations of accountants in the Netherlands they do not audit companies, and are restricted to work of a book-keeping or tax computational nature.

There are about 5,000 members of NIVRA, of whom 50 per cent are in public practice. In order to qualify, a student must obtain the Diploma by way of professional experience and examination and – unlike the UK – by means of postgraduate study in accountancy following a first degree in economics. There is no requirement for a student to be apprenticed to a registered accountant and the broadness and theoretical foundation of NIVRA examination forms a sound basis for flexibility in accounting practice. Like the UK chartered institutes, the Dutch counterpart is engaged on investigatory work, management and tax consultancy work.

The Code of Ethics is laid down by the Ministry of Economic Affairs.

UNITED KINGDOM AND REPUBLIC OF IRELAND

These are considered together because their professional organisations are very similar.

Professionalism in accounting stems from the Joint-Stock Companies Acts of 1844 which required annual appointment of Auditors and 1856 which allowed the appointment of an auditor who was not himself a shareholder, and also allowed him to employ persons to conduct an audit at company expense. The Chartered Institutes in Scotland (dating from 1854) and in England and Wales (from 1880) together with that in Ireland (from 1888), and the Association of Certified Accountants formed in 1904 are currently recognised by the Department of Trade and Industry for the purpose of conducting audits of limited companies.

There was then the need to fulfil the requirements of the professional accountant in industry as distinct from the audit function. The Institute of Company Accountants was formed in 1928, and in 1974 amalgamated with the Society of Commercial Accountants to form the Society of Company and Commercial Accountants, whose prime function is the development of control techniques and procedures within commerce and industry throughout the world as an aid to more effective and efficient management. The Society seeks recognition of the profession of the qualified in-company accountant throughout Europe, and is the first professional accounting body to institute a post-graduate diploma in European Studies.

Other bodies with specialist functions in the accounting profession are the Institute of Cost and Management Accountants and the Chartered Institute of Public Finance and Accountancy.

Summary – Methods of qualifying as Accountant/Auditor

	Years to Qualify (Post School)	*Post School Education*
Belgium	7/9	Full-time degree and/or professional examinations
Denmark	5/8	Full-time bachelor and masters degrees plus seminars or part-time courses
France	10	Diploma in accounting studies and a thesis on accounting
Federal Republic of Germany	10	Holders of specified degrees with subsequent professional examinations
Greece	5	Specialised
Italy	4/7	Full-time degree doctoral thesis followed by state examination or part-time accounting diploma followed by state examination
Luxembourg	6	Full-time degree
Netherlands	7/8	First degree full-time; part-time accountancy diploma
Republic of Ireland and UK	5	Full-time/part-time professional examinations

2. Accounting Systems

Introduction

There are four types of accounting system, each of which exists within Europe.

(1) *Macroeconomic* – in which accounting is regarded as a tool in the furtherance of national economic objectives which are set and communicated by government.
(2) *Microeconomic* – which operates on the overriding belief that what is good for the individual firm is good for the economy. Reports are produced to demonstrate the efficiency of the company as a going concern. Accounting practice is based upon economic theory, and the legal outline encourages conformity with business practice but does not prescribe rules or procedures.
(3) *Uniform accounting* – uniformity in the presentation of accounting information. At national level, uniformity is ensured by the enactment of legislation which lays out standard forms of accounts, rules and procedures. Within this system the function of accountants is to comply with the law and there is no room for independent judgment.
(4) *Pragmatic* – which is based on the principles that *(a)* the accounting function is to serve business, and *(b)* business is an art and responds on an *ad hoc* basis to the requirements existing at that time. Accounting reports are produced primarily for entrepreneurs who are considered to be the best judges of what information is required.

All these systems are found in Europe but considerable diversity exists depending on each country's stage of economic development and in part from different national cultural influences.

BELGIUM

The developing accounting system in Belgium, with its dependence on taxation legislation, implies a macroeconomic orientation. The emergence of proposals for a uniform chart and plan of accounts modelled on the French system is likely to increase this orientation.

There is, however, a difference in disclosure standards between quoted and unquoted companies. Although Belgian company law does not detail the format of financial statements, it stipulates the following balance sheet headings – fixed assets, realisable assets, bonds issued, secured and unsecured liabilities, and shareholders' equity. Published accounts only occasionally have notes appended, showing the basis of valuation of assets, depreciation formula and any changes in accounting principles.

Fixed assets are shown at cost less depreciation, but proposals for the reporting of intangibles are:

(1) discount in share issues can be written off over the life span of the issue;
(2) initial expenses can be capitalised and written off over not more than 10 years, and
(3) Research expenses can be amortised over 10 years.

Inventories are reported at the lower of cost or net realisable value, but the tax authorities do not usually consider the "last in first out" and base stock methods as acceptable in calculating costs.

Liabilities are shown under the divisions of long-term and medium-term profits and capital resources.

Profit and Loss accounts are not required to be presented in a standard form.

DENMARK

The Danish accounting system remains orientated towards taxation accounting except in the case of larger companies, and even under new legislation is very heavily creditor-based. It may still, therefore, be described as falling within the macroeconomic pattern.

The law requires that ten per cent of the annual net profits after tax will be transferred to a legal reserve until this equals ten per cent of the paid up share capital: thereafter five per cent of the net profit after tax must be transferred until the statutory reserve amounts to twenty-five per cent of the paid up share capital.

Financial reporting follows the general pattern of other Community countries with modifications.

Fixed assets are reported at cost less accumulated depreciation, but the annual depreciation provision need not be on a consistent basis. Assets may be revalued but the surplus can be used only for the issue of bonus shares or writing down other assets.

Inventories are stated at up to 30 per cent less than the lower of cost or realisable value, costs being calculated by any method except "last in first out",

Profit and Loss accounts are prepared to give a satisfactory explanation, in line with the company's operation, of how the profit and loss has been arrived at.

FRANCE

With the prescriptive requirements of the Plan Comptable, the French accounting system is a uniform approach. In addition the aims underlying the Plan Comptable and the insistence that financial reports should conform with the tax legislation sets this uniform system within a macroeconomic framework.

France is one of the few countries which adheres strongly to uniform accounting. The accounting process is based on double-entry book-keeping principles. The principles are in the Plan Comptable prepared by Ministerial Commission in 1947 and amended in 1950 and 1957. The Plan is a codified system of accounting, providing charts of accounts, forms and classifications of financial statements valuations and reporting procedures and the basic methods of recording transactions.

It has ten groups of accounts and each group has ten main accounts including Fixed Assets, Inventories, Accounts Receivable, Operating Expenses, Profit and Loss and Cost accounts. Every main account is identified with two-digit account numbers – e.g., manufacturing profit and loss account number 98, and depreciation and provisions 68. Supporting and sub-supporting accounts are identified by third and fourth digits, e.g., amortisation of buildings 6811.

The objectives of the Plan are to provide precise accounting data which will promote more reliable natural economic and fiscal policies.

The Plan requires the valuation of inventories at weighted average cost subject to the lower of market or cost doctrine. Assets are shown at cost and price-level adjustments are not permitted. The basic rules for depreciation of assets are:

(1) an asset can be depreciated only by its legal owner;
(2) depreciation must be taken regardless of the current period's operating results;
(3) if depreciable assets are self-constructed they must be completed before depreciation can be commenced;
(4) aggregate depreciation can never exceed total purchase or construction costs, and
(5) depreciation must be on approved dates.

In addition to the Plan, accounting procedures are governed by tax regulations, the Companies Act and stock exchange requirements.

FEDERAL REPUBLIC OF GERMANY

Although the German system of accounting is in a transitional state, until the 1940s it clearly followed the macroeconomic path and operated within a macroeconomic business environment. Since then the accounting system has been less suitable for the environment in which it operates. Accounting practice has remained rigid and prescribed, whilst its environment has required a more flexible pragmatic approach to accounting systems.

The Public Corporation Law 1965 and the Commercial Code contain regulations relating to accounting principles. The main provisions are:

(1) fixed assets are to be reported at cost less accumulated depreciation;
(2) current assets are to be stated at the lower of cost, net realisable value and replacement value;
(3) intangible assets may be carried if they are acquired from third parties, and
(4) all liabilities, including unrealised losses, have to be fully provided for and unrealised profits can be taken up.

In the Federal Republic, as in many other EEC countries, the influence of taxation is very significant. Uniform accounting has been the fundamental feature of the German accounting scene since 1920.

The generally accepted accounting regulations and concepts are:

(1) the concept of accounting for an economic entity and for a definite period of time,
(2) the concept of historical cost, and
(3) the concept of continuity.

Those for the preparation of financial statements are:

(1) *completeness* – all economic activities which are accountable have to be accounted for;
(2) *prudence* – the financial position should not be presented too favourably;
(3) *the concept of valuation* – the financial statements must not state the current value of the business though it must give a summary of individual assets and liabilities, and
(4) *the concept of net realisable value* – current assets should be stated at values which can be realised and fixed assets have to be depreciated over their useful lives.

The following are the main features of accounting.

(1) The Annual Accounts follow the model set out in the Public Corporation Law of 1965 except in the cases of transportation, banking and insurance.

(2) Foreign subsidiaries' accounts are not consolidated.
(3) The "concept of valuation" prevails where in conflict with the "true view".
(4) Depreciation provisions can appear among liabilities.
(5) Intangibles can appear in the balance sheet only when they have been acquired for value.
(6) Inventories are usually valued at average prices.
(7) Expenses for research and development can be capitalised.
(8) It is not necessary to disclose the amount of firm contracts for capital expenditure not incurred at the date of the final accounts.
(9) AGs must set up a legal reserve by transferring 5 per cent of annual profits until the reserve equals one tenth of the share capital or a higher amount as laid down by the articles.

GREECE

Introduction

As a general rule books on an enterprise must be maintained in the Greek language, and the entries made in the Greek currency (drachmae). However, foreign enterprises operating in Greece may request approval to use a foreign language. Enterprises established in Greece with foreign capital may be permitted to state their capital in terms of the currency in which that capital was imported and to keep their books of account and issue their financial statements in that currency.

Generally, before the legally required books may be used the pages must be pre-numbered and the books authenticated (i.e. stamped or perforated) by the tax authorities. Furthermore all entries in the books are to be supported by proper documentation such as invoices, receipts and statements.

Accounting Records

(1) *First Category Books* – business enterprises having gross revenue from the previous year of less than 7 million drachmae are only required to maintain a book of purchase.
(2) *Second Category Books* – business enterprises having gross revenue from the previous year of 8 million to 20 million drachmae are only required to maintain a book of revenues and expenditures.
(3) *Third Category Books* – business enterprises having gross revenue from the previous year of 20 million to 25 million drachmae are only required to maintain books of revenues

and expenditures and an inventory book, in which all the year-end balances of all assets and liabilities are to be recorded.

(4) *Fourth Category Books* – corporations, limited liability companies, and branches of these foreign companies. Other forms of business enterprise having gross revenue from the previous years of more than 25 million drachmae are also included in this category. Enterprises in this category must use a double-entry book-keeping system based on accepted accounting principles.

Enterprises offering services must keep second category books. Specified enterprises with gross revenue over 50 million drachmae are required to maintain day-to-day inventory records. Manufacturing companies that are required to maintain these records must also keep a book showing the costs of production.

Recording transactions in the Books and Records

The Tax Records Code provides certain time limitations for recording transactions in the books. For example cash transactions must be recorded within three days following the issuance of the related invoice, the detailed ledger cards must be updated within 20 days following the date of entry in the journal, the quantity of goods purchased or sold must be recorded in the inventory records within five days following the date of receipt or shipment, and all transactions relating to the preparation and recording of the detailed inventory list, the balance sheet, and the profit and loss statement must be recorded within two months of the prior year's end.

Valuation of Assets and Liabilities

The Tax Records Code prescribes the valuation method for carrying the following items on the balance sheet:

(1) Inventories should be valued at lower of cost or market. Any cost method is acceptable provided that it is maintained consistently. However if standard cost valuation is used, all variances must be allocated on the basis of goods sold and inventories on hand at year-end. Variances relating to cost of goods sold must be charged to profit and loss, and variances relating to inventories on hand must be charged to a balance sheet account and transferred to the following year's profit and loss account.

(2) Fixed Assets are carried at acquisition cost less accumulated depreciation.

(3) Bad Debts are carried at their initial amount less accumulated write-offs. It must be noted that bad debts are only deductable

for tax if they are recorded on the books and the insolvency of the debtor can be proved.

(4) Claims and liabilities in foreign currency are converted into drachmae at the official conversion rates as of the balance sheet date.

(5) Securities, in the aggregate are carried at their acquisition cost at any previously used lower cost or at their average market cost during the 15 days prior to the balance sheet date, whichever amount is lower.

Accounting Books Committee

In addition to the authority given to the Minister of Finance and the competent tax authority, the Tax Records Code also established the Accounting Books Committee. This committee has authority to decide whether an enterprise should maintain inventory records as well as the method for maintaining them. The Committee can also give opinions on certain specified Tax Record Code matters.

ITALY

The Italian system of accounting is not sufficiently advanced to fit within any of the four patterns. However, to the extent that the legal framework within which it is confined is largely influenced by fiscal policy considerations and because of the role played by government-promoted institutions, it is likely that any development of the system of accounting will adopt a macroeconomic orientation.

The accounting practices are governed by the 1942 Civil Code, which regulates the recording and valuation of a company's assets and liabilities, and the items to be disclosed in financial statements. Though the law does not prescribe a fixed form of financial statement a format has developed from practice.

Fixed assets are valued at cost less depreciation and are not usually revalued because the surplus would be taxable as income.

Depreciation rates are formulated and agreed by the tax authorities.

Intangible assets are reported at cost and amortisation is governed by the life of the assets.

Inventories are at the lower of cost or net realisable values, but tax law specifies the use of "last in first out" to ascertain the cost price.

Investments are valued according the best judgment of the directors. For valuation purposes the law makes no distinction between short-term and long-term investments.

Companies are required to appropriate an amount of not less

than five per cent of their annual net profit after tax to a non-distributable legal reserve until the reserve is equal to twenty per cent of the subscribed capital.

LUXEMBOURG

There is unquestionably a macroeconomic orientation of the accounting system with its dependence on the taxation legislation. The Code de Commerce states that the accounting records should be kept by companies. These include a statement of assets and liabilities and a journal for recording daily transactions.

It is also necessary to publish annually in the official gazette the final accounts which must include the following:

(1) a balance sheet;
(2) a profit and loss account;
(3) a distribution of profits statement;
(4) a statement of capital, and
(5) particulars of the directors and auditors.

All SA (*Sociétés anonymes*) must disclose in their balance sheets the following groupings:

(1) fixed assets;
(2) current assets;
(3) shareholders' equity;
(4) secured and unsecured liabilities, and
(5) bonds.

Company law requires that 5 per cent of the net profits after tax but before appropriations be transferred to a non-distributable legal reserve until this equals 10 per cent of the subscribed capital. If accumulated losses exceed 50 per cent of the subscribed capital, shareholders must vote for the continuation of the company. If accumulated losses exceed 75 per cent of the subscribed capital, 25 per cent of the shareholders can demand its winding up.

Reported items include:

(1) fixed assets at cost less depreciation – the rate of depreciation must be agreed with the tax authorities;
(2) inventories, valued at the lower of cost or net realisable value, and
(3) dividends when paid in cash.

Non-reported items include:

(1) deferred taxes;

(2) contingent liabilities;
(3) turnover, and
(4) cost of sales.

No provisions are required for future pension rights or proposed dividends.

NETHERLANDS

The system of accounting and reporting practised in the Netherlands, at least in the case of the larger quoted companies, contains most of the characteristics of the microeconomic approach. Not only has the business community supported such an accounting orientation but government has also given statutory recognition in its implementing legislation both to the respectability of the accountant's role and to the need to preserve a flexible approach to changing conditions.

The instrument of statutory control over the format of annual accounts is the Annual Accounts of Enterprise Act 1971. This act defines the acceptable standards, requiring a balance sheet, a profit and loss account, and among other facts the basis of valuing assets and liabilities.

Accounting in the Netherlands has been influenced by Professor Limpberg (see Limpberg Institute) whose ideas on replacement value accounting – where buildings, plant and machinery and inventories are revalued at the lower of two market values: replacement and proceeds value – are universally employed.

Tax laws have not influenced the accounts as in France and the Federal Republic of Germany, but sets of financial statements are required for the tax authorities.

Fixed assets are reported at cost less accumulated depreciation – the tax authorities accept rates decided by management, providing they are reasonable.

Intangible assets appear at cost less accumulated amortisation.

Inventories are reported at the lower of cost or market value, and cost in this respect can be calculated by the first-in first-out method.

In the UK assets are grouped as, say, current assets and in the Federal Republic of Germany as revolving assets, but in the Netherlands assets are not grouped, as it is necessary to distinguish between the various classifications e.g., debtors – trade, special and intercompany.

Bank overdrafts, creditors, provisions and other liabilities are also shown separately. A feature in the Netherlands is that, unlike for instance in the United Kingdom, a company may own its own shares.

Profit and loss accounts must disclose sales or revenue either as *(a)* absolute amounts or *(b)* percentage change over the previous financial year, and must also present it in a way that conforms with the practice of other companies in a like industry.

UNITED KINGDOM AND REPUBLIC OF IRELAND

The system of financial accounting operated within the UK and the Republic of Ireland is of the pragmatic approach. It is noticeably lacking in any theoretical foundation and relies for its authority on the use of a few well-tried and useful "ground rules" or concepts developed over time and supported by an authoritative, well-regarded, self-disciplining profession.

The Companies Acts are the major statutes for controlling accounting and reporting, and they are systematically and periodically revised by committees appointed on an *ad hoc* basis, deriving their recommendations largely from expert testimony and appropriate papers submitted by interested organisations.

All limited liability companies, both public and private, must file annual returns with the Registrar of Companies within a specified time after the annual general meeting. The balance sheet must show fixed assets under separate headings with details of acquisitions and disposals during the year and a note of any shortfall between recorded and realisable values. Details must also be shown of current assets, assets which are neither fixed nor current, land held, loans (other than from banks), separately classified reserves, redeemable shares and redeemable debentures available for re-issue.

The profit and loss account must state the amount of turnover where it exceeds a given amount, and a description of the method by which it is calculated. Details are required of directors and their remuneration and pensions.

Consolidated statements in the form of group accounts must be prepared, consisting of a consolidated balance sheet and a consolidated profit and loss account directly attributable to the parent company.

Fixed assets are valued basically at historical cost but have (relatively) frequent application to current values. Any increase in value is taken to capital reserve and is not (generally) available for distribution.

Current assets valued in realisable terms under the figure shown should be noted. Inventories are valued at historical cost less any amounts written off to reduce to net realisable value or replacement price if this is lower. The method of determining cost according to flow is not usually disclosed, although any consistently applied method is permitted – the last-in first-out method is not allowable for tax purposes; first-in first-out or average is probably the most frequently used method.

Liabilities are distinguished as between those of short- and long-term maturity, secured or unsecured.

Income statement – turnover is shown although the cost of sales and gross profits according to differentiated products, groups or activities need not be stated. Sales are noted net of VAT. Depreciation must be shown. Directors' remuneration is shown, as are extraordinary and non-recurring items.

Taxation accounting is not practised in the UK or Republic of Ireland and consequently considerable differences can arise between accounting profits and taxable profits.

3. Taxation

Introduction

From very early days, when people first joined together to form a society or community, one of the methods of ensuring its continuity was the payment of money or personal services to a central body. The tax systems of older countries reflect the economic, social or geographical relationships peculiar to those countries. These systems usually developed at a time when countries were able to pursue separate and independent tax policies without regard to their effects on other countries. Tax systems therefore differed radically in approach and type.

As communications between countries increased, so did awareness of the international impact of national tax systems. Following World War II the need for reconstructions and other economic measures accelerated this trend. The government's increasing need for revenue was reflected in its increasing interference in the national economy. Funds for restoration or reconstruction had to be generated by the community and consequently many taxes were imposed to provide this badly needed revenue. Special tax incentives were given to businesses to encourage their participation in the reconstruction. This resulted in each country developing a complex tax system based upon its individual needs, and without regard to repercussions elsewhere. Because these laws placed undesirable economic burdens upon businesses wishing to engage in international transactions they often obstructed increasing business contacts between countries. Several international organisations were established in Europe to find solutions to these problems and encourage international communication. The European Economic Community and the Organisation for

Economic Cooperation and Development have both participated in this endeavour through their work on tax harmonisation and model treaties.

In addition to these internal changes in Europe, however, other major events were taking place elsewhere. An unprecedented number of colonies became independent sovereign countries, each struggling to discard its colonial structure and develop its own. Tax systems therefore had to be modified to meeting changing needs, effective administrations established and staff recruited and trained. Regional cooperation developed between these newly independent countries to solve these and other problems. In many cases, national welfare depended upon international trade and commerce, which had to be further stimulated. Tax treaties were among the measures introduced to relieve undesirable economic burdens on international transactions, and these treaties were often between countries having dissimilar economic structures. Even more than in former years governments used taxation as a tool to combat recession and inflation. It would seem that inflation is considered the main cause of economic disturbances, since almost everywhere tax measures have been introduced to keep the rate of inflation as low as possible, and in many European countries these efforts have been proved successful.

Tax measures introduced or strengthened during recent years have taken various forms. Some countries have increased personal allowances, sometimes even indexed them, e.g., in the United Kingdom. At the same time income tax brackets have been revised so as to reduce the nominal tax burden by reducing or nullifying the effect of the progressive rate on inflation-related income rises. In several countries the rate is automatically adjusted according to the official cost-of-living index. In the business sphere specific provisions have been aimed at maintaining an economically sound system of depreciation. This was achieved by the allowance of specially accelerated depreciation rates, or by the re-introduction of a system of revaluation of assets, or by altering capital-gains taxation to take account of inflation.

In the face of economic recession, too, governments have resorted to taxation as an effective means of giving momentum to the economy. A matter of great concern was the fact that industrial investment was lagging behind, and various stimulating measures have been introduced. Investment incentives were granted in various forms. In some countries such incentives were geared to investment in economically weak areas, and sometimes these have been coupled with disincentives for investments in areas with a high degree of activity so as to reduce tensions in the labour market. In other countries general investment allowances or investment credits have been introduced or increased – measures for increased or accelerated depreciation allowances can probably be viewed as incentives for investment for expansion and modernisation. One of the major problems in this connection is the progress of technology, which easily leads to labour-saving manufacturing processes, thus increasing structural unemployment. A special feature is that several countries provided special tax incentives connected with research and development and exploration costs. The application of modern technological devices aims at more efficient and cost-saving manufacturing processes, thus increasing the rate of productivity, although this may again result in increased unemployment.

NATIONAL TAX SYSTEMS

BELGIUM

Types of taxes imposed

Although the Belgian corporate income tax is in principle not a schedular tax but a unitary one (i.e., all income components from whatever source are lumped together to form world-wide income), two taxes can be distinguished:

(1) the corporate income tax which is levied on Belgian sources of *resident* companies, i.e., companies which are established in Belgium, and
(2) the tax on *non-resident* companies which is levied on Belgian sources of income of companies which are established abroad.

The corporate income tax is levied by assessment while the tax on non-resident corporations is levied either by assessment or by withholding.

Some types of income are subject to the system of *pre-payments*.

(1) An immoveable pre-payment is levied on income from real estate. The basic rate of this levy is 3 per cent of the "cadastral income" of land, buildings and equipment. The "cadastral income" is a presumptive income determined by the Land Register, but has no connection with the actual economic rental value.
(2) A moveable pre-payment is generally withheld from income from certain moveable properties (dividends, interest, royalties).
(3) Professional pre-payment for employees and companies. The professional pre-payment is mainly a withholding tax on wages and salaries paid to employees. It has, therefore only minor

importance for companies. However both resident and non-resident companies which are engaged in certain business activities may be subject to a lump sum pre-payment. For resident companies the pre-payment varies from Bf 300 to Bf 1200. For non-resident companies the pre-payment is fixed at Bf 1200. This pre-payment is creditable against any final tax assessment. Any excess over Bf 20 is refundable.

Types of company taxpayers

(a) Resident

All companies, associations, organisations or establishments which have legal personality, which have their registered office or main establishment or place of management in Belgium, and which are occupied with operations of a profit-making nature (i.e., industry, trade or agriculture) are subject to corporation tax.

NV/SA and SCA/VGA companies whose invested capital does not exceed Bf 5,000,000 may elect to have the profits taxed to the individual partners, provided that the number of partners does not exceed 15.

(b) Non-resident

Companies, associations, institutions or organisations whether with legal personality or not, which do not have their registered office, main establishment or place of management in Belgium are subject to the non-resident income tax.

DENMARK

Types of taxes imposed

Legislation concerning the taxation of companies is spread over twelve statutes. In addition to these direct taxes a company may also be liable to capital duty import, excise duty and other levies.

Types of company taxpayers

Companies are divided into resident, non-resident and those which are exempt. Residents are generally subject to tax on their world-wide sources of income, non-residents are taxed only on income derived from enumerated sources.

(a) Resident

The following taxpayers are liable to corporate tax:

(1) registered A/S and ApS;

(2) other entities in which the participants are not subject to personal liability and which distribute their profits in proportion to the capital contributed;
(3) savings banks;
(4) cooperatives;
(5) mutual insurance companies, and
(6) other legal entities such as associations to the extent that they have income from business activity.

Residence is in most cases determined by the place of incorporation. A company may therefore be deemed resident even if its management and business activity is abroad. As a result a company may find itself liable to both Danish and foreign income taxes. If a treaty exists, the terms of the treaty will prevail over Danish domestic rules with the exception of rules concerning relief for foreign trade. If no treaty is in force a measure of unilateral relief is afforded.

(b) Non-resident
A non-resident company is liable to Danish tax on:

(1) income from immoveable property situated in Denmark;
(2) business income from a permanent establishment in Denmark, and
(3) dividends received from Danish sources.

In addition, the tax payer is also assessed on its "special income" — that is, income derived from any sale of business assets and real property in Denmark. Dividends are taxed by withholding sufficient to satisfy the total liability from that source.

(c) Exempt
Certain companies and enumerated types of activity are granted tax exemption. Among these are activities performed by the state, churches, municipalities, schools, hospitals, the central bank and some cooperative activities.

FRANCE

Types of taxes imposed

The most important direct tax on companies is the corporate income tax (*impôt sur les sociétés*) currently imposed at a 50 per cent rate whether or not profits are distributed.

Where the distributed profits have not borne corporate income tax at the full 50 per cent rate or where the distributed profits were earned before 1 January 1965 or over five years before distribution, an equalisation tax (*précompte*) is imposed at a rate of 33 per cent on the grossed-up dividend.

In addition to the corporate income tax, branches of foreign companies are also subject to a "deemed" distribution withholding tax of 25 per cent (or lower rates provided by tax treaties) on profits net of corporate income tax – whether or not remitted to the foreign head office. Foreign companies, individuals or legal entities who receive dividends, interest, royalties, and certain other income from French sources, and who are not connected with the operations of a permanent establishment in France, are subject to other withholding taxes.

A 25 per cent tax is imposed on dividends, and under certain conditions the rate is reduced in accordance with tax treaties. French tax treaties generally adopt the OECD definition of permanent establishment. A French branch of a foreign company is not recognised under French law as a separate legal entity and thus cannot benefit from tax treaties.

Types of company taxpayers

The French tax system is based on the principle of territoriality, thus the tax law is not applicable beyond French territorial limits. There are, however, exceptions – e.g., tax consolidation and special but temporary foreign investment tax incentives. For corporate income tax purposes France is defined as Metropolitan France (excluding Monaco), Corsica and overseas departments of Guadeloupe, Martinique, Guyana, Réunion and Saint Pierre et Miquelon.

There are three bases upon which corporate income tax liability of resident entities may arise, legal form, doing business or election.

(a) Legal form

The following entities are subject to corporate income tax by virtue of their French legal form alone:

(i) a stock corporation (SA);
(ii) a limited liability company (SARL);
(iii) a limited partnership with shares (*société en commandite per actions*);
(iv) a cooperative (*société coopérative*) and its central organs.

(b) Doing business

Corporate income tax liability also attaches to all other legal entities carrying on business or profit-making activities, including public institutions, state organisations with financial autonomy and department or local government organisations.

Civil companies (*sociétés civiles*) are normally taxed as partnerships but corporate income tax liability at the company level may arise in three cases:

(1) if they engage in industrial or commercial operations (e.g., mining, subdivision and sale of land);
(2) if their structure is closer to that of an SA/SARL/limited partnership with shares/cooperative, or (for the limited partners) limited partnership, or
(3) if they elect to be taxed as corporations.

(c) Election

The following entities may elect before 1 April of each year to be subject to corporate income tax: general partnerships, limited partnerships, joint ventures and civil companies. Such an election is irrevocable and may not be made if these entities originate from the transformation of an SA/SARL, limited partnership with shares or other *société de capitaux*.

The opposite election (that of a legal entity subject to corporate income tax to be taxed as a partnership) is no longer available in the absence of a transformation into one of the various types of partnerships (generally termed *société personnes*).

FEDERAL REPUBLIC OF GERMANY

Types of taxes imposed

Resident German companies, branches and permanent establishments of non-resident businesses are subject to corporate income tax on profits either world-wide or German-source only, depending on whether they have unlimited or limited tax liability. For financial years ending after 31 December 1976 the general rate for resident companies is 56 per cent on undistributed and 36 per cent on distributed profits.

The new Corporation Income Tax removes the previous double taxation of a company's profits (on the corporate and on the shareholder level) by introducing an imputation tax system permitting resident shareholders to claim a credit of corporate income tax of 36 per cent paid by the distributing company on profit distributions.

In addition to corporate income tax, companies are subject to the following direct taxes.

(1) *Trade tax* – a tax collected by and for the municipalities which apply multiples of generally 240–450 per cent to the basic federal rate. The trade tax is calculated on two bases, business income and business capital (up to 1 January 1980 payroll was a base). The exact burden is variable but is normally in the range of 12–20 per cent of taxable income for corporate income tax purposes.

(2) *Net worth tax* – a federal tax, the revenue of which goes to the state.
(3) *Capital levy* – under the Equalisation of Burdens Law paid by German companies in existence at the date of the currency reform in 1948.

The imputation tax system does not affect the composition of trade tax, nor does it eliminate the double tax burden for net worth tax purposes. Net worth tax will continue to apply to the shareholder level and the underlying assets (company level).

Types of company taxpayers

(a) Resident

German corporate income tax law distinguishes between taxpayers subject to "unlimited" and "limited" tax liability, which distinction broadly corresponds to "residents" and "non-residents". Corporate taxpayers with unlimited tax liability are subject to taxation on income from both German and foreign sources (Germany in this context means the Federal Republic, the German section of the continental shelf, and West Berlin). Conversely limited tax liabilities applies only to the German-source income of non-resident enterprises and also covers corporations, associations, estates and trusts not subject to unlimited tax liability having sources of income in Germany subject to withholding taxes.

Unlimited corporate income tax liability applies to six categories of taxpayers:

(i) companies, including the AG, GmbH, KGaA, colonial companies and mining companies with independent legal existence;
(ii) cooperatives, whether registered or unregistered;
(iii) mutual insurance companies;
(iv) other legal entities organised under private law;
(v) clubs, institutions, foundations and trusts without independent legal existence, and
(vi) commercial enterprises operated by public entities.

(b) Non-resident

The Corporate Income Tax Law sets out two types of taxpayer with limited tax liability:

(i) non-resident companies, unincorporated associations and estates and trusts which have neither domicile nor place of management in Germany; they include branches, and are taxable only on German-source income of a special type;
(ii) domestic companies, unincorporated associations, and estates and trusts which are not subject to unlimited tax liability –

such entities are subject to taxation on any German-source income (usually investment income) from which tax is deducted at source.

GREECE

Types of taxes imposed

The basic direct tax on corporations (whether resident or non-resident) is corporation income tax which has a surcharge in favour of the Agricultural Insurance Fund (OGA).

For industrial and mining companies the shares of which are quoted in the Athens Stock Exchange, corporation income tax for retained profits is reduced. Commercial companies even if they are listed on the stock exchange do not benefit from the above reduction and must thus pay the normal corporation income tax for retained profits.

Distributed dividends are only taxed in the hands of the recipient, although the distributing company must withhold tax in accordance with a standard scale.

Corporate income tax is levied on the retained profit of the company. In addition the company must withhold the amounts specified above on distributed dividends. The first 60,000 drachmas of dividends received by each shareholder are tax free.

Types of company taxpayers

Residents

Resident companies are defined as those that have their seat of their place of management in Greece and those companies which are incorporated in Greece. Only the SA is subject to corporate income tax in Greece on its retained profits by reason of incorporation in Greece. Resident companies are subject to "world-wide income tax" i.e., they are taxed on income from both domestic and foreign sources.

Non-residents

A corporation is considered to be a non-resident if neither its seat (incorporated in Greece) nor its place of management are situated in Greece. A non-resident corporation is taxable on its income derived from Greek sources or from its local permanent establishment.

The Greek income tax law treats all foreign enterprises operating in Greece – whether corporate or otherwise – under the category "foreign companies" and taxes them as corporations (SA).

ITALY

Types of taxes imposed

The income taxes applicable to companies are corporate income tax (*Importa sul reddito delle persona guiridiche*) and local income tax (*Importa locale sul reddito*).

Resident companies are subject to corporate income tax on all income or revenue, even if produced abroad. They are subject to the local income tax on their income, but foreign income is not subject to this tax unless it derives from business activities carried out abroad where the company does not have a permanent establishment with separate management and accounts.

The local income tax is not applicable to income (including dividend income) arising from participations in resident or non-resident companies and partnerships of any type.

Types of company taxpayers

(a) Resident

Corporate taxpayers are resident in Italy for the purposes of income tax if they have been incorporated in Italy or if they have their administrative headquarters or principal business purpose within the territory of Italy. The entities subject to corporate income tax are:

(i) stock corporations (SPA);
(ii) limited liability companies (SrL);
(iii) partnerships limited by shares;
(iv) mutual insurance companies, and
(v) other public and private entities having as their enclosure or main purpose the exercise of business activities (including organisations not having legal personality).

(b) Non-resident

Corporate taxpayers are not resident in Italy if they have neither their legal seat, nor their administrative headquarters nor their principal business purpose within the territory of Italy. Non-resident corporate taxpayers include non-resident companies, partnerships and entities of all types, whether or not having legal personality. Non-resident companies are subject to tax in Italy only on income produced in Italy.

A general concept is that the principles for calculating income chargeable to corporate income tax are equally applicable to local income tax unless otherwise stated. The rights to levy a tax on income may be limited by tax treaties entered into by Italy with other countries.

LUXEMBOURG

Types of taxes imposed

The Law of 4 December 1967 governs taxation in Luxembourg. The following taxes are levied:

(1) corporate income tax;
(2) municipal business tax;
(3) ground tax;
(4) tax on total salaries and wages paid;
(5) net worth tax; and
(6) annual tax.

Taxes (2) and (4) were introduced during the German occupation and have been maintained since with only relatively minor changes.

Types of company taxpayers

(a) Resident

A company is considered to be resident if either the statutory seat or the place of management is in the Grand Duchy. The following types of entity are subject to tax on their world-wide income:

(i) Luxembourg public limited companies (SA) and limited liability companies (SARL);
(ii) cooperative societies, agricultural associations;
(iii) religious societies recognised by the government (whatever their legal status);
(iv) mutual insurance companies and societies for the welfare of employees;
(v) foundations;
(vi) non-profit making organisations, either
  (1) other organisations of civil law (*droit privé*) which have a "collective" character and have an income which is not directly taxable in the hands of other taxpayers, or
  (2) *patrimoines d.affectation* and *patrimoines vacants;* and
(vii) public utility corporations.

A number of companies and other entities are specifically exempted from corporate income tax, principally for social or economic reasons. The following are exempt:

(1) the entities listed under (iv) and (vi) supra having an exclusively cultural or charitable purpose of serving exclusively the public interest – on such part of their income which is not derived from industrial or commercial activities;
(2) government or local utility companies supplying water, gas and electricity;

(3) professional organisations which do not engage in business activities; and
(4) certain specific entities with a social function such as employee pension funds.

(b) Non-resident

A company which does not have its statutory seat or place of management in Luxembourg is considered non-resident. A non-resident company is liable to tax on its Luxembourg source income.

The taxable income of a non-resident taxpayer includes, *inter alia,* all profits and gains made through a permanent establishment in Luxembourg.

A permanent establishment is statutorily defined as any installation or facility which is fixed to a definite location and appropriated to the use of any business other than an ambulatory one. The following are specially named, but not exclusively as permanent establishments, by law:

(i) the place of management of the business;
(ii) branch offices, manufacturing establishments, warehousing, purchasing, sales or other offices and all other facilities which serve the owner or co-owner of the business or his permanent representative such as a manager in the conduct of the business; and
(iii) building or construction projects, if the duration of the individual project or that of several connected projects carried out in the same community, exceeds or is likely to exceed six months.

This definition is subject to modification by treaty.

NETHERLANDS

Types of taxes imposed

The corporate income tax is the only tax on the profits of companies. It is not a schedular tax but a unitary one, i.e., all income components from whatever source are lumped together to form worldwide income.

The present Corporate Income Tax Act (VPB) became effective on 1 January 1970, succeeding the Corporate Income Tax Ordinance 1942 as revalidated by the Royal Decree of 17 September 1944. The Corporate Net Wealth Tax and Business Taxes were abolished in 1947 and 1950 respectively.

In addition to this direct tax a number of other indirect taxes and duties are also imposed. An entity is also liable to capital duty, excise duties, import duties and land tax.

Types of company taxpayers

The Income Tax Act imposes a tax on all companies, resident and non-resident. In the case of residents, the income which is subject to taxation is their world-wide source income; for non-residents only income derived from the enumerated specific domestic sources is taxable.

Resident
Companies listed are subject to corporate income tax as resident if they are –

(1) incorporated under the Dutch law, or
(2) "actually situated" in the Netherlands. Fulfilment of either one of these criteria is sufficient to meet the requirements of resident tax liability.

The following companies are subject to corporate tax once they meet the requirements for residency (VPB2):

(1) NVs, BVs, limited partnerships with a capital wholly or partly divided into shares and any other entity with capital wholly or partly divided into shares;
(2) cooperative societies;
(3) mutual insurance companies and other associations which on the principle of mutuality act as insurance or credit organisations;
(3) entities with or without legal personality to the extent they conduct an enterprise;
(5) "funds for joint account," i.e., funds whose purpose it is to make gains for the benefit of their participants by means of investing for joint account, provided the participants' interests are evidenced by negotiable certificates, and
(6) a specified number of public authority enterprises, e.g., mining and transportation enterprises.

Non-resident
To be classified as a non-resident company an entity must be one of the following (VPB3):

(1) an organisation with legal personality;
(2) a limited partnership in which capital is divided into shares;
(3) a partnership without legal personality, provided the capital has been fully or partly divided into shares;
(4) an association with or without legal personality to the extent it conducts an enterprise, or
(5) a doelvermogen, which is any form of organisation whether or not recognised by Dutch law, which receives Dutch-source

income, including trusts, foundations and funds – it is a catch-all.

VPB1 generally imposes a tax on all companies listed in VBP2 (residents) and VPB3 (non-residents). In the case of residents the income which is subject to taxation is their world-wide source income: for non-residents only income derived from the enumerated specific domestic source is taxable.

REPUBLIC OF IRELAND

Types of taxes imposed

The system of taxing company profits and the principles by which such profits are compiled were brought into line with a decision by the EEC Commission to recommend that company taxation within the community be harmonised on the basis of the imputation system.

All the profits, wherever arising, of a company resident in the state are within the charge to corporation tax. If a non-resident company carries on a trade in the state through a branch or agency all income arising through the branch or agency is liable to corporation tax. Profits in this context include capital gains in addition to income.

Relief is given under corporation tax for trading losses and tax capital allowances which were unrelieved under the old system but which could have been carried forward against future profits under the old system if it had continued to apply to the profits of companies.

Because the legislation is new (Corporation Tax Act 1976) a great deal of the legislation has not yet been ruled on by the Irish Courts. However, a substantial body of case law in the United Kingdom is very similar in some areas. Decisions of the UK Courts are not binding in Irish Courts but they do have persuasive force.

Types of company taxpayers

Irish law does not distinguish between limited and unlimited companies or between public and private companies.

All types of corporate bodies are liable to corporation tax subject to specific exemptions:

(1) companies which qualify as charities;
(2) trustee savings banks;
(3) bodies formed to promote athletic or amateur games or sports, and

(4) credit unions with effect from the date of their registration under the Industrial and Provident Societies Act.

Some corporate bodies are liable to corporation tax at a reduced rate:

(1) associations registered as companies with limited liability but without the addition of the word "limited" to their names;
(2) companies established solely for the advancement of religion or education;
(3) companies which are precluded by their constitution from distributing profits among members;
(4) the Agricultural Credit Corporation, and
(5) certain public utility societies.

Ireland gives wide-ranging reliefs from company taxation by way of industrial incentives, e.g., accelerated depreciation, investment allowances, export sales relief and Shannon Relief.

The tax exemption enjoyed by agricultural and fishery cooperatives was terminated from 6 April 1976. However, from 1 April 1978 the exemption has been restored subject to minor modifications:

(1) sales to the Intervention Agency are not treated as exempt transactions;
(2) additional conditions must be met before sales are treated as exempt, and
(3) restrictions on the carry-forward of losses from the non-exempt to the exempt period.

There are a number of special rules applicable to cooperatives:

(1) loan interest is payable by them in full;
(2) dividends are deductable on arriving at their taxable surpluses (the dividends do not carry a tax credit);
(3) trading bonuses and discounts paid to members are allowed in arriving at the taxable surpluses of the cooperatives.

Resident
For corporation tax purposes a company is resident in Ireland if the management and control of its business is exercised there.

Non-resident
A non-resident company which does not trade in Ireland through a branch or agency is liable to Irish income tax on income arising in Ireland.

For trading companies not resident it is necessary to distinguish trading *in* Ireland from trading *with* Ireland.

UNITED KINGDOM

Types of taxes imposed

Corporation tax is charged on the world-wide profits (income and capital gains) of companies resident in the United Kingdom and on the profits of non-resident companies related to a trade carried on in the United Kingdom through an unincorporated branch, agency or permanent establishment. The UK source income of a non-resident company which is not related to a UK branch, agency or permanent establishment is liable to income tax.

The relevant legislation is contained primarily in the Income and Corporation Taxes Act 1970 and the Finance Act 1965 (capital gains) as modified by subsequent annual Finance Acts. Most of the administrative and procedural aspects are set forth in the Taxes Management Act 1970.

Companies may also be liable to the following taxes and duties:

(1) value added tax;
(2) customs and excise duties;
(3) stamp duties on legal documents and on contributions to the capital of the company;
(4) municipal taxes ("rates") which are based on the rental value of the property occupied and are collected by local authorities;
(5) social security and other contributions in respect of employees, and
(6) income tax in the case of closely-controlled UK resident companies.

Types of company taxpayers

UK tax jurisdiction extends to England, Wales, Scotland and Northern Ireland. The Isle of Man and the Channel Islands (Jersey, Guernsey, Alderney and Sark) have separate jurisdictions over their own taxes.

Resident

Companies resident in the United Kingdom (wherever incorporated) are charged corporation tax at a single rate on their total world profits – income and capital gains – for each accounting period whether or not the profits are distributed and whether or not they are remitted to the United Kingdom.

For this purpose the term "company" comprises not only entities incorporated under the Companies Acts or otherwise whether limited or unlimited, but also unit trusts authorised by the Department of Trade and any unincorporated association other than a partnership.

A corporate member of a partnership is charged to corporation tax on its share of the partnership profits as part of its total taxable profits for the related accounting period.

Certain entities are specifically exempt from tax at least within the scope of their normal activities including the following:

(1) charitable, religious and scientific research organisations;
(2) approved pension funds;
(3) registered trade unions;
(4) approved housing associations;
(5) certain other non-profit making organisations and mutual associations.

A company is resident in the United Kingdom and taxable on its world-wide profits if its central management and control are situated there. The normal primary test of residence is the location of the directors' meetings, irrespective of where the company is incorporated or where the physical activities of the business are carried on. It is unlawful for a UK resident company to transfer its residence overseas without the consent of the Treasury.

Non-resident

The extent of UK tax liability of a non-resident company is in most cases determined by the relevant double taxation treaty, to which reference should be made. In general the treaties limit the taxation of industrial and commercial activities in the United Kingdom to the profits attributable to a permanent establishment in the country. Where a non-resident company is so taxable, the computation of liability on the chargeable profits of the permanent establishment corresponds in general to the computation for a UK resident company.

FISCAL HARMONISATION

In the European Economic Community it seems to have been found necessary to treat the tax systems of the member states as a major exercise capable of encyclopedic treatment. Unfortunately fiscal harmonisation is making slow progress – only in the field of sales taxation (value added taxation) and to a lesser extent the taxation of capital contributions is harmonisation really under way.

The alignment of corporate and personal income taxation cannot now take place until all tax systems are simultaneously adjusted, which in turn requires a high degree of cooperation in monetary matters and in the area of national economic and social policies. Even when that day arrives the experience of federal unions such as Switzerland, Brazil and the United States of America shows that federal complexity and state differences remain.

Those who wish to proceed to undertake a detailed study of the full complexities of taxation in Europe should write to:

The International Bureau of Fiscal Documentation,
Minderspoort, Sarphatistratt 124,
PO Box 20237,
1000. HE Amsterdam,
Netherlands.

Not all their literature is relevant but in the context of Europe the following will be helpful:

Guides to European Taxation

Volume 1 – *The Taxation of Patent Royalties, Dividends, Interest in Europe*
Volume 2 – *The Taxation of Companies in Europe*
Volume 3 – *The Taxation of Private Investment Income*
Volume 4 – *Value Added Taxation in Europe*

To this should be added their monthly journal, *European Taxation,* with articles concerning tax laws of European countries, and the Supplementary Service which is in four sections –

Section A – corporate tax rates
This lists the corporate tax rates for direct and indirect taxes in Western European countries, including the cantonal and municipal taxes of the Swiss Cantons. This section also includes concise summaries of the major factors influencing taxation of corporate income in each country.

Section B – individual tax rates
This contains descriptions of the taxes on the income of individuals, and lists the full tax rates (where available). Where helpful, worked examples clarify the practical application of the taxes in assessing an individual's tax liability.

Section C – tax treaties
This section contains the full texts (in English) of more than a hundred tax treaties signed by European countries with countries both inside and outside Western Europe. Each monthly supplement usually contains two more treaties.

Section D – abstracts from official reports
This includes the texts of such material as –

EEC advice on VAT
EEC Directive on Harmonisation of Turnover Taxes
EEC Directive on Capital Movement
EEC Directive on Mergers and Take-Overs

EEC Directive on Parent-Subsidiary Relationships
OECD Draft Conventions
UK Richardson Committee Report

All the above publications are updated and retained in loose-leaf binders (except the monthly journal).

VALUE ADDED TAX

The introduction of a turnover or value added tax (VAT) into the tax system of all members of the European Community has helped contribute to simplification of the operations of companies working within the Common Market, and also provided a common basis for assessing the VAT element of the "own resources" system for financing the Community budget.

Securing agreement on the necessary legislation has been difficult, and further proposals await or are in the process of adoption. It was only in 1979 that the VAT yield (a rate of up to 1 per cent within the harmonised VAT base) became the third element of the Community budget revenue, and it will be 1980 before all Community countries are expected to contribute on that basis.

This section summarises the Community VAT legislations, adopted or proposed to date.

A common tax basis

The development of the Common Market and removal of trade barriers among the original Six by 1968 highlighted the need to harmonise indirect or turnover taxes on goods moving between Community countries. In April 1967 the Council of Ministers adopted two important Directives on the matter. The First Directive established the principle of harmonisation of legislation of member states concerning turnover taxes; the Second Directive laid down the structures and procedures for application of the common system of value added tax.

Initially the Council of Ministers had envisaged the Community legislation coming into effect by 1 January 1970, but difficulties in some member countries required extension of this date under the Third, Fourth and Fifth VAT Directives to 1 January 1973.

Meanwhile on 21 April 1970 the Council made a further decision to introduce the "own resources" system of financing the Community budget from customs duties, agricultural levies and a percentage of the uniform basis of assessment of VAT – all elements which had some direct connection with Community policies. It was envisaged that the new scheme would come into effect on 1 January 1975.

The three new members, Denmark, Ireland and the United Kingdom, had already introduced VAT into their tax systems before joining the Community in 1973, but the decision to rely on VAT as an element in financing the budget required agreement on the "uniform basis of assessment" or bundle of goods and services on which the tax for Community purposes would be levied throughout the member countries. This proved a long and complex task and the introductory target date had to be postponed. It was not until 17 May 1977 that the Council of Ministers adopted the key Sixth Directive on VAT establishing the uniform basis of assessment. The provisions of the Directive apply to the supply of all designated goods and services effected within the country by designated taxable persons and to the import of goods. The Directive defines in details such taxable transactions, sets out various exemptions, and makes special provision for small undertakings which could encounter difficulties if the full tax procedures were applied.

Because of difficulties in some countries over national legislation, the Sixth Directive as it affects the Community budget only became fully operational in 1980, by which time the limit of 1 per cent of the uniform basis assessment had been reached. However, near the end of 1979, the Upper House of the Parliament of the Federal Republic of Germany refused to ratify the Sixth Directive, linking it to a dispute over German frontiers. A mediation committee, comprising both houses of Parliament, is seeking a solution to the problem.

The British position

The Sixth Directive did not require any radical changes in the British VAT system. Such modifications as were necessary were included in the Finance Act 1977, and by Treasury orders which came into effect on 1 January 1978. In general, the UK system of relief from VAT, either by zero rating or exemption, remains unaffected. The most significant change has been with regard to exports or services where the old zero rate group "9" has been replaced by a new group with entirely new rules governing eligibility for zero rating. Full details of the changes in UK laws were given in a special November 1977 supplement to Customs & Excise Notice No. 701 and in VAT News, No. 13, both available from local Customs & Excise offices.

Regarding small businesses, countries with a VAT exemption above the 5,000 million EUA specified in the Sixth Directive can retain this figure or increase it in order to keep pace with inflation, and so maintain its value in real terms, provided such action is within the letter and spirit of the Directive. Thus the UK was able to increase the exemption level of £7,500 to £10,000 in the 1978 budget and to £13,500 in 1980.

Further legislation

The Sixth Directive did not solve all the problems and divergencies of member states and the Commission has sent the Council a number of further proposals (the Seventh Directive is considered under "Proposed Legislation" below).

The Eighth Directive on VAT and two related Directives were adopted in principle by the Fiscal Council on 16 October 1979. The Eighth Directive is concerned with the refunding of VAT to firms established in a Community country other than that in which goods or services have been invoiced inclusive of tax. The new measure will substantially improve the present situation for firms publicising or expanding their operations in other member countries, whether on a temporary or a permanent basis. The Directive is of particular interest to exhibitors at international fairs and to international carriers in that it will make it possible to accord equal treatment in respect of VAT in areas of trade where such treatment is now very uneven, because conditions governing tax refunds are more restrictive in some countries than others. The UK has made provisions to introduce such a scheme following adoption of the Eighth Directive.

The two other Directives adopted by the Council relate to mutual assistance and information in combating indirect (VAT) tax evasion and tax avoidance and to the use of procedures to enable one member state to recover VAT and other consumption taxes due in another member state. Both these Directives extend earlier legislation relating to direct taxation and agricultural and customs levies.

The Ninth Directive on VAT, adopted by the Council in June 1978, provided for a derogation from the original date of implementation of the Sixth Directive (1 January 1978) to 1 January 1979 for seven countries (excluding Britain and Belgium) that had not then ratified the Directive in national law.

Proposed legislation

Used goods and works of art

A draft Seventh Directive contains proposals for a common system of VAT to be applied to works of art, collectors' items, antiques, and used goods. The original proposal for the Sixth Directive included a special scheme for second-hand goods, but so many problems arose during discussions that it was decided (Article 32 of the Sixth Directive) to deal with them under a separate directive. The problems involved included the definition of used goods, the actual application of VAT to used goods and the status ("taxable persons" or private person) of the seller.

"Used goods" are taken to mean goods which, after manufacture and marketing, have reached the final consumer, thereby completing a commercial cycle and which after a lapse of time, presumed to have entailed some use, re-enter a second commercial cycle when supply transactions in them begin again. These goods are grouped into three main categories:

(1) used goods in general, i.e., any consumer durables that lose their value during successive commercial cycles;
(2) certain used goods such as cars and boats, where changes of ownership are usually officially recorded, and
(3) works of art, antiques and collectors' items, whose value as a rule increases over time.

The purpose of the special scheme is to avoid or to mitigate the impact of cumulative taxation on such goods and to prevent distortions of trade working to the detriment of traders wishing to resell used goods or works of art. Sales and imports of works of art by the artist himself are to be exempt from VAT and no problem would arise where supplies of used goods between taxable persons were already covered by normal tax schemes or where transactions are carried out between private persons who are not liable to VAT.

The Commission originally proposed that the amount subject to tax of a transaction would be a standard percentage – 30 per cent – of the selling price but following consultation with the European Parliament and trade associations concerned the Commission has introduced a number of amendments. These do not alter the original options, but provide for an alternative scheme involving taxation of the difference between the selling price and the purchase price. Any taxable person reselling used goods (other than cars, trailers, pleasure boats, motor cycles or private aircraft) would have to opt for one or other of the schemes – either 30 per cent of the selling price or the difference between the selling price and the purchase price, for a tax period of one year. It would always be open to the seller, however, to be taxed under the normal tax system.

These amendments have been welcomed by British art and antique dealers who have pressed for the alternative scheme of taxing the difference between the selling and the purchase price on works of art and antiques.

Private cars, trailers, motor cycles, pleasure boats and private aircraft are not included in the scheme as these items are subject to rules that make it possible to identify successive owners.

Moveable tangible property on hire

A draft Tenth Directive proposes application of VAT to the hiring out of moveable tangible property. Some member states are encountering difficulties as regards the application of VAT to goods which are hired out in a member state by a supplier established outside that country, so it is felt that Article 9(1) of the Sixth Directive, which defines the place where a service is supplied, needs clarification. The aim is to create a legal fiction. The proposed Tenth Directive specifies that "in the case of the hiring out of moveable tangible property, other than forms of transport, the supplier shall be deemed to have established his business at the place where the property is at the time it is actually made available to the customer."

Forms of transport are excluded because a supplier is nearly always established in the country where he hires out vehicles and problems of control would arise since such property could by definition easily cross frontiers.

Rates of VAT

Community legislation in the field of VAT deals with the system, structure and basis of assessment but not with the rate of VAT. All Community countries are free to decide their own rates of tax.

VAT Directives: summary

The following is a summary of adopted and draft legislation, with a short synopsis of each Directive.

Adopted legislation

First Directive	Harmonisation of legislation of member states concerning turnover taxes.
Second Directive	Structure and procedures for application of the common system of value added tax (superseded by Sixth Directive).
Third Directive	Introduction of VAT in the member states.
Fourth Directive	Introduction of VAT in Italy.
Fifth Directive	Introduction of VAT in Italy.
Sixth Directive	Common system of VAT: uniform basis of assessment.
Eighth Directive	Arrangements for the refund of VAT to taxable persons not established in the territory of the country.

Ninth Directive	Harmonisation of laws relating to turnover taxes.

Draft legislation

Draft Seventh Directive	Common system of VAT to be applied to works of art, collectors' items, antiques and used goods.
Draft Tenth Directive	Application of VAT to the hiring out of moveable tangible property.
Draft Eleventh Directive	Provides for the exclusion of the French overseas departments from the scope of the Sixth VAT Directive.

CHAPTER 8

GENERAL POLICIES OF THE COMMUNITY

1. The European Social Fund

Main areas

The priorities of the European Social Fund are mainly the provision of aid for jobs for young people, migrant workers, workers in the hard-hit textile and clothing industries, the handicapped and workers leaving agriculture. A further heading of aid for women workers is now planned. The number of persons benefiting at the present time from projects aided by the Fund is approximately one and a quarter million. The chief beneficiary has been the United Kingdom, receiving more than one-third of the funds.

The main areas of intervention may be summarised as follows:

(1) *Agriculture*
In accordance with the Community policy to cut down the number of inefficient farms, 38,000 agricultural workers have been trained for other work, about half going into the building and metalwork industries, others to the electrical and electronic sectors. The number leaving agriculture has slowed down, mainly because of the high level of unemployment elsewhere, but also because of the emergence of a new tendency, particularly among the young, to seek work in agriculture. Community policy pays special regard to the need for stable employment and the avoidance of rural depopulation. The French and Germans receive most aid under this heading, the United Kingdom least.

(2) *Workers in textiles*
The intensity of competition from third world countries has led to widespread bankruptcy and unemployment in the textile sector. Community policy has stressed the need for restructuring, so aid has taken two main forms: the training of workers who leave the industry for other employment, and the training of workers for higher qualifications within the industry. Nearly 30,000 workers have benefited from the Social Fund, with the United Kingdom obtaining most.

(3) *Migrants*

The bulk of applications for aid were for the specialised teaching of children of migrant workers, with special programmes for integrating them into the educational system of the state. Language teaching and vocational preparation figure high. Germany is the biggest recipient of aid under this heading, with the United Kingdom and France coming next. Some 80,000 children will benefit under these schemes and 150,000 adults, with the addition of a further 180,000 benefiting from applications approved earlier but yet to be carried out.

(4) *Young people*

The majority of applications have been so-called "anti-crisis" training programmes, launched by the national training authorities. The most significant development has been the increasing number of local or regional initiatives. An increase of applications from voluntary organisations in the United Kingdom is significant. Over half a million young people have benefited, with the United Kingdom being the biggest recipient of aid, followed by France and Italy.

(5) *The handicapped*

The objectives vary considerably, ranging from improving techniques in the rehabilitation of the handicapped (e.g., use of audio-visual aids) to demonstrating the suitability of the disabled, after proper training, for a wide range of jobs – the computer industry in particular. The training of special instructors has also called for Social Fund aid. Some 5,000 people have benefited directly, both in demonstration projects and training of instructors; this has a multiplier effect and is stated to have contributed directly towards the reintegration of 25,000 disabled people into working life. Germany has been the biggest recipient in this sector.

Fund aid in the United Kingdom

The greater part of the assistance given by the Fund to the United Kingdom (54 per cent in terms of allocations) has been in support of the training and retraining of unemployed people: the training and work preparation of young people also accounted for a sizeable proportion (30 per cent). Also assisted were the handicapped – through schemes of employment rehabilitation and specialised vocational training – and migrant workers and their families (in United Kingdom terms principally new Commonwealth migrants), workers in the textile and clothing industries and, to a much lesser extent, those leaving agriculture.

An analysis of the numbers trained in 1977 is given below.

Age Group	*Agri-culture*	*Textiles Clothing*	*Young People*	*Migrants*	*Regions*	*Handi-capped*	*Total*
Under 25	259	1,102	74,995	12,500	23,781	605	113,242
25 35	216	11	–	NA	5,528	608	6,363
35–50	84	719	–	NA	10,423	1,112	12,338
50+	24	540	–	NA	2,778	1,100	4,442

(Ref: COM (78) 476 Final)

There is good evidence that training supported by the Social Fund helps to improve the employment situation. The major programme operated under the Training Opportunities Scheme (TOPS) provides training opportunities for the unemployed and those becoming redundant: in 1977 training was given under TOPS to some 100,000 people.

The Training Services Agency (TSA) programme of special measures for young unemployed people has, by means of grants for long-term training, provided many extra places for young people. About 30,000 special measures trainees were supported by government funds in 1977, of whom about 6,000 were aided by the Fund.

The Manpower Services Commission's Work Experience Programme (WEP) for young people was extensively supported by the Fund. It is worth noting that a recent survey of a sample of young people who had completed WEP courses indicated that 84 per cent had been in full-time employment at some time since leaving WEP, and that 72 per cent were still in employment. Most of the private companies helped by the Fund have been retaining workers in the assisted areas or in textiles and clothing, and often in both. Many have changed their type of production in order to keep going and therefore to maintain employment. It is difficult to say to what extent the amount of training was greater with Fund aid than it would have been without: the Government gives a high priority to vocational training and would no doubt have allocated a great deal of money to its various programmes in any case. The United Kingdom Government does, however, take into account the possibility of aid from the fund when deciding the size of its programmes. The possibility of Fund aid has also helped to sway the decision of private companies to set up new factories or to preserve existing employment in the poorer regions, thus generally improving the employment position there.

2. Transport

Introduction

Forty per cent of public investment in the Community and eleven per cent of private investment are absorbed by the transport sector, which employs six million people and constitutes six per cent of the European Community's gross national product. In 1976 the Nine injected 27,500 million EUA into their road networks, rail systems and inland waterways. This is equivalent to the total tax revenue of a country the size of Belgium.

A European transport policy is necessary for three main reasons.

(1) The Nine need to draw the maximum benefit from their expenditure in this sector. A certain amount of coordination is needed simply on account of the geographic proximity of the countries. It is also an advantage in relations with outside countries.

(2) The Community is founded on the principle of a common market in which goods and services move freely. The volume of trade between the Nine has quadrupled since 1958. Transport is directly involved both as a major industrial sector and as a service linking manufacturers with consumers across open frontiers.

(3) The European Treaties – drawing the logical conclusion of all this – confer on the Community the responsibility for removing distortions in competition and discrimination in this sector whether they are the result of tariff policies, public subsidies, taxation methods or national regulations on commercial practices. Accordingly, since 1955, direct international tariffs were introduced for transporting coal and steel by rail to ensure the same price/distance relationship no matter how many national frontiers were crossed. In 1968 a system was set up (and is currently being revised) which catered for the establishment by road transport organisations of international tariffs based on cost prices. In 1971 the Commission also proposed common rules for imputing costs for infrastructure so as to harmonise vehicle taxation regulations and to eliminate distortions of competition.

Road transport

Cars and lorries have traditionally been subject to national regulations and standards which hinder the free movement of goods within the Community. The measures taken to remedy the situation are varied.

(1) There are numerous European directives to harmonise the national norms to which vehicles are subjected – brakes, lighting, windscreens, sound levels, etc. To cover in particular the five-axled articulated or semi-articulated lorries whose inter-

national movement is hindered by different national regulations on maximum weight and dimensions (50 tonnes in the Netherlands, 32 in the UK), the European Commission has proposed – so far in vain – that these provisions be harmonised at a limit of 44 tonnes as long as certain environment protection and safety regulations are respected.

(2) Crossing frontiers has been made easier for individual travellers and for public transport. In broad terms, no authorisation is required for tourist transport (buses and coaches). In the goods sector, traditionally subject to authorisation and quota systems, Community action has eliminated first one and then another of these barriers for a series of forms of transport. As for the rest, a quota of Community permits created ten years ago enabled a certain number of operators to travel between all member countries without the need to obtain bilateral authorisations valid for the passage from one country to another. In the long term the Community's objective is to eliminate all quantitative restrictions in this sector.

(3) The quality and safety of road transport have been improved by Community regulations which specify maximum permitted driving hours per day and week. The control of these provisions is assisted by the use of the tachograph, installed in heavy road vehicles. Tachographs automatically record the speed of the vehicle, the time of day, how far the vehicle has travelled, and for how long the vehicle has been driven. They were widely specified by national rules on the Continent as a safety device and to ensure limits on drivers' hours and were adopted as a Community standard. Since 1977, another directive has been concerned with the improvement of the mutual recognition of national certificates and qualifications so that transporters from one country are able to set up in business in other countries.

(4) The Commission has now proposed the introduction of a Community driving licence. New driving tests would no longer be necessary when changing country of residence.

Railways

The financial situation of European railways has frequently been precarious. The difference between income and operating costs amount to an average 50 EUA per head in the Community. Though economical on energy consumption, rail has been the main competitive target for other forms of transport and its role in the transport of industrial goods has diminished. Since the early 1960s the Community has tried to harmonise the rules of financial compensation and public service obligation. Aids for infrastructure and subsidies to cover operating deficits have generally been taken into consideration. Greater transparency has thus been achieved and in 1975 the Nine specified the means for financial redress and a clearer definition of the relations between the rail and public authorities –

(1) autonomy in the administrative, economic, and accounting management of the networks;
(2) the operation of networks in accordance with economic needs, including the freedom to fix transport rates, and
(3) greater commercial and technical cooperation between European networks to offer them the advantages of an enlarged market and standardised infrastructure and equipment.

To facilitate and re-establish financial equilibrium, the European Commission demanded that member states bear the financial consequences of their intervention and of the obligations which they put on the rail companies. It also argued for –

(1) the establishment of multi-annual industry programmes, particularly for investment (infrastructure, rolling stock): these programmes aim to increase productivity and at the same time the variety and quality of services;
(2) the removal of economic and technical barriers to free movement and close cooperation between different European countries, and
(3) an extension of combined transport services (rail and road, for example).

Inland waterways

Europe's rivers and canals play a vital role in the movement of heavy industrial goods: total tonnage transported in 1976 was 680 million tonnes. Over 60 per cent of traffic used the Rhine and surrounding tributaries.

Since 1976 the approvals for navigability given by Community countries have been mutually recognised. The European Commission is proposing the creation of a Community certificate based on uniform standards as well as the adoption of common rules governing qualifications for seamen and their living and working conditions.

To clean up this sector, all ageing and unsuitable barges must be eliminated, equipment modified and means allocated to monitor market trends. On a recommendation from the Commission, Community countries have already scrapped numerous decrepit barges and the owners have been compensated. Improvements in the European network of navigable waterways must be continued. The Commission has undertaken a general study of this problem. It is also concerned about the completion of the Rhine-Maine-Danube canal which will link the North Sea to the Balkans in the mid-1980s, and the possible harmful practices of Eastern European companies which operate within a different economic system.

Maritime transport

Around 85 per cent of Community external trade is conducted by sea. A common policy has developed in this sector in recent years.

Concern for safety at sea and the anti-pollution campaign following the *Amoco Cadiz* disaster in March 1978 have resulted in new measures being taken in conjunction with the Intergovernmental Maritime Consultative Organisation (IMCO). In particular two European directives were adopted in November 1978, one on the qualifications of deep sea pilots operating in the English Channel and in the North Sea, the other on the safety standards applicable to tankers entering and leaving Community ports. The European Commission is also preparing actions to strengthen safety and pollution prevention standards in ports. In 1977 when the first common decision was taken concerning maritime transport, the Nine decided to discuss periodically their relations in this field with other countries. One of the first problems was the competitive challenge faced by Community shipowners from a large number of East European companies largely subsidised by their public authorities. In September 1978, the Nine decided to monitor the traffic passing through their ports. All shipping lines from Eastern Africa and Central America are now being monitored, particularly in relation to their tariffs and cargo.

Developing countries want to be guaranteed a certain share of world traffic. Following four years of discussion, the Nine agreed in May 1979 to ratify the United Nations code of conduct which allocated an equitable share of the traffic to national shipping companies while a substantial share was left for other transporters. It should be mentioned, however, that the Nine decided to let them continue competing with each other (and to operate on a basis of reciprocity in their relations with other market economy industrialised countries): such competition must, however, be fair.

The European Commission is drafting a regulation which will enable European competition rules to be applied to maritime transport.

Air transport

From an investigation into the extent of government involvement in the determination of air fares in the Community, the Commission concluded that in most cases governments are actually responsible for setting them and other commercial conditions.

The Commission accordingly decided to open discussions with the member states with a view to improving the structure of the air transport sector and to intensifying competition between airlines.

With this in mind it included the subject of competition in the Memorandum prepared for the Community institutions and other interested parties, which assesses the situation of air transport in the Community within a world context: One of the proposals in Part 3 of the Memorandum is that a procedural regulation be issued, applying the rules of competition to air transport. The Commission however, has not sufficient powers to apply the rules of competition systematically and effectively to airlines, as air transport is not covered by a regulation laying down examination procedures and penalties for infringements. The short and medium term action of the Community should therefore be concentrated on measures which bring increased flexibility and innovation to air transport between the member states of the Community. Increased possibilities of market entry air innovation could be introduced whilst basically maintaining the network of reliable services by designated scheduled airlines. Full freedom of access to the market could, however, only be envisaged at long term. The short and medium term should be concentrated on specific actions which should be coherent with the conceptual framework.

Specific actions, short and medium term

Intra-European tariffs are often criticised by public opinion and the European Parliament. Such criticism is frequently founded upon comparison with tariffs in force on the North Atlantic or within the USA, it does not always take into account the difference in costs between North Atlantic and domestic US operations and intra-European operations, intra-European costs being much higher. Comparison is also often made directly between the normal economy class tariffs for intra-European services and lower tariffs on the North Atlantic, which again is misleading. It should also be remembered that there are tariffs in Europe lower than those in the USA though hindered with restrictive conditions of sale.

In any event, the Commission considers that there is a scope for improvement and that it is time for a rethinking of the tariff structure. The present scheduled structure has as its basis economy tariffs which include payment for services which are useful to probably the majority of business and government travel. The "economy" tariff is therefore of necessity fairly expensive and *ad hoc* modifications of the system have been introduced from time to time to make reforms and to allow scheduled air carriers to meet competition in particular from non-scheduled air carriers. This led on certain routes to a profusion of tariffs which are not only somewhat non-transparent to most users but which may also be irrational, whilst on many other routes tariff options are limited. Changes in the tariff structure for scheduled air transport may, it is claimed produce tariffs more suitable for the leisure market and for point-to-point traffic.

Given the situation as it is, the aim should be to offer users a broader range of tariffs without jeopardising the economic situations of the airlines. An initial step could be that member states ask the airlines to introduce travel arrangements permitting a reduction of tariffs on the most important traffic links, preferably in a multilateral framework.

In scheduled intra-Community passenger services these arrangements could provide for:

(1) The introduction of a third class.
(2) Introduction of special tariffs for a certain percentage of the capacity offered on condition that the fare is paid in advance and is not refunded if the passenger decides to postpone his flight.
(3) Basic no-frills point-to-point tickets for which additional services could be purchased such as reservation, and interchangeability.
(4) Offer of a specified percentage of weekly capacity available on the routes in question at a tariff not exceeding 50 or 60% of the economy class tariff with suitable conditions of sale.
(5) Introduction of a European roundtrip ticket.
(6) General implementation of standby-tariffs.

The governments, the airlines, their regional and world associations could make appropriate proposals.

In a Community arrangement it should be envisaged that should airlines show reticence to introduce these reduced tariffs the governments responsible should allow the establishment of a limited number of services with such tariffs by other operations on the routes in question.

Wider conceptual framework

If an airline requested traffic rights in order to carry out a new route between member states, a new type of scheduled service, or an existing service at a considerably lower price accompanied by new marketing measures, then it should not be prevented from being so authorised unless the airline(s) already designated decided to offer a similar service or tariff. These carrier(s) could naturally choose to refrain from matching the proposed offer in situations where they judged the new activity unprofitable.

If such a policy were introduced directly, it might have disruptive effects. The inclusive of certain criteria might therefore prove desirable to minimise these potential effects possibly along the following lines:

(1) The new carrier might be asked to show that its proposed new activity would be profitable in order to avoid predatory market entry; licensing authorities could keep watch on the ability of the carrier to expand its activity in view of its resources.
(2) A tariff reduction justifying market entry should be of a certain minimum size to be defined in order to preserve a certain stability.
(3) The number of new traffic rights that a carrier could obtain each year under these rules could be limited to avoid sudden disruptions.
(4) In order to give a carrier, already designated or not, the time to build up a new route, it should be possible to give protected traffic rights for a limited number of years.

The graduated introduction of such policies would counteract abuses of dominant positions in favour of lower prices and work towards removal of obstacles which one member state can now operate to the detriment of airlines of another member state. The elements would not intervene unduly in the normal licensing procedures of the member states and would preserve the primary responsibility for their own commercial action of the airlines and the operation of scheduled services in accordance with the comprehensive framework of the bi-lateral agreements.

Passenger services should be the subject of separate discussions from freight services as it may prove less difficult to reach agreement on the latter case.

European infrastructure network

Many actions taken by the Community affect transport as a whole, in particular the following.

(1) The introduction of a market monitoring system which will provide quantitative and qualitative information on the development of international road, rail and sea transport and which will help predict user requirements and the transport facilities available.
(2) Policy for ports: the ports tend to act as the linking points between the different forms of transport and the European Parliament put forward a case for a common policy in this sector. In liaison with the European Commission, representatives from the principal European ports have had regular meetings since 1974.

(3) The promotion of combined road/rail/sea transport: the use of containers facilitates cooperation between the different forms of transport and permits a more rational use of infrastructure, greater energy saving and a cleaner environment. The European Commission has already managed to simplify the formalities for combined transport when crossing frontiers, but it is necessary to stimulate the extension of these techniques.

(4) Harmonisation of the different national systems for Summer Time has been proposed to simplify matters for transport users.

The big question which affects all forms of transport and all users is to know what new transport infrastructure we will need in the next twenty years. This is a crucial problem for the future of the Community but it is all too often still dealt with only in national terms. When governments are evaluating individual projects they tend quite naturally not to take into account the advantages or costs which could arise outside their borders. The growing traffic between the Nine calls for another approach. Without getting too involved itself in national projects the Commission wishes to ensure that the Community interest is fully taken into account in the development of new infrastructure projects and that the Community as a whole contributes to the planning and financing. The Commission has created a financial facility capable of according aid or loans at low interest rates to projects of Community interest. Such projects are already the subject of periodic meetings of officials of the Nine and the exchange of information. It has also launched a research programme on the Community interest in certain major projects such as the cross-Channel link, links with the new members, Greece, Spain and Portugal, the development of combined road/rail transport, an inventory of problem regions and the bottlenecks in the European transport system as well as Europe's transport needs to the year 2000.

3. Energy

Electricity, petrol, gas, solid fuel, liquid fuel – whatever form it takes in today's society, energy is essential in industry, farming and commerce as well as being necessary for home comfort and many leisure activities. Two facts are important:

(*a*) energy consumption per head is generally speaking greater in those countries with the highest standard of living and the best working conditions, and

(*b*) energy consumption has risen at a steady rate except during periods of economic recession.

But energy, indispensable though it may be, is no longer ours for the taking. Oil price increases have reduced the rate of economic growth in the Community countries. Maintaining our standard of living and ensuring further progress demands reliable energy supplies in sufficient quantities at reasonable prices and of the type most suited to our needs. Especially while most people want to see further improvements in the quality of life, few are prepared to reduce the quantity of goods and services available to them.

From the end of the Second World War up to 1973, Community countries and their 260 million inhabitants – whose standard of living is one of the highest in the world – have benefited from reliable and stable energy supplies. Important changes took place in this period however. In contrast to the pre-war situation, all Community countries came to depend heavily on external energy supplies to an extent that they now constitute 54 per cent of the total energy consumption.

At the end of 1973 under the impact of politico-military events in the Near East, the situation deteriorated abruptly, marked by oil supply difficulties at the beginning and, for some countries, supply embargoes. The situation subsequently stabilised, but the threat continued to hang over oil trade, and was made more pronounced by events in Iran. There followed abrupt price increases, oil costs rising threefold at the end of 1973. Further price rises – more moderate and staggered – have been unilaterally imposed since then.

The energy crisis which struck in 1973 was not the only cause of the world economic recession which set in at about the same time, but it is one of the fundamental elements.

Community approach to the energy problem

The first efforts by European institutions to coordinate action by Community member states in the energy field date back to 1962, well before the crisis.

The European Coal and Steel Community was formed in 1951, and the European Community for Atomic Energy was created in 1957. The problems in the coal industry caused by rising oil imports and the development of peaceful applications of nuclear energy demanded a global European approach to energy problems.

The Treaty founding the European Economic Community made no specific mention of an energy policy. Solidarity is, however, an obligation for the Nine: they have to increase the security of energy supplies and ensure that no distortions or imbalances which could compromise the realisation of the Common Market and of economic union arise from their energy import policies. The degree of dependence on imports is not in fact the same everywhere, certain member states being better endowed than others with indigenous resources.

The energy crisis has made the need for a common policy more urgent.

(*a*) Western Europe has been shown to be very vulnerable. Supply boycotts and restrictions together with sharp price rises have caused innumerable economic problems in European countries.

(*b*) Isolated and uncoordinated national actions have proven to be ineffective; when dealing with the oil producing countries, consumer countries must react with solidarity.

(*c*) Research into ways of reducing dependence on external supplies has become indispensable. Reduced dependence cannot be brought about by the play of economic forces on the market. It involves by contrast a collection of measures covering a multiplicity of factors. A global energy policy which is in tune with long-term economic and social policy is required.

(*d*) Such a policy will help avoid isolated or uncoordinated national efforts and the duplication of effort which this often implies, particularly in the field of scientific research.

(*e*) Only in this way can we draw from the economic and political weight of the entire Community.

Action taken

A common energy policy is emerging little by little by means of convergent actions undertaken by the member states and through decisions being taken by the Community institutions. The process is of course slow and may appear less than spectacular.

(1) The solution to the Community's energy supply problem cannot in the foreseeable future be found by reducing the quantities of useful energy used by agriculture, industrial, commercial or domestic users. Energy supplies have to be assured whilst maintaining a high standard of living, economic expansion and social progress.

(2) It is necessary to save energy by using it more rationally.

(3) Supply security and reliability, both in quantity and price are better assured on the whole by indigenous supplies than by imports. A high level of autonomy must therefore be sought at an acceptable cost.

(4) Diversifying energy sources is also a way of achieving the object of supply security and stability. It is dangerous to depend greatly on one sole energy source such as oil, but on the other hand a massive dependence on nuclear energy could also pose serious difficulties.

With these general principles in mind the Commission has mapped out a framework of directions for action and drawn up numerous proposals. A Community action programme was established in 1974, aiming to reduce the primary energy demand in 1985 by 15 per cent. Various specific measures were recommended:

(1) heating of buildings, improving heating installations, improving insulation and reducing thermal losses;
(2) better use of energy in industry;
(3) operation of household appliances, and
(4) promotion of public transport.

The next need is to secure resources.

(*a*) *Solid fuel.* Community coal production should be maintained at the level of 250 million tonnes of consumed energy, while brown coal and turf (peat) production should be increased. Coal imports from third countries should also be increased.

(*b*) *Nuclear energy.* More nuclear power stations should be built to provide an installed capacity of at least 160 GW and if possible 200 GW by 1985.

(*c*) *Hydrocarbons* should be developed by the exploitation of the large oil and natural gas resources on Community territory and in its territorial waters. The Commission has been granting aid for several years to Community development projects covering new techniques for the prospection and exploitation of hydrocarbons in the difficult conditions encountered in the North Sea. The European Investment Bank provides finance for oil and gas production installations as well as the construction of oil and gas pipelines. To provide better supply security for oil and oil derivatives, the Community has introduced a compulsory storage arrangement corresponding to 90 days consumption. Stocks must also be kept at electricity power stations to ensure at least one month's operation.

It is not surprising that progress is slow and laborious, but it is clear that in this very basic sector the objectives are unanimously agreed. A coherent body of common regulations and actions already exists and progress towards a common policy is based on clearly defined guidelines, but research into new forms of energy, solar, geothermal, wind and wave power as well as research into the liquefaction and gasification of coal must be pursued. A stable supply of energy at an acceptable price is a prerequisite for all economic development, without which social progress would be impossible.

4.The Environment

Europe's environment is menaced on two broad fronts, which for the purpose of analysing the threat can be divided into –

(1) the natural environment (rivers, lakes, the atmosphere, wild life preservation, etc.) and
(2) the man-made environment (towns and cities, etc.).

In reality, however, the natural and man-made environments are interrelated and interdependent. The European Commission has defined the environment as "the combination of elements whose complex interrelationship make up the settings, surroundings and the conditions of life of the individual and of society as they are or as they are felt."

In the natural environment indiscriminate use of pesticides can result in the death not only of plant pests but also of wild birds and other fauna. Pesticide residues can also find their way into the food chain and eventually cause human health problems. Man-made pollution invariably finds its way into the natural environment. Domestic and industrial effluents are washed down by the rivers to the sea and atmospheric pollutants are dispersed by the winds and return to the soil in rain. Toxic wastes discharged by industry contaminate micro-organisms and find their way by complex (and mostly uncharted) pollution pathways into the food chain. In the man-made environment the situation is worse. Europe, already one of the most densely populated regions in the world, is in the throes of an urban explosion which if allowed to continue unchecked could lead eventually to the destruction of much that we value in our culture, heritage and society.

Trends are such that the next twenty years could see the creation in the Community of what has been described as a giant "megalopolis" – an urban agglomeration sprawling from the Ruhr in West Germany through "Randstad Holland" and the industrial crescent of Antwerp–Brussels–Lille to Paris in the south and from there over the Channel to join London bursting at the seams. The problems confronting Europeans are compounded by the fact that it is becoming more and more difficult to get away from them. If Belgium's urban development continues at current rates then the whole country will be built up by the year 2030.

But escaping from the towns, however, does not necessarily mean escaping from pollution. For example, holidaymakers on the Mediterranean – and there are over 30 million of them a year – may not be aware of it, but pollution in the Mediterranean as a whole has reached dangerous levels. Pollution on the Atlantic coastline, however, is lower, thanks to the ocean's greater capacity to absorb and neutralise pollutants.

Estimated Damage Costs of Air Pollution in the United Kingdom 1970
(£ million)

	Economic cost	*Social cost*
Painting		6.3
Corrosion	42.0	
Textiles	33.0	
Total damage costs	75.0	6.3
Laundry and household goods	0.5	164.0
Exterior cleaning of buildings		1.5
Window and office cleaning	5.0	
Total soiling costs	5.5	165.5
TOTAL	80.5	171.8

(*Source:* Programmes Analysis Unit, Didcot, Berks., 1971.)

The problem

The United Nations Conference on the Human Environment held in Stockholm 1972 alerted public opinion to the environmental problems. Many governments have subsequently turned their attention to the formulation of environmental policies. Progress has not been fast but most European governments are pursuing environment programmes, with varying degrees of success and efficiency.

Given that all nine Community member states are actively engaged in environmental protection policies at national level, it may reasonably be asked why the Community as such has concerned itself with the environment sector. There are four very good reasons.

(1) Many environmental problems have to be tackled on an international or intra-Community basis.
(2) As a Community we have set ourselves economic goals which have implications for environment.
(3) We are living in a Community in which desperate economic action at national level can disrupt the normal functioning of the Common Market.
(4) In some circumstances the Community institutions are better equipped to react to changing environmental policy requirements.

When the EEC came into being the member states agreed that the "essential objective of their efforts would be the constant improvement of the living and working conditions of their peoples." They went on to pledge (Article 2) that their task would be "to promote throughout the Community a harmonious development of economic activities, a continuous and balanced expansion, an increase in stability, an accelerated raising of the standard of living and closer relations between the states belonging to it."

Action taken

The need for a Community environmental policy has long been recognised, and has already been agreed by the Council of Ministers. It is designed –

(1) to prevent, reduce and as far as possible eliminate pollution and nuisances;
(2) to maintain a satisfactory ecological balance and ensure the protection of the biosphere;
(3) to ensure sound management of, and avoid any exploitation of, resources or of nature which cause significant damage to the ecological balance;
(4) to guide development in accordance with quality requirements, especially by improving working conditions and the settings of life;
(5) to ensure that more account is taken of environmental aspects in town planning and land use, and
(6) to seek common solutions to environmental problems with states outside the Community, particularly in international organisations.

A number of international organisations deal with environmental problems and in order to avoid duplication of efforts the Community cooperates with them and follows their work closely. These organisations include OECD, the Council of Europe, NATO, WHO, UNESCO, and the United Nations Economic Commission for Europe.

The Community as such has also played an important role in international action to combat pollution, particularly in international conventions. So far the Community has signed and ratified the following:

(1) the Paris Convention for the Prevention of Marine Pollution from Land-based Sources;
(2) the Barcelona Convention for the Prevention of Marine Pollution in the Mediterranean, and
(3) the Bonn Convention for the Prevention of Chemical Pollution of the Rhine.

A decision on whether the Community should participate in the European Convention for the Protection of International Watercourses against Pollution is pending. It also represents the Nine in the UN Conference on the Law of the Sea as it relates to pollution control. Relations with non-member countries have been developed and the Community has now signed technical co-operation agreements with the United States, Canada and Switzerland; agreement in principle on similar arrangements has been reached with Japan. In the context of the Euro-Arab dialogue, the European Commission is chairing a specialised group from the European side on marine environment and the development of coastal areas.

The Community will continue to take part in international measures to combat pollution and safeguard the environment. In the future programme, however, special attention will be given to co-operation with the developing countries. This co-operation would essentially be geared to ensuring that polluting industries are not transferred from Europe to the developing world at the expense of the latter's environment. In other words, the Nine will help the developing countries – especially those linked to the Community via the Lomé Convention – to ensure that new techniques in the industrial and farming sectors do not result in excessive pollution and the creation of "pollution havens".

Development projects will also attempt to ensure that dangers inherent in agricultural development, such as erosion, overgrazing and deterioration of forests, can be forestalled. Europe still has a long way to go on the environmental protection front and if our environment is to be adequately safeguarded and the quality of life maintained and improved, greater efforts will have to be made at all levels – regional, national and international – to introduce and pursue policies that take account of the so-called environmental "limits," such as the capacity of the natural environment to absorb and neutralise pollution and the capacity of man to withstand the pressures of modern society.

The Community intends to continue its efforts to improve the dissemination of information relating to environmental protection and will give priority to the following tasks.

(1) The inventory of information sources on the environment agreed under the first programme.
(2) The establishment of a co-ordinated body of information services known as Euronet.
(3) The setting up of an information system on national and Community environmental legislation.
(4) The creation of an information network dealing with the technological aspects of pollution control.
(5) The establishment of a specialised information network covering congresses and conferences on the environment.

(6) The setting up of a databank on chemicals likely to contaminate the environment.

The Community will also continue its work in promoting public awareness of environment problems, while on the social front action will be taken to improve the working environment by humanising working conditions. The European Foundation for Living and Working Conditions will develop its work in this field. By agreeing to continue EEC environment action, the member states have accepted the need for a Community environment policy and have recognised the part the EEC institutions can play in shaping and protecting the European's environment of the future. The Community as such will continue to pursue its goal of growth and stability, but in the knowledge that these make sense only as a contribution to better conditions in general, not only by raising the standard of living but by improving the quality of life.

If as part of the second EEC action programme the Community is to develop a method of environmental "mapping," it seems likely that future maps will show a gradual but nevertheless positive improvement in Europe's environment.

5. Regional Policy

One of the aims of the Community's industrial policy is to achieve not just growth but balanced growth. Before the Community was established, considerable prosperity gaps existed not only between the original six member states but between regions within them. This divergence was in some ways even further highlighted with the accession of the three new member states in 1973.

Such disparities have resulted in a serious population decline in poorer areas as people have drifted towards the more prosperous industrial centres. This in turn has led to over-crowding in many areas, particularly in the megalopolis stretching from the Ruhr in the Federal Republic of Germany to Paris and across the Channel to London. Such a development with all the serious social and environmental consequences that it entails, brings as many "regional" problems to rich areas as it does as to poor ones. The ECSC Treaty recognised these trends and provided for Community loans to attract new industries into declining coal and steel regions and to train redundant workers for new jobs. More than £556 million has been spent so far on giving workers new skills, and reconversion loans totalling £178 million have created new jobs in coal and steel areas.

The Treaty of Rome followed up this example by providing money for regional development. The European Investment Bank was created to raise money for investment in industrial and other projects in the poorer areas, where some 75 per cent of its funds go. Ways in which the Bank might further develop its operations to provide more money for investment in areas particularly badly hit by unemployment or to help certain critical industries currently under pressure are being examined. The Social Fund also spends most of its resources on helping re-train workers who face unemployment in the less-favoured regions, and the Guidance Section of the Farm Fund was designed to modernise farms and make agriculture more efficient.

It was not until 1975 that a Community regional policy was formally adopted and a Regional Fund established. This fund was given £520 million for an initial three-year period (1975–77) to help finance industrial and infrastructure investments in areas of greatest need. A further £1,47 million has been voted for the 1978–80 period.

The Fund is used to make non-repayable grants to eligible investment projects, in association with governments' own regional aid systems and the infrastructure expenditure of national public authorities. It can make grants equivalent to up to 20 per cent for industrial and some service investments in areas benefiting from national regional aids, and it can in the same area contribute up to 30 per cent of the cost of infrastructure works that are directly linked with the development of industrial activities. A key requirement is that money from the Fund should be additional to national expenditure and not be used simply to reimburse national authorities.

The Commission administers the Fund with the help of a Regional Fund Committee. A Regional Policy Committee plans future strategy. Both are made up of representatives of the Commission and of the member states. While the processing of applications and the general administration of the current Fund has been rapid and efficient, its initial size was disappointing, being only half of the original figure proposed by the Commission. This inadequacy was underlined in the first annual report on the operation of the Fund in 1975 where it was pointed out that the prosperity gap between the richest and poorest areas of the Community had actually widened since 1970.

Clearly, a more determined effort on the part of the richer member states is urgently needed to narrow this gap and bring about a more balanced development of the Community, on which the success of so many other policy areas depends.

6. Education

The Community is proud of its cultural diversity and is conscious of the need to preserve it. Education therefore remains very much the responsibility of individual member states and the Community has no intention of aiming at a harmonised education system. However, European co-operation in education has a very important part to play in many aspects of the development of the Community, and it was with this in mind that, in 1976 the Council adopted a first programme of action in the education field.

Six priority issues were identified. They cover:

(1) improved educational facilities for Community and non-Community migrants and their children;
(2) closer relations between educational systems;
(3) compilation of up-to-date educational documentation and statistics;
(4) increased co-operation in the field of higher education;
(5) the teaching of foreign languages, and
(6) equal educational opportunities for all.

Within the programme particular priority was given to the need for measures in the education field to prepare young people for work and to facilitate their transition to working life.

Working closely with an Education Committee on which it and the member states are represented, the Commission has undertaken a number of Community projects. These include collaboration with the member states on pilot schemes designed to improve the education of migrant workers' children; the institution of a system of grants for joint study programmes between higher education institutions in different Community countries, and grants for study visits by teaching and research staff and administrators. Discussions on modern language teaching are in progress. The study of European integration is also encouraged.

The Commission has drawn up a report analysing the problems encountered in preparing young people for working life and in facilitating the transition between school and work. It suggested a number of ways in which these problems might be tackled within the framework of existing educational systems and a series of major pilot projects is being prepared as part of an action programme which should have an allocation from the Community budget of £8.5 million over the period 1981–6 with additional financing by the member states.

A new Centre for Vocational Training was opened in Berlin in 1976, as was the European University Institute in Florence where postgraduate work is carried out by students from all parts of the Community. There are, in addition, seven European Schools for the education of children of Community officials. The 10,000 pupils learn at least two Community languages other than their own.

7. Fishing

By decision of the Council of Ministers during 1980, the European Community is committed to developing a new Common Fisheries Policy which is to operate from 1 January 1981. Detailed negotiations will be taking place to reach agreement on effective conservation measures, fair allocation of catches and proper controls to ensure compliance.

Conservation cannot be confined to national waters. This is because fully grown fish caught in one country's waters may have been spawned in seas of other member countries. Cod for instance which matures in British waters is normally spawned off German and Dutch coasts. Herring spawned near British coasts drifts to fishing areas off Danish and other continental coasts and then return in the third or fourth year back to Scottish waters. Distribution of catches will have regard to traditional fishing activities, to the special needs of certain regions dependent upon fishing and to the loss of catch potential in third country waters. Once quotas have been allocated between member countries, controls will be exercised by each state within the waters under its jurisdiction. The European Commission will have powers to verify that member states have implemented the regulations.

The aim of the new policy is to provide a fair basis for rebuilding a viable European fishing industry by restore depleting stocks within European waters under a system of Community management and law. For Britain a fair Community Fishing Policy will go some way towards restoring in due course, the massive damage caused to the industry by the extensions of fishing limits by Iceland, Norway, the Faroes and the Soviet Union, and the catastrophic decline caused by uncontrolled over-fishing in the North Sea and North Atlantic.

CHAPTER 9

COMMUNITY POLICIES ON AGRICULTURE AND INDUSTRY

1. The Common Agricultural Policy

In all countries, however industrialised, agriculture is a key factor: the Common Agricultural Policy has been a crucial element in the first twenty years of the European Community. Without a policy for agriculture, it would have proved impossible to introduce a customs union which provides the economic base for the Community. The introduction of a single Community policy in place of the various national policies has reconciled deep conflicts of interest amongst member states and made it possible for the Community to trade on an international basis with some of the most sensitive issues in international relations.

The European Community is one of the world's major food producing areas. Its farmers and growers can produce 90 per cent of the food needed by the Community's 258 million consumers. This high level of production is a valuable insurance in an unpredictable world where there is a danger of recurring food shortages.

Pressure on the global food supply became evident only in the early seventies. The soaring world prices of those years had eased by the mid-seventies, but the world's population is expected to double over the next generation while its capacity to produce enough food to meet its needs may be held back by a shortage of energy, the excesses of the climate or even political events in distant parts of the world. It is this long-term uncertainty in food supplies which persuades almost all governments – and the EEC as a whole – to have agricultural policies designed to ensure a reasonable level of domestic food production.

The Community was especially glad of its food-producing capacity between 1973 and 1976 when the balance of supply and demand for foodstuffs on world markets was seriously upset. Food prices in the member states during this period were kept below world prices and the Community was able to add to its normal food aid commitments by providing extra grain to the hardest-hit developing countries.

Agriculture responds to the basic but permanent consumer need for food. All farm policies aim to guarantee a sufficient and regular supply. Demand and supply rarely coincide – farming is particularly sensitive to atmospheric and biological factors – and shortages can easily occur. Retail prices are also affected by supply problems, as in turn is the consumer, who in Community countries spends an average of 26 per cent of his budget on food. The percentage of income spent on food is decreasing, however, as the standard of living rises. Food prices no longer appear to be the decisive determinant of consumption levels. Prices also depend greatly on commercial and industrial costs, since it is now exceptional for a product to pass directly from the farmer to the consumer.

For the eight million full-time workers in European agriculture, the land is the principal source of income. Through technical progress and productivity increases, earnings have risen but have not always kept pace with other sectors of the economy.

Public authorities have been obliged to intervene to support agricultural markets and improve the organisation of production whilst taking account of social and economic problems at the same time. This type of intervention – more or less transparent – is now commonplace throughout the world: all governments give great attention to this sensitive sector which is both difficult to manage and often politically very important. Agriculture's contribution to national wealth and to exports is continually declining, however, though its importance for rural management is growing.

In 1960 one in five of the working population was a farmer or farm worker: the figure is now about one in twelve, but in certain countries or regions agriculture is still the mainstay of employment. It provides a living for 25 per cent of Ireland's working population, there are a million wine producers in France and Italy, dairy farming employs nearly two million people in France alone, and beef and sheep production is fundamental to the economy of large parts of the United Kingdom.

THE POLICY IN PRACTICE

Article 39 of the Treaty of Rome defines the five fundamental objectives assigned to the Common Agricultural Policy:

(1) to increase productivity by promoting technical progress and by assuring the national development of agricultural production and the optimum utilisation of the factors of production, in particular labour;
(2) to ensure a fair standard of living for the agricultural community;

(3) to stabilise markets;
(4) to assure the availability of supplies, and
(5) to ensure that supplies reach consumers at reasonable prices.

But the Treaty did no more than lay down guidelines for developing a common policy. The detailed business of providing a single system of price support for agriculture in place of the different national systems was a matter for prolonged negotiations. The main elements of the system were completed by the late sixties but the policy has been continually changing and developing since then.

To best meet the objectives, various markets for farm produce have been progressively organised, based on three fundamental principles – the single market, Community preference and joint financial responsibility.

The single market

The single market implies total trade liberalisation and therefore the removal of customs duties and non-tariff obstacles and the harmonisation of administrative, health and veterinary regulations. It also implies common management rules, common prices, identical competition rules and uniform protection arrangements at Community frontiers. Applied uniformly throughout the Community, these management rules differ according to the characteristics of the different products. Three main types of market organisation exist.

(1) *Intervention measures.* For the principal cereals, sugar, milk products, beef and veal an intervention price system is used. When market prices fall below a set price the Community intervenes to acquire a certain quantity which is then stored: when the market corrects itself, it is resold. For other products – pig-meat, certain fruits and vegetables and table wines – market support comes via other more flexible measures such as storage assistance, withdrawals of produce from the market, or aid for distillation.
(2) *Additional product aid* covers only 2.5 per cent of production – wheat, olive oil, certain oleaginous products and tobacco. Reserved for products in which the Community is a net importer, it helps maintain relatively low prices for consumers whilst guaranteeing a certain income for producers.
(3) *Flat-rate per hectare,* or aid determined by the *quantity produced* covers only a limited segment of production – cottonseed, flax and hemp, silk-worms, seed and dehydrated fodder.

The uniform application of these mechanisms requires that the guaranteed prices used are common throughout member states. These prices are fixed each year by the Council of Ministers.

Community preference

Community preference is the indispensable corollary for the single market. Protection for the European market against low-priced imports and fluctuations on the world market is assured by customs duties or levies which act as a "sluice-gate" at Community frontiers. If prices of imported products are lower than those in the Community, a levy is imposed equal to the difference between the two prices; free access to the Community market is maintained without distorting competition in the common markets. If, on the contrary, world levels are higher than in the Community, a levy is imposed to dissuade sales to the world market, in so far as it is necessary to guarantee supplies to European consumers.

Joint financial responsibility

Such responsibility arises logically from the two preceding principles. It formalises the solidarity between the regions of the Community and facilitates the operation of the system in practice. Management of the system is the responsibility of the European Commission, and for practical reasons expenditure and revenue are also the Community's responsibility. This common financial responsibility is embodied in the European Agricultural Guidance and Guarantee Fund (EAGGF) which is an integral part of the Community budget. As a sign of the importance of agriculture in the process of European unification, this financial instrument, provided for in the founding treaty and set up in 1962, represents two-thirds of the Community budget. It has two sections, guarantee and guidance.

(1) The "guarantee" section finances all public expenditure arising out of the implementation of the common organisation of the market:
   (*a*) a variety of *interventions* aims at regularising the internal market (4,200 million EUA in 1978) – purchases by intervention bodies, storage costs of these bodies, direct income assistance, and subsidies to facilitate the marketing of products competing with low-priced imports, and
   (*b*) *export refunds* (3,000 million EUA in 1978) – financial aid which compensates for the difference between Community and world market prices.

(2) The "guidance" section contributes to the financing of the common policy to improve agricultural marketing and produc-

tion structures by supporting individual farm improvement projects; partially reimbursing general modernisation work: giving assistance to farms in the naturally worse-off regions, and financing schemes to recognise markets (e.g., the reconversion of vineyards).

The policy has progressed much more slowly than market policies, and European aid has often merely supplemented national subsidies. Annual credits from this section have been limited to 325 million EUA since 1973, but expenditure has increased regularly and rapidly over the last ten years.

On 20 March 1979 the European Commission recommended that the Community give a new boost to structural policy by using existing instruments and by introducing new measures of a regional nature.

ACHIEVEMENTS OF THE POLICY

Agricultural productivity has increased very rapidly at 8.8% per year on average from 1961–1971 and 6.2% per year since then. This has been due to technical progress, farm rationalisation and the reduction of the total number of farm workers by about one-third between 1968 and 1978, a reduction which has been induced by the productivity gap between industry and agriculture.

Agricultural incomes have increased since the creation of the Common Market but the increases have not been even. The situation varies greatly from country to country, from product to product and from farm to farm. The greatest divergence has been recorded between the regions of the north and the south of the Community. In addition the gap between the net value added per farm worker and non-farm worker varies on average between 10% and 70% depending on the country. Much remains to be done in this area.

Supply security has been assured and Europe no longer suffers from shortages, even though self-sufficiency in all products has not yet been reached. For certain products, such as protein foods for animals and tropical products, Europe will always depend on outside suppliers. The regularity of supplies as regards price and quantity results from the links established between the Community and supplying countries.

Prices. The assurance of reasonable prices for consumers has been established for the majority of products. The price index has risen at a speed comparable with that for foodstuffs and services, whilst being slightly higher than that for manufactured products. Europe was sheltered from the price inflation which hit the world sugar market in 1974, and the cereal market in 1974–75.

Market stability has also been realised over the last fifteen years. European prices have been little influenced by the world market and have scarcely deviated from the objectives set, but the prices policy has had repercussions at the production level, and in certain sectors surpluses have emerged which have had to be dealt with – generally by expensive experience and unpopular means. Some of these surpluses have been conjunctural and arise from the risky nature of farming, which sometimes imposes production targets above normal demand. But more serious are those of a structural nature which are massive and permanent.

Each year the EAGGF finances stocks of butter and milk powder which are difficult to sell, and sugar production outstrips domestic needs. In these sectors the Common Agricultural Policy is subject to other constraints. In the worst-off regions, milk production has a social dimension since it is practically the only source of income for the small farmers. The competition between butter and margarine which is made from cheap imported products is linked to the absence of an overall policy in the supply of fats. European sugar production has had to cope with the importation of 1.4 million tonnes of sugar taken in by the Community through its Third World co-operation policy.

The single market objective has been disrupted by monetary disorders. To offset the effects of monetary movements in the agricultural industry, Community countries introduced in 1969 the "green" exchange rates to translate the common agricultural prices expressed in European units of account into national currencies. Monetary Compensatory Amounts (MCAs) were introduced to balance out the difference between the green rates and commercial rates and the effects of exchange rate fluctuations. The object is to ensure that member states do not lose any export competitiveness, but despite all the attention given to the introduction and management of this system, competitive distortions have appeared, benefiting those countries least affected by inflation, and the guidance role of the common prices has not been able to play its part fully. The cost of the system has also risen greatly, and in 1978 was close to 900 million EUA.

Finally, farmers in the south of France and in Southern Italy are being threatened by the prospect of the *enlargement of the Community* to bring in largely agricultural competitor countries – Greece, Portugal and Spain. The Community must now give greater attention to the problems of Mediterranean agriculture – often poor and backward – and to some of its produce such as table wines and certain fruit and vegetables. Significant actions were undertaken in this direction in 1978, particularly in the fruit processing sector.

Faced with various difficulties, the Commission is recommending an overall strategy based on the following principles.

(1) The single common agricultural market should be a basic rule. Through the European Monetary System, which came into force in March 1979, we can hope for greater stability, which will reduce the need for introducing new compensatory amounts. On the other hand the common organisation of the market should be extended to cover alcohol, potatoes and sheepmeat.

(2) It is no longer possible to finance production surpluses indefinitely. Market balance must be re-established by a more rigorous price policy which would still enable producer income to rise. The first corrective measures have already been taken in the milk sector (a co-responsibility levy imposed on producers, premiums for the non-marketing of milk and for the reconversion of herds) and for wine production (wine quality policy). These measures must be strengthened and completed. Selective social aids can possibly be granted to those small farmers who are unable to adjust.

(3) The structural modernisation policy must be amplified and the credits available increased from 325 to 700 million EUA per year. Whilst taking account of the problems specific to certain markets, the Commission proposes to concentrate its assistance on those types of farms where structural change involves special difficulties. The Commission also proposes to adapt structural measures more to the needs and possibilities open in the regions, where income levels and economic prospects are alarmingly low. Apart from the action already decided on to help Mediterranean regions, agricultural development programmes – some specific and others integrated into general regional development programmes – should be launched to help the poorer regions.

Cereals

Market management arrangements for cereals and the price levels decided annually for grains are fundamental to the working of the Common Agricultural Policy and the economics of farming in the Community, as cereals constitute a large proportion of total farm production and are the chief expense incurred by most livestock farmers.

Under the Community system a target price is set for each type of cereal. This price is fixed at the level which it is hoped producers will achieve on the open market in that area of the Community where grain is in shortest supply – Duisburg in the Ruhr Valley.

Like all the official cereal prices in the Community, the target price is not an on-farm price, but a price when delivered to store or merchant.

All other prices are linked to the target price. The first line of defence is the threshold price, which applies at all ports round the perimeter of the Community. Threshold prices are calculated so that when grain landed at Rotterdam has been transported to the Duisburg deficit area, it will sell at about the target price or a little more. The threshold price is the same at all ports, but is stepped up seasonally, reflecting the trend of storage costs for the home crop over the year.

Each day variable levies are calculated in Brussels, making up the difference between the lowest c.i.f. offers on world markets and the threshold price. These levies are payable on each consignment shipped into the Community from non-member countries, so producers need fear no undercutting by imports.

Import control is effective in controlling home market prices only so long as imports are coming in and there is no internal surplus. Intervention, or buying in, becomes necessary when home production exceeds demand.

The intervention price for each cereal runs parallel to the target price, pitched at 12–20 per cent below it, moving up in seasonal steps during the cereal year. The old system of derived regional support prices has been replaced by a single intervention price for barley, maize and wheat, so all feed grains are supported at the same level and special measures apply to keep up returns for high quality wheat.

For the trader who decides to sell grain to intervention there are eleven main centres in Germany, in France, in Italy and in the UK, eight in Denmark, five in Ireland, two in Belgium, and one in the Netherlands. These main centres have further sub-centres, all of them committed to paying the fixed price for grain delivered to them provided it meets certain quality and quantity standards. Obviously grain will be offered at intervention only if those holding it are unable to get a better price on the open market. Grain which cannot be sold in the Community market is usually exported.

When Community prices are higher than world prices an export subsidy or restitution is necessary to bridge the price gap. The level of refund is determined by Commission officials on the basis of various facts such as world prices, the amount of the surplus at home and future trends. Restitutions are also payable for derived products such as malt and starch. When world prices are higher than in the EEC, levies are imposed on cereal exports. Producers of drum wheat (the hard grain which is used for making pasta) qualify for a special deficiency payment to encourage them to grow more of a product which is heavily imported from non-member countries.

Sugar

Largely because of the importance of sugar production to developing nations and the attractions of sugar beet to arable farmers in Europe, the Community imposes more discipline on the sugar sector than on any other commodity. The system combines quotas, support buying, and penalties for over-production.

The Community's sugar needs are met partly by imports from developing countries whose economies depend to a large extent on the production of cane sugar, but mainly from domestic beet production and cane sugar from the French overseas territories.

Under the Lomé Convention, the Community is committed to importing about 1.3 million tonnes of cane sugar each year from developing countries such as Fiji, Mauritius, the Caribbean sugar producers and India. This arrangement runs for an indefinite period and guarantees these overseas producers a price linked to the Community's internal support prices.

With the Community, a target price is fixed each year for sugar production in the main surplus areas. EEC producers enjoy the full intervention price on a limited quantity of sugar amounting to 9,136,000 tonnes. This basic quantity is then divided among the member states which allocate quotas for the sugar companies in their territories.

Each year the Council determines a maximum quantity over and above the basic quantity: for 1977/78 this maximum quantity was 35 per cent more than the basic quantity. But whereas the basic quotas qualify for the full intervention price, any sugar which is produced between basic and maximum quotas is subject to a production levy which reduces the effective level of support. Sugar produced outside these quotas – so-called "C" sugar – does not qualify for support. The Community may forbid its sale on the domestic market or may restrict its export, depending on the state of the markets at home and abroad. The production disciplines which apply to the companies are reflected in the prices assured to farmers for their sugar beet. Beet which is to be used for "A" quota sugar is guaranteed a higher price than for "B" quota. There is no fixed minimum price for beet produced outside the quotas.

Free market imports of white sugar, raw sugar and molasses from outside the Community are subject to threshold prices with variable levies payable in the same way as for cereals. Export levies and other restrictions may be applied when world prices are above

Community levels. Export refunds may be paid when world prices are low. In order to meet the severe shortage of sugar in 1974 and 1975 resulting from rising world demand and a poor EEC crop, the Community agreed a special import scheme under which 500,000 tonnes of sugar was bought on the world market and made available to EEC consumers at heavily subsidised prices.

Milk and milk products

The common price policy for milk came into operation in April 1968 at the same time as the final regulations for the closely linked beef and veal markets were introduced. A common target price was established for milk, this being the price which it was thought producers should receive for their milk delivered to dairy, subject to market outlets being available inside and outside the Community. Only about a quarter of the milk produced on Community farms goes for liquid consumption, so the emphasis in price management is on milk products. The policy is to maintain the target price by providing intervention for butter and skim milk, and for cheese in Italy where little butter is made. Community producer prices are protected more from low import prices by threshold prices, which are set out for 12 "pilot" products. The importer pays a levy to cover the difference between the world c.i.f. price and the threshold price. Threshold prices for other products are calculated from the pilot products.

The Community dairy farmers are currently producing more milk than can be used for domestic consumption, so a programme has been agreed for the dairy sector designed to boost demand and reduce output. The measures include a levy on production known as co-responsibility levy, assistance to encourage producers to leave dairying, consumer subsidies on butter, special aid to users of skimmed milk powder and subsidies for school milk.

Each year the Community provides in excess of 200,000 tonnes of skimmed milk powder to developing countries under the World Food Programme. The heavy reliance of New Zealand on the British market for milk products led to agreement that the Community should import certain quantities at a special fixed price. No long-term agreement has been reached on cheese imports.

Beef and veal

In recent years the Community's beef and veal market has been subject to strong cyclical tendencies, with an acute shortage and high prices during 1972/73 and an abundance of supplies and low prices developing in 1974. During 1974, intervention became an important element in a market organisation which until then had depended largely on control of import prices.

The free Community market in beef and veal came into operation from the beginning of April 1968, after a four-year transition period. The guide price is central to the arrangements, acting as a target price which it is hoped producers will achieve, and also serving as a trigger mechanism for import control and intervention at home.

The intervention arrangements provide an alternative outlet at a guaranteed price (90 per cent of guide price) when market prices become unattractive to producers. Greater flexibility was introduced to the system in 1974, because of the reluctance of some governments to undertake support buying and a shortage of storage space. A new system of direct seasonal payments for beef cattle was introduced to encourage more orderly marketing, and the European Commission has now proposed that direct payments should become an integral part of the beef support system in conjunction with intervention.

Live cattle which are imported into the Community have to bear a customs duty of 16 per cent and beef imports bear a duty of between 20 and 26 per cent depending on type. These duties are part of the common external tariff, although they can be temporarily suspended or reduced, as they were during 1972–3. The levy arrangements, on the other hand, are flexible.

Levies on beef and beef cattle are fixed every week, comprising the difference between the price at which the consignments are imported (including duties) and the guide price, but the proportion of levy payable by the importer depends on the state of the home market. This is assessed on representative market prices, usually known as reference prices, which are calculated in each member country and then brought together as a Community reference price, weighted for the size of the cattle population in each country. Thus depressed markets in one country do not have a disproportionate effect on the Community reference price.

Fruit and vegetables

More responsibility is given to producer organisations in the operation of the fruit and vegetable markets than in other sectors, largely because of the difficulties of operating a rigid system of support for commodities which are invariably seasonal, usually difficult to store and where marketing problems are often local or regional rather than national.

Imports can be controlled by imposition of a countervailing

duty when the price of imports falls below the reference price for two successive days. This reference price is virtually a minimum import price based on cost of production and marketing. It can be seasonally stepped and is additional to customs duties, which vary between 10 and 21 per cent for vegetables and between 7 and 25 per cent for fruit.

For home markets management basic prices for cauliflowers, tomatoes, table grapes, peaches, apples and pears are fixed annually by the Council of Ministers, Member states may fix buying-in prices at between 40 and 70 per cent of the basic price. When market prices are below this buying-in price for three successive days, a state of serious crisis is declared and member states must intervene to stabilise the market.

Producer organisations are entitled to fix a reserve or fall-back price for each commodity, at which price they may intervene with some help from Community funds. In practice this means that they will not market produce at below this level.

Strict grading standards apply for fruit and vegetables and all intervention is paid for at grade II prices, so encouraging producers to place their better quality output through the market.

To increase the effectiveness of producer organisations, the Community provides for disciplines on their members as well as grant aid to help with their setting up.

Wine

Wine proved one of the most difficult products for which to evolve a common policy. It was a subject for discussion, proposal and counter-proposal for some seven years, but agreement was eventually reached in April 1970 as part of the package of measures which marked the introduction of the definitive phase of Community financing.

The final arrangements abolished all quotas on imports, introducing a customs duty and a variable levy system to bring imported wines up to the price level of their Community equivalent. They also provided for supervision of plantings, an intervention mechanism and common terms for trade with third countries.

It was decided that the strength of ordinary table wines must be between 8.5 and 15 degrees of alcohol (there were different criteria for high quality wines and aperitifs) and that wine growers in Luxembourg and Germany should be free to increase the alcohol content of their wines by up to 3.1 per cent through the addition of sugar to compensate for lack of sunshine.

Measures for improving quality and taking some vineyards out of production were agreed when the so-called "wine war" between

France and Italy was resolved in the spring of 1976. France had imposed a 10 per cent levy on Italian wine imports which was later removed.

DECISIONS ON FARM PRICES 1980–81

Summary

The Council of Farm Ministers reached final agreement on the 1980/81 farm prices package at their meeting of 28 and 29 May 1980. The package they agreed increases agricultural support prices in the Community between 5.5 per cent and 7.5 per cent – except for milk, beef and sugar, where the increases were limited to 4 per cent. The overall average of the package is a rise of 4.8 per cent in the official farm prices throughout the Community. The main decisions were:

(1) butter intervention price up by 2.3 per cent; skim milk powder by 4.8 per cent;
(2) co-responsibility levy on milk producers up from 0.5 per cent to 2.0 per cent;
(3) existing agreements for sugar maintained for a further year;
(4) introduction of a beef cow subsidy of £12 per head;
(5) continuation in the UK of beef premium scheme;
(6) continuation of special UK butter subsidy at 13p per 500 g;
(7) agreement reached on a Community-wide regime for mutton and lamb.

What the decisions mean

Farmers in the Community will get an overall increase of 5.7 per cent against a Community inflation rate of 12 per cent – in 1979 they received 6.6 per cent as against 8.8 per cent inflation. In the UK farmers will get slightly less at 4.7 against an anticipated inflation rate of 21.6 per cent.

For consumers the effects will vary from commodity to commodity, but the settlement is expected to increase household expenditure throughout the Community by ½ per cent. In the UK the price package will add 0.7 per cent to the food price index and 0.2 per cent to the retail price index.

British consumer will also benefit from the retention of the special UK butter subsidy at 13p per lb, wholly refunded from Community sources, and worth in total about £108 million.

The agricultural budget

Community expenditure on farming support in 1980 will now reach 11,500 million EUA, 11 per cent more than in 1979.

This compares with an annual growth in expenditure of 23 per cent between 1975 and 1979. Of this total, some 4,900 million EUA will go to supporting the dairy industry; 1,200 million EUA on beef and 1,600 million EUA on cereals. The anticipated expenditure in 1981 will be 13,000 million EUA. The UK contribution to the budget is now fixed at about 600 million EUA for 1980, and is unaffected by the farm price decision.

Milk

The target price will rise by 4 per cent, but within this the butter intervention price will rise by 2.3 per cent, and the skimmed milk powder price by 4.8 per cent. This has been done to keep down the effect of the butter increase on consumers. The co-responsibility levy rises from 0.5 per cent to 2.0 per cent, and will not be less than 1.5 per cent for the following two years. It will be payable on all milk sold to dairies, with the exception of milk produced in mountainous regions. Producers in less favoured areas will only paid 1.5 per cent on the first 60,000 kilos of production. Investment aids to dairy farmers will be limited to those following a farm improvement plan under a Community modernisation scheme, and will also be limited to the investment needed to generate income for one-and-a-half people.

The premium scheme for the non-marketing of milk, begun in 1977, will cease on 15 September 1980. The premium scheme for the conversion of dairy herds to beef production is scheduled to cease at the end of the marketing year (31 March 1981) – but may be extended after further discussions.

Policies to encourage the consumption of butter continue, with a butter subsidy of 13p per lb in the UK, fully financed by the Community. Other schemes, such as Christmas butter, will be considered in the autumn.

Beef

The rise in intervention price is limited to 4 per cent, but specialist producers are to get a £12 a head suckler cow subsidy paid direct. This will help farmers' incomes at a time when prices are low, but will not affect the price of beef in the shops.

The system of beef premiums is to continue in the UK.

Cereals

The overall average price rises by 5.3 per cent. For wheat and barley, the increase in target prices (which affects the price of imports) is 6.3 per cent and for rye it is 2.5 per cent. Intervention prices for wheat and barley, which set the floor in the home market, go up by 4.5 per cent.

Sugar

The minimum price for sugar beet in the Community rises by 4 per cent; for white sugar intervention prices go up by 4.5 per cent. Commission proposals to limit growers' quotas to correspond as nearly as possible to consumption, with an allowance for traditional imports from ACP countries, were rejected. The second objective, to make the cost of disposing of surpluses fall on producers, should be accepted in time for future price discussions.

Sheep

The council reached agreement on proposals for a common regime for mutton and lamb. Under the agreement all producer prices in the Community will be brought to a common reference level over the next four years. This year UK producers will get a 17 per cent increase in the guaranteed price, paid in the form of a deficiency payment, and funded entirely from the EEC budget. In the rest of the Community an intervention system will be used. This means British lamb will not be sold into intervention. The full detail of the sheep regime has still to be worked out, since it depends on making satisfactory import arrangements with New Zealand.

Monetary decisions

The compromise agreed in the Council included a 1 per cent reduction in German monetary compensation amounts, which effectively reduces the value of the price rise to 3.5 per cent for German producers. The MCAs for the Benelux countries are cut by 0.2 per cent.

These changes, plus actual currency movements, mean that the green rates used for converting the European currency unit (ECU) prices to national currencies are almost on a par with commercial exchange rate values. Thus the common prices of the CAP provide virtually the same level of market support for producers in all Community countries except Germany, where support prices are still about 9 per cent higher than the fixed Community price.

The current green rates are given below and apply to cereals, eggs, poultry, pigmeat, wine, fish, beef, milk products, and sugar.

Prices of the main commodities

Commodity	COMMON PRICE LEVEL		1980/81 Marketing year
	European currency units (ECU)	£[1]	
MILK			
Target price for milk	22.26 ecu/100 kg	14.18p/litre	1 June 1980 –
Intervention price for butter (82% fat)	291.60 ecu/100 kg	1804.00 /tonne	31 March 1981
Skimmed milk powder	121.51 ecu/100 kg	751.73 /tonne	
BEEF AND VEAL			
Guide price	160.76 ecu/live 100 kg	99.45 /live 100 kg	2 June 1980 – 5 April 1981
PIGMEAT			
Basic price	158.72 ecu/100 kg	98.19 /100 kg	1 November 1980 – 31 October 1981
CEREALS[2]			
COMMON WHEAT			
Target price	214.01 ecu/tonne	132.40 /tonne	
Reference price for breadmaking wheat	175.20 ecu/tonne	108.39 /tonne	
Single intervention price	155.88 ecu/tonne	96.44 /tonne	
BARLEY			
Target price	194.32 ecu/tonne	120.22 /tonne	
Single intervention price	155.88 ecu/tonne	96.44 /tonne	
RYE			
Target price	197.31 ecu/tonne	122.07 /tonne	1 August 1980 –
Single intervention price	163.82 ecu/tonne	101.35 /tonne	31 July 1981
MAIZE			
Target price	194.32 ecu/tonne	120.22 /tonne	
Single intervention price	155.88 ecu/tonne	96.44 /tonne	
SUGAR[3]			
Minimum beet price	33.10 ecu/tonne	20.48 /tonne	1 July 1980 –
White sugar target	455.50 ecu/tonne	281.80 /tonne	30 June 1981
White sugar intervention	432.70 ecu/tonne	267.69 /tonne	

(1) Prices in sterling converted at the green rate of £1 = 1.61641 ECU.
(2) Prices at the first day of the marketing year, which are then subject to monthly increments.
(3) Minimum beet price for the UK is £21.45 per tonne. Derived UK intervention price for white sugar is 444.80 ECU or £275.18 per tonne.

Green rates

		New green rate 1 ECU equals	
Belgium/Luxembourg	Bf	40.5191	1
Denmark	Kr	7.72336	
Germany	Dm	2.75175	2
France	Ff	5.84700	
Ireland	Ir£	0.659274	
Italy	L	1 157.79	
Netherlands	Fl	2.79391	3
United Kingdom	£	0.618655	

(1) For milk and milk products Bf 40.7264
(2) For milk and milk products Dm 2.78260
(3) For milk and milk products Fl 2.80821

2. Steel

Introduction

The establishment of the European Coal and Steel Community (ECSC) in 1951 was a first step towards the later, more ambitious creation of the European Economic Community; thus the coal and steel industries of member countries have had a long history of co-operation and common policies, which served them well in the economically buoyant post-war years.

In the 1970s, however, the steel industry was faced with the unpleasant needs of contraction and redundancy. Action in one Community country affects the industry in other member states and world developments also affect the steel industry in the Nine. This makes the need for common policies on modernisation, quality and levels of production all the greater if jobs are to be safeguarded in future, and if those made redundant are to be helped to find alternative employment.

THE COAL AND STEEL COMMUNITY

The ECSC was created by the Treaty of Paris, signed in April 1951. At that time coal and steel were the two commanding heights of the national economies, supplying energy and materials for most industrial activity. The Treaty created an ECSC High Authority, aided by a high-powered Consultative Committee, a Common Assembly, a Council of Ministers, and a Court of Justice.

The objects of the ECSC, as laid down in the Treaty, were economic expansion, growth of employment, a rising standard of living, and rational distribution of production at the highest level of productivity, while safeguarding continuity of employment. The Treaty proposed implementing these objectives by abolishing *(a)* duties and quantitative restrictions on trade in coal and steel between member states, *(b)* discrimination by producers in prices, delivery terms or transport rates and *(c)* restrictive practices tending towards cartels or exploitation of markets. In addition the ECSC was given powers to take action over a wide field of activity in the coal and steel industries, including investment, production, wages and movement of workers, transport charges and commercial relations with non-member countries.

Control of the industry, of course, lies in the hands of national producers, whether public or private, but the rules of the Paris Treaty provide for free trade in basic iron and steel products within the Community and a pricing system requiring producers to publish all their prices at selected basing points. Transport charges have also to be published or notified to the European Commission (formerly the High Authority). The administration of the pricing system and all questions relating to restrictive practices and market sharing agreements are the primary responsibility of the Commission.

In 1967 the Six decided to merge the institutions of the ECSC, Euratom (the Atomic Energy Authority) and the European Economic Community. As far as the ECSC was concerned, this meant that the European Commission replaced the High Authority, though the Consultative Committee remained in being. The Assembly, Council of Ministers and Court of Justice were merged into the existing Community institutions. The Consultative Committee was enlarged on the accession of Britain, Denmark and Ireland in 1973 to consist of not less than 60 and not more than 84 members, representing equal numbers of producers, workers and consumers and dealers from the member countries. Last year Sir Derek Ezra, Chairman of the National Coal Board, was elected Chairman of the Consultative Committee.

The powers of the High Authority have devolved on the Commission which therefore, within the institutions, exercises important responsibilities for the Community coal and steel industries.

Financing activities

The ECSC budget is adopted each year in accordance with the procedures laid down in the Paris Treaty, and is distinct from the general Community budget. After consulting the European Parliament, the Commission has powers to adopt the budget.

Most of the budget resources come from the coal and steel industries in the form of levies on production. The current levy rate remains as fixed in 1972 – 0.29 per cent. The money so raised is channelled back to the industries for various purposes, such as retaining of redundant workers, interest relief, grants towards modernisation, research, and so on. For some time now, however, the levy rate has not produced enough revenue to meet the needs of the ECSC and the Commission has asked the Council of Ministers to supplement its income by a transfer to the ECSC budget of customs duties related to coal and steel products. So far the Council has been reluctant to do this, and has preferred to supplement ECSC requirements by grants from the Community budget and concessions on ECSC obligatory budget contributions.

The Commission adopted an ECSC budget of 180 million EUA (£120 million) for 1979, but has warned that greater resources are needed for the future.

Grants and loans

Under Articles 54 and 56 of the Paris Treaty loans are available to assist investment projects, although the ECSC does not provide general cash requirements or working capital. Such projects include modernisation and conversion of steel plant, and the provision of loans, often at low interest rates, for the establishment of new employment in areas of coal and steel production. There are also loans for house building or modernisation of existing dwellings for those working in the industries. Here loans may be granted to cover up to 20 per cent of the investment cost for new dwellings and 35 per cent for the modernisation of existing ones. The interest rate is usually 1 per cent and the repayment period about 20 years. By 1978 about 5,600 low cost homes had been built or converted in Britain under the scheme.

The ECSC also helps workers affected by fundamental changes in the coal and steel industries through grants in the form of tide-over or resettlement allowances, and the financing of vocational training for workers having to change their employment. Such grants, however, are conditional upon the member country paying an amount at least equal to the ECSC contribution (except in certain cases).

The tables show the range of loans from the ECSC and the number of workers helped in 1978.

Since 1973, 28,000 coal workers and 30,500 steelmen in the United Kingdom have benefited from ECSC help, a total of nearly 60,000 people. Throughout the Community calls for help from the steel industry have been particularly heavy in the last two years. From 1976 to 1978 the ECSC contributed 44 million EUA

ECSC Loans from 1954 to 1977 (in million EUA)

	Total	*Benelux countries*	*Denmark*	*Germany*	*France*	*Ireland*	*Italy*	*UK*
Iron-ore Mines	96	1	–	33	10	–	15	37
Conversion	457	86	–	132	116	–	56	67
Steel Industry	3,020	273	33	835	629	–	666	584
Coal Industry	886	3	–	395	88	–	7	393
Power Stations	130	9	–	56	60	–	5	–
Housing	233	56	1	124	34	1	15	2
Retraining	1	–	–	–	1	–	–	–
Research	4	1	–	2	1	–	–	–
Miscellaneous	13	5	–	8	–	–	–	–
Total	4,840	434	34	1,585	939	1	764	1,083

(Source: *Grants and Loans from the European Community.*)

Readaption of Workers 1978

	COAL INDUSTRY		STEEL INDUSTRY IRON-ORE MINING		TOTAL	
	Amounts made available (EUA '000)	*Workers*	*Amounts made available (EUA '000)*	*Workers*	*Amounts made available (EUA '000)*	*Workers*
Belgium	2,525	1,619	2,433	2,186	4,958	3,805
France	3,742	960	12,413	9,349	16,155	10,309
Germany	8,783	8,479	791	3,381	9,574	11,860
Italy	–	–	1,320	2,528	1,320	2,528
Luxembourg	–	–	1,398	541	1,398	541
UK	17,735 (total for 1977 and 1978)	9,121	11,378	13,025	29,113	22,146
Total	32,785	20,179	29,733	31,010	62,518	51,189

(Source: *European Community.*)

(approximately £30 million) to help 48,000 steel workers in the member states.

Assistance for research

The ECSC also provides financial assistance to cover expenditure directly incurred for purposes of research, including staff, equipment and operating expenses. The grant usually covers 60 per cent of such expenditure. A contribution may also be made on a case-by-case basis for carrying out social and medical research.

Community policy for steel

In recent years the Community steel industry has been faced with the prospect either of erosion from low cost third country competition or of erecting protectionist national barriers against collapse. As it is there has been a serious contraction in the industry since 1974, with the workforce falling by 107,000 from 792,000 to 685,000 at the end of 1978 as a result of failing markets. The European Commission estimates that by the end of 1980 a further 81,000 jobs could be lost.

In accordance with its responsibilities under the European Coal and Steel Community the European Commission has put forward proposals – known as the Davignon Plan – to help the industry, while seeking internationally an equitable share of the steel market. The Plan was approved in principle by the Council of Ministers on 19 December 1978. Although the Commission's current *Forward Programme for Steel* notes a welcome increase in the Nine's steel exports to non-member countries in 1978, the industry is still working at only 66 per cent of capacity.

Background to crisis

Between 1946 and 1974 there was an enormous expansion in the world production of steel, rising from 112 million to 708 million tonnes. The most dramatic expansion was in Japan, where its share of the market rose from 2.5 per cent to 16 per cent in 25 years. In 1974 Community steel accounted for 22 per cent of world production, employed nearly 800,000 workers and was responsible for 7 per cent of the Community's industrial production.

In 1975 world crude steel production dropped by 9 per cent, and the major steel producers – Europe, the USA and Japan – found themselves operating well under capacity. The Community industry was hardest hit, operating at about 60 per cent of capacity compared with the USA at 77 per cent and Japan 74 per cent. For the Community this has meant cutbacks in production, a slump in prices, deterioration of employment and a financial loss for the whole Community industry in 1977 of 3,000 million EUA (about £2,000 million). In addition, a number of European steel plants are old and ill-equipped to face competition from new steel producers in countries such as South Korea and Spain.

The community role

The Paris Treaty that established the ECSC provided guidelines for its members on commercial policy, including a pricing system, notification of transport charges and Commission responsibility on questions of restrictive practices and market-sharing agreements.

Within this framework the Commission put forward proposals,

adopted by the Council in December 1977, (i) to levy temporary dumping duties on steel imported below Community published prices; (ii) to negotiate bilateral agreements to stabilise imports, and (iii) to raise by an eventual 15 per cent the internal Community guidance prices of steel products.

These measures have now been incorporated into the short-term Davignon Plan. The Plan aims to put a ceiling on already surplus production capacities in the Community, and to establish compulsory minimum prices for particularly sensitive products and recommended prices for other products. The anti-dumping restrictions have continued against imports from countries selling in Europe at prices lower than the production costs of their most efficient factories, while arrangements have been made with exporting countries such as Japan, South Africa, and Eastern European countries to limit their exports. As a result European steel imports which amounted to 12.4 million tonnes in 1976 fell to about 11 million tonnes in 1978, while exports rose by nearly 9 million to total 30 million tonnes, thus saving 55,000 jobs in the European steel industry.

Longer term plan

In October 1978 Viscount Davignon put forward proposals for a longer term plan providing Community financial help to modernise the steel industry, and help for redundant workers. The Plan seeks to prohibit national subsidies which increase production capacities or which distort competition within the Common Market; to grant Community loans to encourage the modernisation and rationalisation of companies in order to create a better balance between supply and demand; to increase Community aid for industrial conversion and diversification in the major steel-making area (by 1985 some 100,000 jobs must be created to compensate for steel industry redundancies); to study ways in which the available work can better be shared (such as reducing retirement age, reorganising shift work, reducing the length of the working week and restricting overtime); to intensify research on better ways to use minerals and energy, and to conduct negotiations with other steel producers to ensure that Community producers do not bear a disproportionate share of the cost of coping with the inadequate level of world steel demand.

The Council of Ministers adopted the principles of the Plan at its meeting on 19 December 1978, subject to further negotiation on the question of national and regional aids, a matter on which the United Kingdom and Italy have reservations.

"Anti-crisis" help

Faced with the prospect of a further 81,000 redundancies in the steel industry in 1979 and 1980, the Commission sent a proposal to the Council and the European Parliament in May that would allocate 132 million EUA (about £90 million) towards easing the lot of those people involved as proposed under the Davignon Plan. The money would supplement grants provided under Article 56 of the ECSC Treaty, and over half (£47 million) would be used in new types of intervention.

The new grants would be payable to those directly affected by modernisation and conversion of plant. Four types of intervention are envisaged.

(1) *Early retirement*: grants would be available for a period of three years to those taking early retirement because of the partial closure or full closing down of their enterprise; or because a vacancy would enable a younger worker to take over, and the retiring age is lower than that provided for under national law.
(2) *Part-time working or a reduced working week:* to avoid closure or prevent redundancies, the Commission would contribute to maintaining earnings. The cost would be shared between the workers, the firm, the government and the Community.
(3) *Introduction of an extra shift* in order to share out work; here again costs would be shared between the workers, the firm, the government and the Community. The Community grant would be a tapering one over three years.
(4) *Limitation on overtime working:* the Commission also suggests supplementing, to a limited extent, the wages of those on low incomes affected by restrictions on overtime (where such restrictions are introduced) to encourage work-sharing. Here the countries most affected would be the United Kingdom and Ireland.

Hopes for the 1980s

It is the hope of both the Commission and the Council that the aids envisaged under the Davignon Plan will themselves become redundant as the steel industry adapts to changed times and markets. The aim is to stabilise annual production at 180 million tonnes by 1983. It is estimated that this goal will require an annual investment of 2,000 million EUA (£1,340 million) in the Community iron and steel industry. In addition the Commission is aiming to create 100,000 jobs between now and 1985 to compensate for redundancies in the industry.

3. Shipbuilding

As the state of the Community shipbuilding industry continues to deteriorate, the Commission has submitted to the Council of Ministers for discussion an emergency scheme of "scrap-and-build," designed to help maintain production levels over a three-year period. Broadly, the scheme envisages the scrapping of two ships for the building of one ship equivalent to half the scrapped tonnage. The shipbuilding industry generally approves the scheme: it is designed, with Community financial aid, both to modernise fleets and to reduce present over-capacity in the Community merchant fleet during a period when orders in Community shipyards are barely adequate for a year.

Bleak prospects

The general state of the shipbuilding industry is still marked by a decreasing order intake, reduced order books, and continuous decline in employment. Since 1975 the workforce has fallen from a Community total of 206,354 to an estimated 138,000–145,000 in 1979 – a loss of 5,000–60,000 people. In the UK, which still remains the largest workforce, about 20,000 people have left the industry in this period. Throughout the member countries the jobs of another 50,000 are at risk if orders remain at their present low level.

These gloomy facts, set out in the Commission's first half-yearly report on the state of the Community shipbuilding industry, set the context for the Commission's scrap-and-build proposals. The report noted that in 1978–79 production in Community shipyards at two million compensated gross register tons (see below) fell below the Commission's initial forecasts of 2.4 million cgrt for 1980; competitiveness had not improved and, unless something was done quickly, the situation could lead to a vicious circle of decline which would make it difficult to adapt the industry to the new conditions of the 1980s. Already the share of new order intakes in the Community tends to be lower than the share of deliveries, whereas with competitors, such as Japan, the reverse is the case. The Commission estimates that the average workload in the industry is less than one year's production, while some yards are already in acute difficulty and facing high unemployment problems.

The present imbalance in the shipping market is largely due to the enormous expansion of world sea-borne trade – particularly oil – in the 1960s and early 1970s, which was expected to continue throughout the decade but was brought to an abrupt halt in 1973. At the end of 1978 total world over-capacity was reckoned at around 100 million deadweight tonnes (see below) – mainly tankers – or some 15 per cent of total world cargo-carrying tonnage.

Forecasts suggest that there could be some improvement in the shipping market, and therefore the shipbuilding industry, after

1982–83, but the Commission warns that unless the Community industry reorganises and improves competitivity, it will have a hard job obtaining new orders against the expanding industries of developing countries such as Korea and Brazil, or of Eastern Block countries such as Poland. Meanwhile interim action is required to keep yards in being while the industry is reorganised and modernised.

Scrap and build

This interim action, as devised by Commissioners Viscount Davignon and Mr Burke in consultation with the industry, is the scrap and build scheme. The Commission notes that the shipowners are deferring making replacements to their fleets while times are bad; but a rush of replacements at a later stage could cause bottlenecks or put burdens on the shipbuilding industry with which it could not cope. A scheme that only encouraged shipowners to place new orders now would aggravate the problems of the shipping market; one which solely favoured the scrapping of old ships would not only have a limited scope (as it would only affect ships flying the flags of member states), but would in no way guarantee the placing of additional orders with the Community industry. What is required, the Commission believes, is action which combines the reactivation of demand with encouragement to scrap old vessels.

The essence of the Commission scheme would be the granting of financial support to a Community-established shipowner who placed an order for ocean-going ships with a Community shipyard, *provided* that, as part of the same operation the shipowner also sent ships to be scrapped representing twice the tonnage to be built, calculated in compensatory gross register tons. To be effective the scheme would also have to be reasonably extensive. To enable shipyards to maintain production levels of between 2.5 million and 3 million cgrt, the Commission believes that the target should be 1 million cgrt of new shipping and 2 million cgrt of scrap a year over a three-year period.

Rules governing the scheme, however, would have to be fairly strict. Ships already due for scrapping during the period would not be eligible for grant, and the Commission suggests that no ship built under the scheme should be allowed immediately to transfer registration to a non-Community country; if this were done within a period of six years, the shipowner should repay part of the subsidy he has received.

The Commission proposes that financial support should consist of *(a)* a variable part to offset the difference between the second-hand price and the scrapping price of a ship, and *(b)* a fixed component to encourage the owner to invest in new ships. The variable proportion would be calculated on a flat-rate basis depending on the type, size and age of the vessel and would range from 10 EUA to 75 EUA per lightweight tonne. This is an average of 32.5 EUA per cgrt. If the scheme reached its target of 1 million cgrt new building and 2 million cgrt scrap, the Commission estimates the cost at 145 million EUA a year, or 435 million EUA over three years. Such costs are equivalent to 15–20 per cent of government aid already paid to the shipbuilding industry in the Community.

The Commission believes that if the scheme were adopted, it would help to maintain employment not only for about 35,000 people in the shipyards themselves but for a comparable number in related or dependent industries.

The Commission recognises that the scheme would be a temporary measure and that it is impossible to guarantee that it would be a success. Much would depend on the attitude of shipowners and the state of the market; the scheme could operate only if the price of second-hand ships and of scrapping them remained within limited margins. If these prices widened the scheme would automatically shut off. The Commission leaves open for decision whether a coordinate national approach would be better. For a number of practical reasons the Commission considered that a Community-financed project would be preferable.

Definitions

Gross register ton (grt): the register tonnage of a ship is the volume below the main deck plus that of the tween decks and superstructures, excluding all open spaces; it is expressed in tons, one ton being 100 cubic feet, or 2.83 cubic metres.

Compensated gross register ton (cgrt): since the normal gross register tonnage of a ship does not reflect the amount of shipbuilding work done (which also represents the degree of sophistication of the ship), the OECD has laid down coefficients for each type and size of merchant vessel (grt x coefficient = cgrt).

Deadweight tonne (dwt): the deadweight tonnage, calculated in metric tons, is equal to the weight of the cargo, fuel, stores, crew and passengers, if any, when the vessel is floating at its normal load-line.

Lightweight tonne: the lightweight tonnage of a ship is equal to the weight of the fitted-out hull and the propulsion machinery in working order.

4. Shipping - Cargo Liners

The European Community's cargo-carrying trade is today threatened by increasing competition from state-trading countries which is seriously undermining the activities of the Community's carriers. The countries of the Comecon group now have a virtual monopoly in their bilateral trade with Community countries, and had already obtained about 20 per cent of the shipping trade on other lucrative routes, such as the North Atlantic and Mediterranean.

The Community accepts that state-trading countries have every right to compete for the cargo-carrying trade: its concern arises from the fact that the competition is unfair. The Commission points out that the non-market economies of Comecon countries mean that their liner shipping trade practices do not reflect the true costs (including profit) of the market economy, hence making it impossible for even the most efficient of the Community shipping lines to compete with them. In addition, the Soviet Union and other Comecon countries impose administrative and trade barriers which prevent member state shipping lines from establishing such agencies in their countries, while they themselves remain free to establish such agencies in the Community. The result has been substantial under-cutting of freight rates in trade between member states and the third countries and between third countries, allowing Comecon operators to cream off the most profitable traffic and put member states' shipowners under constant financial pressure.

Since the early 1970s the Soviet Union has been swiftly expanding its cargo fleet and has plans to expand still further. It now carries 95 per cent of its own bilateral trade with Community countries, and is becoming increasingly successful in cross-trades between third countries. Operating outside the international liner conference, Comecon countries – mainly the Soviet Union, Poland and East Germany – are reported to have captured 18 per cent of the eastbound and 22 per cent of the westbound liner conferences' North Atlantic cargo traffic. Their fleets carry between a fifth and a quarter of traffic between Northern Europe and the west coast of South America, between Gulf of Mexico ports and the Mediterranean, and the Europe-East African route. They now also carry 12 per cent of traffic between Japan and the west coast of the United States. While these proportions are less alarming than the bilateral carrying figures, the Commission points out that they are likely to increase unless corrective action is taken.

This can be done only by governments, since Community liner companies have no effective way of competing successfully with the state-trading countries' fleets at commercial level.

Proposals for action

Briefly the Commission's view is –

(1) that member states and the Community should define the objectives to be pursued in relation to cargo liner shipping by state-trading countries;
(2) that the member states should set up monitoring procedures enabling them to follow the activities of the liner operators of state-trading countries using Community ports;
(3) that member states and the Commission should regularly examine developments in this area through approved consultative procedures, and
(4) that the Council, in certain circumstances and on a proposal from the Commission, should take powers to place quantitative restrictions on cargo carried to and from Community ports in state-trading country vessels. These restrictions could be applied generally, by certain member states only, or in a specific area or trading range.

Policy considerations

The Commission sent, in the late 1970s, a proposal to the Council concerning negotiations for Community accession to the UN Convention on a Code of Conduct for Liner Conferences. The Code, not yet in force, deals with such subjects as liner conference membership, cargo sharing, voting arrangement in conferences, consultation between shipowners and shippers and procedures for charging freight rates and resolving disputes.

Basically its objective is to enable the developing countries to share with the traditional carriers in the transport of world trade. Member states have been divided on the Code: some have sought to ratify it, others are hostile. Efforts are now in hand to achieve a common approach.

The threat from the Comecon states is a separate issue, but here again members do not see eye to eye. This partly reflects the sizes of their merchant marines (see below) and partly political relations with the Soviet Union and Eastern European countries.

The Commission points out that while some may argue that the state-trading countries must be allowed to earn hard currencies in the West through the sale of shipping services to pay for Western commodities and technology (the Soviet Union earned about 600 million dollars in 1976 from its international shipping), only a small part of Comecon's foreign trade can be covered by the income resulting from shipping. It seems unlikely, therefore, that the placing of limits on these countries' participation in the Community's cargo liner traffic would have a negative impact on the Community's trade with them. In any case the state-trading countries would not have much scope for shifting their demand pattern geographically as both the United States and Japan are preparing legislation to counteract the impact of state-trading operators on their cargo liner trade.

EEC Liner Fleets (million tons)

Britain	6.5
Germany	3.6
Netherlands	2.1
France	1.6
Denmark	1.4
Italy	1.3
Belgium	.3
Eire	.04
Luxembourg	–
	16.8

(Source: *UNCTAD*)

The London *Times* of 21 April 1978 quoted –

World total	73.0
USSR	6.5
USA	4.0

There is also the question of existing agreements, such as bilateral agreements between the member states and the Soviet Union or other state-trading countries (which usually grant each of the contracting parties most favoured nation status in maritime relations) and broader international agreements such as the Helsinki Agreement. The Commission argues that its proposals are not contrary to the spirit of the latter; as for the former, the proposals might well require some re-negotiation of the bilateral agreements, but member countries could claim that these had not been meaningfully observed by their state-trading partners. GATT rules also allow for the application of defensive measures in certain circumstances.

Whatever the difficulties, however, the Commission considers the position sufficiently serious for the Council to take action on a shipping policy as soon as possible.

5. Textiles and Clothing

The textile and clothing industries are important for the Community economy, providing approximately 10 per cent of industrial jobs, and accounting for some 8 per cent of the Community's industrial activities. For a number of reasons, however, the industries are in difficulties. In a Communication to the Council of Ministers the European Commission has put forward guidelines for a policy of innovation and rejuvenation.

Present difficulties

The textile and clothing industries consist, in the main, of small or medium-sized firms, particularly in the clothing industry, with a wide diversity of products and outlets, and marked fluctuations in demand. They also contain a high proportion of women workers and tend to be heavily concentrated in certain regions.

The industries have already been in difficulties for many years, mainly as a result of slow internal demand and the rapid industrialisation of textile production in the third world. This has led to a cut-back in the numbers of jobs available and the closing down of many factories. The economic crisis of 1974–75 particularly affected textiles and clothing because it coincided with a sharp increase in imports of inexpensive textiles. Even the most dynamic firms have found it hard to keep up or intensify efforts to innovate or modernise, though the situation varies from country to country. There has been an obvious drop in textile production, particularly clothing, in Holland, while despite the crisis Italian and Irish textile production have shown a certain revival since 1976.

In order to safeguard the Community industries and allow time for rationalisation and modernisation, the Community has negotiated limitation agreements with 23 low-cost supplying countries, and devised similar arrangements for six countries with which it has preferential trade agreements, with Taiwan and the state-trading countries. These agreements cover 127 categories of textile products and include either *quantitative limits* (quotas) for categories of sensitive products, or a *mechanism* for *potential limitation* which can be applied to sensitive products from present small suppliers, or to less sensitive products which may become sensitive in time.

These arrangements, negotiated under the Multifibre Arrangement (MFA), have helped to lift the threat to the Community industries caused by the enormous influx of low-cost textile products from developing and other countries in the last two or three years, but the Commission emphasises that this is only a limited reprieve. The agreements are due to expire in 1982: the interval, the Commission insists, *must* be used to adapt to new conditions of both Community and international competition. Unless this is done the textile agreements will merely have provided a false sense of security, particularly as the MFA itself expires at the end of 1981 and it is not yet known whether it will be possible to renew it and, if so, on what terms.

Objectives and guidelines

The Commission suggests that the main objectives must be greater competitiveness integrated into the international trade system, and based on company initiative channelled to developing points of strength.

The Commission seeks particularly to help small firms where management finds it difficult to adapt to adversity, and in consultation with the industry will be looking into ways and means by which the public authorities can help them in special fields, such as product and marketing policy, sales promotion, statistical information about markets and the provision of a proper balance between production, marketing and research. Here the Commission is particularly concerned that small firms should be able to benefit from accurate market information, and is taking further steps to provide harmonised statistics for the Community as a whole, particularly for the clothing industry.

This must be supplemented by research and innovation, specialisation and the use of new technologies. Examples would be the launching of new products adapted to changes in life style (sports, leisure, furnishings), fully exploiting changes in fashion and the use of new materials. To this end the Community is already partly financing a first common research programme, and there are plans to extend it in agreement with the international trade association, Comitextil. The Commission also arranged a European conference on technological innovation, aimed at providing information for company directors – particularly of small and medium-sized firms – of the potential of existing technology and technology about to become operational: this conference was organised by the European Association for the Clothing Industry in conjunction with the Commission.

The Commission points out that most of its objectives can be carried out only by firms themselves. However, subject to certain conditions, Community aid is available to supplement national aids to the industry for restructuring while the European Social Fund has an important part to play in helping workers affected by changes to their livelihood.

Promoting international sales

The Community is the world's leading exporter of textiles and clothing and it therefore has a firm basis from which to expand sales in its traditional markets and to find new ones. The Commission suggests that firms could be helped here by intensified national and Community financial support for special short-term projects, such as prospecting for new markets and finding out how to penetrate them, organising deputations abroad, advertising campaigns, industrial fairs, specialist exhibitions, and so on. This offers a vast range of possibilities for inter-company collaboration at national and Community level and for the co-ordination of national efforts.

Meanwhile the Community will continue to try to reduce the barriers to international trade, insisting that reciprocity by both industrialised and developing countries is essential. The Commission will also try to promote a code of practice on international trade in textiles and which should benefit importers and exporters alike.

Cooperation with the third world

The Community has already pointed out to developing countries the risks they run in the present world context in letting textiles and clothing account for a disproportionately large share of their industrialised efforts, and has suggested that they should encourage diversification of their industrial activities in their development plans. On the other hand, some of their activities concerned with semi-finished products complement Community products, and should be encouraged within the framework of rules framed at Community level. Meanwhile, as noted, the Community has made agreements with about 40 suppliers to control the influx of imports from low-cost countries until 1982.

In this connection the Commission has recently submitted recommendations to the Council concerning the conclusion of agreements between the Community and India, Bangladesh and Sri Lanka: identical in substance, they consolidate the draft agreement drawn up at the end of 1977 to control trade in textile products. These cover all MFA products of wool, cotton and man-made fibres originating from the three countries; call for voluntary restraint at agreed levels on exports to the Community of certain categories of products; provide for a consultation procedure to cover categories of products not initially subject to limitation where certain thresholds are exceeded; establish a checking system of products subject to limitation, and include a flexibility clause allowing the transfer of a certain percentage of the quotas from category to category, or from one year to another.

In exchange for limitation, the agreements contain an undertaking by the Community not to introduce further quantitative restrictions under GATT or the MFA, or measures having an effect equivalent to quantitative restrictions.

6. Lawn Mowers

This industry has been highlighted as a small industry affecting many people and illustrates the human aspects of the Community.

A flourishing industry

The Community market in lawn-mowers is an expanding one. At present 28 million householders own a lawn-mower; the industry produces three million lawn-mowers a year and consumers spend approximately £180 million on these machines. The industry, which is growing rapidly, employs about 10,000 workers in a total of some 60 firms. 15 per cent of the mowers are exported outside the Community while 16 per cent are accounted for by intra-Community trade. Thus the erection of internal barriers must inevitably hinder expansion of this export trade.

The lawn-mower trade in the Community is a small but flourishing one employing approximately 10,000 workers. Noise from lawn-mowers, however, is often an environmental nuisance, and several member countries have begun to introduce laws requiring manufacturers to produce quieter machines. Unfortunately, the permitted maximum noise levels differ in each country, thus creating internal barriers to trade that flout Community principles.

To avoid this, and take account of environmental nuisance, the Commission has sent the Council of Ministers a proposal adopting common permissible noise levels depending on the mower's cutting width. The draft directive is concerned *only* with the design of lawn-mowers and *not* with conditions of use.

Aim of the proposals

The Commission's aim is to halt immediately the development of increasingly noisy mowers and, by using all the resources of present-day technology, to enable limits to be set to permissible noise levels, and to provide for further reductions of these limits as soon as new techniques have been developed.

At the first stage, if the proposal is adopted, the Commission envisages the immediate elimination of particularly noisy models, while others will remain on the market for the time being. The Commission recommends, however, that before 31 December 1983 the Council should take action to reduce permissible noise levels further, such measures to enter into force on 1 January 1986.

The draft directive includes technical details regarding methods of measuring and disciplining permitted noise levels, and recommends a system of self-certification by manufacturers. This would mean that each mower would have an indelible certificate on which the manufacturer certifies that the mower complies with the provisions of the directive, and indicates the sound-power level. Such an inscription, however, would not be required for electrically powered lawn-mowers the cutting width of which is less than 30 centimetres.

CHAPTER 10

COMMUNITY POLICIES ON TRADE

The community and world trade: the effects of recession

Economic recession is tending to erode the pristine principle of free trade in the western world. The problem is made worse because the fall in demand in industrial countries has coincided with increasing competition in sensitive sectors from the developing world and the state-trading countries. The European Community, as the world's biggest trade negotiating body, has heavy responsibilities in this field. The Community has already, in the Multifibre Arrangement under GATT, introduced restrictions (and in some cases a quota system) on the import of textiles from developing countries: the Commission has proposed ordered restructuring of the steel and shipbuilding industries to meet the fall in demand. The footwear industry is suffering from low-cost imports and contracting markets for its own exports. Japanese penetration of the Community's market has led to Community/Japanese talks on the Community's distorted balance of trade with Japan, and to voluntary Japanese restrictions in certain key industrial sectors.

The Commission's aims

Pressure towards protectionism arises not only in the Community but also in the USA. The international situation, therefore, is very different from that when the GATT Toyko Round began with the Declaration of 1973 (see below). The Commission's aim in these difficult circumstances has been to persuade member countries to adhere to the basic principles of the Treaty of Rome – fair and free competition – and not adopt protectionist beggar-my-neighbour policies that could destroy the Community. It has sought to regulate the flow of trade so that in a contracting market available outlets are equitably shared as far as possible. This policy has broadly been adopted by the Community in such international forums as the GATT and OECD; internally, however, Commission proposals for structured contraction of certain industries will lie on the table. As an example let us examine footwear.

Footwear

Though the problem is not the most acute, the number of shoes imported into the Community from third countries is also causing alarm, particularly in the Republic of Ireland. From 1973 to 1975 imports remained steady at around 180 million pairs of shoes a year. By 1977 this figure had risen to 300 million pairs a year, the bulk of the increase coming from Hong Kong, Taiwan and South Korea. These three countries have been particularly hard-hit by recent restrictions imposed on shoe imports by the USA, Canada, Australia and Japan. The Commission estimates that these restrictions have released a potential 50 to 100 million pairs of shoes on the market from low-cost countries. In addition US import restrictions have badly affected Italian shoe exports for the American market, normally 47 million pairs. Under Article 135 of the Act of Accession Ireland has been authorised to adopt protective measures for her footwear industry against a general list of suppliers. More recently the Irish have requested the introduction of quantitative restrictions on imports into Ireland of certain categories of footwear. The Council has agreed that the Commission should continue talks with the main supplier countries, and the request will be re-examined in the light of the outcome of the talks.

In October 1977 the Commission decided to set up a Joint Committee for the footwear industry, its function being to assist the Commission in studying the social and economic problems. The 38 members of the committee are equally divided between worker and employer representatives at European level. This is the first time official contacts have been established between the two sides of an industry for which the Treaty does not specifically prescribe a common policy. For statistical purposes, the Commission has been operating a prior automatic licence surveillance system on the import of shoes into the Community. This is a temporary measure, however, and is being replaced by a more flexible system which will not require the use of prior automatic licences. The present system applies to imports from Brazil, Hong Kong, South Korea, Malaysia, Pakistan, Spain, Taiwan, Czechoslovakia, Poland and Rumania.

Challenges to other industries

We have seen the problems in the steel, shipbuilding, shipping, textiles and clothing industries. The petro-chemical industry is vulnerable to a number of threats, and the plastics industry is another case in point.

To meet some of these problems the Commission is considering legislation and has introduced measures that would effectively permit the establishment of crisis cartels; some of the measures involved have been discussed in the preceding chapter. These actions represent a significant departure from the free trade principles that have always been the basis of the Community's competition policy: the cartels would be exempt from the provisions of the Treaty against restrictive practices.

1.Gatt Multilateral Trade Negotiations

The General Agreement on Tariffs and Trade was established in 1948 as a multilateral trade treaty, embodying reciprocal commercial rights and obligations as a means of expanding and liberalising world trade. Since then it has become the main forum for multilateral trade negotiation with its headquarters and professional secretariat in Geneva. At present over 100 countries participate fully in the GATT, or are indirectly involved in the negotiations.

The basic aim of the GATT is to liberalise world trade through non-discrimination, consultation and the avoidance of quotas, with the major focus on the reduction of tariff barriers to trade. Since 1948 there have been a series of "rounds" of tariff-cutting negotiations, of which one of the most successful, the Kennedy Round, was concluded in 1967. Enlargement of the Community, however, and a US decision to introduce 10 per cent import charges and to terminate the dollar's convertibility to gold, created a new situation requiring further negotiations and clarification. This resulted in the Toyko Declaration of September 1973, the outcome of which is at present under discussion in Geneva.

Objectives of the Tokyo Declaration

The six major objectives of the Toyko Declaration are:

(1) to find an appropriate common formula on application of tariffs with as wide a general acceptance as possible;
(2) to reduce or eliminate non-tariff barriers or, where this is not appropriate, to reduce or eliminate their trade-restricting or distorting effects, and to bring such measures under more effective international discipline;
(3) to examine the possibilities of the co-ordinated reduction or elimination of all barriers to trade in selected sectors;
(4) to examine the adequacy of the present multilateral safeguard system with a view to furthering trade liberalisation;
(5) to include agriculture in the negotiations, taking account of the special problems in this sector, and
(6) to treat tropical products as a special and priority sector.

The Community offer

The Community has been negotiating on the reduction of tariffs for industrial products by the application of the Swiss formula, whereby the higher the original duties the greater are the tariff reductions. By agreeing on a co-efficient of 16 in this formula the Community would be prepared to accept an average weighted reduction in tariffs of about 40 per cent.

The Community has emphasised, however, that in making this offer the final size of the tariff reductions will only be known at the end of the negotiations. Any such tariff cuts must be spread over eight years with a pause for review after the first five annual reductions to see whether conditions are suitable to continue with the other three. In addition the Community has indicated that it reserves the right to take into account the offers made by other developed countries and to adjust its own offer in consequence. It has also made clear its determination to seek for a differential and more favourable treatment for the developing countries, with special preferences for the least developed amongst them. Such preferential treatment could include the staging of tariff reductions and improvement in the General System of Preferences. The Community has also made an offer concerning agricultural products: leaving aside grains, rice, meat and dairy products which are dealt with multilaterally under other auspices, the Community proposes that tariff reductions should be applied to about 100 other products including horsemeat, edible offal, plants, vegetables, fruit, animal fats, jams and marmalade, preserved fruit, sauces and bourbon whisky. If agreed the offer would cover imports of about 1,000 million EUA. Taking into account the multilateral negotiations on the other products mentioned above, the Community offer on agricultural products would amount to about 5,000 million EUA on the basis of the 1976 imports.

The Community position in the GATT

The tariff positions of the MTN (Multilateral Trade Negotiations) partners participating in Geneva remain very different. Whereas with the Common External Tariff on more than half the Community MTN imports there is no duty at all, and on others there are mainly tariffs of between 5 and 10 per cent (with hardly any duties higher than 20 per cent), in the US, Canada and Australia tariffs are proportionately higher, in some cases exceeding 50 per cent. The EEC and the USA also have a high degree of tariff bindings compared with other developed countries. Further, the US Trade Act creates difficulties in reducing tariff disparities of certain mandatory exceptions insisted upon by Congress, while the growing intervention of the state in many national economies has introduced a number of non-tariff barriers – such as health and environmental specifications – which indirectly hamper international trade. Here the GATT Secretariat has listed more than 800 such measures, and part of the work of the Trade Negotiating Committee has been to produce draft codes, not only for technical barriers but for customs valuation, government procurement and countervailing duties and subsidies. Over the years government and public sector purchasing have come to represent an increasingly large proportion of total trade. The MTN has aimed to establish the principle of equality of treatment for foreign and national suppliers based on an integrated draft code advocated by the Nordic countries, Canada and the Community. This recommends the institution of international procedures of notification, consultation and surveillance and the settlement of disputes, to ensure better equality of opportunity in the award of contracts. In particular it lays down the criteria as to qualifications and the terms for suppliers and appeal procedures designed to eliminate discrimination. Because of the complexities, however, a number of details have still to be determined. The problem of export subsidies and countervailing duties has also caused difficulties, largely because US legislation in respect of the latter does not conform to Article 6 of the GATT. Other partners of the GATT have insisted that the US alter its legislation in this respect, while resisting US proposals to eliminate certain export subsidies altogether. The Community and the US have had long discussions on this matter and an "Outline of Discussion" is among the negotiating documents in Geneva. Other difficulties before the negotiators include both the improvement of the international safeguard system, which authorises parties to the GATT to derogate from the rules regarding freedom of trade in certain exceptional conditions, and finalisation of the international framework governing the trade of developing countries. The Community has indicated that it believes agreement on the first is, in present economic circumstances, a precondition for an increased liberalisation of trade. On the second, it has been in the forefront in upholding the needs of the developing countries.

2. Countries Outside the EEC

OTHER EUROPEAN COUNTRIES

The Community is at the centre of a huge industrial free trade area of 300 million people in Europe. This was brought into being in July 1977 when the last industrial tariffs were abolished between it and the European Free Trade Association – Austria, Finland, Iceland, Norway, Portugal, Sweden and Switzerland. EFTA came into being after the signing of the Stockholm Treaty in 1959, following the establishment of the EEC. Its members prefer a free-trade area to a customs union. EFTA is the Community's best customer, taking 25 per cent of its exports and supplying 15 per cent of its imports.

Any European democracy can apply to join the Community and since the early 1960s both Greece and Turkey have had association agreements with the Community designed to lead to membership at a later stage through the gradual establishment of a customs union. The agreement with Greece was partially frozen during the military dictatorship but following the restoration of democracy in July 1974 normal links were established and negotiations for its accession to the Community began in July 1976. The Community has preferential trade agreements with both Spain and Portugal, both of which applied in 1977 for Community membership. It has a non-preferential trade agreement with Yugoslavia which both sides are aiming to expand into a wider co-operation agreement.

NORTH AMERICA

Post-war administrations in the United States have consistently supported the unification of Europe and seen the Community as the means to this end. The relationship between the two has been one of partnership and close co-operation. Twice a year the Commission holds high-level consultations with the US Administration covering bilateral and multilateral economic and commercial relations and issues such as energy, investment, industrial policy, the environment, relations with developing countries and the supply of raw materials. The Community also has agreements with the United States regarding the supply of nuclear fuels and for the exchange of scientific information in the fields of energy, research and development, and the environment.

Apart from the EFTA countries as a bloc, the United States is the Community's most important single trading partner followed by Japan and Canada. The Community is the United States' most important partner (after Canada). In 1976, the Community exported goods woth £10 billion to the United States and took £15.6 billion worth of its exports.

Since 1976, the Community's relations with Canada have acquired a new dimension through the conclusion of a framework agreement for commercial and economic co-operation. The framework agreement embodies a unique approach: it is the first time that the Community has committed itself, on a non-preferential contractual basis, to economic and commercial co-operation with one of its major industrialised partners. The activities developed under the framework agreement add to the traditional close contacts between both partners, and are monitored by twice-yearly wide-ranging consultations on bilateral and multilateral economic and commercial issues. The Community and Canada have also co-operated in the nuclear field since 1959 under the Euratom/Canada Co-operation Agreement.

JAPAN

Since 1975 there has been a regular dialogue between the Community and Japan, mainly involved with commercial problems. Until the early 1970s trade between the two was relatively unimportant and was roughly in equilibrium. But by 1977 Japan enjoyed a trade surplus of £3,466 million with the Community.

The Community is trying to correct this imbalance as well as extend consultation between the two to cover general economic as well as trade matters. It is seeking voluntary restraints on Japanese exports to the Community in key sensitive areas as well as greater access to the Japanese market for Community goods. Some concessions have been made and the talks are continuing.

AUSTRALIA AND NEW ZEALAND

Although it has begun to diversify its trade towards Asian countries Australia is still an important trading partner for the Community and regular consultations take place between the two on matters of mutual interest relating to trade. Australian exports to the Community in 1975–76 were approximately £564 million. Imports from the Community were worth approximately £891 million.

In the decade or so before the United Kingdom joined the Community its share of New Zealand exports fell steadily. However, as a traditional supplier of dairy products to the United Kingdom that country's "renegotiation" of its membership of the Community, concluded in 1975, contained special concessions for the continued import entry of New Zealand's dairy products and this arrangement has now been extended beyond 1977. In 1976, Community imports from New Zealand were worth £456 million, compared with exports of £331 million.

CHINA

China's interest in Western technology obviously opens a market of great scope. China's exports are at present of only peripheral interest to the West, and ideology as well as self-interest make her reluctant to commit herself to a balance of payments deficit. She has made it clear that she would prefer to be regarded as a developing rather than a developed country.

Background

Though Britain and France recognised the People's Republic of China at an earlier date, it was not until 1970–71 that relations between China and all member states of the Six were normalised. Political recognition brought with it a rapid development of trade, but based entirely on bi-lateral agreements. By Community decision these expired towards the end of 1974 and the Commission sent a memorandum to China and other state-trading countries suggesting broad provisions for a possible trade agreement between them and the EEC.

Early in 1975 the Chinese invited Sir Christopher Soames, then Vice-President of the Commission specially responsible for external relations, to pay an official visit to China, which he did from 4–11 May. As a result the Chinese appointed an Ambassador to the Community and, in January 1976, indicated that they were interested in opening negotiations towards a trade agreement. Because of internal changes in China little progress was made until February 1977.

Chinese attitude to the community

The warm welcome given to the latest Community trade delegation signified the regard with which the Chinese view the Community. Although, as seen from Peking, it may be a grouping of a capitalist nature, the Community finds favour as a means of strengthening the independence of Western Europe *vis-à-vis* the super-powers of Russia and America. According to a European Parliament report, the Chinese leaders divide the world into three categories: the USA and USSR make up the First World, the developing countries the Third, and in between the developed countries, such as Western Europe, Japan and Canada, compose the Second.

Although her sympathies lie clearly with the Third World, China believes that the Second World should unite to check the economic and military hegemony of the First. Hence she has firmly supported the principle of the European Community as a uniting force in Europe. If she should seek technological help from abroad, it is natural that China should look to the Community as a possible major supplier.

Patterns of Chinese trade

Chinese external trade is under exclusive control of the state. Only the state import and export companies – known as "corporations" – are authorised to sign purchase or sale contracts and are the sole negotiators. Each of the eight corporations, under the Ministry of External Trade, has the responsibility for a particular sector of the economy, covering imports and exports. There are representatives of these corporations in the chief provincial towns as well as abroad.

Under Chairman Mao, scarred by earlier memories of Western exploitation of China, the country's external trade was based on the principle, which directs all aspects of Chinese life, of "independence, autonomy and self-reliance," and tended to be minimal. The present Chinese leaders, however, are interpreting this principle more widely to mean, according to an article in the *People's Daily*, that "China can learn much from the experience and products of other countries," a judicious use of foreign goods being necessary in order to give the country a solid economic base.

Chinese leaders see their country, with an 80 per cent peasant population, as part of the developing world. Precise information about development is scanty, but the EP Document, subject to reservations, suggests the following:

(1) China is the world's leading producer of cereals (first place for rice, second for maize after the USA, third for wheat after the USSR and the USA);
(2) it occupies fifth place in the list of iron and steel producers (though compared with the Community, for instance, the output is small);
(3) it takes third place for coal, after the USSR and the USA (400–420 million tonnes in 1975);
(4) its oil production is rising steadily, and
(5) it is the world's leading producer of cotton goods.

External trade

Since 1970 China has considerably increased her trade with the outside world, but it still represents less than 5 per cent of the national product, and only about 2 per cent of world trade – roughly the same as Taiwan with only 15 million inhabitants, compared with China's estimated 800 million.

Since diplomatic relations were established in 1972 Japan has become the People's Republic's leading trading partner. Both proximity and the broadly complementary economies of the two countries account for this. In 1974 Japan accounted for 27 per cent of China's external trade, involving a Chinese trade deficit of about $700 million. China also trades heavily with Hong Kong, the latter importing most of its food and raw materials from the mainland.

Here China has a considerable surplus ($1,300 million in 1975) in balance of payments. The European Community is China's second most important trading partner (in 1975, $742 million worth of imports, $1,322 million worth of exports, corresponding to a Chinese deficit of $580 million). West Germany is the major supplier, followed by France and the UK. Since 1972, after the lifting of the American embargo and restoration of political relations, trade between China and the USA has developed fairly rapidly.

The main Chinese imports (they include scarcely any consumer goods) are raw materials and semi-industrial products (lead, copper, nickel, iron and steel products, rubber, chemical fertilizers); cereals and other agricultural products, and capital goods. But the pattern is already beginning to change, following improvements in China's own agricultural and industrial development. Imports of chemical fertilizers, for instance, are expected to drop rapidly as installations built by foreign firms come into operation; iron and steel products are also expected to fall. This will enable China to make better use of its resources to buy capital goods and "turnkey" or nucleus factories, so vital to its development. Mainly for political reasons, China prefers to turn for these capital goods to Second World countries.

To meet her import bill China has to export but, as her leaders admit, what she has to offer is not normally of particular interest to the Second World. She is trying to diversify and develop exports of manufactured products but, with the exception of fabrics and cotton goods, none have yet been exported in large quantities. She is also seeking to increase her production of oil, which in 1976 exceeded her own internal needs.

Mainly for ideological reasons, it has been Chinese practice to pay for imports in cash or by barter. Faced with large trading deficits, however, she has recently adopted a more flexible position in this matter. She has been prepared to finance her wheat purchases from the USA and Canada by means of short-term credits and, since 1972, has made increasingly frequent use of the system of deferred payments for the purchase of capital goods and turnkey factories. Since 1974 the yuan is quoted daily against other foreign currencies. The trade deficit is also financed by occasional gold sales on the London market.

China would prefer, however, to trade by barter wherever possible – for example with capital goods or factories being paid for in raw or semi-processed materials produced through these installations or exploited by them. There has been talk of some such projects with Western countries, such as a consortium of German firms supplying mining equipment in exchange for the annual delivery of 10 million tonnes of coal. Such tentative plans were abandoned during the political struggle in China in 1976, but may well be explored further in negotiations in the new trade agreement.

3. Community Relations with other Trading Areas

THE MEDITERRANEAN

In accordance with an overall Mediterranean policy adopted by the Council of Ministers in 1972 a series of agreements has been negotiated with all states in the region. These are designed to establish a vast industrial free-trade area complemented by industrial co-operation and financial assistance to Mediterranean countries by the Community.

The first of these arrangements was signed in 1976 with the Maghreb States – Morocco, Algeria and Tunisia. Such co-operation agreements open a vast field of action for economic, technical, financial and institutional co-operation; marketing and sales promotion; encouragement of private investment and long-term contracts for the delivery of petroleum products. Over the first five years, the Community's financial contribution to these countries will be around £160 million in the form of loans and grants. Their raw materials and industrial products can enter the Community free of customs duties and quotas and most of their agricultural produce receives tariff concessions.

Similar agreements have since been signed with the Mashreq States – Egypt, Syria, Jordan and the Lebanon. The financial aid involved up to 1981 will be more than £120 million.

Beyond specific links with a number of Arab countries, an important development is that the Community as a whole is engaged in the Euro-Arab Dialogue. This brings together the Community of 260 million people and, through the League of Arab States, the whole of the Arab World of 120 million people. This is an important forum for both sides.

In 1976 the Community's exports to Arab League countries represented 13.5 per cent of total exports. This was more than exports to the United States and Japan combined. In the same year, the Community's imports (mainly oil) from these countries represented about 20 per cent of total imports, again higher than imports from the United States and Japan. The Community is also the Arab League's biggest trading partner.

The dialogue proceeds mainly at the level of joint working parties of experts which meet in European and Arab capitals at intervals.

The talks cover agriculture and rural development, industrialisation, basic infrastructure, financial co-operation, trade, scientific and technological co-operation, cultural, labour and social questions.

The global Mediterranean policy also applies to Israel, with which the Community has a preferential trade agreement which was broadened in 1976 to include economic co-operation. Both sides are moving towards a free-trade area which will come into being fully in 1985.

The Community is also in the process of establishing a customs union with Malta and Cyprus.

THE THIRD WORLD

The Yaounde and Lomé Conventions

There have been two Yaounde Conventions: Yaounde 1 was signed in 1963 and Yaounde 2 in 1969. Both were concerned with relations between the Community and former French, Belgian, Dutch and Italian colonies who wanted to go on being associated with the Community after their independence.

The Conventions provided for the duty-free entry for certain exports from the developing countries including the output of infant industries, a similar arrangement for exports from the Community into most of the countries and a new European Development Fund for these associated countries.

Following the 1973 enlargement of the Community, Yaounde was replaced by the Lomé Convention.

The Lomé Convention, which brings together more than 500 million people from African, Caribbean and Pacific (ACP) developing countries, including 22 members of the Commonwealth, is a unique arrangement between developed and developing countries. This uniqueness rests on a number of distinctive factors.

(1) It is a contractual agreement and the security it offers enables the developing countries to plan their economies with greater confidence.

(2) Being global, it encourages regional and inter-regional co-operation. By its global nature, too, it is also non-aligned and embraces developing countries represented by governments of varying political persuasions which negotiated together.

(3) It is unprecedented in its scope and in the specific definition of its terms, which embrace financial aid, guaranteed access to markets, the stabilisation of export receipts, special treatment for a number of products, industrial co-operation and so on.

(4) It gives the developing countries responsibility for establishing their priorities and for planning and carrying out schemes with Community assistance, thereby creating a relationship based on equality.

What exactly does the Lomé Convention offer the third world signatories, whose number has now risen to fifty-six members?

In the area of trade and co-operation 99.4 per cent of the ACP products can enter the Community duty-free except for agricultural products for which the Community has joint marketing organisations. All the Community asks in return is to be given most-favoured-nation treatment, which means that the ACP countries should not discriminate against it in relation to their other trading partners in the developed world. There is also a special protocol on sugar, which is of particular importance to some ACP countries, providing a guaranteed price on about 60 per cent of their total exports. It involves reciprocal guarantees of purchase and delivery of specified quantities of sugar and a semi-indexation of prices. The amount involved is 1.4 million tonnes of raw sugar (about 1,221,500 tonnes of white sugar). The price offered for this sugar must be within the range of prices for sugar in the Community. The system has been in operation for the 1975–76 and 1976–77 seasons and has had a stabilising effect compared with the wild fluctuations in the world market in recent years.

An innovation of the Lomé Convention is the Stabex system which is designed to protect the ACP countries against price fluctuations of commodities on which they depend. A list of key commodities, principally agricultural, has been drawn up; when an ACP country's earnings on any one of them falls below an agreed reference level a compensation fund advances it the difference. The country concerned repays this to the fund when the situation improves, but the poorest of the ACP (half of them) need not do so. This system of insurance against bad years guarantees the ACP countries, which often depend almost exclusively on a single product, that their earnings from commodities covered by Stabex are assured, thereby enabling them to plan their economies with more confidence. The Stabex system has an allocation of £150 million for the first five years of the Convention.

The Stabex money is part of the European Development Fund (EDF) which has £1,240 million at its disposal for financial and technical co-operation, of which £840 million is in the form of grants, £172 million for loans at special rates and £38 million for risk capital. In addition there is a special fund of £60 million to help ACP countries in the event of natural disasters.

First established under the Treaty of Rome, a second and third fund were set up, the two Yaounde Conventions and the present fund, under the Lomé Convention. The Convention also supports regional and inter-regional co-operation and around 10 per cent of the funds available are reserved for projects of this type. There is outside the EDF a further £156 million in loans available from the European Investment Bank for which the EDF lowers the interest. Outside the funds for the ACP there are £64 million available for the French Overseas Countries and Territories (Reunion, French Guinea, Martinique and Guadeloupe).

The Community is determined to help develop and diversify ACP industrial production. This involves the development of research and technology, information exchange, the establishment of contact between firms and so on. These activities are being directed by a Committee on Industrial Co-operation and carried out by a Centre for Industrial Development.

LATIN AMERICA

In 1971 the Community and 22 Latin-American countries formed the Latin-American Co-ordination Committee and the Community has unofficially advised both the Central-American Common Market, the Andean Group and the Latin-American Free Trade Area on the technicalities of economic integration. The Community helps promote Latin-American exports to Europe and it has non-preferential trade agreements with Argentina, Brazil and Uruguay, and an economic and commercial co-operation agreement with Mexico. All Latin-American countries are beneficiaries of the Community generalised system of preferences. In addition, several of them benefit from the Community food aid and Community financing of agricultural development projects.

ASIA

The Community has, with very few exceptions, active relationships with all of the countries of Asia in regard to both trade and economic co-operation and it extends food aid and technical and financial assistance to most of these countries. Practically all of the developing countries of Asia are beneficiaries of the generalised system of preferences. The Community has concluded commercial co-operation agreements with India, Bangladesh, Pakistan and Sri Lanka. A similar co-operation arrangement is in operation with the Association of South-East Asian Nations (ASEAN) – Indonesia, Malaysia, Philippines, Singapore and Thailand.

EASTERN EUROPE

Relations between the Community and the East European state-trading countries have not always been easy, largely because of the unwillingness of the latter to have normal dealings with the Community or to recognise the political, economic and legal realities on which it is based.

The Community for its part has for several years expressed its readiness to enter into negotiations with these countries. More particularly, the Community's commitment to working for increased economic co-operation between the eastern and western halves of our continent was demonstrated by its signature of the Helsinki Final Act in August 1975.

In November 1974, the Community proposed to each of the state-trading countries that negotiations should begin with a view to concluding trade agreements. In view of the continued reluctance of the state-trading countries to respond to this proposal, the Community has sought meanwhile to ensure a continuation in the traditional flow of trade pending the opening of normal trade relations. It has unilaterally opened import quotas for each state-trading country and these lists are revised each year.

The Community has also entered into a series of sectoral negotiations with a number of state-trading countries. For example, an agreement between the Community and Rumania covering trade in textile products was concluded recently, while similar negotiations with Poland and Hungary are under way. Negotiations for the conclusion of framework agreements on fishing rights were initiated in 1977 with the Soviet Union, Poland and East Germany, but have not produced concrete results.

4. Community Aid

Food aid

The Community with its member countries is the largest donor of food aid at international level. The aid takes the form of donations of cereals, skimmed milk powder and butter-oil. Essential aspects of food aid are continuity and careful management. Aid cannot be used in an *ad hoc* way for disposing of occasional EEC surpluses, for that could have a disruptive effect on the agriculture and even the economies of developing countries. It must be on a reliable basis. A high standard of management is also essential: reconstitution of skimmed milk powder, for instance, demands strict hygiene and appropriate distribution conditions.

Criteria for aid

The object of the Community Food Aid programme, as agreed by the Council of Ministers in March 1977, is to raise nutrition standards, to help in emergencies, and to contribute towards the economic development of recipient countries.

The Community has been particularly anxious to help the poorest developing countries and the main criteria taken into account in allocating aid are the basic food needs of the recipient, a per-capita income below approximately £150 a year, and an adverse balance of payments. The Commission emphasises, however, that these criteria must remain flexible so as to be able to cope with the needs of countries facing particular difficulties such as hostilities, the influx of refugees, resettlement problems or natural disasters. If this were not so, several countries in the Middle East and Africa would fail to qualify despite real problems, particularly with refugees.

Cereals

The Commission had hoped that the Council would agree to an increased allocation of 1,135,000 tonnes of cereals in 1979 rather than maintain the 1978 level of 720,500 tonnes. The demand for aid from 52 governments and eight international organisations has risen to 3,226,520 tonnes wheat equivalent, compared with a call from fewer countries for 2,650,000 tonnes in 1978.

According to the UN Food and Agriculture Organisation (FAO), requirements for cereals imports of the most seriously affected and food-priority countries increased by 14 per cent, and this appears to be part of a long-term trend. The situation is serious, as world reserve food stocks have diminished while, due to drought, crop failure or other reasons, the demands for food aid from Pakistan, Vietnam, Bangladesh and Egypt have increased.

Hopes of replacing the 1971 International Food Aid Convention by a new one have not materialised, so the old Convention will continue for a further period unchanged. The Convention, however, only lays down minimum obligations on donor countries, and the Commission intends to recommend a higher Community allocation in future.

Another 566,500 tonnes of grain will be provided by individual member states in addition to the contribution of the Community *per se*, bringing total EEC cereal aid to a minimum of 1,287,000 tonnes.

Powdered milk and butter-oil

The Council decided to provide in the 1979 budget for 150,000 tonnes of skimmed milk powder and 45,000 tonnes of butter-oil. In the light of increasing demand, the Commission had asked for an allocation of 55,000 tonnes of butter-oil. The oil is particularly useful in assisting economic development in the reconstitution of liquid milk in dairy industry projects, whereas difficulties of supervision and distribution create problems in the proper use of skimmed milk powder.

Transport costs

The Food Aid Programme has been criticised for confusion over transport costs in delivering aid. It has been seeking to rationalise these costs and agree on basic criteria as part of its efforts to achieve better management of food aid, but the discussions will not be finished before the present programme should be adopted. The Commission proposes, therefore, that the same procedures should apply as in previous years, with the payment of transport costs limited to the poorest countries, namely those with a GNP per head of approximately £75 or less, and in general for African countries with a GNP per head of £135 or less. Exceptions to these rules would be made for countries receiving considerably increased quantities of aid. The total cost is expected to be less than 10 per cent of the estimated cost of the foodstuffs at Community prices.

Other types of aid

Started on a "symbolic scale" in 1976, Community aid to non-associated developing countries (i.e., those outside the Lomé Convention) is expected to increase to 140 million EUA in 1980. Directed towards a population of 1,250 million in Asia, Latin America and Africa (Angola and Mozambique), 900 million of whom in 1976 had a GNP per head of under $200, the Community contribution is obviously minute in relation to need. The Commission would like to see such aid increased substantially in the future. Meanwhile, it believes that such money as is available should be concentrated mainly on the poorest regions and on valuable projects geared to rural development rather than "abstract allocations" to individual recipients.

Geographical allocation

The Commission points out that in determining the allocation of aid among the three continents, the basic criterion must be the size and level of need of the different regions. In addition, however, there is a certain minimum threshold of intervention below which no significant projects can be implemented. There needs also to be a reasonable balance in Community assistance to the different regions.

In 1979 Asia received 73 per cent of available aid, Latin America 20 per cent, and Africa 7 per cent. Most of Africa, of course, is covered by the Lomé Convention: should Angola and Mozambique decide to accede to the Convention, the African allocation would be partly or wholly redistributed among the other target regions.

If the money is to be used effectively, the selection of projects requires great care. The criteria proposed include the technical possibility of achieving the desired objectives, the manner in which earlier projects have been implemented and the rate of disbursement and the degree of co-operation established with the responsible authorities.

While aid will be directed essentially towards the poorest countries, more prosperous countries will also be helped if the projects concerned are clearly in favour of the very poorest regions or population groups in those countries (as in two projects in Peru and Ecuador).

The Commission would also like to see aid for one year concentrated on a substantial project in one country to ensure its getting off the ground rather than finance a small project each year in every eligible country. An example is the Mahaweli Ganga irrigation scheme in Sri Lanka, a major programme for harnessing and distributing the country's water resources. The Commission intends to propose a substantial contribution to this scheme in the 1980 programme. As several member countries are also expected to contribute to this project, progress here should make a real impact on the development of the country.

Efforts to encourage projects of a regional character have not, hitherto, met with much success, but the Commission intends to go on trying.

Types of project

The major target for aid – rural development – will cover schemes designed directly or indirectly to help the poorest groups, particularly by increasing the supply of foodstuffs. Integrated rural development projects accounted for nearly a quarter (24.6 per cent) of total programme funding over the period 1976–79. In future greater emphasis will be given to fisheries and aquaculture, rural roads and forestry development, all of which experience shows offer real potential for development. Irrigation and water supplies (averaging 16.1 per cent of past funding) will continue to attract aid. The Commission also proposes to devote more attention to assistance in project preparation. Many of the poorest developing countries have found it difficult to prepare a sufficient number of acceptable projects capable of rapid implementation, and could benefit from technical help in this field.

About 7–10 per cent of the aid money will be held in reserve for long-term reconstruction or prevention projects following catastrophe.

The Commission notes that co-financing represents an important proportion of aid under the non-associates programme. In the past a large number of projects have been co-financed with various international aid organisations, notably the Asian Development Bank and the Inter-American Development Bank. Co-financing with Community member countries has, however, been limited to date, although a few such projects were started in 1978 and 1979. The Commission would like to see this form of co-operation expanded.

CHAPTER 11

EDUCATIONAL AND RESEARCH FACILITIES IN THE COMMUNITY

1. Education

The European University

European University,
Badia Fiesolana,
5 Via dei Roccettini,
50016 San Domenico de Fiesole,
Florence, Italy.
Tel. (055) 477931 Telex. 58528 IVE

The European University was inaugurated in Florence in November 1976. It would be difficult to find a more beautiful setting for a university than the Badia Fiesolana on the slopes leading up to Fiesole from Florence. The buildings include a twelfth century church and a monastery. The university is a graduate school open to students intending to read for a doctor's degree or to do advanced research in specialist fields.

The objectives of the university are:

(1) to assist outstanding research students in preparing doctorate theses or in doing advanced research, and
(2) to provide a research centre co-operating closely with other centres of learning in order to foster knowledge and understanding of the problems of our time, whether in historic perspective or in their present day setting.

Whilst seeking to keep its programmes as flexible as possible, the Convention has established four departments:

(1) History and Civilization,
(2) Economics,
(3) Law, and
(4) Political and Social Sciences.

The University is administered by three authorities.

(1) The High Council, composed of representatives of the governments, and which must meet at least once a year in Florence.

(2) The Principal, whose task it is to carry out or supervise the carrying out of acts and decisions pursuant to the Convention and who is responsible for the administration of the University.
(3) The Academic Council, consisting of eight professors from different universities within the Community.

The qualifications for admission are as follows.

Belgium – possession of a licence for graduates from Belgian universities.
Denmark – a candidate's degree for graduates.
France – possession of a *Mâitrise* for graduates from faculties of literature and human sciences, of a *Diplome d'Etudes supérieures au approfendies* for students of law and economics, or a degree from an Institut d'études politiques or Grande Ecole for graduates from French universities.
Germany – successful completion of studies or other qualification for obtaining a doctor's degree for students from universities in the Federal Republic.
Italy – a lauria for graduates from Italian universities.
Netherlands – possession of a doctoral examination for graduates from Dutch universities.
United Kingdom/Republic of Ireland – a good honours degree (at least upper second) from British or Irish universities.
Others – possession of an equivalent degree or being a Ph.D candidate for students from other universities. A limited number of places are available for nationals of states which are not members of the European Community – in exceptional cases, for example, persons with professional experience which enables them to participate in the research work, when the conditions mentioned above may be modified or waived.

Scholarships are available from member states; the University does not provide scholarships of its own.

The College of Europe

College of Europe
Dyver II
B–8000 Brugge
Belgium
Tel. (050) 335334

The College of Europe is the oldest of the institutes of European studies. It was founded in 1949, in the aftermath of the Second

World War, to prepare young university graduates for dealing with problems of society, economy and institutions, not at the level of a single country, but of that of Europe seen as a community of destiny and civilization. The college offers to holders of university degrees one year of complementary studies devoted to present problems of the unity and integration of Europe.

Those associated with the college since its formation include Don Salvador de Madariaga, the Spanish statesman, thinker and writer, M. Jean Ray, Belgian Minister of State and former President of the Commission of the European Communities, Hendrik Brugmans, Dutch historian and Charlemagne Prize winner, Henri Janne, former Belgian Minister of National Education, Jan Tibbergen, Nobel prize for Economics 1969, and Alphonse de Vreese, Judge at the Benelux Court of Justice.

The College of Europe is placed under the authority of an Administrative Council composed of the representatives of the countries and institutions which contribute to its budget. The Council is directed by Francois-Xavier Ortoli, Vice-President of the Commission of the European Communities.

Professor Jenzy Lukaszewski is the Rector and presides over the Academic Council, which is composed of professors, and elected representatives of the assistants, students and former students.

The College merits its name not only by the orientation of its programme but also by the composition of its student and professorial body. Each year some twenty nationalities are represented among the students. Some ten nationalities are represented among the professors assuring the presence of diverse university traditions, schools of thought and methodological approaches in the College.

Established at Bruges, the College is within easy reach of the headquarters of the main institution of the European Community. The two working languages are English and French. The College accepts from one academic year 140 university graduates (e.g., MA or at least BA in the Anglo-Saxon type system, "licence" in the French and related systems).

There are four specialised fields of European studies, administration, economics, law and (added in 1976) conservation of historic towns and buildings, admitting architects, art historians and urbanists. Each of the first three fields of study consists of at least six courses forming a coherent unit of at least 180 hours of teaching. Students admitted choose the specialised field of study which corresponds best to their previous university education, but they must add to their major field of study three courses chosen freely from the multi-disciplinary part of the programme.

2. Management

Management Centre Europe

4, Avenue Des Arts
B 1040 Brussels
Belgium

Management Centre Europe, founded in 1961, is the European headquarters of the American Management Association and the largest international management organisation in Europe today. The AMA's network of centres – each devoted to the continuing task of management development – are located in the USA, Canada, South and Central America and Specialist units include the Foundation for Management Research, the Society for the Advancement of Management, and the Graduate School of International Management.

The AMA is the largest publisher of business management books in the world, has eight different management periodicals and a computer-based management information service with over 100,000 items in its memory.

In 1980 this extensive international organisation welcomed more than 100,000 participants to its centres worldwide.

Alone amongst the operational centres of the global organisation, Management Centre Europe is a truly international centre. Located in Brussels – capital of Europe – since its conception, its activities cover the whole of Europe and Scandinavia, giving it a unique role amongst management organisations in Europe, This "uniqueness" is based on three major elements of MCEs operating philosophy.

First, it is very much a Centre, a meeting place for managers from all over Europe and beyond to come together, learn and share experiences in a completely international yet neutral environment (the Centre's staff of 65 reflect this internationalism – currently there are twelve different nationalities working in MCE).

Second, MCE, in common with AMA policy and philosophy, is a totally self-financing, non-profit-making organisation, which receives no aid – financial or otherwise – from any source, has no political or sectarian views, and promotes no beliefs or doctrines except the professionalism of management.

In this lies MCEs independence, an independence that very few organisations, national or international, can claim. It means that MCE exists as an unbiased organisation purely to raise the quality of management, to make available the latest management techniques, and to help management adapt to changing environments.

Third, its faculty of professional management education staff is drawn from the world of business, and in this way MCE has available a huge reservoir of experience in the business world. Because of this MCE programmes are not overly theoretical, but based on the practical up-to-date experiences of practising managers. In simple terms it advocates the education of management by management.

Alone, each of these points would be admirable, together they provide MCE with a unique style, that is passed on to participants as a special experience in management development.

The international environment, the independence as a self-funding organisation, and the practical experience of the working managers that make up the faculty, create an organisation that is different from other management development groups in Europe. It is normal for a programme with twenty participants to have as many as eight or nine different nationalities, and as the world gets smaller and Europe's nations come close together, this additional experience is invaluable in the development of today's and tomorrow's managers. As many of MCE's programmes are aimed at the practical, they involve participation for the people on the programme. This sharing of experiences by participants of different nationalities and cultures from large and small companies, creates an especially significant exchange of ideas and techniques.

A fourth point that makes MCE different from many of its competitors around Europe is the depth and diversification of its work, and the flexibility that comes from its independent status.

Today, MCE has five main operating divisions. These are Programme Division, Top Management Programmes, In-Company Programmes, Executive Compensation Service and Multi-Media.

Programme division

This division handles all public programmes for the Centre. These include international conferences, meetings, seminars, information briefings and round tables. The division is divided up into operational sectors such as Marketing, Finance, Personnel, EDP, etc., each controlled by a programme director.

Top management programmes

All senior executive programmes are handled by this division, includ-programmes for the Presidents' Association, a membership operation with 2,500 members worldwide. All programmes run by the division are specifically orientated towards the management problems of the chief executive and his immediate subordinates.

In-Company programmes

This new division, set up in 1975, deals with the ever-growing demand for development programmes individually tailored to a company's need. Although public programmes have still an important role to play in management development, there are many cases where it is more cost-effective and productive to bring the MCE programme to a chosen location, and immerse all a company's chosen personnel in the subject at the same time.

MCE offers a series of standard programmes which are adaptations of public courses, and also builds up specific programmes on a one-off basis for clients. In certain cases a member of MCE staff will define the management development needs of an organisation and suggest a complete plan of action over an extended period, utilising a series of both public and in-company programmes.

Executive compensation service
This division is the publishing arm of the organisation with the emphasis on management information. It publishes a series of widely used Management Remuneration Surveys on a comparative and national basis. These surveys are almost certainly the biggest selling salary surveys of their type in Western Europe, and MCE has the largest coverage of any organisation in this field.

Additionally, it publishes research studies on management and has recently diversified into the whole field of management personnel information with a series of publications covering employment, tax, labour relations and fringe benefit programmes for Europe. This division also publishes the monthly newsletter *Industrial Relations Europe*, which has come to be regarded by international personnel and industrial relations managers as one of the most authoritative, up-to-date reviews available.

International Management Institute

IMEDE
PO Box 1059
CH–1001 Lausanne
Switzerland

IMEDE was established in 1957 as an independent educational institution to promote advance management concepts and methods within the international business community. The University of Lausanne provides patronage and co-operation. However, the two institutions are independently operated. The governing body of IMEDE consists of a ten-person Board of Trustees composed of leading international business men, educationalists and governmental representatives. The IMEDE faculty members are drawn from the international academic and business communities. Since its founding, the Institute has been guided by senior professors at Harvard University Graduate School of Business Administration, who have aided in the design and development of the programme of instruction.

During the past two decades IMEDE has earned an international reputation as a leader in the development of executive talent for upper-echelon management.

Synopses of three of their many courses are given below.

MBA (Master in Business Administration)
This course is directed at young men and women already successfully engaged in their careers with a minimum of two years practical experience and holders of a university degree or equivalent.

The objectives of this programme are:

(1) the development of fundamental managerial skills, and
(2) the broadening of the mind in dealing with the new "publics" of the enterprise – government agencies, unions, movements, industrial policies in foreign countries, in a truly international environment and a practical, as opposed to academic, orientation.

PED (Programme for Executive Development)
The Programme for Executive Development is designed to assist managers in mid-career to make the transition from functionally orientated positions to future positions as general managers. This is effected through the development of analytical skills, i.e., those required to solve business problems, and interactive skills, i.e., those required to put decisions into action.

Candidates must hold a responsible position and be sponsored by a business or firm or government agency. A degree from a recognised university, or equivalent experience is required and the average age of the participants is 37.

SSE (Seminar for Senior Executives)
This seminar is designed to reinforce the general management viewpoint – as opposed to the operational viewpoint – for experienced executives at the upper level of management.

Applicants must be experienced executives of approximately 40 years of age holding senior positions in their companies and nominated and sponsored by their organisations.

One of the great strengths of the IMEDE programme is the wide diversity of the participants – a wide variety in terms of managerial and cultural backgrounds, industries and functions that allow participants to gain a fuller understanding of international business operations and problems.

Centre for Education in International Management

CEI
4 Chemin de Conches
1232 Conches
Geneva
Switzerland

The CEI – Centre d'Etudes Industrielles – Centre for Education in

International Management, was founded by Alcan as a company training centre in 1946. The centre was opened to other users in 1956, and became a foundation under Swiss law in association with the University of Geneva. The Foundation board consists of 15 members from 12 countries, with two members only from Alcan.

Some twenty educational programmes are offered every year in Geneva, the longest, the MBA programme, lasts 35 weeks; others vary from one week to eight weeks.

The main characteristics of CEI is that everything is international, and as opposed to certain other schools that follow a one-method approach (usually the case method) the CEI believes that it is necessary to apply a variety of teaching methods in order to achieve various educational objectives.

The CEI is under the supervision of the Geneva government but receives no government subsidies. Since most participants are company-sponsored, it is considered normal that companies should finance the school's activities through tuition fees.

The CEI has a Business Associate Programme and some sixty leading international firms belong to this network. The objective is to solve problems in management education on a joint basis, and to keep the CEI current.

Although all courses are successful, it may be prudent to mention the international financial management seminar, which provides insights into changing economic and financial environments. Emphasis is placed on foreign exchange management (the CEIDEAL game is featured). Other areas examined include the state of the international money and capital markets, and international funds management.

The Administrative Staff College

Administrative Staff College
Greenlands
Henley-on-Thames
Oxon, RG9 3AU, U.K.

Henley was founded in 1946. It is the longest established management school in Europe and the seed-bed for many developments in management education in the UK and the rest of the world. Many thousands of senior managers from industry, commerce, financial institutions and the public service and from all over the world have attended the college's courses.

The development of managers involves many facets such as varied job experience, job rotation in line and staff positions, overseas postings: but management education is an indispensable element in the process. The overriding aim of Henley is to play its vital part in producing managers who will run efficient, effective and profitable enterprises.

Currently, the main features of the College contribution are:

(1) *Management Science*. The analytical methods and techniques which will assist the drive to efficiency, cost consciousness and profitability.
(2) *Human motivation at work*. Development of policies which will encourage effective working groups which are adaptable to change.
(3) *The Environment*. The social economic and political framework within which all organisations must operate.

Managers thus widen as well as deepen their understanding and will be better prepared for future responsibilities. The major programmes encompass all these features. The shorter courses deal with specific aspects.

There are. however, certain principles which reflect Henley's philosophy – a philosophy which has given the College its unique reputation and which, even in times of uncertainty and turbulence, continues to stand the test of time. It applies with particular force to the major programmes.

The fact that the College's students are mature and experienced men and women and that their experience is an invaluable resource, means that a balanced use of adult educational methods must be used to ensure an integrated approach to learning. Groups of people are selected with great care to give a blend of backgrounds and skills. Members are then able to evaluate information critically and from different viewpoints, to compare and contrast experiences and to assist their own effectiveness as an example of a managerial team at work (Henley was a pioneer of group or syndicate learning methods).

Students learn to distinguish the formulation and execution of policy – the role of the manager, from the presentation and analysis of the facts – the role of the expert. They have the opportunity to stand back from their job and position in society and to think about what they are doing and how they are doing it.

The College has always believed that its main function is the development of the individual, both as a person and in his or her knowledge and skills. The role of the staff is important in guiding and counselling and in encouraging members to experiment with new ideas and methods in a non-threatening atmosphere.

The major programmes run by the College are as follows.

(1) *The General Management Course* lasts for just over nine weeks, and is intended for managers in mid-career who need to broaden

and deepen their understanding in order to move successfully into senior positions.

(2) *The Senior Course* is for managers holding a position of high responsibility who need to be brought up-to-date (4 weeks).

(3) *The International Management Programme* is for key executives who influence policy and strategies in multinational enterprises (4 weeks).

(4) *The Masters' Programme* is for young managers who have begun their careers and need development before assuming more senior positions (2 years on a modular basis). It leads to an MBA degree.

(5) *The Research Programme* involves individually-based research for a higher degree.

The College also runs a Management Development and Advisory Service, a Centre for Employment Policy Studies, and a Centre for International Management. Seminars, Workshops and Short Courses are held regularly.

3. Accountancy

European Accounting Association

European Accounting Association
20 Place Stephanie
B–1050 Brussels
Belgium

The purpose of the Association is to provide a forum for persons professionally concerned with or interested in accounting research and education. It serves as a focal point of communication for its members residing in and outside the European Economic Community. It also provides a framework for the better dissemination of information on accounting research and pedagogy and serves as a network for the exchange of accounting information at an international level.

A person professionally qualified and concerned with or interested in accounting research and education is eligible for membership of the Association subject to acceptance by the High Council. The Association has no citizenship requirements nor an official language.

In addition to individual members, membership is also open to institutions such as business and professional firms, financial institutions, government agencies, universities and other organisations subject to approval by the High Council.

The Association is continually invited by the European Economic Commission to set up groups of experts to give opinions and views on accounting harmonisation problems.

Some examples of other research completed include the following.

(1) The Investment Process in Finnish Industrial Enterprises from the 50 largest Finnish enterprises.
(2) Economic Analysis and Financial Planning in a Changing Environment.
(3) Cost Accounting Models as a source for relevant information for management decisions.
(4) Planning and Control Systems for Diversified Accounts.
(5) Teaching Accounting to Non-Financial Managers.
(6) Inflation Accounting.
(7) Enterprise Valuation – a Cash Flow Approach.
(8) Company Reporting.

Limpberg Institute

Limpberg Institute
Mensinge 2
1083 H.A. Amsterdam
Netherlands
Tel. 020–440222

The Limpberg Institute is the inter-university institute for accountancy at Amsterdam, Netherlands. It was founded in 1974 as an inter-university institute of the State Universities (Rotterdam and Groningen), the Municipal University of Amsterdam, the Free University (Amsterdam), the Catholic College (Tilburg) and the Netherlands Institute of Registered Accountants (NIVRA).

The purpose of the Institute is to promote scientific research and education in accounting and auditing. Its tasks can be summarised as follows:

(1) initiating research projects to be executed by the Institute itself or by groups outside the Institute;
(2) stimulating and co-ordinating research undertaken by its affiliates;
(3) aiding in the preparation of students for the accounting and auditing professions and in the continuing education of practising members of these professions, and
(4) stimulating and encouraging publications on accounting.

The Institute is governed by a Council whose president is Professor J.W. Schoonderbeek (on behalf of NIVRA). Its research projects are the responsibility of a Scientific Committee chaired by Professor G.G.M. Bak (Catholic College, Tilburg) and managed by M. J.F. Van Dijk.

In 1977 the Ministry of Education and Sciences allocated public funds to the Institute.

4. Computer -Assisted Research

The European Computing Services Association

ECSA is the European Body which represents organisations engaged in computing services throughout Europe. A large proportion of European computing skill and experience is represented within the software, service bureaux and consulting organisations which are members of their national associations. ECSA was formed after the 1975 Brussels Conference where it became clear that European co-operation and the unification of the industry's views on many strategic issues were required. The nations which are represented in ECSA are Belgium, Denmark, Finland, France, West Germany, Italy, Netherlands, Norway, Republic of Ireland, Spain, Sweden and the United Kingdom.

The objectives of ECSA are as follows.

(1) To promote and protect the computing services industry in the member countries.
(2) To represent the industry to International, European and National organisations where appropriate.
(3) To promote international co-operation in the computing services industry and the transfer of skills in the interests of professional computing.
(4) To provide a platform for discussions with manufacturers and the public data communications carriers.
(5) To promote internationally acceptable standards of professional behaviour.

ECSA has established a number of key areas in which it is actively establishing and pursuing policies on behalf of the computing services industry in Europe: these include policies for:

(1) overall development of computing in the European Economic Community;
(2) data transmission in the Community and on a world-wide basis;
(3) industry-wide statistics in the ECSA Nationals;
(4) co-operation with the industry representational institutions in the United States and Japan (see address at end);
(5) significant social and legal issues impacted by computing;
(6) professional standards of conduct within the member nations, and
(7) a sharing of technology with developing nations.

For these purposes ECSA has established dialogues and regular meetings with organisations which include the Commission of the European Communities, the International Telecommunications

Union, the Group of Post and Telecommunications in Europe, the Council of Europe and the European Parliament.

ECSA has established standard working groups on Telecommunications, Statistics, and Social and Legal Factors. In addition ECSA has published three Annual Surveys on the European computing services industry market.

Through their membership of the individual national industry associations, some 750 companies are represented within Europe. Details of the services they offer to clients are available from the European Computer Services Association Secretariat at the following addresses:

United Kingdom	*United States of America*	*Japan*
5th Floor Hanover House 73/74 High Holborn London WC1V 6LE	ADAPSO 11th Floor 1925 North Lynn Street Rosslyn Arlington Virginia 22209 USA	JSIA Kozo Kekaku Engineers Inc. Nippon Holstein Kaiken 4-38-13 Honcho Nakano-Ku Tokyo Japan

Euronet-Diane

Euronet-Diane is a Community-wide network of computerised information which enables subscribers to extract information from data bases and data banks in different member states simply by picking up the telephone.

The new network, which became operative in February 1980, opens up vast possibilities in the increasingly important field of information. The world's store of computerised information is equivalent to 50,000 volumes the size of the Bible. While not all this information will be immediately available to Euronet-Diane subscribers, the system already covers the broad spectrum of human knowledge – scientific, technical, economic, legal and social. Subscribers can switch into this vast store of valuable information whether they are twenty or two thousand miles from the computer. What is more, subscribers can have this access for the cost of a local telephone call.

The idea of creating the Euronet-Diane network was born in 1970 as the faster rate of industrial, economic and social evolution brought in its train greater demands for easily obtainable accurate information on a wide range of subjects. Access also had to be cheap. The seventies saw the creation of numerous information services making use of advanced technology, notably computers. However, these services were independent of one another and were frequently incompatible. In addition they were usually set up to answer the needs of a specific group, such as research chemists or constitutional lawyers, and were therefore developed in isolation. As long ago as 1971 the European Commission proposed to the Council of Ministers the development of a Community-wide network for scientific and technical information and documentation that would be quick and cheap. The Council gave the go-ahead for the plan, fully appreciating the need for a co-operative effort between the member states to rationalise the development of this new industry by sharing research, technical management and staff costs.

The network spans the whole Community. There is a monitoring centre in London and four pocket switching exchanges in Frankfurt, London, Paris and Rome. These exchanges are equipped with computers which are connected through high-speed links which have been doubled in case of breakdown. "Host" computers throughout the Community as well as "user" terminals in Amsterdam, Brussels, Copenhagen, Dublin and Luxembourg can be connected to the nearest switching exchange.

In practice, then, a subscriber in London who wants to find out what research has been done recently in France in a certain subject and where this information is available can simply pick up the telephone. The user terminal transmits the request to the switching exchange which relays it to the host computers linked to the network. The hosts are the information centres – data bases and data banks.

Although the scheme is still in its infancy, it already offers a wide choice of data bases filled with references, abstracts of articles, books, conference proceedings and other sources, all containing specific data, facts, figures and formulae. According to the team which manages the system it is particularly useful to organisations working in the fields of aerospace, agriculture and veterinary science, all branches of engineering, computers and electronics, human sciences, medicine, metallurgy, patents, petroleum and pharmaceuticals. For researchers and development scientists its attractions lie in the fields of biology and biomedicine, chemistry, environmental sciences, mathematics, nuclear sciences, physics and social sciences. Each subscriber is given a password which gives him access to the whole network. There is a short training course to teach users how to get the best out of the system.

As a result of Community financial efforts host computers of different makes have been connected to the network. A common command language has also been created so that it is not necessary for the subscriber to learn the language of different host computers to make his requests understood. It is thus possible for a subscriber to use only one terminal for access to any of the 23 host computers connected to the network and through them to the 130 or more data banks and data bases stored in their memories.

Having created an esperanto of computer jargon the Commission, thanks largely to the help of the European Parliament, has launched a programme for computer-assisted translation of the data itself. It covers all the official Community languages but for cost reasons has been limited to certain fields. However, the Commission is to consider a full-scale research programme into fully automatic translation. If this goes ahead it is not too much to expect that in a few years time a Sicilian doctor will be able to put a question in Italian to a German data base specialised in the medical field, that his question will be automatically translated into German and that the answer provided by the German data base will be automatically translated into Italian before appearing on the screen in front of the doctor.

So far £13 million, four-fifths of it paid out of Community funds and the rest by the national administrations, has been spent setting up the network, but obviously a great deal more money will have to be invested to perfect the system. For example, the Commission will certainly investigate the possibilities of a link-up between Euronet and the new videotex technology which enables a subscriber to telephone for information which is then displayed on his television screen. Another problem is copyright. At the moment there are nine different national legislations regarding copyright. Eventually a single copyright claim for the whole Community could be envisaged, but at the present time it will be necessary to work out a system to ensure payment and the recovery of royalties for authors and publishers whose publications are traded as computerised information from one member state to another.

In 1976 the number of queries to computerised information services was about 60,000. By 1985 this is expected to exceed 2 million. Euronet-Diane is the Community's response to this challenge.

5. Post-Graduate Degrees

There are many post-graduate degrees which cover European Integration. Apply to:

Madam Jacqueline Lastenoise
University Information
Commission of the European Communities
Rue de la Loi 200
B1049 Brussels
Belgium

APPENDIX 1

NEW ENTRANTS

Introduction

In this section some details of the events leading up to the entry of Greece into the Community on the 1 January 1981 are recorded for historical interest, although in the main Greece has been included under the respective chapters of the book. As with the Six, then with the Nine, new entrants, such as Greece, Spain and Portugal, have to have achieved political and economic stability before they are eligible for full membership, whilst, therefore, Greece has already joined the Community and it is expected that Spain and Portugal will become new entrants on 1 January 1983, because of past unsettled political and economic factors in all three countries, it would be incorrect to treat them on a standard basis. The information presented, which includes details of the transitional arrangements for Greece, although not in a common framework will present the reader with some idea of the problems facing the Community during 1981–1983.

GREECE

Greece signed the Treaty of Accession to the European Communities on 28 May 1979 after three years of hard negotiation. She joined the Community as a full member on 1 January 1981. The Treaty allows for a general transition period of five years for Greece to accommodate to Community requirements, with an extension of a further two years in the case of certain agricultural products. There is also a seven-year transitional period for the achievement of full freedom of movement within the Community for Greek workers, although firms and professional people will enjoy freedom of establishment from the beginning.

Historical background

Greece was the first European country to become an associate member of the Community under Article 238 of the Rome Treaty. The Agreement came into effect on 1 November 1962, but was suspended five years later when in 1967, democracy in Greece was overthrown by a *coup d'état*. With a change in the political situation, relations were resumed in 1974, and on 12 June 1975 Greece applied to join the Community as a full member: negotiations started the following year in July 1976 and were concluded on 3 April 1979, the signing of the Treaty taking place in Athens on 28 May 1979.

The Customs Union for industrial products

Greece accepted the *acquis communautaire* (or achievements of the Community to date) as the basis of the Agreement. Since 1974, under the Association Agreement, with the exception of ECSC products (coal and steel), approximately two-thirds of the Community's industrial exports to Greece have been duty-free, while Greece has adopted the Community's Common External Tariff (CET) for the same products with regard to third countries. Apart from coal and steel, Greek industrial exports have also entered the Community duty-free.

Under the Treaty there will be a five-year period for the progressive elimination of remaining customs duties on Community imports into Greece, and for the progressive alignment of the Greek tariff on CET. Greek tariffs will be reduced in six stages, starting with the present reduction of 10 per cent, followed by a further 10 per cent reduction in 1982 and four further annual reductions of 20 per cent, so that all tariffs will be eliminated by 1 January 1986. Alignment to the CET follows the same timetable.

Quantitative restrictions will be abolished immediately on accession, except for 14 special industrial products (including certain fertilisers, engineering products, vehicle components, and so on) for which Greece has requested extra protection during the transitional period. These quotas will be progressively increased during the five-year transitional period and will be abolished by 31 December 1985. Measures of equivalent effect to quantitative restrictions will be abolished from accession, with the exception of the Greek system of cash payments and import deposits which will be phased out over three years.

General reciprocal safeguard mechanism

A general and reciprocal safeguard clause has been included in the Treaty along the lines of Article 135 of the Accession Treaties in the UK, Denmark and Ireland. In addition, a special emergency measure has been agreed in cases of serious economic difficulties.

External relations

During the five-year transitional period Greece will be allowed to maintain quantitative restrictions towards GATT and state-trading countries for a small number of products, but will apply the Community's Generalised Preferences Scheme from accession, subject to a five-year transition for certain products. Subject to transitional measures Greece will also apply the Community's preferential agreements with third countries, and the Multi-Fibre Arrangement regarding textiles.

Agriculture
The full application of the Common Agricultural Policy (CAP) will not come into force until the end of the five-year period, with a further two-year extension for certain sensitive products such as tomatoes and peaches. For Greek products such as drum wheat, processed fruit and vegetables, as well as olive oil, where prices are significantly lower than Community prices, full price support and income subsidies will be gradually phased in over the five-year period. Producers of cotton, dried figs and raisins will benefit from the new systems of deficiency payments. Meanwhile, to avoid abrupt changes in producer costs or in prices, Greece will gradually phase out existing national state subsidies, chiefly on fertilisers and live-stock rearing, and will also eliminate all restrictions on Community agricultural products.

Social affairs
Although full freedom of movement of Greek workers in the Community will not be achieved until the end of the seven-year transitional period, priority will be given to Greek workers, as nationals of a member country of the Community, where it proves necessary to recruit workers from outside the Community. Workers already employed in other Community countries will progressively be able to bring in their families over the five-year period, and they will be eligible for family allowances after three years in cases where the family does not live in the same country as the Greek worker. Greek workers will then receive the same treatment as other Community workers.

Financial arrangements
From the date of accession Greece will contribute in full to the Community's own resources system, but because she will not be receiving full financial help from the CAP during the transitional period she will inevitably be a net contributor to the Community budget rather than a beneficiary of it. To avoid this a special financial mechanism has been agreed to cover the five-year period. Own resources contributions come from customs and agricultural levies supplemented by Value Added Tax (VAT) or a direct GNP contribution. During the transitional period the amount of duties accruing from VAT or GNP will be paid in full with other levies from 1 January 1981. The Community, however, will refund Greece

a proportion of the GNP/VAT element starting with 70 per cent in 1981 and falling to 10 per cent in 1985. It has been agreed that Greece can delay implementing the Sixth Directive relating to the common system of VAT for three years. The Commission estimates that, with the application of the special mechanism, and on the basis of a hypothetical 1979 budget, Greece's net benefit from the Community budget will amount to about £54 million in 1981.

The drachma will be included in the ECU basket of currencies by the end of the five-year period. Greece will also be able to maintain restrictions on certain capital movements until 1 January 1986.

SPAIN

Spain applied for membership of the European Community in July 1977. The opening of formal negotiations on 5 February 1979 followed the presentation by the European Commission of a favourable Opinion on Spanish entry at the end of November 1978.

In its Opinion the Commission made clear that Spanish entry would require considerable and difficult economic adjustments both for the Community and for Spain, and recommended a ten-year transitional period after entry before final economic integration.

Background

Spain first approached the Community regarding associate membership in 1962. This was then unacceptable, but in 1970 the Community concluded a trade agreement with Spain as part of its efforts to frame a coherent approach to trade relations with Mediterranean countries.

Following the death of General Franco and the return of democracy in Spain, the new Spanish government made it clear in February 1976 that it wished to adapt the 1970 agreement with a view to Spain's eventual integration into the Community. This led in July 1977 to a formal request for membership, supported by all the political parties represented in the Spanish government, by both sides of industry and by the majority of the population. The opening of negotiations was approved by the Council of Ministers in December 1978.

Both the Council and the Commission urged, however, that prior to the opening of negotiations proper, a beginning should be made to concert policies, particularly as regards tariff barriers. On 24 January, therefore, at the joint EEC–Spain Committee (which is responsible for administering the 1970 agreement), the Commission asked for changes in those Spanish measures which hinder sales in Spain for Community exporters. These measures include import quotas, the Buy Spanish Act and administrative difficulties, which have resulted in considerable distortion of trade. Whereas since 1970 Spanish exports to Community countries have risen by 665 per cent, trade in the other direction has increased by only 248 per cent.

The economic picture

The economic buoyancy that heralded the first enlargement of the Community in the early 1970s no longer applies today. Though economic prospects are brighter than they have been, unemployment remains high, and a number of basic industries, hit by recession, are already struggling to remain viable in contracted markets.

Spain started industrialisation late, and though about 38 per cent of the civilian labour force is engaged in industry, 75 per cent of firms employ less than six workers and only 22 per cent employ more than 500 people. Spain's major industries – textiles, steel, shipbuilding and fishing – will inevitably add to the surplus capacities already prevalent in these industries among the Nine. Furthermore, Spanish industry has developed within strong protective barriers and the removal of these barriers will inevitably cause hardship to the more vulnerable enterprises.

There are also problems with agriculture. About 55 per cent of the land area is used for agriculture; agriculture accounts for 9 per cent of GDP and engages 20 per cent of the population. Spain's mainly Mediterranean products will compete not only with the southern regions of France and Italy, but cause problems with other Mediterranean producers – Algeria, Morocco, Tunisia, Israel, Cyprus and Turkey – with which the Community has preferential trading agreements.

The Commission has already drawn attention to these problems and is frank about them in its Opinion. Nevertheless it maintains that the opening of the Spanish market should be welcomed by other Community exports (in particular the motor industry) and should provide an opportunity for better penetration of Latin American markets where Spain has a long historical relationship.

Recommended action

Although Spain has great potential for development it will take time, in most sectors, for her to parallel the economies of the Nine, and interim measures should be applied for a period of up to ten years. If, in the course of the transitional period, conditions were such that the timetable for integration could be adjusted in a given sector, a decision to that effect could be taken by the Council.

Meanwhile, the Commission considers that as far as her *industry* is concerned, Spain must meet three requirements:

(1) elimination of the present imbalance by the dismantling of tariffs between the Community and Spain – this was intended, but failed to happen under the 1970 agreement (at present the Community has reduced its tariffs by about 57 per cent, as against 26 per cent on the Spanish side);
(2) harmonisation of the basic conditions of competition, especially from the angle of taxation and aids, and introduction of VAT, and
(3) speedy involvement of Spain in industrial restructuring schemes and in the common disciplines adopted for Community industries in crisis.

Regarding *agriculture* the Commission admits that the Common Agricultural Policy is likely to boost production, particularly in Mediterranean products.

Enlargement, therefore, is likely to bring with it a more than proportionate increase in problems linked with farm structural shortcomings and with differences in farmers' incomes. It will therefore be necessary to step up efforts to reduce productivity differences between farms in the Community. To avoid hardship, structural reform will have to be accompanied by adequate regional aid to the poorer areas.

The Commission considers it inevitable that, to begin with, membership of the Community will mean loss of jobs in Spain as, for the first time, Spanish industry and agriculture will be subjected to Community competition. Also the removal of barriers to freedom of movement of workers could accentuate the flow of Spanish workers to other Community countries, already grappling with high unemployment. It is largely because of these social problems that the Commission believes that adaptation of the Spanish economy to Community rules and responsibilities must be gradual, and why a long transition period is necessary.

Strengthening the Community

The Commission emphasises again that to ensure the success of enlargement and particularly of the integration of Spain, it is essential that the Community takes steps to improve its decision-making capacity, such as a greater use of majority voting and by giving the Commission greater discretion to decide on technical matters. Unless this is done, further enlargement will accentuate differences between the member states and is liable to aggravate the Community's difficulties in adopting and implementing common policies.

Spain and the other applicant, Portugal, have made it clear that they are not interested in joining a diluted Community. It is essential, therefore, the Commission insists, not only to maintain what has been achieved (*acquis communautaire*) but to strengthen the core of the Community so that it can take on its new responsibilities. Action here should parallel negotiations for enlargement.

Spain will, of course, be a full member of the Community from the first day of entry into force of the Act of Accession; it will participate during the transitional period as a full member, with both the rights and duties that this entails.

PORTUGAL

The Portuguese government places great importance on eventual full membership of the European Communities. Its application was presented in Brussels in March 1977 and the Opinion which outlined the major advantages and disadvantages of Portuguese accession was issued in Brussels on 23 May 1978. Substantive talks are now taking place for full membership.

Geography

Portugal covers an area of 35,000 square miles, and has a coastline of 528 miles. There are three climatic zones:

(1) North-western, with abundant rain, moderate winters and hot summers;
(2) North-eastern, with long cold winters and hot summers, and
(3) Southern, with little rain, moderate winters and long, hot summers.

The population is 9.6 million. The islands of Madeira and the Azores together with the mainland, form the administrative area called Metropolitan Portugal.

Lisbon, the capital, is the most important port, with modern cargo and passenger facilities, and three significant shipyards. The city and its environs have steel works, engineering firms, flour mills, oil and sugar refineries, and other industries including textiles, cement, chemicals, fertilisers and cork products. Nearby Setubal is the centre of the motor vehicle assembly industry and the largest of the country's shipyards, Setenave. Oporto, the second major city, is the centre of the cotton textile industry and the port through which wine shipments are sent.

Agriculture is carried on throughout mainland Portugal. Plans for agrarian reform since the Revolution of April 1974 have been confused and inconsistent.

Foreign policy

The 1970s did not only see a considerable change in Portugal but brought an end to her reign as an African colonial power. The new democracy places great importance on a role as part of the European Economic Community, and is already a member of NATO and acceded to the Council of Europe in September 1976.

The economy

A lower level of investment added to the government's restrictive economic policies has slowed GDP growth to 3.4 per cent in 1978 compared with 5.7 per cent in 1977. In fact all domestic demand components decelerated in 1978 and the main contribution to growth came from external account. Portugal is one of the ten economies which have been defined by the OECD as a newly industrialised country along with such countries as Spain, Greece, Yugoslavia and Mexico. In fact after many years of sustained economic growth per capita GDP at US $1,811 is relatively high and industrial production accounts for 45.9 per cent of GDP, although employment in agriculture at around 30 per cent is still too high for an industrial economy.

Management of the economy has continued on essentially the lines of a stabilisation programme agreed with the IMF in May 1978. A tighter monetary policy has been implemented as well as a monthly devaluation of the escudo to keep Portuguese exports competitive. Annual inflation as measured by the implicit GDP deflator is running at 20 per cent and unemployment is 8 per cent of the 3.6 million work-force.

Trade

Since 1973 bilateral trade has been governed by the EEC/Portuguese Free Trade agreement which, because of Portugal's low level of industrial development, reflected the special concessions she enjoyed within EFTA prior to the UK's accession to the EEC. Portugal's economic difficulties following the Revolution of 1974 prompted further concessions by the EEC in 1976, including the acceleration by one year (to 1 July 1976) of the final EEC duty reductions.

EEC–Portugal Free Trade Agreement

The Agreement came into force on 1 January 1973, the date of UK and Danish accession to the European Communities. Agreements with the other EFTA states came into force simultaneously. The FTA was designed to continue the move towards free trade between UK and Portugal in manufactured and some processed agricultural goods begun during the UK membership of EFTA. At the same time it provides eventually for the same facilities to be extended to trade between Portugal, the original Six and Ireland.

The FTA in its original form provided for the gradual removal of import duties on manufactured goods and the protective element in processed agricultural goods by 1 July 1977. However, because of Portugal's low level of industrialisation in relation to that of EEC and the rest of EFTA, the concessions granted her under Annex G of the Stockholm Convention establishing EFTA were reflected in Protocol 1 of the FTA. This allows Portugal to retain duties on a variety of goods until 1 January 1980 and on a smaller range until 1 January 1985.

The main text of the Agreement, in common with all the EEC–EFTA FTA's contains the following points:

(1) the abolition of existing and prohibition of new quantitative restrictions (Article 14);
(2) the prohibition of monopolies and cartels (Article 26);
(3) provision for anti-dumping measures to be taken (Article 28), and
(4) permission for industrial safeguard and balance of payments restrictions (Articles 28, 29 and 30).

Protocol 1 to the FTA provides for annual tariff ceilings to be established for imports into the EEC of Portuguese paper and board, cork and some textile items. The full Common External Tariff may be applied to imports in excess of the ceilings. There is provision for the ceilings to be raised automatically each year by 5 per cent, for this increase to be withheld in cases of sectoral difficulty and for the ceilings to be suspended if imports do not reach 90 per cent of the levels set for two successive years – this has happened with some textile and cork items. Ceilings on paper are due to be removed at the end of 1985; those on textiles in 1980. In addition the UK (and Denmark) may open, until 1984, annual zero duty tariff quotas for paper and board.

Protocol 1 (Article 6) also offers protection to Portugal's nascent industries – with certain provisions by imposing tariffs of up to 20 per cent. Such tariffs must be removed by 1 January 1985.

Protocol 2 lays down the arrangements for and lists the processed agricultural goods covered by the FTA.

Protocol 3 sets out origin and documentation rules. Questions on these matters are normally handled by HM Customs and Excise.

Protocol 6 concerns imports of motor vehicles into Portugal. In particular it allows the maintenance of annual quotas for made up vehicles and sets out the arrangements for the removal of fiscal duties by 1980.

Protocol 8 sets out the levels of duty reduction on certain agricultural goods traded in both directions. It also provides for tariff quotas to be opened for EEC imports of Portuguese port, madeira and muscatel wines.

In order to assist Portugal's post-revolution economic recovery, two new protocols were concluded in 1976 – an Additional Protocol containing trade provisions and limited social security rights and a financial protocol granting up to 200 million EUA to Portugal for approved projects. An interim agreement embodying the trade provisions came into force in November 1976. This allowed for some items of EEC origin due to become duty free in 1980 to be transferred to the slower duty reduction timetable, ending in 1985. It also modified the protection available to nascent industries and extended this to certain other industries that suffered during the revolution by allowing tariffs of up to 20 per cent to be applied. These provisions have yet to be used, but such tariffs must be removed by 1 January 1985. For Portuguese exports, EEC customs duties were removed from 1 July 1976 on most goods covered by the agreement. The existing ceiling and quota arrangements on paper and board, some textiles and fortified wines were modified and the EEC opened new zero-duty quotas for certain types of paper.

APPENDIX 2

ABBREVIATIONS

One of the difficulties posed by many EEC documents is their tendency to refer to organisations, agreements, systems and procedures by their initials.

ACP	African, Caribbean and Pacific countries.
ADR	*Accord dangereux routier* – the European agreement on the international carriage of dangerous goods by road.
ASEAN	Association of South-East Asian Nations – Indonesia, Malaysia, Philippines, Singapore and Thailand set up in 1967.
BDA	Federal Association of German Employers.
BEUC	*Bureau europeén des unions consommateurs* – (European bureau of consumers unions) 29 Rue Royale, 1000 Brussels.
BIS	Bank for International Settlements, established 1930 by the central banks of Belgium, Britain, France, Germany, Italy and Japan. It serves as a meeting place for the governors of the central banks.
BLEU	Belgo-Luxembourg economic union formed in 1921, these countries pool their foreign currency holdings, operate a single balance of payments regime and combine their foreign trade statistics.
CAP	Common Agricultural Policy.
CARICOM	Carribbean Community and Common Market (formerly CARIFTA) – a regional community whose principal objective is economic integration. It introduced a single like tariff on 1 January 1976 and at present has 12 members.
CCC	Customs Co-operation Council – Studies questions of co-operation in customs matters to attain harmony and uniformity. Governments of 83 countries are members.
CCCN	Customs Co-operation Council Nomenclature – the standard of goods for customs tariff purposes now used by most countries.

CCT	Common Customs Tariff of the EEC, less accurately referred to as CET (Common External Tariff).
CEEP	*Centre Européen de l'Entreprise Publique* (European centre for public enterprises), 15 Rude de la Charite, 1040 Brussels.
CEFIC	*Conseil européen des fédérations de l'industrie chemique* (European council of chemical industry federations). Avenue Louise 250 BTE 71, 1050 Brussels.
CEN	*Comité européen de normalisation* (European committee for standardisation), whose members are the national standardisation organisations of Austria, Belgium, Denmark, Finland, France, Federal Republic of Germany, Irish Republic, Netherlands, Norway, Portugal, Spain, Sweden, Switzerland and the United Kingdom. General Secretariat, Rue Brederode 2 BTES, 1000 Brussels.
CEPAC	*Confédération européenne de l'industrie des pâtes papiers et cartons* (European confederation of pulp, paper and board industries) 14 Rue de Crayer, 1050 Brussels.
CEPT	Conference of European Postal and Telecommunications Administrations — founded in 1959 to promote closer relations between members and harmonisation and improvements of their administrative services. 10500 Stockholm, Sweden.
CERN	*Centre Européen Recherche Nucléaire* (European centre for nuclear research). 1211 Geneva 23.
CIDST	*Comité d'information et de documentation scientifique et technique* (committee for scientific and technical information and documentation). Jean Monnet Building, Rue Acide des Gasperi, Luxembourg–Kirchberg.
CIPEC	*Conseil intergouvernemental de pay exportateurs de cuivre* (intergovernmental council of copper exporting countries). 177 Avenue de Roule, 92200 Neuilly-sur-Seine.
COCCEE	*Comité des organisations des pays de la CEE* (committee of commercial organisations in the EEC) 3 avenue L. Gribaumont, 1150 Brussels.
COMECON	Council of Mutual Economic Assistance set up in January 1949 to promote the development of the economies, science and technology of USSR, Bulgaria, Cuba, Czechoslavakia, East Germany, Hungary, Mongolia, Poland and Rumania.

DG	Directorate-general. The staff of the Commission is divided into 19 directorates-general. Berlaymount Building, 200 rue de la Loi, 1049 Brussels.
EAGGF	European Agricultural Guidance and Guarantee Fund – finances the EEC's common agricultural policy.
EBU	European Broadcasting Union. Ancienne Route 17A, PO Box 193, 1211 Geneva 20.
ECGD	Export Credits Guarantee Department.
ECMT	European Conference of Ministers of Transport founded in 1953 to achieve the maximum use and most rational development of Europe's inland transport. 19 European countries are members. 19 Rue de Franqueville 75775 Paris Cedex 16.
ELEC	European League for Economic Co-operation.
EMBO	European Molecular Biology Organisation. Meyerhofstr 1, 6900 Heidleberg, 1 Postfach 1022 40.
EMU	Economic and Monetary Union.
EOE	European Options Exchange – set up in Amsterdam in April 1978 to facilitate trading in options in securities of European-quoted companies. A Dutch venture *not* linked with the Community.
ETUC	European Trade Union Confederation – unites 18 trade union organisations from 15 countries. 37-41 Rue Montagre aux Herbes Potagenes, 1000 Brussels.
ETUI	European Trade Union Institue. The centralising body for trade union affairs. Boulevard d' l'impératrice 66 (BTE4), 1000 Brussels.
FAO	The United Nations Food and Agriculture Organisation, which has its secretariat in Rome.
FIGED	Federation International des Grandes Enterprises de Distribution (federation of large retail distributors) EEC group of FIGED, 117 Avenue Castel, 1200 Brussels.
GNP	Gross National Product.
IBRD	International Bank for Reconstruction and Development – also known as the World Bank. 1818 H. Street NW, Washington DC 20433.
ICC	International Chamber of Commerce. 6-14 Dean Farrar Street, London SW1H 0DT.
IEA	International Energy Agency. 2 Rue André Pascal, 75775 Paris.
ILO	International Labour Office. 87 New Bond Street, London W1Y 9LA.
ISO	International Standards Organisation. 1 Rue de Varennbe, 1211 Geneva 20.

NIMEXE The nomenclature for the foreign trade statistics of the EEC is the harmonised nomenclature that EEC countries have adopted to classify goods for compiling their foreign trade statistics.

OCED
OECD Organisation for Economic Co-operation and Development – established in 1961 as the successor to the OEEC (Organisation for European Economic Co-operation). 2 Rue André Pascal, 75775 Paris Cedex 16.

OJEC Official Journal of the European Communities.

SNAKE Community joint float – this is the informal description of the EEC scheme aimed at narrowing the margins of fluctuation between community currencies. Under this scheme the central banks of participating countries act as necessary in their own markets to ensure that the spot exchange rate of each participating currency is never more than 2¼ per cent different from its declared central rate.

STABEX Export earnings stabilisation scheme – a system set out in Title II of the Lomé Convention which aims to guarantee the stabilisation of earnings from exports by the ACP states to the community of certain products.

TIR Transport International Routier – a *carnet* issued to international road transport operators which allows loaded vehicles to cross frontiers with minimum facilities.

UNICE *Union des industries de la communauté européene* – brings together national employers' associations, including the Confederation of British Industry. It has regular meetings with the EEC Commission and maintains frequent contact with individual directorates of the Commission. 6 Rue de Loxum, 1000 Brussels.

WEU Western European Union – the member states of the EEC seek to co-ordinate their defence policy and equipment and to co-operate in political, social, legal and cultural affairs. 9 Grosvenor Place, London SW1X 7HL.

APPENDIX 3

BIBLIOGRAPHY

After much research throughout the Community the author recommends additional reading for those who wish to study the Community in more detail. As the Community is always changing the economic reviews are recommended.

General

1. *The Annual General Report on the Activities of the European Communities* (published by the European Communities)
2. *Economic policy for the European Community. The way forward.* (Alec Cairncross and others – published by Holmes and Meir New York)
3. *European Economic Interpretation* (Bela Bolossa – published by North-Holland Publishing Co. Amsterdam)
4. *The Law of the European Economic Community* (K. Lipstein published by Butterworths London)
5. *Financing the European Community* I. Druker – published by Leydon Sythoff)
6. *Business Atlas of Western Europe* (Gower Press Farnborough)
7. *Company Policy for the EEC* (Financial Times Ltd. London)
8. *Economic Surveys of Member Countries* (OECD Paris) 19–21 Issues per year – finance, money, the economic situation and policy
9. *Company Law* M.C. Oliver (Macdonald & Evans, Plymouth UK)
10. *European Banking to 1985* (Graham and Trotman Ltd. London) Analysis and forecast of likely developments in banking practices
11. *Sources of Corporate Finance in Western Europe* (Graham and Trotman Ltd. London) Directories and companies sources of company finance in Europe. Chapters deal individually with countries giving notes on depreciation and other investment allowances, incentives – and special sources of information.

Some reading from Community countries

Belgium

1. *Economic and Technical*

(Office Belge du Commerce Extérieur
Boulevard E Jacquemain 162
Brussels

Bulletin for the foreign press giving economic and technical information.

2. *Belgium News*

Ministère des Affairs Etrangères
et du Commerce Extérieur
Rue des Quatre Bras 2
B1000 Brussels

Series of booklets on various economic subjects.

Denmark

1. *Danmarks Nationalbank Monetary Review* (Quarterly)

Holmens Kanal 17
1093 Kobenhaven K

2. *Economic situation in Denmark*

Den Danske Landmansbank
12 Holmens Kanal
DK1092 Kobenhaven

France

1. *Bulletin Manual D'Information Financiers et Boursieres*

Societe General Siege Social
1429 Boulevard Haussman
Paris 9E

Monthly economic review.

2. *Business Newsletter* (fortnightly)

French Commercial Counsellor
12 Stanhope Gate
London W.1

Germany

1. *Latest from Germany*

Embassy F.R. Germany
23 Belgrave Square
London SW1X 81Z

Weekly news bulletin.

2. *Economic situation in the F.R. of Germany*

Villemombler ST76
5300 Boon–Duisdorf

General quarterly economic review.

Italy

1. *Economic Review*

Banco di Roma
Dinizione Centrale
Casilla Postale 2442
00100 Roma

6 issues a year.

2. *Basic Data on the Economy of Italy*

US Department of Commerce
Government Printing Office
Washington DC20402
U.S.A.

Republic of Ireland

1. *Economic Services*

Central Statistics Office
St. Stephens Green House
Earlsfort Terrace
Dublin 2

(A series of monthly booklets of statistical information).

2. *Ireland in Figures*

Allied Irish Banks
Landsdown House
Ballsbridge
Dublin 4

Netherlands

1. *Business Comments from the Netherlands*

Algemene Bank
32 Vijzelstraat
Amsterdam

Monthly Economic Survey.

2. *Economic Review*

Rotterdam Bank NV
Rotterdam

Quarterly review

APPENDIX 4

PRESS AND INFORMATION OFFICES
OF THE EUROPEAN COMMUNITY

BELGIUM
1040 BRUSSELS
Rue Archimede 73
Tel. 735 00 40/735 80 40

DENMARK
1045 COPENHAGEN K
4 Gammeltory
Postbox 144
Tel. 14 41 40

FRANCE
75782 PARIS CEDEX 16
61, rue des Belles-Feuilles
Tel. 501 58 85

GERMANY
53 BONN
Zitelmannstrabe 22
Tel. 23 80 41

1 BERLIN 31
Kurfurstendamm 102
Tel. 8 92 40 28

GREECE
ATHENS 134
Vassilisis Sofias 2
T.K. 1602
Tel. 743 982/83/84

IRELAND
DUBLIN 2
29 Merrion Square
Tel. 76 03 53

ITALY
00187 ROME
Via Poli, 29
Tel. 678 97 22 to 26

LUXEMBOURG
Batiment Jean Monnet B/O
Rue Alcide de Gasperi
Luxembourg-Kirchber
Tel. 430 11

NETHERLANDS
THE HAGUE
29, Lange Voorhout
Tel. 070-46 93 26

UNITED KINGDOM
LONDON W8 4QQ
20, Kensington Palace
Gardens
Tel. 727 8090

CARDIFF CF1 9SG
4 Cathedral Road
Tel. 371631

EDINBURGH EH2 4PH
7, Alva Street
Tel. (031) 225.2058

PRESS AND INFORMATION OFFICES OUTSIDE THE COMMUNITY

CANADA
OTTAWA, Ont. KIR 7S8
Inn of the Provinces -
Office Tower (Suite 1110)
350 Sparks St.
Tel. 238 64 64

JAPAN
102 TOKYO
Kowa 25 Building
8-7 Sanbancho
Chiyoda-Ku
Tel. 239-04 41

LATIN AMERICA
CARACAS (VENEZUELA)
Quinta Bienvenida
Calle Colibri
Valle Arriba
Caracas 106
Postal Address:
Apartado 67076
Las Americas
Tel. 92 50 56 - 91 47 07

SANTIAGO, CHILE
Avenida Ricardo Lyon 1177
Santiago 9
Postal Address:
Casilla 10093
Tel. 25 05 55

SWITZERLAND
1202 GENEVA
37-39, rue de Vermont
Tel. 34 97 50

TURKEY
ANKARA
Kavaklidere
13, Bogaz Sokak
Tel. 27 61 45/46

UNITED STATES
WASHINGTON, D.C.
20037
2100 M Street, N.W.
Suite 707
Tel. (202) 862-9500

NEW YORK, N.Y. 10017
1 Dag Hammarskjold Plaza
245 East 47th Street
Tel. (212) 371 3804

Reference has been made to the first Diploma in European Studies. If any readers would like to receive details of the Diploma, they should write to:

The Education Secretary
Society of Company and Commercial Accountants
40 Tyndalls Park Road
Bristol
U.K.

INDEX

INDEX